# The Language of Politics

**Series Editor**

Ofer Feldman, Doshisha University, Kyoto, Japan

**Editorial Board**

Christ'l De Landtsheer, University of Antwerp, Antwerp, Belgium

Catalina Fuentes-Rodríguez, University of Seville, Sevilla, Spain

Augusto Gnisci, University of Campania "Luigi Vanvitelli", Caserta, Italy

Michael Hameleers, University of Amsterdam, Amsterdam, The Netherlands

Ken Kinoshita, Faculty of Socio-Environmental Studies, Fukuoka Institute of Technology, Fukuoka, Japan

Michael Alan Krasner, City University of New York, New York, USA

Sam Lehman-Wilzig, Bar-Ilan University, Ramat Gan, Israel

Hongna Miao, Nanjing University, Nanjing, China

Katarzyna Molek-Kozakowska, University of Opole, Opole, Poland

Gene Segarra Navera, National University of Singapore, Singapore, Singapore

Debbita Ai Lin Tan, Universiti Sains Malaysia, Penang, Malaysia

Annemarie Walter, University of Nottingham, Nottingham, UK

Ruth Wodak, Lancaster University, Lancaster, UK

Sonja Zmerli, Sciences Po Grenoble, St. Martin d'Hères, France

The Language of Politics series is an interdisciplinary, critical, and analytical forum for the publication of cutting-edge research regarding the way language is used by political officials. It focuses mainly on empirically-based research aiming to analyze and discuss the role, function, and effects of the vocabulary used by politicians and other officials in Western and non-Western societies. Such language can be broadcast live in venues such as parliamentary debates and deliberations, election campaign assemblies, political party conventions, press conferences, media interviews, and even non-broadcast (but later reported) speeches in front of support groups or during international negotiations – in traditional as well as social media (e.g., Facebook, Twitter). It can include polite, respectful, and deferential public speaking, or conversely, impolite verbal discourse, debasing and derisive comments, and the use of crude, vulgar, or abusive terms – including curses and obscenities – through irony, sarcasm, cynicism, ridicule, and mockery, to demean, degrade, humiliate, and insult individuals, the political opposition, or groups in society.

The series is located at the intersection of several social science disciplines including communication, linguistics, discourse studies, political sociology, political science, and political psychology. It aims to bring together multiple political and social theories and concepts; qualitative, quantitative, or mixed methodological approaches; and in-depth, empirical, communication- and language-oriented analyses. By addressing critical issues such as the use of words, terms, and expressions in parliamentary debate and political negotiations, and their effect from novel perspectives, it can expose the weaknesses of existing discourse analysis concepts and arguments, or reassess the topic in other ways through the introduction of different ideas, the integration of perspectives from disparate sub-fields or even disciplines. By challenging existing paradigms, authored books in the series will enrich current debates surrounding several complex, discourse relationships: between politicians' and citizens; between decision-makers and their colleagues; and in general, the way language shapes political culture in an increasingly globalized world. All proposals and books in this series are peer-reviewed by international experts in the aforementioned fields.

Ofer Feldman
Editor

# Communicating Political Humor in the Media

## How Culture Influences Satire and Irony

Springer

*Editor*
Ofer Feldman
Doshisha University
Kyoto, Japan

Kyoto University
Kyoto, Japan

ISSN 2731-7617     ISSN 2731-7625 (electronic)
The Language of Politics
ISBN 978-981-97-0725-6     ISBN 978-981-97-0726-3 (eBook)
https://doi.org/10.1007/978-981-97-0726-3

© The Editor(s) (if applicable) and The Author(s), under exclusive license to Springer Nature Singapore Pte Ltd. 2024

This work is subject to copyright. All rights are solely and exclusively licensed by the Publisher, whether the whole or part of the material is concerned, specifically the rights of translation, reprinting, reuse of illustrations, recitation, broadcasting, reproduction on microfilms or in any other physical way, and transmission or information storage and retrieval, electronic adaptation, computer software, or by similar or dissimilar methodology now known or hereafter developed.
The use of general descriptive names, registered names, trademarks, service marks, etc. in this publication does not imply, even in the absence of a specific statement, that such names are exempt from the relevant protective laws and regulations and therefore free for general use.
The publisher, the authors and the editors are safe to assume that the advice and information in this book are believed to be true and accurate at the date of publication. Neither the publisher nor the authors or the editors give a warranty, expressed or implied, with respect to the material contained herein or for any errors or omissions that may have been made. The publisher remains neutral with regard to jurisdictional claims in published maps and institutional affiliations.

This Springer imprint is published by the registered company Springer Nature Singapore Pte Ltd.
The registered company address is: 152 Beach Road, #21-01/04 Gateway East, Singapore 189721, Singapore

Paper in this product is recyclable.

*To the Hatanis—*
*Akifumi, Asaya, and Usa*

*Who love trains, green cars, and to laugh.*

# Preface

This is the second published volume of a project concerning contemporary political humor in a variety of societies and groups around the globe. It follows the first volume entitled *Political Humor Worldwide: The Cultural Context of Political Comedy, Satire, and Parody* (2024), but is distinguished by its focus on political humor in different mass media—print, broadcast, and social networking services (SNS). Its value for readers who are interested in political behavior, communication, and culture is likely to be found in three areas. First, the relationship between culture (encompassing norms of behavior, attitudes, belief, etc., in all walks of life), and expressions of humor about politics, the political system and institutions, and office holders and aspiring politicians, as manifested in a variety of media channels. In particular, this entails how cultural factors (e.g., social structure, social relationship, historical experiences, economic system, and individualism/collectivism) affect the content, type, and style of humorous expressions in channels of communication in a given country/society. Second, the way graphic artists, satirists, comedians, cartoonists, parody programs writers, users of SNS, journalists and columnists, as well as general readers, utilize the media to voice satire, parody, jokes, and other expressions of humor, through which they target policymakers, the administration, and the political processes. Third, political humor's social, political, psychological effects or potential effects as displayed by the media in any given polity.

As with the first volume, this book has an outstanding collection of chapters written by experts in research areas such as political behavior, communication, linguistics, and cultural studies. They all bring multinational and multidisciplinary diversity, as well as an array of theoretical/conceptual approaches and research methods, to detail how culture is relevant (or affects) political humor, also offering potential avenues for future research on the nature and effect of this type of alternative political communication.

The common thread that runs through these two books is that expressions of humor in politics—whether in face-to-face communication such as during parliamentarian deliberations and election campaign speeches, or through the mass media—reflect multiple facets. Such expressions are accepted and appreciated by members of one society as amusing and result in laughter, yet they could be regarded as rude and unpleasant to members of another society. Thus, at the heart of this project lies the notion that culture is a powerful element affecting and determining the content, nature, and characteristics of humor regarding political issues and personnel, and as well as reaction to these.

The two volumes form a collection with strong internal coherence and abundant cross-references among their contributions, and our intent and hope is that they will be read and used together as a unified, polyphonic, and interdisciplinary contribution to the study of the fascinating yet under-researched subject of political humor.

As the editor of this book, I sincerely thank all the contributors for their commitment and support to this project and their timely contributions despite their very busy schedules; their competence and patience made the completion of this volume possible. I hope that the process of writing their chapters has been a rewarding endeavor for them as well. I am especially grateful to Sam Lehman-Wilzig, who, as in previous projects, carried out the language and copy-editing task. All the contributors are deeply indebted to him for his meticulous editing work that improved the quality of our publication. My thanks to Sonja Zmerli for her continual support and sense of humor during this project, and to Hongna Miao for friendship and valuable talks from which I have greatly benefited. Many thanks also to Yuriko Kôno, Aya Ojiri, and Chie Sakuragi, for helping in research, coding, and communication matters regarding this volume. Furthermore, I am deeply indebted to Einat Maoz for years-long friendly and unwavering encouragement and kindness, and to Efraim Gantz and Asher (Ashi) Nutovitz for moral and professional support and advice through difficult times. My great respect and heartfelt gratitude to Tatsushi Mayama, a scholar, colleague, and friend, without whose support this intellectual journey in Doshisha University over the last 20 years wouldn't have been possible. Finally, special thanks to Juno Kawakami, our editor at Springer, for her thoughtful guidance and counsel throughout the whole process. Needless to mention, as in my previous projects, none of the above-mentioned individuals bear any responsibility for any mistake or flaws in this book—except perhaps my three grandsons Akifumi (4.5 years old), Asaya (2.5 years old), and Usa (200 days) to whom this book is dedicated.

Kyoto, Japan                                                                                   Ofer Feldman

# Reference

Feldman, O. (2024). (Ed.), *Political Humor Worldwide: The Cultural Context of Political Comedy, Satire, and Parody*. Springer.

# Contents

1. Humor and Politics in the Media: A Conceptual Introduction ..... 1
   Ofer Feldman

## Part I  Humor in Political Cartoons

2. The Relationship Between Culture and Political Humor in Japanese Manga ..... 21
   Roman Rosenbaum

3. A Tale of Two Presidents: Indonesian Humor as Depicted in Political Cartoons ..... 45
   Danang Satria Nugraha

4. Mocking the Inept: Brazilian Cartoons and Criticism of the Jair Bolsonaro Government ..... 73
   Bruno Mendelski and Marco André Cadoná

5. How Political Cartoons Reveal Türkiye's Cultural Dynamics: An Analysis of Three Satirical Magazines ..... 93
   Ayşe Deniz Ünan Göktan

6. Spanish Humor and Political Culture Through Cartoons: Multimodal Discursive Analysis of *Forges*'s Socio-political, Graphic Universe ..... 119
   María del Mar Rivas-Carmona

7. Far-Right Political Humor in Australia: Culture, Coloniality, and Exclusion ..... 145
   Kurt Sengul and Jordan McSwiney

**Part II  Political Humor in the Broadcast Media**

8  **Televised Political Satire in Poland: Historical Roots and Social Implications of Stereotypical Representations of Politicians and Politics** .................................... 165
Agnieszka Kampka and Katarzyna Molek-Kozakowska

9  **Sexist Humor in Public Facebook Comments Delegitimizing Female Politicians Within Montenegro's Patriarchal Culture** ...... 183
Milica Vuković-Stamatović

10  **Exploring Attitudinal Meaning in Iranian Political Humor Targets as Distributed Through Social Networks** ................. 203
Alireza Jalilifar and Yousef Savaedi

11  **Mocking the Powers that Be: The Case of Culture and Political Humor in Malaysia** ........................................ 223
Debbita Ai Lin Tan

**Part III  Political Humor in the Print Media**

12  **Politically Related *Senryû* Verses in Daily Newspapers as a Manifestation of Humor in Japan** ......................... 243
Ofer Feldman and Ken Kinoshita

13  **Depicting "*La Grieta*": The Role of Political Satire and Humor in Argentinean Polarization** ................................ 273
María Isabel Kalbermatten

**Part IV  Conclusion**

14  **The Complexity of Media Political Humor: Research Considerations** .................................................. 295
Sam Lehman-Wilzig

**Index** ............................................................. 305

# Contributors

**Marco André Cadoná** Department of Science, Humanities, and Education, and Program in Regional Development (PPGDR), University of Santa Cruz do Sul (UNISC), Rio Grande do Sul, Brazil

**Ofer Feldman** Faculty of Policy Studies, Doshisha University, Kyoto, Japan

**Ayşe Deniz Ünan Göktan** Kadir Has University, Istanbul, Türkiye

**Alireza Jalilifar** Shahid Chamran University of Ahvaz, Ahvaz, Iran

**María Isabel Kalbermatten** Gustavus Adolphus College, St. Peter, Minnesota, USA

**Agnieszka Kampka** Department of Sociology, Institute of Sociological Sciences and Pedagogy, Warsaw University of Life Sciences, Warsaw, Poland

**Ken Kinoshita** Faculty of Social and Environmental Studies, Fukuoka Institute of Technology, Fukuoka, Japan

**Sam Lehman-Wilzig** Department of Communications, Peres Academic College, Rehovot, Israel

**Jordan McSwiney** Centre for Deliberative Democracy and Global Governance at the University of Canberra, Canberra, Australia

**Bruno Mendelski** Department of Business Management and Communication, and Graduate Program in Regional Development (PPGDR) and Administration (PPGA), University of Santa Cruz do Sul (UNISC), Rio Grande do Sul, Brazil

**Katarzyna Molek-Kozakowska** Department of English, Institute of Linguistics, University of Opole, Opole, Poland;
Department of Creative Communication, Vilnius Gediminas Technical University, Vilnius, Lithuania

**Danang Satria Nugraha** Department of Indonesian Language, Sanata Dharma University, DI Yogyakarta, Indonesia

**María del Mar Rivas-Carmona** Faculty of Philosophy and Letters, University of Córdoba, Córdoba, Spain

**Roman Rosenbaum** Japanese Studies, School of Languages and Cultures, University of Sydney, Sydney, Australia

**Yousef Savaedi** Farhangian University of Ahvaz, Ahvaz, Iran

**Kurt Sengul** Department of Media and Communications, The University of Sydney, Camperdown, Australia

**Debbita Ai Lin Tan** School of Languages, Literacies and Translation, Universiti Sains Malaysia, Penang, Malaysia

**Milica Vuković-Stamatović** Faculty of Philology, University of Montenegro, Podgorica, Montenegro

# Chapter 1
# Humor and Politics in the Media: A Conceptual Introduction

**Ofer Feldman**

**Abstract** This chapter presents a general introduction to the book. It draws upon and summarizes the key aspects of humoristic expressions in politics as detailed in the previous volume in this series of two books on political humor. It first reintroduces the definition and the scope of political humor, suggesting that humor about political matters is a highly contextual and subjective phenomenon that can be perceived differently by individuals, with different cultures shaping its content, nature, and characteristics. This is followed by a short presentation of the theoretical approaches that guide the subsequent chapters. The chapter also discusses key aspects in the analysis of political humor: first, that humoristic expressions related to politics can be employed for positive and negative purposes, illustrated by examples on the role played by stereotypes and prejudice in creating ethno-national humor; and second, that members of the public, political elite, and the media employ humorous expressions in politics while using different means for different goals. The final section of this chapter details the structure of the book, briefly describing each of the contributions.

## 1.1 Introduction

This book's overall project views political humor as a form of comical expression communicated via any medium that addresses aspects of, or directed at, the power structure, including the political system and process, political institutions, political leaders, and subject matters in the public sphere. Such expression is found in verbal messages including jokes, puns, parody, comedy, satire, and metaphors, and in non-oratorical discourse and visual representations such as graffiti, caricatures, cartoons,

O. Feldman (✉)
Faculty of Policy Studies, Doshisha University, Kyoto, Japan
e-mail: ofeldman@mail.doshisha.ac.jp

© The Author(s), under exclusive license to Springer Nature Singapore Pte Ltd. 2024
O. Feldman (ed.), *Communicating Political Humor in the Media*,
The Language of Politics, https://doi.org/10.1007/978-981-97-0726-3_1

pictures, or *manga* (comic or satiric strips). The latter are detailed in the ensuing chapters.[1]

Arguably, political legitimacy implies deference to the government, its institutions, and representatives. This is the primary tenet underlying all types of political systems. Humor that is aimed at the power structure and public officials, through such venues as parody, comedy, satire, and jokes, is created and circulated by members of the public (or journalists and political pundits) on the assumption that this might satisfy a need for disrespect of political authority and a relief from the trivial stress and frustrations people feel toward political leaders, institutions, or policies. In this sense, such humor can be seen as weapons of political criticism and contempt, as methods of individual coping with disliked policies, politicians, and circumstances, and as an instrument to get even with oppressors.

Such humor draws upon two noteworthy concepts. First, the common experiences and stereotypes around which identities and perceptions toward the self and the other are formed. Very often it satisfies needs that are more psychological and symbolic than political, more in the domain of amusement instead of pursuing and realizing public goals. In this respect, it is a discourse of persuasion and opinion, and attitude formation and change, almost always against the political elite, oppressors, and the "other." On this premise, the rhetoric of political humor is ultimately political.

Second, political humor relies on the semantics and pragmatics of political language, contextual information, the culture, norms, values, and beliefs of a given society or an ethnic group, and the political culture of a given country (Bergson, 2008, p. 11). Humor in general, and humor about political issues and personnel in particular, are thus seen as a highly contextual and subjective phenomenon that may be interpreted differently by individuals. It can be funny for some people and evoke laughter, but could also result in unexpected or unpleasant outcomes, including nervousness and embarrassment, by offending and upsetting others.

The idea that context affects political humor is also central to the project that resulted in this book, focusing especially on cultural circumstances. Our assumption is that humor doesn't develop in a vacuum; it evolved as part of the interaction between individuals and their surroundings. As a form of alternative communication between individuals, humor is therefore influenced by specific circumstances, language, religion, history, and social values and norms. People from different cultural backgrounds, Western and non-Western—Asian and Middle Eastern societies, individualistic and collectivist cultures—perceive, interpret, use, and are affected by humor, as well as with other means of communication in different ways (see Feldman, 2021). There are cultures and political cultures in which humor plays an important role in social life, where humor in its diverse forms is accepted, and cultures where humor is not encouraged in everyday life.

Focusing on different countries and groups, the following chapters examine the extent to which cultural factors are related to (reflect, shape, determine) the content,

---

[1] This chapter draws on Feldman (2024). The interested reader should see this reference for a detailed discussion of the theoretical background, methodological perspectives, and numerous examples related to the topic.

nature, and characteristics of humor in selected countries and social groups. The message emanating from this work is about the distinctive power of humor: studying political humor leads to a better understanding of political rhetoric, information processing, attitude formation and change, persuasion, and political engagement.

In this chapter, following a brief theoretical consideration, I detail three selected aspects at the heart of political humor relevant to the ensuing chapters: Sect. 1.3 discusses first the notion that political humor can be employed for both good and bad purposes, followed by a discussion on the role played by stereotypes in affecting ethno-national humor. Section 1.4 details each of the three main groups—the public, politicians, and mass media –that employ humorous expressions in politics, detailing the means they use and their goals in doing so. Finally, the chapter details the structure of the book and briefly describes each of the contributions.

## 1.2 Theoretical Considerations

Along with studies in such fields of knowledge as anthropology, philosophy, literature, and history, research in the fields of psychology, sociology, and linguistics have paid considerable attention to, and developed theories, explaining humor's role and effect in society, and especially the circumstances that enable humor to be effective, interesting, and amusing. Warren and his team (2021) noted more than 20 different psychological theories that attempt to identify a set of psychological conditions, or characteristics prompting laughter, and the perception that something is amusing. These are split into three predominant theories, often linked to each other and sharing the same concepts, that explain humor appreciation: superiority, incongruity, and relief/release. The three theories and their relevance to political humor are detailed hereon.

### 1.2.1 Superiority Theory

Superiority Theory suggests that the purpose of humor is to demonstrate one's superiority, dominance, hostility, derision, or power over others or some objects, and also over the persons' own former position or a former version of themselves (Lintott, 2016; Smuts, 2006). This theory works well in the realm of political humor, as laughs can easily be gained at the expense of other individuals or groups in society. It is often demonstrated in racist and sexist attitudes that intend to derogate or humiliate members of minorities such as ethnic groups, women, LGBT, and physically handicapped persons (see Feldman, 2023a, 2023b), and in humor demeaning members of certain populations. Here is a joke that falls under this category that ostensibly shows the "superiority" of a Romanian in comparison to Russians.

A Romanian engineer came to visit his friend, a Russian engineer, in Russia, and saw that he had a beautiful apartment with seven rooms. The Romanian, surprised by this wealth, asked his friend how does a person in a communist country manage to build himself a 7-room apartment?

The Russian: Do you see that big bridge over there?
The Romanian: Yes.
The Russian: I planned it. So you take a stone here, a stone there, a bag of cement here, a bag of cement there, and that's how I build it.
A year later, the Russian engineer went to visit his friend in Romania and to his surprise saw that his friend had a huge villa with 24 rooms, a private pool, and tennis and golf courts.
The Russian: How does a person in a communist country manage to build himself a villa like this?
The Romanian: Do you see that big bridge over there?
The Russian: No.
The Romanian: That's it.

## 1.2.2 Incongruity Theory

The Incongruity theory of humor focuses on its cognitive or intellectual aspects. It is based upon the idea that humor results from a contrast between what is logically expected and what actually takes place or what is said i.e., the mismatch between two or more normally unrelated ideas or events that are brought together in an unanticipated, inappropriate, or surprising manner. Consider the following examples:

Customer: Waiter, there is a dead fly in my soup.
Waiter: I know, the heat kills them.

An old Jewish man reads about Einstein's theory of relativity in the newspaper and asks his scientist grandson to explain it to him.
The grandson explains: "Well, grandpa, it's sort of like this. Einstein says that if you're having your teeth drilled without Novocaine, a minute seems like an hour. But if you're sitting with a beautiful woman on your lap, an hour seems like a minute."
The old man considers this profound bit of thinking for a moment and says, "And from this he makes a living?"

Employee comes back from a business trip to Brazil.
Boss: How was your trip?
Employee: It was fine but I don't like Brazil. The whole country is nothing but soccer players and hookers.
Boss: You do know that my wife is Brazilian, right?
Employee (flushing): Oh really? Which team does she play for?

## 1.2.3 Relief/Release Theory

Third, the Relief/Release theory relates less to what makes something funny and more to the purpose of laughter and its physiological effects—the release of tension—asserting that humor and the resulting laughter are necessary to discharge energy and stress (Smuts, 2006). Here, humor appears as a socially acceptable vehicle to relieve tension about such sensitive issues as aggression, violence, racism, and sexual impulses that individuals might find difficult or uncomfortable to discuss (cf., Freud, 1960, pp. 797–803). As opposed to the previous theories, the relief/release theory is not of much use in the study of political humor because while it describes the process of laughter, it does not contribute to the discussion of purposeful humor that the incongruity and superiority theories provide. The following is an example of a joke that could be said to fall under this category:

> Two elderly couples were enjoying a friendly conversation when one of the men asked the other, "Jack, how was the memory clinic you went to last month?"
> "Outstanding," Jack replied. "They taught us all the latest psychological techniques visualization, association—it made a huge difference for me."
> "That's great! What was the name of the clinic?"
> Jack went blank. He thought and thought, but couldn't remember. Then a smile broke across his face and he asked, "What do you call that red flower with the long stem and thorns?"
> "You mean a rose?"
> "Yes, that's it!" Jack turned to his wife. "Rose, what was the name of that clinic we went to?"

Taken together, the three theories are an essential framework for presenting the variety of classical approaches. They are, however, incomplete and by themselves not adequate to fully describe the phenomenon. As such, scholars proposed comprehensive theories encompassing all aspects of humor development within a framework that makes sense of contemporary matters.

## 1.2.4 Comprehensive Theories

Examples of comprehensive theories include *John* Morreal's (1983) theory that combines the traditional approaches of superiority, incongruity, and release, emphasizing that all laughter results from a pleasant psychological change of the individual in response to the humorous stimulus, and Avner Ziv's model for understanding humor (Ziv, 1984). The latter emphasizes five specific functions rather than psychological change: aggressive, sexual, social, humor as a defense mechanism, and intellectual function. Here is a brief description of each of these functions.

### 1.2.4.1 The Aggressive Function

The aggressive function of humor involves the victimization of individuals (e.g., lawyer humor, psychiatrist humor), groups (e.g., ethnic humor), or institutions (e.g., political humor), through ridicule or disparagement, creating a sense of superiority in the perpetrator. Consider the following example of this kind of humor:

> Questions: What's the difference between a good lawyer and a great lawyer?
> Answer: A good lawyer knows the law. A great lawyer knows the judge.

Patient: "Doctor, I keep thinking I'm a dog."
Psychiatrist: "Lie down on the couch and I'll examine you."
Patient: "I can't, I'm not allowed on the furniture."

God creates the world and decides that for the Holy Land he's going all out. He tells the angels of his plans: "The place will be flowing with milk and honey; there will be beautiful mountain ranges and gorgeous deserts; a fine coast with nice beach; not too big a country so the people can stay together; great weather with no hurricanes, typhoons, snowstorms; etc." At some point the angels stop God and ask: "Don't you think you're exaggerating a bit? OK, they might be your Chosen People, but this is extreme!"
To which God replies: "Just wait; I haven't told you who I'm giving them for neighbors."

### 1.2.4.2 The Sexual Function

The sexual function deals with socially acceptable ways to express and reduce sexual tension i.e., what society consider taboo. Sexual humor can indicate enjoyment, anxiety, or disappointment in sex, allowing people to challenge such taboos in a pleasant manner. An example in this regard:

A man goes to a psychologist and says, "Doc, I got a real problem, I can't stop thinking about sex."
The Psychologist says, "Well let's see what we can find out," and pulls out his ink blots. "What is this a picture of?" he asks.
The man turns the picture upside down then turns it around and states, "That's a man and a woman on a bed making love."
The Psychologist says, "Very interesting," and shows the next picture.
"And what is this a picture of?"
The man looks and turns it in different directions and says, "That's a man and a woman on a bed making love."
The Psychologists tries again with the third ink blot, and asks the same question, "What is this a picture of?"
The patient again turns it in all directions and replies, "That's a man and a woman on a bed making love."
The Psychologist states, "Well, yes, you do seem to be obsessed with sex."
"Me!?" demands the patient. "You're the one who keeps showing me the dirty pictures!"

### 1.2.4.3 The Social Function

This function of humor is characterized by two aspects. First, relationships within a group, the social system within which personal acquaintance and interaction between and among group members exist. Second, society as a whole or social phenomena. Humor's role is to reform aspects of these. On the one hand it includes, among other things, strengthening group relations, cultivating social intimacy, and reinforcing group cohesiveness. On the other hand, humor can be used to exclude members from the group (Ziv, 1984, p. 3). Humor in this sense can be a way of improving society, working as a social corrective by acting as a safety valve for the release of tensions and frustration. Satire, for example, conveys a social message, expresses many social problems and aspirations, and its aim is to educate through humor. In this book, satire in political cartoons, broadcast and the print media are exemplars in this regard.

Political cartoons, as discussed below, are also satirical representations that are essentially discursive and intertextual. They question power relations, indicate societal injustice, and reveal corruption. Satire enables cartoonists to tackle serious and sensitive issues in a way that motivate thinking, and encourage debate. It is utilized in political cartoons in several ways including highlighting specific characteristics or behaviors of political leaders by stressing the divergence between what leaders say and what they do, by ridiculing their actions, decisions, and statements, and by criticizing specific policies, ideologies, or societal issues associated with the leaders and political parties.

As such, satire has tremendous cultural significance in Indonesia, for example, with a long history of mixing comedy and satire into daily life through folklore, traditional performances, and oral storytelling (see Chap. 3). Political cartoonists have utilized satire to criticize Indonesia authority, and to express discontent of political leaders and policies, providing social commentary on governance, political climate, and socioeconomic challenges, that contribute to public discussions. Likewise, for more than two centuries satirical cartoons in Spain (Chap. 6) were able to serve as a loudspeaker and reference for transcendent issues such as the Franco dictatorship, democratic transition, territoriality, and anticlericalism. In Brazil, satire depicted in political cartoons was able to criticize Jair Bolsonaro's ultraconservative agenda (see Chap. 4), and also in Japan (Chap. 2) satire of contemporary socio-political discourses through *manga* played an important role in molding public attitudes and the agenda. In the broadcast media, satirical sketches in Poland include historical references, ethnic stereotypes, and representations of individual political leaders (Chap. 8), and in the print media, satire in Japan (see Chap. 12) is expressed in humorous verses that focus also on political leaders, policies, and political issues.

### 1.2.4.4 The Defensive Function

As a defense mechanism, humor is a means of providing us with a way to deal with our anxieties. Two characteristic forms of humor as a defense mechanism are identified, both assisting in protecting an individual's self-image and emotional balance. First, humor acts as a form of self-inoculation against what scares us in a form of "gallows humor" or "black humor," the type that makes light of a subject often considered taboo, serious, or painful to discuss; for example, death, crime, discrimination, terrorism, and genocide, including the Holocaust. It is instrumental in actively helping us to handle threats and horror instead of yielding to it, and can be described as the humor of survival (Ziv, 1984, p. 58). Here are examples of "black humor:"

> "Did you hear about the guy whose left side was cut off? He's all right now."

> In a bar, a guest and a German bartender were having a conversation. They talk for some time until they come to the topic of religion. "Yeah, I'm Jewish," says the man. The bartender is in shock: "I'm terribly sorry for the Holocaust, oh my God, we did horrible things to you." The Jewish man doesn't know how to react. It feels wrong to just respond with "It's okay..." The bartender cuts the silence first:"If there is anything I can do for you, just say." The Jew thinks for a moment. "Oh umm, could I possibly get free beer?"

The bartender: "Oh, I mean if I could I totally would, but the owner would kill me if he found out…".
The Jew: "Yeah, don't worry, it is not your fault. After all, you're just following orders, right?".

The second characteristic form of humor as a defense mechanism is self-disparagement or self-deprecating humor i.e., the ability to laugh at oneself or groups we belong to. By revealing the speaker's weakness, self-disparaging humor aims at discharging any hostility towards themselves by impeding aggressive motives, gaining sympathy from others who identify with the humorist's shortcomings, and at the same time enabling them to actively grapple with their fear and drawbacks. Sigmund Freud (1960, p. 111) noted that self-deprecating jokes by Jews point to the positive attributes of the Jewish people at the same time that they poked fun at perceived negatives. Here is an example in this context:

> Two beggars are sitting side by side on the street in Rome. One has a cross in front of him, the other a Star of David. Many people go by, but only put money into the hat of the beggar sitting behind the cross. A priest comes by, stops and watches throngs of people giving money to the beggar sitting behind the cross, but none give to the beggar sitting behind the Star of David. Finally, the priest goes over to the beggar behind the Star of David and says: "Don't you understand? This is a Catholic country. People aren't going to give you money if you sit there with a Star of David in front of you, especially if you're sitting beside a beggar who has a cross. In fact, they would probably give to him triple the amount just out of spite to you."
> The beggar behind the Star of David listened to the priest, turned to the other beggar with the cross and said: "Aaron, look who's trying to teach us marketing."

### 1.2.4.5 The Intellectual Function

Finally, based on wordplay and absurdities, intellectual humor provides temporary release from strict rules and rational thought, an escape to the absurd. The intellectual function of humor involves understanding and problem solving. Understanding is a part of the thought process, and the enjoyment of humor calls for an intellectual activity like the kind required in problem solving. Here are related examples:

> Question: "How many dead are there in this cemetery?"
> Answer: "Everyone."
>
> "Once I had multiple personalities, but now we are feeling well."
>
> "I used to be indecisive. Now I'm not sure."
>
> Two men are sitting in a pub and looking through the window.
> One says, "Do you see the two ladies across the road? One is my wife and the other one is my mistress."
> "You just took the words out of my mouth," replies the other.

Perhaps also included in this category is the Japanese *dajare* (literally, "wordplay"), a linguistic device similar in spirit to a pun that relies on similarities in the pronunciation of words to create simple jokes. These homophones (and Japanese has plenty of these), have a different "spelling." Most of the time the pun relies on the phrase being spoken (different from writing when different kanji i.e., logographic Chinese characters, are used for the same sounds). Thus, while speaking, one can use context or explain later, but when writing something down, kanji specify the meaning apart from the pronunciation. *Dajare* are also associated with *oyaji gyagu* (literally "old man gag" or "old man joke"), which is the Japanese equivalent to dad ("old man") jokes in English (see Toshiko, 2022).

Here are a few example of *dajare* that use the same syllables twice, carrying a different meaning the second time yet still making a somewhat coherent phrase and a completely meaningful sentence to make a pun:

> ***Arumikan*** (aluminum can) *no ue ni* (on it's top) ***aru mikan*** (an orange).
> There is an orange [*mikan*] on an aluminum can.
>
> ***Ikura*** (salmon roe) *wa* ***ikura*** (how much, regarding the cost of something)?
> How much is the salmon roe?
>
> ***nyûyôku*[2] *de* (in New York) ***nyûyoku*** (taking a bath)
> Taking a bath in New York
>
> ***Sukii*** (ski) *ga* ***suki*** (like).
> I like skiing.
>
> ***Iruka*** (dolphins) ga ***iruka*** (are there)?
> Are there dolphins?

Other *dajare* use similar sounds twice:

> ***Futon*** (a Japanese style mattress) *ga* ***futton****da* (blown away)
> Futon was blown away

Or, sentences with more than one meaning:

> *Nê,* (Hey) *chanto* (properly) *ofuro haitteru* (take a bath)?
> Hey, do you take a bath properly?
>
> *Nêchan* (your sister) *to* (with) *ofuro haitteru* (take a bath)?
> Are you taking a bath with your sister?

Here, *nê* is used as an interjection, while *chanto* means "proper," but the meaning quickly changes when combining both, as *nêchan* means "sister."

## 1.3 Comparison and Stereotyping Aspects in Humor

### *1.3.1 Good and Bad Purposes*

Considering the above theories on general humor, political humor can be employed for both benevolent and malevolent purposes. On the one hand, humor creates positive action (laughter) through a shared experience between the person providing the mirth

---

[2] A diacritical mark, for example, ê, ô, or û over the vowel indicates that it is a long vowel.

and the person enjoying the humor's benefits (the laughing person). Humor facilitates communication between individuals across social strata and hierarchies; it serves as a bonding tool and solidarity that ties people together, creates a friendly atmosphere in a given social group, a sense of belonging that can enhance teamwork in the workplace, a tool for healing, helping to relieve stress, and maintaining social justice (e.g., Friedman & Friedman, 2019; Warren et al., 2021).

Conversely, humor may serve as mocking discreditation and thus function as a tool for ridiculing, criticizing, demeaning, humiliating, belittling, and manipulating other people (Feldman, 2023a, 2023b). A political debaser can use "humor" i.e., debasing attack on a given victim, and then "protect themselves" by later saying to those who don't like such speech and criticize them: "I didn't really mean it; it was just in jest." (I thank Sam Lehman-Wilzig for his observation in this regard.) Such humor may stem from the need to reinforce one's own self, often at the expense of other people and relationships with them in order to enhance one's superiority, domination, and self-esteem. A large number of cases involve comparisons between good and evil, heaven and hell, and winners and losers, with rhetorical devices usually being employed, as discussed in the following section.

### *1.3.2 Stereotyping Groups and Ethnic Communities*

Stereotypes, images, along with prejudice, enter also political humor in jokes regarding different groups of people, religions, classes, genders, and professions, as indicated in the following examples regarding "blond women," and then (ignorant) policemen:

> A young, touring ventriloquist puts on a show in a small town. With his dummy on his knee, he starts going through his usual dumb blonde jokes.
> Suddenly, a blonde woman in the third row stands on her chair and starts shouting, "I've heard enough of your stupid blonde jokes. What makes you think you can stereotype blonde women that way? What does the color of a woman's hair have to do with her worth as a human being? It's men like you who keep women like me from being respected at work and in the community, and from reaching our full potential as people. Its people like you that make others think that all blondes are dumb! You and your kind continue to perpetuate discrimination against not only blondes, but women in general, pathetically all in the name of humor!"
> The embarrassed ventriloquist begins to apologize. The blonde then yells: "You stay out of this!... I'm talking to that little shit on your lap!!!"

> Two policemen are standing on the street in New York City. A foreigner approaches them looking slightly panicked. "Parlez vous Francais?" He asks them. The policemen, not knowing a word of French merely shrug their shoulders at the man. Frustrated, the man asks them, "Ustedes hablan español?" Again, the policemen merely shrug. The foreigner continues with the same result with Dutch, Russian, and German. Eventually, he leaves, knowing that there's no hope for him to communicate with the officers. "I keep telling you we should learn more languages!" says one policeman to the other. "Why?" responds the other, "That man knows five, and it didn't get him anywhere."

Other examples include cultural stereotypes regarding naïve Native Americans, smart Jews, and "poor" Palestinians:

> A Native American hitchhiker was picked up by a slick city man who was driving past the reservation.
> As they were driving along, the Native American noticed a brown paper bag on the dashboard and inquired as to its contents.
> The city man replied, "It's a bottle of wine, I got it for my wife."
> The Native American looked forward at the road, nodded his head solemnly, and said, "Good trade."

> Two Jews were standing and talking on a Moscow street. One of them did not have official papers permitting him to be in Moscow at the time. When a police officer approached them to verify their documents, the Jew with the documents told his friend not to worry as he began to run from the officer.
> The officer began to chase him. When he finally caught up, the officer asked him to show his documents, which he did. The officer asked him, "Why did you run away from me when you have the right documents?"
> "My doctor told me to run one mile each day," responded the Jew.
> "But why didn't you stop when you saw me running after you?" asked the officer.
> "I thought your doctor told you the same," said the Jew.

> Question: "How many Palestinians does it take to change a light bulb?"
> Answer: "None! They sit in the dark forever and blame the Israelis for it!"

### 1.3.3 Comparing National Groups

Likewise, here are examples of humor related to the concept of national character, defined as the traits apparent in the consciousness and behavioral tendencies shared by most of the population (e.g., Feldman, 1997). This is how cultural stereotypes find their way as classic jokes to illustrate differences in national character:

> An international cruise ship, where every nationality in the world is represented on board, was sailing across the ocean. Suddenly, the ship springs a leak and begins to sink. The captain put the women and children in lifeboats. But there weren't enough boats, so he had to persuade the men to jump into the water. One by one, the captain called up each national group, said something to them, then they jumped. Later, a reporter asked him, "How did you persuade each nationality to jump?" "It was easy," explained the captain.
> "To the American I said that if he jump into the sea, he'd be a hero.
> To the British, if you jump you are true gentleman!
> To the Australian, don't be a wuss, all your mates are down there in the drink.
> To the New Zealander, strap on this bungee cord—she'll be alright!
> To the Russian, all the vodka was washed overboard, I can see the bottles floating past...if you're quick you can grab them.
> To the French, please do NOT jump into the water.
> To the German, according to regulations, all the men must jump into the sea.
> To the Italian, beautiful woman are swimming in the sea!
> To the Chinese, ingredients that look delicious are floating in the sea!
> To the Japanese, everyone else has already jumped.
> To the South Korean, the Japanese guy has already jumped.
> To the North Korean, this is your chance to defect! This is your chance to go into exile!"

Another joke in this regard relates to the Japanese people, referring to their sensitivity to relations with others i.e., having a strong tendency to compare themselves with people from other countries, and a great concern about their image and the way others see them. The joke is about an international essay-writing contest endorsed by the United Nations on the topic of elephants.

> The Englishman went for a few days to India and came back to write an essay on "The Manners of Elephants in India."
> The Frenchman went for a couple of hours to the Paris zoo and wrote about the "Love Life of an Elephant."
> The German disappeared into the library for several weeks and came back with a book on the "Physiological Structure of Elephants."
> The Spaniard wrote a scientific treatise on "The Elephant and the Art of Bullfighting."
> The Soviet writer wrote about "Elephants and Marxism."
> The American wrote about "How to Raise Elephants in your Backyard for Fun and Profit."
> The Pole wrote on "The Elephant and the Polish National Question."
> For the Japanese it took the longest time and he came back with two books. The first: "Effects of the Japanese Economy on the Elephant's Life;" the second, much longer than the first, was entitled "What Do the Elephants Think of the Japanese."
>
> But this is not the end of the story. The Japanese Ministry of Foreign Affairs, cautioned that because of Japan's low reputation it is better not to publish the books. And the Ministry of Education made sure that all other books from other countries were translated into Japanese.
>
> The moral of the story is how sensitive the Japanese are about the opinion of others and how eager they are to learn from abroad (Thanks to Peter Berton; see also, Berton, 1998).

## 1.4 Creating and Exploiting Political Humor

Three groups—the public, politicians, and the mass media—employ humorous expressions in politics through different means in order to realize different goals.

The general public use humoristic expressions as a means of venting power and resisting the power structure and social injustice. As "the powerless," they overtly try to make fun of the political system, institutions, and political oppressors that regulate, restrict, and discipline them. Humoristic expressions are a reaction of citizens to the stress they feel in this regard in their everyday life. Vehicles of such humor in Europe and the U.S. include artistic work in posters, photograph, pictures, and film (Baldi, 2024; Brzozowska & Chłopicki, 2024; Sills & Monaghan-Geerneart, 2024); and live shows performances such as satiric, comedy, and parody theater, and festivals and carnivals where groups compose and perform humorous and satirical lyrics, criticizing political powers from the local to the national levels, spreading quickly and widely through the internet and social networks (e.g., Rivas-Carmona & García-Manga, 2024).

Freud (1960) observed that jokes, for example, especially serve the purpose of aggressiveness toward, or defense from, people in high positions for the abovementioned reasons. Humor is thus used by those who have no political power as a means of political criticism, as methods of an individual challenging restrictive policies and stressful political situations, and as an instrument to get even with oppressors.

1 Humor and Politics in the Media: A Conceptual Introduction

Consider, for example, the following joke that was told while U.S. President Donald Trump was in office:

> An Israeli doctor says: "In Israel, medicine is so advanced that we cut off a man's liver, put them on another man, and in 6 weeks, he is looking for work."
> The German doctor says: "That's nothing, in Germany we take part of a brain, put it in another man, and in 4 weeks he is looking for work."
> The Russian doctor says: "Gentlemen, we take half a heart from a man, put it in another's chest, and in 2 weeks he is looking for work."
> The American doctor laughs: "You all are behind us. Two days ago, we took a man with no brains, no heart, and no liver and made him President. Now, the whole country is looking for work!"

For their part, politicians are well aware of the power of humor. American presidents in particular, starting from George Washington and Abraham Lincoln through John F. Kennedy, Ronald Reagan (who was known as *"The Great Communicator"* and the "Master of the Joke," see Harris, 2009), and Barack Obama, used humor while campaigning and in office (e.g., Phillips-Anderson, 2024)—probably because they knew that even a mediocre joke or a witty remark during congressional deliberations, public speeches, or media interviews can affect their interaction with the electorate and the public (Krasner, 2024).

In particular, when used wisely humor can affect politicians' contact with the public along two dimensions. First, humor allows politicians to control the immediate social situation by focusing attention on themselves, re-establishing deference, and creating temporary unity in the audience. Second, humor enables politicians to decisively influence the audience's perception of the potentially damaging issue at stake, thereby redefining the situation to the politicians's advantage. Using witty remarks allows the leader to influence the choice of schema by which journalists and the wider public perceive the situation (Krasner, 2024; see also Feldman, 2022).

Last, the mass media—through which journalists, columnists, political pundits and critics, and subject matter experts (as well as general readers who contribute articles to the opinion column pages or letters to the editors, see Chap. 12)—create and spread humor. The printed media, newspapers and magazines provide the public with comic columns, humorous scripts, editorial cartoons, and *manga*. The internet includes such sites as Facebook, YouTube, Instagram, Twitter, and TikTok that have turned into arenas for humoristic messages, cartoons, and jokes of politicians between each other and with the public (see Rastrilla et al., 2023).

Broadcast media too, including movies and in particular television, provide the public with humor in the form of comedy shows, standup performances, joke tellers, humorous advertisements, and witty comments. Most notably are televised satirical programs in the U.S., including late-night talk shows such as *The Daily Show, The Colbert Report,* and *Saturday Night Live,* where politicians and aspiring politicians, their characteristics and customs, are the focus of the majority of jokes told, overwhelmingly negative in tone; relatively little humor concerns itself with policy or process (e.g., Baumgartner et al., 2014).

Such political satire or comedy constitute a very powerful force. Exposure to political humor in these channels matters as such programs serve as a major source of news for viewers, especially youngsters. They enrich their viewers with knowledge of events and activities, affect their political attitudes and level of political involvement, prompting discussion about politics with friends, family, and coworkers, and influencing viewers' support for certain candidates. As this is known to politicians they try to appear on these programs to their own advantage (e.g., Baym & Jones, 2013; Compton, 2018; Feldman, 2013; Goldman, 2013; Ross & Rivers, 2017).

## 1.5 Overview of the Volume

Overall, three intellectual goals motivated this volume's contributors. The first is to clarify the relationship between culture (broadly defined, involving norms of behavior, attitudes, beliefs etc., in all walks of life) and political humor, as appearing in a variety of media. Accordingly, each author focused on one country, and examined how cultural factors (e.g., social structure, social relationship, historical experiences, religion, economic system, majority/minority relations, individualism/collectivism, and national character) affect the content, type, and style of the humorous expressions in the media in a given society.

The second goal is to probe the source of this humor: Who utilizes humorous expressions and for what reason? Chapters detail graphic artists, satirists, cartoonists, parody program writers, users of social networking services (SNS), comedians, journalists and columnists, and general readers, as their humorous expressions target politicians, the political system, minorities, and the "self." The third goal is to discuss the social, political, and psychological effect or potential effect of political humor in a given polity.

To these ends, the book is divided into three parts. The first part, *Humor in Political Cartoons,* gives particular consideration to the effect of culture on political cartoons published by daily newspapers, in magazines, and books. Chapter 2 examines the relationship between culture and political humor as reflected in Japanese *manga* in both directions. It first assesses how expressions of political satire and humor echo changes in Japanese cultural attitudes and the society's status quo, further detailing the extent to which graphic artists, satirists, and cartoonists have shaped popular attitudes about important historical events, thereby actively engaging in the political decision-making process. The chapter looks also at the way contemporaries' brand of graphic political humor utilized Japan's ideogrammatic culture to defamiliarize political norms and its role in directing attitudes towards the Japanese nation in the international arena.

Chapter 3 elaborates on political cartoons in Indonesia during the presidential periods of Susilo Bambang Yudhoyono and Joko Widodo. By employing a Critical Discourse Analysis approach the chapter analyzes a selected collection of political cartoons to demonstrate the way the two presidents, their personalities and policies, were depicted in these cartoons, revealing the power of humor as a form of social commentary and political critique in Indonesia. Chap. 4 draws attention to the way an award-winning Brazilian cartoonist illustrated President Jair

Bolsonaro's administration. Considering the idea that humor is an important feature of Brazilian's cultural tradition, the chapter maintains that through cartoons political humor provided a form of criticism and opposition to Bolsonaro's anti-democratic and anti-human rights agenda. By condemning and ridiculing government actions, these cartoons raised awareness of important social and political issues, including the Covid-19 pandemic, the electoral system and democracy, conservative values, and the environment, contributing to a critical view and stance towards the central government.

Aiming at exploring how cultural dynamics operate through political humor in the Republic of Türkiye (Turkey), Chap. 5 focuses on the characteristics of humor through the political cartoons published during thirteen months in three satirical magazines. The analysis reveals diverse attitudes in the different magazines. In one, political authority is criticized by adopting elements of black humor, concern, and despair as prominent themes. The second inspires readers with hope, encouraging action especially among women, through editorial strategies that refer to a culture of struggle. In the third magazine, cartoons are mostly based on populist dualities, seeking to construct an alternative historical narrative. It utilizes cultural characteristics in the process of a neo-conservatist, political Islamist, cultural hegemony project, undermining the genre potential of Islamic humor.

Chapter 6 centers around the notion that humor and political culture have always been connected in contemporary Spain. It specifically analyzes the relationship between political culture and contemporary humor by looking at a selection of cartoons by Antonio Fraguas i.e., *Forges*, an influential artist who portrayed Spanish social and political reality over the past 50 years. The final chapter in this section, Chap. 7, presents the case of Australia, utilizing Critical Discourse Analysis and Thematic Analysis to examine far-right political humor and its relationship to the country's culture. It details the way far-right humor is articulated, shaped, and transformed by the cultural context in Australia, shaped by (among other things) its settler colonial reality, its strong multicultural legacy, its proximity to Asia, and cultural, social, and political ties to the U.S. and the U.K.

The second part of the book, *Political Humor in Broadcast Media*, introduces case studies that examine the relationship between culture and political humor in Television, SNS, and YouTube. Chap. 8 looks at satire on Polish television by examining three case studies of popular, televised, parody programs. The chapter describes how historical references are readdressed for comic effect, and how stereotypes are reproduced to satirize ruling elites or expose personal immoralities and incompetence. Moreover, it reveals how satire draws on cultural schemes and metaphors of governance, power, and partisan politics, notably severely ridiculing autocracy and corruption. Political satire in Poland appears as supporting citizenship, on the one hand, by elucidating the processes behind the power, and weakening trust in politicians among citizens, on the other hand.

Focusing on Facebook, Chap. 9 assesses the degree to which sexist humor targeting female politicians appears in Facebook comments within the patriarchal culture of Montenegro. The analysis distinguishes between comments that prompted humorous reactions and those that reduced female politicians to sexual objects, presented them as conforming to traditional gender roles in the society, or played on the stereotype of women's inferiority. It considers the former as humorous and the latter as sexist. Although a large proportion of the commentary was sexist, most often such comments were not recognized as humorous. Those that were recognized as humorous included references to women's bodies and appearance, the sexual objectification of female politicians, personality flaws stereotypically associated with women, and encouraging women to prioritize family over politics.

SNS is at the center of Chap. 10 that aims to identify the targets or the stereotypical victims that are culturally addressed in political humor distributed in Iran through social networks. Utilizing the Appraisal Model, the chapter details the extent to which social status, economic conditions, and religious views form political humor within the Iranian socio-political context. It reveals that the closed socio-political context within a country affects the selection of the targets and the tone of the humor. As for YouTube, Chap. 11 looks at comedic acts performed by Malaysian comedians that are also accessible via YouTube. The chapter probes the extent to which the essence of culture, including being polite, civilized, and maintaining/saving face, are related to the activities of two comedians. Based on Brown and Levinson's framework on politeness, the chapter suggests that off-the-record and negative politeness strategies prevail in the parody of one performer, and that the other's jests were unequivocal, direct utterances in which the communicative intent was clear, the targeted group was also clear in linguistical and contextual terms, exhibiting negative politeness. In both cases, restraint in the Malaysian context is observed.

The third part of the book, *Political Humor in the Print Media,* draws attention to Japanese and Argentine newspapers. Chapter 12 elaborates on *senryû*, satirical and humorous verses in Japanese dailies, as a manifestation of humor in this country. At the center of the chapter are 3,443 verses contributed by general readers as they were published in two national newspapers during 2022 and 2023. The chapter reveals that a large number of these verses focused on political issues, processes, and decisionmakers, as a vehicle to mirror public sentiment towards political institutions and leaders, policy initiatives and decisions, and society as a whole –on the one hand using such rhetorical devices as satire, irony, and ridicule, and on the other hand expressions of optimism, hope, and empathy. Chapter 13 discusses "*la grieta*" in Argentinian society, the deep and irreconcilable division fragmenting and polarizing the nation. It significantly affects political, social, cultural, and even beyond that, personal relationships—friendships, families, and workplaces in Argentina. Leading newspapers in this country align themselves with different sides of *la grieta*, adopting either a progressive, conservative, or a center-right stance, reflected in their satirical approaches through political columns and editorial cartoons. In this way, the chapter notes, the print media reinforced existing beliefs, deepening the ideological and political divide.

The fourth and final part of the book, *Conclusions* consists of one chapter suggesting guidelines and directions for future research in political humor. In particular, the chapter proposes several methodological questions regarding political humor research. These includes the extent to which political humor is addressed to both/all sides of the political spectrum, the elements underlying the effect of political humor, the focus of its influence (governmental policy, personnel, and/or ideology, or on the general public), and the effect of a given medium on a specific social group.

It is the contributors' sincere hope that readers will find this book useful and that it will stimulate further research into the fascinating yet under-studied topic of political humor.

## References

Baldi, B. (2024). Humor and cynical political parody in Italian movies and newspaper cartoons. In O. Feldman (Ed.), *Political humor worldwide: The cultural context of political comedy, satire, and parody* (pp. 159–174). Springer.

Baumgartner, J. C., Lichter, S. R., & Morris, J. (2014). *Politics is a joke! How TV comedians are remaking political life*. Westview.

Baym, G., & Jones, J. P. (Eds.) (2013). *News parody and political satire across the globe*. Routledge. https://www.routledge.com/News-Parody-and-Political-Satire-Across-the-Globe/Baym-Jones/p/book/9781138109377

Bergson, H. ([1911]2008). *Laughter: An essay on the meaning of the comic* (trans. C. Brereton & F. Rothwell). Macmillan. https://www.templeofearth.com/books/laughter.pdf

Berton, P. (1998). The psychology of Japan's foreign relations. In O. Feldman (Ed.), *Political psychology in Japan: Behind the nails that sometimes stick out (and get hammered down)* (pp. 283–302). Nova Science Publ.

Brzozowska, D., & Chłopicki, W. (2024). Cultural wars in Polish political humor. In O. Feldman (Ed.), *Political humor worldwide: The cultural context of political comedy, satire, and parody* (pp. 117–138). Springer.

Compton, J. (2018). Inoculating against/with political humor. In J. Baumgartner & A. B. Becker (Eds.), *Political humor in a changing media landscape: A new generation of research* (pp. 95–114). Lexington Books.

Feldman, L. (2013). Cloudy with a chance of heat balls: The portrayal of global warming on The Daily Show and The Colbert Report. *International Journal of Communication, 7*, 430–451. https://ijoc.org/index.php/ijoc/article/view/1940

Feldman, O. (1997). Culture, society, and the individual: Cross-cultural political psychology in Japan. *Political Psychology, 18*(2), 327–353. https://doi.org/10.1111/0162-895X.00060

Feldman, O. (2021). Introduction: Assessing cultural influences on political leaders' discourse. In O. Feldman (Ed.), *When politicians talk: The cultural dynamics of public speaking* (pp. 1–14). Springer. https://doi.org/10.1007/978-981-16-3579-3_1

Feldman, O. (2022). Introduction: Political interviews—an analytical model. In O. Feldman (Ed.), *Adversarial political interviewing: Worldwide perspectives during polarized times* (pp. 1–21). Springer. https://doi.org/10.1007/978-981-19-0576-6_1

Feldman, O. (Ed.). (2023a). *Political debasement: Incivility, contempt, and humiliation in parliamentary and public discourse*. Springer.

Feldman, O. (Ed.). (2023b). *Debasing political rhetoric: Dissing opponents, journalists, and minorities in populist leadership communication*. Springer.

Feldman, O. (2024). Humor and politics: A conceptual introduction. In O. Feldman (Ed.), *Political humor worldwide: The cultural context of political comedy, satire, and parody* (pp. 1–28). Springer.

Freud, S. ([1905]1960). *Jokes and their relation to the unconscious*. Norton.

Friedman, H. H., & Friedman, L. W. (2019). Laughing matters: When humor is meaningful. *Journal of Intercultural Management and Ethics, 4*, 55–71. https://papers.ssrn.com/sol3/papers.cfm?abstract_id=3418980

Goldman, N. (2013). Comedy and democracy: The role of humor in social justice. *Animating Democracy*. http://animatingdemocracy.org/sites/default/files/Humor%20Trend%20Paper.pdf

Harris, M. K. (2009). The political application of humor. *Honors Capstone Projects—All. 497*, 1–41. https://surface.syr.edu/honors_capstone/497

Krasner, M. A. (2024). Political humor in American culture: From affability to aggression. In O. Feldman (Ed.), *Political humor worldwide: The cultural context of political comedy, satire, and parody* (pp. 217–238). Springer.

Lintott, S. (2016). Superiority in humor theory. *The Journal of Aesthetics and Art Criticism, 74*(4), 347–358. https://doi.org/10.1111/jaac.12321

Morreall, J. (1983) *Taking laughter seriously*. State University of New York Press.

Phillips-Anderson, M. (2024). Founding contradictions, contemporary expressions: Political humor in American culture. In O. Feldman (Ed.), *Political humor worldwide: The cultural context of political comedy, satire, and parody* (pp. 31–47). Springer.

Rastrilla, L. P., Sapag, P. M., & García, A. R. (Eds.) (2023). *Fast politics: Propaganda in the age of TikTok*. Springer.https://doi.org/10.1007/978-981-99-5110-9

Rivas-Carmona, M. M., & García-Manga, M. C. (2024). The cultural background of political humor "sung" by the Spanish people. In O. Feldman (Ed.), *Political humor worldwide: The cultural context of political comedy, satire, and parody* (pp. 193–214). Springer.

Ross, A. S., & Rivers, D. J. (2017) Digital cultures of political participation: Internet memes and the discursive delegitimization of the 2016 US Presidential candidates. *Discourse, Context & Media, 16*, 1–11. https://doi.org/10.1177/1461444821989621

Sills, L., & Monaghan-Geerneart, P. G. (2024). The power of funny: Indigenous high art as quiescence and rebellion. In O. Feldman (Ed.), *Political humor worldwide: The cultural context of political comedy, satire, and parody* (pp. 175-191). Springer.

Smuts, A. (2006). Humor. In J. Fieser & B. Dowden (Eds.), *Internet encyclopedia of philosophy*. http://www.iep.utm.edu/h/humor.htm

Toshiko. (2022). 10 Common Japanese Jokes (Oyaji Gyagu). JW. https://jw-webmagazine.com/common-japanese-jokes/

Warren, C., Barsky, A., & McGraw, A. P. (2021). What makes things funny? An integrative review of the antecedents of laughter and amusement. *Personality and Social Psychology Review, 25*(1), 41–65. https://doi.org/10.1177/1088868320961909

Ziv, A. (1984). *Personality and sense of humor*. Springer.

**Ofer Feldman** is Professor of Political Psychology and Behavior at the Faculty of Policy Studies, Doshisha University, and an Affiliated Professor at the Center for Southeast Asian Studies, Kyoto University, Kyoto, Japan. His research centers on the psychological underpinnings of mass and elite political behavior in Japan. He has extensively published journal articles, books, and book chapters on issues related to political communication and persuasion, political leadership, and political culture. His books include *The Rhetoric of Political Leadership* (2020, edited), *When Politicians Talk* (2021, edited), *Adversarial Political Interviewing* (2022, edited), *Political Debasement* (2023, edited), *and Debasing Political Rhetoric* (2023, edited). In 2021 he was elected Honorary Chair of the Research Committee on Political Psychology, International Political Science Association.

# Part I
# Humor in Political Cartoons

# Chapter 2
# The Relationship Between Culture and Political Humor in Japanese Manga

**Roman Rosenbaum**

**Abstract** The development of humor in Japanese, politicized, graphic art has a long and illustrious history ranging from early manifestations of *fûshiga* (satirical drawings) via *jiji manga* (Western style cartoons) to the modern *manga* media. Nowadays, Japanese manga culture manifests itself as a powerful tool across the political divide to shape domestic as well as global perception of the nation. While the open denigration of politics via pop-cultural representations is generally regarded as a cultural taboo in Japanese society, the visual medium of manga provides a powerful counter-hegemonic space where discontent, Criticism, and satire can be expressed more freely than via conventional media. This chapter will not only illustrate how expressions of political satire and humor reflect changes in Japanese cultural attitudes and the society's status quo, but also how graphic artists, satirists, and cartoonists, have helped to shape popular attitudes about landmark historical events, thereby actively engaging in the political decision-making process. The chapter further examines how today's brand of graphic political humor utilized Japan's ideogrammatic culture to defamiliarize political norms and thereby might be more influential than ever in manipulating attitudes towards the Japanese nation in the global political amphitheater.

## 2.1 Introduction

Japanese comics do not exist in a vacuum; they are closely connected to Japanese history and culture, including such areas as politics, economy, family, religion, and gender.[1] Therefore, they reflect both the reality of Japanese society and the myths, beliefs, and fantasies that Japanese have about themselves, their culture, and the world (Ito, 2008, p. 26). Modern manga culture in Japan intrinsically links political

---

[1] All translations are mine unless otherwise stated. In Japanese, vowels can either be short or long; a diacritical mark, for example, â, ê, î, ô, or û over the vowel indicates that it is a long vowel. Personal names are given in the Japanese order i.e., family name first.

---

R. Rosenbaum (✉)
Japanese Studies, School of Languages and Cultures, University of Sydney, Sydney, Australia
e-mail: roman.rosenbaum@sydney.edu.au

© The Author(s), under exclusive license to Springer Nature Singapore Pte Ltd. 2024
O. Feldman (ed.), *Communicating Political Humor in the Media*, The Language of Politics, https://doi.org/10.1007/978-981-97-0726-3_2

humor with the issues du jour in contemporary society. Yet one person's sense of humor is another's insult, as attested by the Muhammed Cartoon controversy that led to the Charlie Hebdo attacks: it is impossible not to reflect on visual humor's power to move (Rosenthal et al., 2016, p. x).

Whereas early forms of cartoons offered political commentary via caricatures, slapstick, and satire, eventually the development of longer narrative structures enabled the portrayal of more sophisticated parodies as well as the allegorical treatment of socio-political and culture issues affecting Japanese society. As the epigraph by sociologist Itô Kinko suggests, comics and manga[2] have historically been established as a more sophisticated medium for social and political storytelling. Moreover, Japanese humor can be as politically subtle as its Western counterpart, but one needs to understand where to look for it and when it is permissible (Davis Milner, 2006, p. 1).

Consider for example of Fig. 2.1 This cartoon features a group of people in white on the left side of the image, representing politicians from the *Kaze no Kai* (Wind Party) right wing faction, who try to work out the validity of a sign created by the painter in black on the right side. The person closest to him shouts: "Hey, are you kidding, that's not us!!" The painter in black represents the cartoonist Yamafuji (1992) who replies: "I am sorry, I ran out of paint and will do the rest tomorrow." The characters on the far-right study of the image debate the sign: "It's weird that the left side is missing! Your stroke order is all wrong!" "What character is that? I have never seen it before." When **controversial right-wing political figure Shûsuke Nomura** established the *Kaze no Kai* during his run for candidature in the 1992 Upper House election, the above political caricature by enfant terrible cartoon superstar Yamafuji savagely attacked his position by replacing the character for "wind" with that of "lice," very similar in Japanese. This caricature took the 'wind' out of the campaign by literally leaving out a single stroke of the pen. Yamafuji's cartoon was a very rare case of criticizing right-wing organizations, and following Nomura's letter of complaint, Yamafuji replied with a letter of apology.

The dramatical historical changes in political humor have been substantiated by Exner (2022, p. 7), who suggested that between 1900 and 1919, a new middle class had replaced the nobility as the main class of newspaper readers, and formerly separate political and entertainment papers merged, now featuring news and entertainment. In addition, during the early 1920s, an audience of middle-class "popular readers" emerged that turned to newspapers more for entertainment than news and opinion, increasing newspapers' incentive to provide humorous content. Given Japan's high literacy rate and the well-developed state of the Japanese press and publishing industry by the 1920s, it is unsurprising that in 1923 publications began to import comic strips that had begun to dominate American newspapers around 1900.

This transformation of the media during the *fin de siècle* period saw manga develop beyond erudite *fûshi* or satirical manga that were able to deal concisely in humorous,

---

[2] The word "manga" will be treated throughout this chapter as a *plural* word denoting an entire spectrum of forms and styles within a single medium (similar to "fish" as the plural).

2 The Relationship Between Culture and Political Humor in Japanese Manga  23

**Fig. 2.1** Ridiculing political parties in Japan. *Source Shukan Asahi*, July 24, 1992. ©*Shûkan Asahi* and Yamafuji Shôji

socio-political commentary, but only in anecdotal, pithy fashion. This short format of comic art was gradually replaced by the development of longer-narrative content arising from Japan's story-telling traditions like *kami-shibai* ("picture card street theater") and the *yonkoma manga*, or four cell strips, by Kitazawa Rakuten (1876–1955), eventually leading to the development of novelistic discourse strategies akin to the rise of the literary novel in the eighteenth century.

Whereas oral Japanese cultural traditions of humor performances like *manzai* and *rakugo* (see Feldman & Kinoshita, Chapter 12) had principally eschewed the expression of political issues, the democratization under Taishô Democracy (1912–1926) enabled local, budding, cartoon artists to flourish when Kitazawa Rakuten founded the satirical magazine *Tokyo Puck* in 1905. Kitazawa's cartoons were influenced by Australian artist Frank Arthur Nankivell, who introduced new lithographic techniques and a satirical stye of cartooning more suitable to Japanese modernity. Later, Kitazawa's own influence extended to Ôten Shimokawa, creator of Japan's first cartoon animation, and further innovations were provided by Okamoto Ippei who introduced sophisticated and refined writing to manga and was one of the favorite cartoonists of the young Tezuka Osamu.

During the descent into the dark valley period of the Asia–Pacific Conflict, manga propaganda was the modus operandi of the media until the early postwar period saw the emergence of a new generation of artists that included Tezuka Osamu. As one of the chief architects in this transition to longer narrative manga, his development of the long story graphic format enabled much more detailed investigations of characters via extensive plot developments, protagonist/antagonist psychological development, and narrative strategy, to explore the relationship between culture and politics. Often this was accomplished via humorous techniques inherited from the early cartoon tradition and *fûshi* manga that sought to combine the various socio-political realms of modernizing Japan. This tradition is still observable in the many political manga pamphlets in contemporary Japan. The following episode, illustrated in Fig. 2.2, from *A heartwarming family's "What are constitutional revisions?"* (Shibata, 2015) depicts how humor is deployed in political manga discourse.

The situational comedy illustrated in Fig. 2.3 arises when grandfather Senzô (92 years old) quietly listens to the family's discussion on "constitutional revisionism." Unexpectedly, he shouts out something unintelligible in Japanese and shocks everyone into silence. In a moment of sublime comedy young Shôta (2 years old) brings grandfather his teeth on a plate.

Grandfather repeats his outburst in more intelligible Japanese: "Silence! Don't you know anything about history?" With everyone aghast, grandfather drops the bombshell in an intriguing crescendo: "The foundation of the Japanese Constitution was created by Americans." This is followed by a long comical narrative on the benefit of revising the Japanese constitution according to the Liberal Democratic Party's (LDP) agenda. The humorous political pamphlet was created by the LDP to promote its political vision via a discussion of constitutional revision in a stereotypical Japanese family. This illustrates how Japanese humor has moved into the mainstream with every-increasing commercialization of popular manga following the

**Fig. 2.2** Debating constitutional revision in manga. *Source* Shibata (2015). ©Liberal Democratic Party (LDP) and Shibata Kôbô

global commodification of Japanese visual culture. Yet this recent example follows in the footsteps of a long history of political cartooning.

According to eminent sociologist Tsurumi (1970, p. 322), "no matter how quietly innocent and touristy the scenery, these [postwar] manga unavoidably complained of the ever encroaching political." The best example for this was the appearance of Keiji Nakazawa's *Barefoot Gen* in 1972 that became the first full-length translation of a manga from Japanese into English to be published in the West. Highly critical of Japanese society it led to the establishment of the "masochist view of history" that still dominates socio-political affairs today. However, it was not until Frederik Schodt's (1983) well-illustrated introduction of manga to the international community in 1983 that the medium gained global attention. At the turn of the millennium, Sharon Kinsella provided one of the first detailed analyses in English of the phenomenon. Kinsella evocatively defines manga as a medium that displays a special responsiveness to the changing political currents of society. While manga's definition evolved according to the prevalent socio-political paradigm from a kind of trickster art, it also institutionalized a new type of democratic medium accessible by cultural amateurs that enabled the transgression of the boundaries of low and high

**Fig. 2.3** Grandfather explains the Japanese constitution. *Source* Shibata (2015), p.13. ©Liberal Democratic Party (LDP) and Shibata Kôbô

culture via humorous means, but also with a focus on the establishment's carefully controlled cultural politics with its own agendas (Kinsella, 2000, p. 6).

During Japan's bubble economy period (circa 1986–1991), the new concept of *seiji manga* (political manga) was able to cross the political divide and mesmerize left-wing intellectuals, class-conscious workers, and students alike, all of whom simultaneously regarded manga as a progressive medium that was able to transgress repressive social taboos (Kinsella, 2000, p. 5). Thus, manga became a unique polyphonic tool kit bridging the socio-political cultural divide and was able to evolve and adapt speedily to each new Japanese historical era. During the following "lost two decades" (1991–2010) the medium was able to reflect rapidly changing social circumstances, transitioning from being anti-establishment to pro-establishment, always adapting to the socio-political trends of the late twentieth century. Beyond this, the medium quickly entered the international arena and is nowadays regarded as one of the key pop cultural exports adopted as a soft power behemoth and able to promote Japan's nation building effort in the global amphitheater. The key to this transition is the ambidextrous ability of humor to influence political decision making, wherein manga can please any subjectivity and provide platforms for modern consumers' sundry identities.

Nowadays, manga offer a pop-cultural platform for creators/readers to address current socio-political events and issues as opposed to the mainstream media. Pop-cultural practices like comics/manga have come to be built on appropriation and hybridization across the arts, contributing to their transcultural success (Berndt & Kümmerling-Meibauer, 2013, pp. 1–2). Graphic art is particularly effective in visually expressing challenging emotional issues such as discrimination, inequalities, corruption, and disenfranchisement, often in disarmingly humorous ways. By presenting these complex themes in a relatable and engaging way, and through the mollifying devices of satire and humor, creators can raise awareness and encourage readers to think more deeply about traumatic and vexing issues.

Yet, besides merely representing a pastiche of transculturality, manga have been adopted to shed light on historical events and their impact on the world today. By reaching far beyond the hegemonic discursive formations of mainstream media, graphic art has enabled authors to express their alternative thoughts and ideas and provide readers with a deeper and more versatile picture of the world around them. This sense of bipartisanship and inclusivity has enabled comics and manga to be used as a platform for activism and social change, by raising awareness of important issues and inspiring readers to express democratic dissent while advocating for change. Whether through the portrayal of characters dealing with social and political issues, the use of satire and humor to critique current events, or the examination of historical events, manga can offer a uniquely powerful and often humorous way to engage the domestic with the global issues around us (Shashank, 2022). While this has been done traditionally via literary devices such as allegory, parody, satire, and other well-established tropes, more recently direct politicization has been the hallmark of the gentrification of the media.[3] Manga illuminate how socio-political humor affects Japanese culture.

The manga discussed in this chapter have been carefully selected to first illustrate how modern manga culture portrays political humor in Japan and second, as a result, affect socio-political engagement with the complex topics that make up our modern world. Some examples discussed include nationalism and war, gender politics, and inclusivity. In a word, manga make it easier to read, digest, and ultimately learn to live within an imperfect world. They might even make it fun.

---

[3] 2 Several manga published by the LDP, for example, advocate for "Constitutional Revision," (Johnson, 2015) and the "promotion of 18-year-old voters" (Kyodo, 2016); these are only two of many more examples.

## 2.2 The Postwar Rise of Graphic Political Expression: Tezuka's *Shôri no Hi Made*

As a pioneer of Japanese manga, Tezuka Osamu has been heralded in Japan as the "God of comics" and is lauded nowadays with a status akin to Walt Disney. His graphic oeuvre redefined manga throughout Japan's long postwar period and continues to influence graphic art today. Before his debut as a professional manga artist, Tezuka produced *Shôri no hi made* (Until the day of victory), when he was only sixteen years old. Drawn in a university notebook of A5 size, Tezuka reimagined the prevailing military discourse as a humorous pop-cultural long narrative manga that was completed during 1945, the final war year (Mori, 2012, pp. 533–534). This early work is full of hidden satire that when carefully scrutinized reveals a plethora of hidden layers adopting the carnivalesque mode to debunk Japan's war effort. Remarkably, young Tezuka had to espouse the prevalent military discourse, but his adoption of levity and satirical content debunked the myth of Japanese imperialism and satirized the stark reality of trauma experienced by his generation. Tezuka's narrative is full of comical cathartic expressions, whereby his generation's childhood comic heroes—both American and Japanese—compete against each other in ridiculous and hilarious one-upmanship.

Tezuka took his inspiration for the title of the work from the solemn wartime ballad by the same name, popularized by the singer Kirishima Noboru in 1944, which was turned into a hit consolation movie for soldiers at the frontline in the Japanese Navy by director Naruse Mikio in 1945.[4] Against this somber background, Tezuka adopted the work into a comical charade that satirized Japan's national effort into a nihilistic carnivalesque that showcased the ridiculous nature of Japan's colonial expansion into Asia. In this early slapstick militaristic manga, Tezuka reversed the outcome of the war, with Japanese fighter planes bombing major American cities. In the initial chapter entitled *kûshû keihô* (air-raid alarm), New York is the first city attacked and destroyed followed by a bawdy scene where American civilians try to cram into packed air raid shelters blocked by a corpulent female figure.[5]

The ensuing, unflattering bawdy scene is frivolous even by today's standards. Tezuka even inserts English and Japanese into his manga discourse, creating early avatars of his favorite future characters. Here Tezuka reverses his own traumatic childhood experience of the *yakeato* generation, those children who witnessed the fire-bombings of major Japanese cities and experienced the "burnt-out" ruins left behind. The juvenile story line represents cathartic one-upmanship shortly before

---

[4] *Imon eiga* (consolation movies) were similar to *imon bukuro* or "comfort boxes" sent at the time to soldiers at the front for encouragement.

[5] While the original intention was to include images from *Shôri no hi made* published by Kodansha as a collected edition of Tezuka's unpublished works in 2012, our request for copyright clearance was denied. The reason provided was that the work was produced before Tezuka's professional debut when he was 16 years old. And since they are of a personal nature and are not published as commercial works, they were deemed inappropriate. Given that they were published in Japanese, I tend to disagree with this verdict, but still respect the assessment of the publisher and I have therefore removed the images. For readers interested in a sample please refer to Holmberg (2012).

the war enters into its devastating final phase with the atomic bombing of Hiroshima and Nagasaki.

Tezuka's naïve story makes on important point, namely that despite the darkest circumstance, humor can save the day. Regurgitating the prevalent military propaganda of the time with a direct hit on the White House, adolescent Tezuka's imaginary bombing of major American cities by Japanese bombers brings up some pop-cultural American household names. The power of comic intertextuality even during the precarious final year of the war immediately becomes apparent in the cross-cultural references of *Shôri no hi made*, when the young teenage Tezuka, plying his craft, leaves nothing unscathed, with local and international comic superstars being exploited for farcical innuendo. When Japanese fighter planes bomb American cities in a scene of fantastic comeuppance, Tezuka's proverbial graphic bombs cause havoc in the household of *Jiggs and Maggie*—two iconic cartoon characters, created by American cartoonist George McManus in his popular comic strip entitled: *Bringing Up Father*.

When their household is destroyed in an aerial attack Maggie immediately blames Jiggs for the mess: "Why did you not come when I called?" Jiggs replies in bewilderment: "Didn't you just do this?" Young Tezuka's playful graphic *cri de coeur* shows the ridiculous side of a senseless conflict. In another chapter entitled *kijû sôsha* (machine gun) one of the Japanese air-raid shelters is attacked by fighter-planes, and a close-up scene of the cockpit depicts Mickey Mouse as the fighter pilot working the machine gun. Disney's Mickey Mouse was well established in Japan at the time and became popularized by leading local cartoonists Shaka Bontarô and the long running series *Norakuro* by household manga artist Tagawa Suihô.[6]

The playful carnivalesque and often absurd mode of the story is developed via the narrative structure of a *gunzô-geki* (ensemble cast) wherein rather than a single protagonist a plethora of popular celebrity manga characters make up the cacophony of voices. Incidentally, the metaphorical structure of the manga remarkably reflects the reality of the US-Japan conflict: beginning with the bombing of Pearl Harbor or Tezuka's American cities and followed by US attacks on Japanese soil. The timeline culminates with a final chapter entitled *shôi kôgeki* or "incendiary bombs" raining on Japanese cities.

In the final stage of the story, the pop-cultural icons of Japanese prewar manga have to deal with the fallout of American retaliation bombing. In the lower panels on the right, Ryuichi Yokoyama's long running *Fuku-chan*—a naughty five-year-old street kid—makes a guest appearance as he is attacked by B-29 bombers.[7] Rather than being somber, the naughty and hilarious episode depicts Fuku-chan trying to count the number of planes approaching, despite the teacher berating him to come inside. The captions show Fuku-chan counting in Japanese: "Oh, its B29s. Let's see

---

[6] Shaka Bontarô's publication of *Mikki no katsuyaku* (The activities of Mickey) published by Nakamura Shoten in 1934 was one of the first to popularize the character in Japan.

[7] Fuku-chan was a *yonkoma* or "four cell" manga series that appeared from 1936 until 1971 in Japanese newspapers and belongs to the longest running strips in Japanese comic history. It also produced three films during the Asia Pacific conflict for propaganda purposes.

11, 12, 13. KABOOM. Teacher! How many kilos of explosive was that? Fuku-chan eventually exits the shelter so that he can count the planes better and is hit as a result.

A vast variety of assemble cast including perhaps Niizeki Kennosuke's *Tora no ko torachan* (Tora the Tiger), mingles with a likeness of Pat Sullivan and Otto Messmer's *Felix the Cat* character, in a grotesquely humorous episode that enables a sense of catharsis from the fire-bombing traumas experienced by a generation of Japanese readers. When *Felix* exits the air-raid shelter to pick up something that looks like food: "Oh, it's a Katsubushi (bonito flake)," the other characters warn him: "Something dropped by the enemy is not good for anything." When he complains: "Why can't I have it?" an explosion occurs: "There, I told you so." Together with popular American comic characters the tragicomic devastation of the war is depicted through childhood laughter via a cacophony of polyphonic pop-cultural voices.

Tezuka's major advances in graphic art were already visible in *Shôri no hi made* but were later taken to their full effectiveness in *New Treasure Island* (1947) and *Astro Boy* (1952). Tezuka was able to develop a new type of graphic visuality via the creation of the long narrative story-manga, that effectively intertwined elements of the literary novel, picture books, and the *kami-shibai* storytelling technique popular at the time, with Japan's robust tradition of socio-political humor.

By conflating amusement and humor with socio-political topics, Tezuka developed a culture of manga that superimposed the two traditions of Japanese humor and current affairs onto the realm of graphic discourse. *Shôri no hi made* already contains early elements of this tapestry that combines the serious elements of the *gekiga* tradition with the comedy of Disney and Japan's cartooning history.[8] Beyond his innovation in narrative structure and presentation, Tezuka also broke away from the tradition of plain humor in manga, instead cultivating sophisticated narrative characters with intricate story lines, an assemblage of persona with ambiguity, and the dichotomy of good versus evil (Ono, 2007, p. 104). Tezuka redefined comic content and initiated the way to realistic tragicomedy later visible in the *gekiga* tradition, leading the medium in the direction of the modern graphic novel.

Here manga are manifest as a socio-political palimpsest, where multiple layers of meaning play against each other in paradoxical comedy. For instance, a 16-year-old schoolboy portraying his indoctrinated fantasies of defeating the enemy inspired by strictly enforced war time propaganda. Or the irony of a child repeating the emperor mythology and the youth who wrote sarcastically about his beliefs that are so far-fetched that they become hilarious and thus debunk and ridicule the military. What is left for posterity is a graphic historical record that pioneered a method of ridicule and laughter for the representation of socio-political consciousness in manga.

---

[8] Developed by avant-garde manga artists Tatsumi Yoshihiro and Matsumoto Masahiko, *gekiga* literally refers to "dramatic pictures" that focus on more serious manga topics for adult consumption.

## 2.3 Sophisticated Everyday Contemporary Humor in *Joshiraku*

Compared to the slapstick collage of Tezuka's early polyphonic comic characters who tragic-comically try to kill each other in a carnivalesque display of countercultural wrath, contemporary manga have taken a completely different trajectory in their application of humor. The example below illustrates the mocking inflation of the mundane every day to the level of sophisticated traditional, artistic traditions in Japanese society, and in so doing belittling the high arts while mocking low brow plebeian preoccupations. In this sense, although manga can be serious they also have the potential to apply humor to any serious aspect of society. To illustrate this point, comic writer Kumeta Kōji along with graphic illustrator Yasu have created a manga version of the historical *rakugo* tradition in Japanese theatres. The work entitled *joshiraku,* an abbreviation referring to "female *rakugo*," is a collection of short, gag, manga episodes laid out in the style of *rakugo* theater performances. It was published from 2009 to 2013 in the *Bessatsu Shônen Magajin* and breaks the taboos of male-dominance in the arts.

*Joshiraku* adopts as its comic raison d'etre the prosaic lifestyle of its female readership that overseas has become known as CGDCT (Cute Girls Doing Cute Things) due to its tendency to lampoon the everyday ludicrous banter of young Japanese females while consciously avoiding newsworthy socio-cultural and political issues. These works surfaced in the new millennium perhaps as a result of the general political disillusionment and overall indifference to politicized narratives pervading the public media. Instead, the new genre was termed *kûkikei*, literally "air-style" works that are "vacuous" due to their affinity to display meaningless banter of young females. This graphic genre represents "slice of life" narrative techniques "without fantastical aspects, which [take] place in a recognisable, everyday setting, such as a suburban high school, and which [focus] on human relationships that are often romantic in nature" (Hirose, 2013, p. 7). Komori (2011, p. 234) has described these narratives as "a type of work that endlessly portrays the mellow mundane lifestyle of young girls."

While the mundaneness of the works in this category reflects the tediousness of life itself in Japanese society, *joshiraku* represents a sophisticated parody of these vacuous conversations by introducing the highbrow cultural form of the *rakugo* comic story tradition to alleviate the lowbrow, boring, daily, meaningless banter of girls, into the century old highbrow cultural artistic tradition. This comedic overinflation and hyperbole injects comic innuendo where there is none, leaving the reader flabbergasted but chuckling along at the superciliousness of the banter. Repeatedly, within the graphic work the purpose of these stories is described as: "in order to enjoy the cuteness of young girls these manga incorporate a degree of inobtrusive conversation that is inoffensive" (Kumeta, 2010, p. 6). Yet quite to the contrary, the individual stories use sophisticated language games that are comic for the Japanese reader but probably would leave its non-Kanji literate readership somewhat baffled. Perhaps this inability to translate linguistic humor is the reason for its untranslatability to the English market.

For example, the title of each episode of the manga reflects the subject of an ancient traditional *rakugo* performance. Chapter one of the manga entitled *Inu to neko no sainan* reflects the traditional *rakugo* title *Neko no sainan* which was based on a *waraibanashishû* (collection of funny stories) publication from 1777 entitled Katsuo (bonito fish). This chapter introduces the performance of Harōkitei Kigurumi (a supercilious pun on the Japanese words for "Cartoon character costume" and "Hello Kitty"). She enters the stage by asking her fellow performers: "Do you favor dogs or cats?" While they protest about the "boring question," a funny discussion ensues with the other characters about the pros and cons of keeping either of the two pets. After suggesting that dogs are better for training various tricks, another character by the name Anrakutei Kukuru with long black hair suggests that she hates the Japanese character for "dog." Her name is a complicated pun that can suggests several different meanings like *anrakushi* (euthanasia) or phonetically "unlucky." The ensuing discussion descends into a hilarious discussion of the Japanese character for "dog" (see Fig. 2.4). The political humor expressed via the female slice of life parody in the images above, destabilizes existing male-dominated textualities by injecting feminine narrative content into the dominant masculine discourse of Japanese society.

**Fig. 2.4** Fun with Japanese Kanji. *Source* Kumeta (2010), Vol. 1, p. 8. ©Kumeta Kôji, Yasu and Kodansha

When asked why she finds the Kanji character confusing, she suggests that she forgets where to put the little dot for the character. By way of explanation, she shows a confusing list of nonsense characters that would amuse Japanese readers. Further discussion leads to evermore confusing renditions of the simple "dog" character that will leave the laughing Japanese reader in tears (see Fig. 2.5).

When one of the playful suggestions appears to actually "impale" the "dot" representing the dog, it triggers outrage from the *rakugo* performer. This is followed by "but isn't it lonely with only one dog?" The mocking answer is a character with multiple dots representing dogs all around it and the exclamation: *datôgai* (owning multiple animals). The following scene then suggests: "I have thought of a new character." And shows a character without any dots at all suggesting "animal loss"—with the final deadpan reply that this is simply the character for "*dai*" or "large," one of the most common characters in Japanese and easily recognizable by everyone. With this the curtain closes and chapter one completes episode one of the *rakugo* performance. The stylistic conventions of the *rakugo* performance are adopted for each of the humorous manga chapters when the narrator closes with *wo ato ga yoroshii yô de*. That's all from me, and now on to the next speaker.

## 2.4 Mocking Domesticity: Ôno Kôsuke's *the Way of the Househusband*

Moving seamlessly from the mocking feminization of *rakugo* theatre to the subversion of Japanese domesticity, traditional gender roles and their socio-political dynamics in Japanese society are humorously deconstructed via the househusband trope. The exaggerated title of the manga—*goku-shufu-dô* literally translates as "the extreme way of the househusband"—is manga artist Ôno Kôsuke's first serialization as well as his first English language publication. Initially published in the online manga magazine *Kurage Bunch* as a limited series in 2018, it garnered enough popularity to begin serialization in the same year. In North America, Viz Media acquired the English language rights and began publication in 2019. Following the popularity of the online version this manga was swiftly adapted into other multimedia environments.

Initially, several animated comic videos with voices of popular Japanese entertainers were produced to promote the release of this manga series. In October 2020, *Nippon TV* adapted *The Way of the Househusband* into a live-action television drama, followed in 2021 by the release of the Netflix anime series. In 2022, the series was developed into a live action film by Sony Entertainment. Similarly, the initial critical reception of the English translation released by Viz Media as *The Way of the Househusband* was positive and sometimes revelatory. Rosie Knight (2021) remarked that the series "breathes life into what many may see as the mundane task of caring for another." She further noted that in this manga, our daily dedication to one another in

**Fig. 2.5** Having fun with the character for "dog". *Source* Kumeta (2010), Vol. 1, p. 10. ©Kumeta Kôji, Yasu and Kodansha

today's fast-paced society bursts with loyalty and honor, so that rather than boring and dull, our domestic interactions become full of heroic adventures.

Eventually the success of the English language adaption led to an Eisner Award in 2020 for Best Humor Publication, only the second time a Japanese work was selected for the award inaugurated in 1992. With the Netflix series now in its second season in 2023 what is the reason for the growing popularity of this farcical housekeeper narrative?

The stories' hilarious premise is that Tatsu—the series protagonist, a former infamous and feared yakuza boss nicknamed "the Immortal Dragon"—has recently retired from crime to become a fulltime househusband in order to support Miku, his career-women wife. In the manga, stereotypes abound and are quickly subverted by role-reversals and the exchange of social responsibilities. The feminization of a die-hard yakuza boss in combination with the masculinity of his "salaryman wife" inject comic catharsis into the Japanese world of strict conformity to traditional gender-roles.

The former yakuza boss applies the skill and intensity of his previous profession as a crime lord, *faute de mieux*, equally efficiently to housework and domestic tasks as a househusband, thereby creating comic innuendo through overlaying the two genres of banal domesticity and yakuza intensity. The episodic series depicts a variety of comedic scenarios, typically wherein Tatsu's banal domestic work as a househusband is juxtaposed against his intimidating personality and appearance, and his frequent run-ins with former yakuza associates and rivals. In this sense, Ôno's *The Way of the Househusband* is similar to *joshiraku* in that both are slice of life comedies that infuse the mundanity of the everyday with heroic battle scenes that elevate the trivial to the fantastic.

This concept of humor arising from the incongruity of a narrative has a long history harking back to Francis Hutcheson in *Reflections on Laughter* from the early eighteenth century, developed further by Immanuel Kant who explained laughter as a response to the absurdity of a situation (Clewis, 2020, p.18). Arguably, the successful blending of mutually exclusive ways of life—that of the violent, albeit traditional, male-dominated machismo, yakuza lifestyle, in conjunction with the contemporary domestic bliss of the stay-at-home-dad that is familiar to the modern readership—has created a global success story.

The background history to this socio-political parody is well known and began in the 1950s during the baby boom in America and Japan. This period was also called the "Golden 50 s" and gave rise to the eponymous Baby Boomer generation. With families after the war trying to make up for lost time, increasing urbanization led to the number of two-income families beginning to increase, and grown children began to remain at home longer because of financial difficulties. In the United States and Europe, women began re-entering the workforce, triggering a slow progression away from the traditional view of the woman as the homemaker, eventually leading to the emergence of the role of the stay-at-home dad whose numbers have been increasing in Western culture, especially in Canada, the UK, and the United States since the late twentieth century. In developed East Asian nations such as Japan and South Korea, this practice is less common due to strict traditional gender roles within entrenched patriarchal societies.

A survey conducted in 2008 in Japan suggested that nearly one-third of married men would accept the role (Kato, 2009). Moreover, amidst the nationwide effort to overturn social stereotypes and a prevailing patriarchal Japanese cultural norm, former Prime Minister Abe Shinzô pledged to raise the ratio of women in managerial positions to 30 percent by 2020 (Aoki, 2016, p. 3).[9] In light of this, "househusbands" and "career women" are vital roles in the manga that comically dispel and subvert traditional gender roles in Japan.

The comedic element in *The Way of the Househusband* resides in the sophisticated use of humorous tropes applied to three stereotypical social roles in Japanese society. Clearly defined social positions like "career women" and "househusband" but also "yakuza" are subverted and blended in the manga. By superimposing stereotypical social/gender roles in the manga, the incongruity of the story creates extravagantly comic situations that create a terse sense of ambiguity that defamiliarizes the readers' experience and expectation. Genre conventions are mixed and lambasted against our expectations with surprises at every page that go against our conventional modes of reading. For example, when Tatsu's menacing facial expression and tough outside appearance continues to intimidate people around him, his wife Miku gets frustrated and tells him to be more *kawaige ni* (cute or loveable) (see Fig. 2.6).

To the delight of his wife, Tatsu buys and cross-dresses with an apron of her favorite anime characters, and then continues to harass him to pose for a photo. Besides the subversion of the politics of traditional gender roles, the manga's narrative humor arises via a series of sophisticated tropes. Repeated use of comically serious situations in the manga highlights the protagonist as a tragi-comic fool whose lack of reaction to embarrassing, undignified, or just plain bizarre situations subverts the reader's expectations of social norms. Yet the image above also illustrates that there is a hidden dimension beneath this fool—dark black, comedic yakuza ferocity, suggesting Tatsu's hidden dimension of the trickster figure in today's intersectional society.

Some of the comic episodes are very contemporary. As depicted in Fig. 2.7, when sidekick Masa—an underling in Tatsu's former gang—is cornered by a rival yakuza group, he pulls out his mobile phone and googles "how to fight many opponents." When pushed around, he indifferently replies: "Dude, chill, I have only got one bar," in a sublime reference to his limited, mobile phone's battery power.

Often the situational comedy reaches extravagant heights and leads the reader along to an imagined climactic, grotesque, yakuza finale, when suddenly an unexpected turn of events dramatically changes the circumstances of the plot development. When Tatsu accidentally runs into former Yakuza boss Torajirô, who after release from prison now owns a food truck that sells crêpes, the reader is prepared

---

[9] Aoki (2016) noted that there appears to be no official data on the number of house husbands in Japan, but numbers can be obtained indirectly from women who claimed spousal tax exemptions for their husband. In fiscal 2013 this number reached around 110,000—more than double compared to 40,000 in 1997.

2  The Relationship Between Culture and Political Humor in Japanese Manga        37

**Fig. 2.6** Immortal dragon with cute apron. *Source* Ôno (2018), Vol. 1, p. 134. ©Ōno Kōsuke and Shinchosha

for a violent climactic finale in accordance with yakuza tradition. Recognizing each other, their rivalry flares up again and Torajiô challenges Tatsu to what can only be a life and death Yakuza style duel. Instead, as seen in Fig. 2.8, Tatsu and Tora settle the unfinished rivalry from their former lives via a duel over who can make the best dessert. The winner being whoever gets more "likes" on *Instantgram*, a wordplay and "bland-name" for *Instagram*. The following photography scene lampoons an entire generation of selfie-addicted teens, but despite their affinity for food preparation and

38                                                                                      R. Rosenbaum

**Fig. 2.7** Gangsters googling how to fight. *Source* Ôno (2018), Vol. 1, p.108. ©Ôno Kōsuke and Shinchosha

artsy photography skills, Tatsu wins with just one single like, and even then, it's just from his partner Miku.

This situational comedy also arises via the trope of melodrama, where everyday mundanity is made awesome via hyperbole and dramatic exaggeration. Tatsu repeatedly exaggerates things, adding an element of bathos to our daily chores. Ôno here adopts a story-telling technique that juxtaposes serious concepts with the trite or ludicrous and creates unexpected anticlimaxes that generate humor.

Ôno's modern-day power couple combines the incongruities of daily life with a sentient sense of lambent wit, with which he amusingly delves into the absurdities of our modern, socio-political lives. Yet, by portraying the humorous fallacies of our daily routines via role reversals, he debunks the underlying stereotypes of female

**Fig. 2.8** Yakuza battle for the best Instagram post. *Source* Ôno (2018), Vol. 2, p. 92. ©Ōno Kōsuke and Shinchosha

domesticity and male chauvinism in relation to the role our political environment plays in perpetuating the sacrosanctity of these outdated social norms.

## 2.5 By Way of Conclusion

> [...] centuries of political repression of comedy by a cast of thousands including Confucius, Tokugawa Ieyasu, Uesugi Yozan, the warrior class and their pompous descendants, the militarists, the industrialists, the civil servants, the politicians, the NHK [Japan Broadcast Cooperation] and the private broadcasters, all of whom saw laughter, or humor or even smiling as dangerous because they signified a revolt against authority (Wells, 1997, p. 152).

Manga have inherited a strong counter-cultural, carnivalesque tradition that has come a long way since the medium's inception through the early Western inspired satirical cartoons by Charles Wirgman and Frank A. Nankivell. Taken on its own domestic trajectory via Kitazawa Rakuten and the development of the long story manga by Tezuka Osamu, today comics are discussed in the *Wall Street Journal* and *The Diplomat*, illustrating their soft power potential in the global amphitheater of socio-political discourse. Make no mistake: these stories are full of political humor, but not everyone is laughing. Modern, sophisticated, polyphonic manga narratives make readers of all generations think about the implications of our past histories and how they can be interpreted from different perspectives depending on our own circumstances.[10] Through parody and satire of contemporary socio-political discourses, manga reflect on how our cultures affect political humor across the stereotypical political fulcrum of Left versus Right agendas, advocating that this is no longer relevant in today's multivalent societies.

The analysis of *joshiraku* and *The Way of the Househusband* are examples of how manga nowadays effectively promote self-understanding through humor and explore our intricate relationship with the society we live in, while at the same time competing with global cultural paradigms. Manga also demonstrate a potential source of identity in modern consumer societies and paradoxically also represent fictitious worlds for identification that provides us with community and a sense of belonging to something larger than ourselves.

Continual innovation of manga media from early satirical cartoons via the counter-cultural *gekiga* revolution of the 60 s and 70 s led to more subtle conceptions of humor that were able to debunk formalities and expose stereotypical cultural expectations. In this way, more sophisticated, erudite forms of humor released the readers from the shackles of social constraints and via tragic-comic release enabled them to laugh at their own predicaments. Thus, modern manga have become an all-inclusive, socio-political, cathartic expression to debate but also commercialize society's most

---

[10] This is not just the case for *manga;* similar educational, narrative methodologies have been employed in the European graphic tradition. See for example, Eric Heuvel (2009) that narrates the controversial story of the Netherlands' involvement in the Second World War, and its sequel Heuvel et al. (2009), relating the main facts about the Holocaust told through the experiences of a fictional family during the Nazi occupation of the Netherlands.

pressing issues. This has been exemplified above via the escapades of a "heartwarming family" arguing about constitutional revision, the incongruity of classical *rakugo* comic storytelling focusing on nonsensical small talk that de-genders male-dominated textualities, and finally the situational humor of a retired yakuza playing househusband in a comedic mashup of cultural stereotypes. All these follow in the footsteps of the counter-cultural iconoclasm of Tezuka Osamu's humorous militarism whereby Mickey Mouse battles with Japanese pop-cultural icons. In this sense, the cartoons presented in this analysis all defamiliarize socio-cultural stereotypes via the expression of political humor in manga.

Through a sense of hilarity, manga tropes incorporate satire, parody, tragi-comedy, and many other modern tropes of culture to undermine contemporary Japan's sclerotic political apparatus. Yet all political humor has a serious underbelly to it and manga's undermining and subversion of the serious has broken many taboos and have increased the inclusivity of minority groups, as well as bringing to the fore LGBTQ + matters and gender discrimination.

Today, readers the world over—adults and children alike—can be greatly influenced by these fictional worlds that offer a space for frank discourse, a safety zone to talk about anything on any controversial topic from sex to violence to war, without the imposition of traditional barriers. In the manga mainstream, people can connect directly and indirectly with their peers, creating a world of their own, impenetrable to their parents, teachers, and other authority figures. It is safe here to caricature authority: teachers, police officers, and even the prime minister (Hashimoto, 2023).

Manga's political subversion graphically illustrates—via grotesque defamiliarization, exaggeration, irony, and humorous analogy – the vital social function of humor in providing a counterpoint to the political depiction of current affairs and social issues relating to abuses of power. Arguably, the graphic carnivalesque mode of laughter in manga is a successful artifice to counteract the fear tactics of modern, socio-political, neo-liberalism and capitalist agendas. Laugher is as liberating as fear is captivating, and it is for this reason that comic relief is a successful antidote to our zeitgeist of precariousness and uncertainty, whether financial or social.

**Acknowledgements** I gratefully acknowledge the permission of the following publishers: *Shinchosha*, Kodansha, Liberal Democratic Party (LDP), and *Asahi Shimbun* for the use of the cartoons by Yamafuji Shôji, Shibata Kôbô, Kumeta Kôji, Yasu and Ōno Kōsuke in this chapter.

# References

Aoki, M. (2016). House husbands gaining acceptance as stereotypes ease. *Japan Times*. https://www.japantimes.co.jp/news/2016/04/28/national/social-issues/house-husbands-gaining-acceptance-japan-gender-stereotypes-ease/
Berndt, J., & Kümmerling-Meibauer, B. (2013). *Manga's cultural crossroads*. Routledge.
Clewis, R. (2020). *Kant's humorous writings: An illustrated guide*. Bloomsbury.
Davis Milner, J. (2006). *Understanding humor in Japan*. Wayne State University Press.
Exner, E. (2022). *Comics and the origins of manga: A revisionist history*. Rutgers University Press.

Hashimoto, A. (2023). Popular culture: Manga. *JapanPitt*. https://www.japanpitt.pitt.edu/essays-and-articles/culture/popular-culture-manga

Heuvel, E., van der R., & Schippers, L. (2009). *The search*. (L. T. Miller, Trans.). Farrar, Straus and Giroux.

Heuvel, E. ([2003]2009). *A family secret* (L. T. Miller, Trans.). Square Fish.

Hirose, M. (2013). The cage named "slice of life:" The animation "keion!" and the imagination of sexuality. *Sugiyama Jogakuen University Language and Expression - Research Papers, 10*, 7–22. http://id.nii.ac.jp/1454/00001918/ (in Japanese).

Holmberg R. (2012). Tezuka Osamu and American comics. *The Comic Journal*. https://www.tcj.com/tezuka-osamu-and-american-comics.

Ito, K. (2008). Manga in Japanese society. In M. W. MacWilliams (Ed.), *Japanese visual culture* (pp. 26–47). East Gate Book.

Johnson, J. (2015). LDP produces manga to make case for constitutional revision. *Japan Times*. https://www.japantimes.co.jp/news/2015/05/11/national/politics-diplomacy/ldp-produces-manga-make-case-constitutional-revision

Kato, M. (2009). Househusband not such a bad gig, one-third of men say. *Japan Times*. https://www.japantimes.co.jp/news/2009/01/14/national/househusband-not-such-a-bad-gig-one-third-of-men-say

Kinsella, S. (2000). *Adult manga: Culture and power in contemporary Japanese society*. Curzon Press.

Knight, R. (2021). Review: The way of the househusband: Comics' greatest wife guy. *WomenWritingAboutComics*. https://womenwriteaboutcomics.com/2021/04/review-the-way-of-the-househusband-comics-greatest-wife-guy

Komori, K. (2011) The parallel relationship of mystery and TV animation works in 2011. In S. Shimada (Ed.), *Real mystery world 2012* (pp. 230–238). Nanundo. (in Japanese).

Kumeta, K. (2010). *Female rakugo*. Kodansha. (in Japanese).

Kyodo. (2016). Japan's political parties deploying mascots and manga to appeal to younger voters. *Japan Times*. https://www.japantimes.co.jp/news/2016/06/09/national/japans-political-parties-deploying-mascots-manga-appeal-younger-voters

Mori, H. (2012). Commentary to vol. 3. Tezuka Osamu complete works. In O. Tezuka (Ed.), *Tezuka Osamu complete works: Works not included in complete manga collection* (Vol. 3, pp. 533–535). Kodansha. (in Japanese).

Nakazawa, K. (1972). *I saw it*. Shueisha. (in Japanese).

Ono, K. (2007). The long flight of manga and anime: The history of comics and animation in Japan. In A. Cholodenko (Ed.), *The illusion of life II* (pp. 99–118). Power Publications.

Ôno, K. (2018) *Gokushufudô (The Way of the Househusband)*. Shinchosha. (in Japanese). https://www.youtube.com/watch?v=LgfyuH6Ofhw&ab_channel=TVSeriesXAnimeXMovieClipTV. (in Japanese with English subtitles).

Rosenthal A., Bindman, D., & Randolph, A. W. B. (2016). *No laughing matter: Visual humor in ideas of race, nationality, and ethnicity*. Dartmouth College Press.

Schodt, F. L. (1983). *Manga manga: The world of Japanese comics*. Kodansha International.

Shashank. (2022). The role of comics and manga in social and political commentary. *GoBookMart*. https://gobookmart.com/the-role-of-comics-and-manga-in-social-and-political-commentary

Shibata, K. (2015). *A heartwarming family's 'What are constitutional revisions?' Liberal Democratic Party (LDP)*. https://storage.jimin.jp/pdf/pamphlet/kenpoukaisei_manga_pamphlet.pdf (in Japanese).

Tezuka, O. (2012). *Tezuka Osamu complete works: Works not included in complete manga collection* (Vol. 3). Kodansha. (in Japanese).

Tsurumi, S. (1970). *Postwar history of Manga II: Manners and customs*. Chikuma Shobo. (in Japanese).

Wells, M. (1997). *Japanese humour*. Palgrave MacMillan.

Yamafuji, S. (1992) Yamafuji Shōji's black angle. In *Shûkan Asahi*. https://sessendo.blogspot.com/2019/12/blog-post_2.html (in Japanese).

**Roman Rosenbaum** is an Honorary Associate at the University of Sydney, Australia. He specializes in Postwar Japanese Literature, Popular Cultural Studies, and translation. In 2008 he received the Inoue Yasushi Award for best refereed journal article on Japanese literature in Australia. In 2010/11, he spent one year as a Visiting Research Professor at the *International Research Centre for Japanese Studies* (*Nichibunken*). He has published extensively on Japanese graphic art and his latest publications include: 'Representation, Recognition and Resistance,' in *Art & Activism in the Nuclear Age*, University of Sydney, Tin Shed Gallery (2022, edited); and *Art and Activism in the Nuclear Age: Exploring the Legacy of Hiroshima and Nagasaki* (2023, Routledge).

# Chapter 3
# A Tale of Two Presidents: Indonesian Humor as Depicted in Political Cartoons

**Danang Satria Nugraha**

**Abstract** This chapter delves into political humor during the presidential periods of Susilo Bambang Yudhoyono and Joko Widodo in Indonesia. By employing a critical discourse analysis approach, the chapter explores the portrayal of these two presidents through the lens of political cartoons, shedding light on the power of humor as a form of social commentary and political critique. Based on a selected collection of political cartoons from the prominent Indonesian publication *Kontan*, the chapter analyzes how these cartoons depicted and satirized the personalities, policies, and governance of Yudhoyono and Widodo. The cartoons captured the essence of their respective leadership periods through caricatures, symbolism, and visual metaphors, offering insights into public sentiment, societal expectations, and critical narratives surrounding these presidents. The analysis reveals the distinct humor styles employed in portraying Yudhoyono and Widodo. For Yudhoyono, the cartoons often highlighted his leadership style, policies, and controversies, employing exaggerated features and witty captions to critique his governance. In contrast, the cartoons depicting Widodo emphasized his down-to-earth persona, tackling economic policies, corruption, and social issues with a satirical edge.

## 3.1 Introduction

### 3.1.1 Background and Significance of Political Cartoons in Indonesia

Political cartoons have a long and illustrious history in Indonesian society, playing an important role in conveying political messages and reflecting societal sentiments since the era when artists such as Raden Saleh and Wakidi used illustrations to criticize the Dutch administration (e.g., Djordjevic, 2014; Nelson, 2019; Susanto et al., 2018; Wee, 2015). Political cartoons have become an important component of

---

D. S. Nugraha (✉)
Department of Indonesian Language, Sanata Dharma University, DI Yogyakarta, Indonesia
e-mail: d.s.nugraha@usd.ac.id

© The Author(s), under exclusive license to Springer Nature Singapore Pte Ltd. 2024
O. Feldman (ed.), *Communicating Political Humor in the Media*,
The Language of Politics, https://doi.org/10.1007/978-981-97-0726-3_3

Indonesian media, catching the attention of the public and officials alike. Political cartoons are significant because they are able to reduce complicated political concerns into visual and frequently funny portrayals (Attardo, 1994; Feldman, 1995; Streicher, 1967). Cartoons can capture the essence of political events and individuals in a brief and accessible manner through brilliant visual analogies, exaggerated caricatures, and sarcastic comments (Attardo, 2001; Feldman, 2000; Tsakona, 2009; Young, 2017). They function as social commentary, providing a critical prism to scrutinize political officials' behavior and policies.

Political cartoons have flourished as a tool for protest and social criticism in Indonesia where freedom of expression and press freedom are prized. Cartoonists have utilized their artistic abilities to challenge power, expose corruption, and draw attention to social injustices (Balakrishnan et al., 2019; Boukes et al., 2015). Furthermore, political cartoons have become vital to public discourse, influencing public opinion, stimulating discussions, and even aiding in political reforms (Dynel, 2013; Dynel & Chovanec, 2021). The emergence of social media and digital platforms in Indonesia has increased the reach and effect of political cartoons (Daniels, 2007; Harun et al., 2015; Hasanah & Hidayat, 2020; Lent, 2014; Nugraha, 2020; Ostrom, 2007; Sen & Hill, 2007). Cartoons are widely shared and distributed online, enabling them to reach a bigger audience and increase their effectiveness. Because of the speed and virality of social media, cartoons have become an excellent instrument for political criticism, in a visually interesting and memorable way aiding citizens in connecting to political topics. Against this context, this chapter aims to look into the political satire depicted in political cartoons during the presidential terms of Susilo Bambang Yudhoyono and Joko Widodo.

## 3.1.2 Overview of the Two Presidents Under Analysis

This chapter focuses on the political humor regarding Susilo Bambang Yudhoyono and Joko Widodo, two significant presidents who changed Indonesian politics in different ways. In a cartoon (Fig. 3.1) that appeared during the middle period of his second presidency in 2012, President Susilo Bambang Yudhoyono, commonly known as SBY, was shown holding a fruit that looks like an apple with a worm inside (symbolizing the problematic issues that he had to handle in his presidency). The fruit contains the text *grasi ola* (commutation or clemency for Ola, an international trader sentenced by Indonesian authorities for her crimes). SBY's eyes are looking at the worm inside the fruit. Amusingly, SBY's face looks confused (symbolizing his difficulties in resolving the issue and its international relations consequences).

In a cartoon (Fig. 3.2) that appeared during the first year of his first presidency in 2014, President Jokowi is shown standing with a bag of fruits next to the juicer. The bag contains the text *calon menteri* (symbolizing that many candidates have been collected for the ministerial selection). The juicer contains the text KPK (Corruption Eradication Commission) with the ordinary trusty man staring at the glass in the output part (symbolizing the ministerial selection process Jokowi conducted to create

**Fig. 3.1** The pitfalls of clemency for drug convicts. Benny Rachmadi, November 12, 2012 (Reproduced from *Kontan*, 2023)

the cabinet to satisfy the civilians). Mirthfully, Jokowi's eyes look at the ordinary man (symbolizing his attention to fulfilling society's needs). Jokowi carefully provided good service by using the best available resources (symbolizing his concern for the welfare of the civilians).

Understanding their backgrounds, leadership styles, and policies is crucial to contextualize the political cartoons that emerged during their respective presidencies. SBY served as the sixth president of Indonesia from 2004 to 2014. As a retired military general, SBY brought stability and a reformist agenda to the country. His presidency was marked by efforts to combat corruption, improve governance, and navigate complex domestic and international challenges. SBY's tenure witnessed significant political and economic developments and controversies that became fodder for political cartoonists. In 2014, Joko Widodo, sometimes known as Jokowi, became president, beginning a new era in Indonesian politics. With a local government and business career, Jokowi stood out from the established political class. He prioritized economic reforms, social welfare initiatives, and infrastructural improvement during his presidency.

**Fig. 3.2** Selecting ministerial candidates who passed KPK screening. Benny Rachmadi, October 22, 2014 (Reproduced from *Kontan,* 2023)

### 3.1.3 Purpose of the Chapter and the Use of Critical Discourse Analysis

This chapter aims to present a complete examination of the political humor that arose in Indonesia during the presidential terms of SBY and Jokowi. Researching political cartoons depicting these two presidents enables an understanding of the underlying narratives, motifs, and critical discourses buried within these visual representations. The chapter investigates political cartoons and their sociopolitical implications using a critical discourse analysis (henceforth CDA) methodology that enables us to see beneath the cartoons' amusing façade. One can decipher the cartoons' social and political signals by examining their visual and linguistic components, offering a more nuanced understanding of the larger discourses surrounding SBY's and Jokowi's presidencies. I will examine how these political cartoons reflected and affected public opinion, challenge power systems, and contributed to creating collective memory via the lens of CDA (Blommaert & Bulcaen, 2000; Fairclough, 2013; Weiss & Wodak, 2007).

To implement CDA for analyzing the political cartoons of SBY and Jokowi, the following steps will be taken:

(1) Collect Political Cartoons: Gather a comprehensive collection of political cartoons featuring SBY and Jokowi during their respective presidencies (the collection was a corpus developed by Nugraha (2022)). The corpus consists of 222 cartoons. The cartoons were downloaded from open online newspaper platform i.e., *Kontan* (n.d.). The download process was undertaken between November 1, 2021 and January 5, 2022. Meanwhile, the coverage of the cartoon publication period is January 1, 2004 to December 31, 2022.
(2) Identify Key Themes: Start by identifying the key themes or topics that emerge from the cartoons i.e., policy issues and leadership styles.
(3) Analyze Linguistic and Visual Elements: Apply CDA to examine the linguistic and visual elements of the cartoons.
(4) Uncover Power Dynamics and Ideologies: Identify how individuals or groups are represented and what power relations were implied; consider the ideologies, political affiliations, or social hierarchies that might be reinforced or challenged through the cartoons.
(5) Examine Social Context: Situate the cartoons within their social context; reflect on how these contexts might have influenced the creation and interpretation of the cartoons; analyze the broader societal issues and concerns reflected in the cartoons and how they related to the political landscape of the time.
(6) Interpret and Discuss Findings: Based on the analysis, interpret the findings and discuss the implications; analyze the patterns, trends, and contrasts that emerged from the cartoons of SBY and Jokowi.
(7) Draw Conclusions: Describe the essential findings and themes that emerge from the analysis of these political cartoons.

## 3.2 The Power of Political Cartoons in Indonesian Society

### 3.2.1 Historical Context and Cultural Significance of Political Cartoons

Political cartoons in Indonesia have a deep-rooted, historical background and hold significant cultural significance within the nation's rich artistic and political traditions. The origins of political cartoons in Indonesia can be traced back to the colonial era when artists like Raden Saleh and Wakidi used illustrations to critique the Dutch administration (Lis, 2014; Susanto, 2018; Vickers, 2020). The historical setting of political cartoons in Indonesia is connected to the country's war for independence and the ensuing nation-building process. Political cartoons evolved as a potent instrument in the battle against colonial domination, mobilizing public opinion, challenging repressive governments, and rallying support for nationalist movements (Cohen, 2016; Protschky, 2011; Spielmann, 2017).

These cartoons exposed the inequities of colonial authority, also helping strengthen Indonesian solidarity. They served as a visual embodiment of national ambitions. Political cartoons played a significant part in the new period of administration after Indonesia gained independence in 1945 (Aragon & Leach, 2008; Cohen, 2019). They evolved as a way to criticize the actions of political leaders, voice public concerns, and hold them accountable. Cartoonists illustrated the nascent nation's difficulties, including political unpredictability, economic hardship, and social inequity. Political cartoons were an important part of the public conversation because they provided alternate viewpoints and challenged the status quo.

Political cartoons strongly emphasize humor in particular—an effective weapon for social critique, allowing cartoonists to approach delicate and divisive subjects through humor (Hill, 2013; Stewart, 2015). Political cartoons expose corruption, highlight social inequalities, and question power, using satire, irony, exaggeration, and parody (Fein et al., 2015; Witek, 2022). They serve as a mirror to society, providing a critical prism through which political realities, power relations, and governance problems may be viewed.

Over and above that, for many Indonesians, political cartoons have developed into a source of cultural identity and pride. They stand for an artistic expression that enables people to participate in politics, express their concerns, and influence the country's direction. Cartoonists are frequently seen as social critics and influencers who use their creative talents to highlight pressing social issues, undermine established hierarchies, and promote constructive change. Understanding political cartoons' influence and function in influencing public discourse in Indonesia requires understanding the country's historical background and its cultural relevance. Examining the cultural and historical contexts of political cartoons in the context of this chapter will lay the groundwork for examining the political comedy published during the administrations of SBY and Jokowi.

### 3.2.2 Role of Humor and Satire in Social Commentary

Humor and satire have long been used as social commentary and critique in Indonesian society. In political cartoons, comedy and satire effectively convey meaningful ideas, challenge authority, and address delicate social and political topics (Kreuz, 1997; Piata, 2016). Understanding the function of humor and satire in political cartoons in Indonesian culture sheds light on the effectiveness and impact of political cartoons as tools for social critique. Admittedly, humor allows vital ideas to be communicated in non-threatening and entertaining fashion (Holbert et al., 2011; Pinar, 2020).

Political cartoonists can call attention to societal and political concerns by using wit, sarcasm, and smart wordplay, rendering them accessible and relevant to various audiences. On the other hand, satire is a type of creative critique that uses exaggeration, parody, and mocking to expose flaws and failings in persons, organizations, and social standards (Rossen-Knill & Henry, 1997; Singh, 2012). Political cartoons with satire reveal hypocrisy, question power relations, and shine a spotlight on societal injustice. Satire enables cartoonists to approach serious and sensitive themes in a way that encourages thinking, sparks debate, and urges viewers to reflect. Humor and satire have tremendous cultural significance in Indonesia that has a long history of mixing comedy and satire into daily life, such as through folklore, traditional performances, and oral storytelling. The use of sarcasm and humor in political cartoons taps into this cultural tendency, making it an excellent medium for engaging with and criticizing the complexity of Indonesian politics and culture.

Furthermore, comedy and satire may be used to avoid censorship and challenge repressive governments (LaMarre et al., 2014; Landreville, 2015). Political cartoonists in Indonesia have utilized satire and comedy to push limits, criticize authority, and express discontent. In this sense, political cartoons are a manifestation of free speech and a form of resistance to attempts to restrict criticism (Meibauer, 2019; Morgan, 2010). By examining the function of comedy and satire in Indonesian culture, particularly in political cartoons, we can better understand how these components create public discourse, impact public opinion, and contribute to social transformation. Examining the use of comedy and satire in political cartoons attacking SBY and Jokowi helps us to reveal the unique ways these cartoons offered social criticism, challenged political authority, and reflected modern Indonesian socio-cultural dynamics.

## 3.3 President Susilo Bambang Yudhoyono: Caricatures and Criticism

### 3.3.1 Introduction to Susilo Bambang Yudhoyono and His Tenure

SBY's administration was a watershed moment in Indonesian politics, and his presidency became a source of examination and criticism in the domain of political cartoons. This section examines SBY caricatures and criticism through the lens of political cartoons, offering light on significant themes, storylines, and societal commentary that evolved under his presidency. The cartoons representing SBY mirrored the political context and issues that Indonesia faced during his presidency. Cartoonists depicted the president and commented on his policies, leadership style, and political decisions using comedy, satire, and visual analogies. The cartoons frequently emphasized corruption, inefficiency in government, and the growing divide between the political elite and regular citizenry.

One recurring topic in the cartoons depicting SBY was his apparent indecisiveness or lack of firm leadership. Cartoonists portrayed him as a weak character who might be swayed by strong interests or unable to take decisive action in response to critical national challenges. These graphic depictions sought to question SBY's efficacy as a leader and highlighted worries about the country's trajectory under his leadership.

Corruption, a long-standing issue in Indonesian politics, was also strongly depicted in the cartoons depicting SBY. Cartoonists frequently portrayed him as complicit or ineffectual in battling corruption, representing him surrounded by corrupt persons or occasions when corruption scandals occurred under his supervision.

### 3.3.2 Analysis of Prominent Political Cartoons Depicting SBY

SBY's administration was characterized by a strong presence of political satire and comedy in the form of drawings and caricatures. Throughout his presidency, SBY experienced several problems and conflicts that were the topic of political satire and commentary. During his administration, political cartoonists and satirists utilized political cartoons to represent SBY's leadership style, policies, and the greater political scene. One prevalent theme in the cartoons was the perception of SBY as an indecisive or passive leader. He was often depicted as hesitant, unsure, or manipulated by powerful interests, reflecting the criticism that he lacked strong and decisive leadership. In addition, corruption, a deeply rooted problem in Indonesian politics, was another prominent theme in that political humor. In a cartoon (Fig. 3.3) that appeared during his second presidency around 2013, President SBY was shown in the middle of a white cloud with a red background (symbolizing the central position over the nation of Indonesia), with four groups of people (symbolizing many interests beyond his tenure). Humorously, SBY's hands are closed, and he has a guilty face, looking uneasy and hesitant as he himself is at the center of powerful interests.

Cartoons often portrayed him as ineffective in combating corruption or being surrounded by corrupt figures. These depictions critiqued his ability to address systemic corruption and raised questions about his commitment to eradicating this issue, a significant concern of the Indonesian public. SBY's military background also became a subject of satire in political cartoons. As a former general, his presidency raised questions about the military's role in Indonesian politics. Cartoons often depicted SBY in military attire or portrayed him in situations that symbolized the military's influence within his government. These visual representations reflected concerns about the balance of power and the potential impact of the military on democratic institutions.

#### 3.3.2.1 Caricatures and Exaggeration of Physical Features and Behavior

Caricatures and exaggeration of physical features and behavior are standard techniques in political cartoons to portray and satirize public figures, including SBY as the Indonesian president. These caricatures employed visual exaggeration to emphasize certain aspects of his appearance, mannerisms, or behavior for satirical effect.

3 A Tale of Two Presidents: Indonesian Humor as Depicted in Political … 53

**Fig. 3.3** Smoke that makes everything wrong. Benny Rachmadi, July 2, 2013 (Reproduced from *Kontan*, 2023)

In one cartoon (Fig. 3.4), President SBY sits with a commoner. Amusingly, they both are daydreaming. SBY daydreams about the arrival schedule of the presidential plane he bought, and the people daydream about the schedule for disbursing aid from the government. By buying the plane, SBY is satirized as a leader with a personality that does not empathize with the country's need priorities, namely financial assistance for the community. His physical appearance was one of the aspects of SBY's image that was caricatured. Cartoonists enhanced key distinguishing traits to create a recognized caricature of the president. These characteristics included his facial expressions, hairdo, and physical size. Cartoonists attempted to catch the reader's attention and generate hilarious or satirical connections with SBY by emphasizing these qualities.

The exaggeration of physical characteristics serves several functions in political cartoons. For starters, it aids in forming a visual identity for the caricatured character. By emphasizing key physical characteristics, cartoonists created a recognized depiction of SBY that stuck out and connected with his identity. This emphasis enabled readers to easily identify the cartoon's target, improving conveyance of the desired message.

Second, exaggeration of physical traits might be employed to communicate certain ideas or remarks. Cartoonists exaggerated particular characteristics to represent or criticize parts of SBY's personality, leadership style, or political acts. For example, an

**Fig. 3.4** Waiting for each other. Benny Rachmadi, July 17, 2013 (Reproduced from *Kontan*, 2023)

exaggeratedly big head can suggest a perceived overinflated ego, whereas a slouched posture may convey indecision or passivity. These visual exaggerations are a shortcut to express complicated concepts or critiques to the audience.

In addition to physical characteristics, cartoonists humorously exaggerated SBY's conduct or idiosyncrasies. This exaggeration included magnifying specific gestures, emotions, or acts connected with the president. Exaggeration is frequently employed in this situation to highlight perceived flaws or to create a comic contrast with the gravity of the position. Using caricatures and exaggeration of physical traits and behavior in political cartoons representing SBY as Indonesia's president was a visual technique to engage readers, deliver messages, and offer social criticism.

#### 3.3.2.2 Depiction of Policies, Controversies, or Governance Issues

The depiction of policies, controversies, or governance issues in political cartoons featuring SBY as the Indonesian president offered a satirical lens through which to examine and comment on his actions and decisions. Political cartoons often portrayed SBY's policies in a simplified and exaggerated manner to convey a specific message or critique. In a cartoon that appeared during his second presidency (Fig. 3.5), President SBY is shown in the policy meeting process from 2009 until 2013. SBY's meeting is about the energy consumption policy. Ironically, over the years SBY always looked to postpone the final policy decision. In this context, he was depicted as the cause of slow decision-making processes. This representation enabled cartoonists to engage a broad audience and spark discussions about the impact and effectiveness of these policies. Accordingly, the controversy surrounding SBY's presidency was also subject to scrutiny and satire in political cartoons. Cartoonists frequently pounced on significant controversies or scandals, such as corruption cases or political scandals, to create visual narratives that shed light on the government's perceived flaws or the president's response. During SBY's administration, political cartoons focused on governance concerns such as bureaucratic inefficiency. Cartoonists portrayed red tape, the delayed decision-making procedures, and the apparent alienation between the government and the people. These depictions aimed to highlight systemic issues and invite critical reflection regarding the effectiveness and responsiveness of the country's governance structures.

Cartoonists can also employ visual metaphors, wordplay, or puns to deliver their critique or commentary. Through these satirical elements, political cartoons provided a critical lens through which the public could reflect on the impact and implications of SBY's policies and governance decisions. By portraying policies, controversies, and governance issues in a visual and satirical manner, political cartoons contributed to public discourse, raising awareness, and challenging the status quo. They offered a unique perspective on the presidency of SBY and invited the public to critically

**Fig. 3.5** Meeting on subsidized fuel. Benny Rachmadi, April 16, 2013 (Reproduced from *Kontan*, 2023)

engage with the policies and actions of the government. The cartoons served as a form of social commentary that encouraged dialogue and reflection on the state of governance in Indonesia during that time.

### 3.3.2.3 The Cartoons' Symbolism and Visual Metaphors

Symbolism and visual metaphors are crucial in political cartoons depicting SBY as the Indonesian president. Cartoonists often use these devices to convey complex ideas, critique policies, or highlight specific aspects of SBY's presidency in concise and visually engaging fashion. One common form of symbolism used in political cartoons is the representation of SBY as a puppet or being manipulated by external forces. In a cartoon that appeared during the latter stages of his second presidency in 2014 (Fig. 3.6), President SBY was shown standing with a bag of merit, handing out star awards to the many hands (this is a symbol of external forces) who contributed during his presidency. Ridiculously, SBY was smiling with satisfaction as he had been depicted as lacking autonomy or control over his tenure. This metaphorical imagery suggested a lack of autonomy or control on his part, implying that powerful interests or individuals were influencing his decision-making. The puppet symbolism critiqued his perceived inability to exercise independent leadership or address issues without external influence. For instance, corruption, a significant issue in Indonesian politics, is often symbolized through visual metaphors in political cartoons. Elsewhere, SBY was depicted as a blindfolded figure holding a scale of justice, symbolizing a perceived failure to effectively combat corruption or uphold the principles of fairness and accountability.

Visual representations of money, bribe offers, or shadowy figures were also employed to symbolize the presence of corruption within his government. Admittedly, these could also have represented public sentiment or perceptions of SBY's presidency, as can be seen in Fig. 3.6, for example. Such symbolic representations and visual metaphors in political cartoons served several purposes. By utilizing symbolism and visual metaphors, the cartoonist created full images that provoked thought, sparked dialogue, and contributed to public discourse on SBY's presidency and the broader socio-political landscape of Indonesia.

## 3.3.3 *Examination of the Critical Discourse Embedded in the Cartoons*

### 3.3.3.1 Power Dynamics and Social Critique

The term "power dynamics and social critique" refers to how SBY's political cartoons represented and criticized the power structures, hierarchies, and social concerns prevalent during his reign. It examines how the cartoons depicted and commented

**Fig. 3.6** Sharing merit badges at the end of the term in office. Benny Rachmadi, October 16, 2014 (Reproduced from *Kontan,* 2023)

on power distribution, the activities of political leaders, and the larger sociopolitical scene in Indonesia. Political cartoons are a type of visual satire that frequently confronts and criticizes individuals in positions of authority. They serve as a forum for social criticism, allowing cartoonists to challenge and expose political people's acts, policies, and behaviors. Political cartoons illuminate the interactions between leaders, institutions, and the general public via the prism of power dynamics.

These cartoons featured SBY as a primary protagonist, emphasizing his status as president and his power. Political cartoons use power dynamics and social critique to challenge established power structures and conventions. They function as a political expression, encouraging public contemplation and dialogue about Indonesian society's governance, social justice, and power dynamics. The cartoons have the potential to be a strong instrument for holding politicians responsible, encouraging civic involvement, and contributing to the larger democratic discussion. Thus, social critique entails critically examining and analyzing social structures, norms, behaviors, and disparities. It seeks to uncover and confront society's defects, inequities, and weaknesses to promote social change, justice, and equity.

### 3.3.3.2 Criticism of Policies or Actions

The cartoons frequently focused on particular SBY policies or activities that the cartoonists found contentious, unsuccessful, or dubious. They exaggerated specific aspects of SBY's policies or activities while making a point through caricatures or comical portrayals. The cartoons' exaggeration and satire highlighted the perceived shortcomings or unfavorable effects of SBY's choices or policies. Therefore, it is critical to remember that while conveying criticism, political cartoons can also be affected by the cartoonist's prejudices, opinions, or political connections. In order to build a sophisticated understanding of criticism of SBY's policies and acts throughout his term, as reflected in the amusing cartoons, a thorough examination of the political cartoons has to consider various sources and opinions.

During SBY's administration, several examples of political cartoons depicted criticism of his policies and conduct. Here are some specific points of critique:

(1) *Corruption*: SBY's handling of corruption concerns was frequently attacked in political cartoons. They portrayed him as ineffectual in battling corruption or called into doubt his dedication to rooting out wrongdoing inside the administration.
(2) *Economic Policies*: Some cartoons critiqued SBY's economic policies, particularly the disparity between economic progress and the well-being of the common populace.
(3) *Human Rights*: Political cartoons highlighted situations where SBY's administration was perceived as failing to handle human rights concerns sufficiently. They frequently portrayed him as ignoring human rights violations or inept in delivering victims' justice.
(4) *Environmental Concerns*: SBY's management of environmental concerns, particularly deforestation and resource exploitation, was criticized. Cartoons showed him as being irresponsible in environmental protection and compromising environmental sustainability for economic gain.
(5) *Political Alliances and Coalitions*: Some cartoons criticized SBY's political alliances and alleged compromises to keep his coalition government in place.
(6) *Ineffectiveness or Inaction*: These cartoons occasionally depicted SBY as an inept or indecisive leader.

Once again, it pays to remember that political cartoons reflect the cartoonists' opinions and viewpoints, and while they provide insights into public feeling, they do not represent common agreement.

### 3.3.3.3 Representation of Public Sentiment

Public opinion fluctuated under SBY's administration, and the Indonesian people expressed positive and negative opinions. Here are a few instances of how the general populace felt while SBY was president:

(1) *Initial Hope*: There was a lot of excitement and hope for change when SBY was initially elected in 2004. Many Indonesians viewed him as a new face and a departure from the past.
(2) *Positive Economic Growth*: The nation's economic growth under SBY's president was one component of his leadership that earned positive reviews. Indonesia's economy grew steadily, bringing in foreign capital and advancing infrastructure construction.
(3) *Dealing with Corruption*: Although SBY vowed to fight corruption, there were doubts in public regarding the efficacy of his anti-corruption initiatives. Some people believed that corruption was still widespread and that high-profile cases frequently led to perceived lenient sentences.
(4) *Human Rights*: Reactions to SBY's record on human rights were in conflict. The handling of cases involving freedom of religion, freedom of speech, and human rights violations by security forces raised concerns, even if his government tried to resolve some human rights issues, such as creating a human rights court.
(5) *Responses to Natural Disasters*: SBY encountered tremendous difficulties in handling earthquakes and tsunamis throughout his administration.

## 3.4 President Joko Widodo: Portrayals and Satire

### *3.4.1 Introduction to Jokowi's Leadership Period*

Under Jokowi's administration, Indonesia saw tremendous political and social transformation. As the nation's seventh president, he faced criticism and comments from various sides on his management style, policies, and governance. A major method for expressing popular opinion and critical conversation about his leadership was political cartoons—an effective medium for social commentary, satire, and critique, offering a distinctive prism to examine and comprehend how the general population viewed his administration.

Jokowi was elected in 2014, riding a tide of popularity as a political outsider known for being a hands-on, proactive leader. His campaign pledges of reform, infrastructure development, and inclusive administration were well received by the population, raising hopes for his leadership. However, as with any leader, Jokowi's term was defined by accomplishments and problems, and political cartoons offered a forum for commenting on these elements. This section examines the many aspects of Jokowi's leadership, as shown in political cartoons, looking at his policy decisions, economic tactics, social programs, environmental efforts, reactions to national crises, and handling of political issues, among others. I attempt to understand the underlying messages, criticisms, and popular opinion regarding Jokowi's leadership style and governance by carefully scrutinizing these cartoons' visual representations, symbolism, and satirical methods.

## 3.4.2 Analysis of Notable Political Cartoons Featuring Jokowi

### 3.4.2.1 Satirical Representation of the President's Personality and Characteristics

Satirical depictions of Jokowi's personality and attributes in political cartoons can vary depending on the context and the cartoonist's point of view. Here are several such satirical representations:

(1) *Simplicity and Informality*: Jokowi is often depicted in a simple and down-to-earth manner, emphasizing his humble origins and relatable personality. He often wore his signature *blusukan*[1] attire: a plain shirt and rolled-up sleeves. This representation highlighted his informal governance approach and connection with familiar people.

(2) *Lack of Strong Leadership*: Some cartoons satirically portray Jokowi as a leader who is perceived as weak or indecisive, through visual cues such as showing him being overshadowed or portrayed as indecisive through exaggerated gestures or expressions. In a cartoon that appeared during his second-year presidency in 2020 (Fig. 3.7), President Jokowi appeared in a plain shirt and rolled-up sleeves (symbolizing a simple and down-to-earth manner). He was also depicted in four action scenes with exaggerated gestures or expressions—as well as weak in front of the mirror (symbolizing his personality as an indecisive person).

(3) *Populist Image*: Jokowi's efforts to connect with the masses and focus on pro-people policies were sometimes satirized as overly populist, depicting him making promises that were seen as aimed at gaining popular support rather than being based on sound economic or political considerations.

(4) *Caricature of Physical Features*: Caricature techniques were often employed to exaggerate certain physical features of Jokowi e.g., his large round glasses, prominent eyebrows, or distinctive smile. These were used to highlight specific aspects of his personality or satirically comment on his leadership.

(5) *Ambiguity in Communication*: Jokowi's communication style, sometimes seen as ambiguous or lacking clarity, was also satirized in cartoons. This style was depicted through exaggerated speech bubbles or visual metaphors that explained his ambiguous or confusing statements. It is necessary to note that these satirical depictions did not accurately reflect Jokowi's character or manner of leadership; rather, they represented the cartoonists' interpretations and points of view.

### 3.4.2.2 Commentary on Economic Policies, Corruption, or Social Issues

Public opinion regarding Jokowi's policies and actions during his presidency in Indonesia was diverse, varying among different segments of society. Here are some key observations regarding public opinion of Jokowi's policies and actions:

---

[1] *Blusukan* (Javanese) *n* (1) activities that monitor a state or situation directly without using the delegation function; (2) directly observing the condition of the people in a certain area.

**Fig. 3.7** When President Jokowi is disappointed with ministers. Benny Rachmadi, July 1, 2020 (Reproduced from *Kontan*, 2023)

(1) *Infrastructure Development*: Jokowi's emphasis on infrastructure development, such as building roads, bridges, and airports, garnered mixed opinions.
(2) *Economic Policies*: Jokowi's economic policies received varied responses. Some supporters credited him with initiatives to promote inclusive economic growth, reduce poverty rates, and increase access to finance for micro, small, and medium-sized enterprises (MSMEs). In the cartoon that appeared at the beginning of his first presidency (Fig. 3.8), President Jokowi discusses the flow of economic trade with his staff. At the same time, pressing environmental problems needed to be resolved immediately. Satirically, his head is quickly covered due to a forest fire (suggesting that he cannot see the facts of the matter).
(3) *Social Programs*: Jokowi's social programs, such as the National Health Insurance Scheme (*BPJS Kesehatan*) and the Smart Indonesia Card (*KIP*) for education, have generally been viewed positively by those who believe in addressing social inequality.
(4) *Environmental Initiatives*: Jokowi's efforts to address environmental challenges, such as combating deforestation and promoting renewable energy, received mixed reviews.
(5) *Political Challenges and Reforms*: Jokowi's response to political challenges and efforts to implement reforms elicited varying opinions. In a cartoon that appeared during his second presidency while fighting the Covid-19 pandemic (Fig. 3.9),

**Fig. 3.8** Smoke exports. Benny Rachmadi, September 18, 2019 (Reproduced from *Kontan*, 2023)

satirically, President Jokowi was satirically shown in the corner of cartoons and receives an award trophy from the Covid-19 virus itself (symbolizing the lack of action regarding his national health policy). Jokowi looked very scared., with his gestures and facial expressions suggesting that he felt guilty.

### 3.4.2.3 Symbolic Elements and Visual Cues Used in the Cartoons

Symbolic components are things, pictures, or people that stand in for intangible ideas or concepts. Cartoonists use these symbols to simplify complicated situations into recognizable and relevant images. With the help of these symbols, the cartoonist can rapidly, visually, and impactfully express a message. Different symbolic components were employed in political cartoons using Jokowi to communicate particular messages or critiques. Here are a few examples:

(1) *Motorcycle*: Cartoons used Jokowi's fondness of riding motorbikes to represent his relatability and tight ties to regular people. This embodied his persona as a realist who was aware of the challenges the typical citizen faced.
(2) *Blusukan Outfit*: Cartoons frequently featured Jokowi wearing his distinctive outfit: a simple shirt and rolled-up sleeves.
(3) *Javanese Cultural Symbols*: Since Jokowi is from Java, cartoons sometimes incorporated Javanese symbols to depict his local identity and cultural

Fig. 3.9 The Covid-19 champion in Asia. Benny Rachmadi, July 22, 2020 (Reproduced from *Kontan*, 2023)

upbringing. These markers emphasized his ties to his culture and heritage, including traditional apparel from Java, well-known sites, or cultural icons.

(4) *Infrastructure and Building*: Cartoon images of building sites, cranes, and roadwork visually expressed Jokowi's emphasis on infrastructure development. The objective was his focus on economic development and his initiatives to upgrade the nation's physical infrastructure.

(5) *Indonesian Flag and National Symbols*: Cartoons starring Jokowi frequently featured the Indonesian flag (Merah Putih) and other national symbols, such as the national emblem (Garuda Pancasila). These emblems emphasized his role as the country's head of state and his duty to the Indonesian people. In a cartoon that appeared in the first year of his second presidency in 2019 (Fig. 3.10), Jokowi's cabinet was shown as a fat man (symbolizing the resourceful capital to provide service for civilians). Ridiculously, he is eating one bowl of tasty food and looking at the new offer of delicious dessert (symbolizing the need for a government that could not be matched with the good possibilities offered by providers from external parties).

Moreover, in political cartoons depicting Jokowi, various visual cues were employed to convey messages, emphasize certain aspects, or evoke specific reactions. Here are a few examples of visual cues commonly found in political cartoons on Jokowi:

**Fig. 3.10** The fat coalition. Benny Rachmadi, October 16, 2019 (Reproduced from *Kontan*, 2023)

(1) *Facial Expressions*: Cartoonists often exaggerated Jokowi's facial expressions to convey various emotions or attitudes. For instance, his serious or stern expression was amplified to depict determination or resoluteness. Alternatively, a smiling or grinning face was used to portray his perceived affability or optimism.
(2) *Attire and Accessories*: Political cartoons can use the choice of attire and accessories as visual signals. Jokowi's distinctive outfit, consisting of a simple shirt and rolled-up sleeves, often represented his casual and hands-on leadership style.
(3) *Movements and Postures*: Cartoonists use movements and postures to accentuate certain characteristics or express a message. Jokowi frequently made exaggerated hand motions that suggested aggressiveness or resolve. His body language could also convey confidence or weakness e.g., standing erect or leaning over.
(4) *Background Information*: Cartoonists frequently incorporate information that adds context or meaning. For instance, a packed office desk with piles of paperwork could be used in a cartoon to represent a hectic or overburdened president.
(5) *Characters or Objects in the Environment*: Cartoonists frequently inserted nearby individuals or objects to interact with Jokowi in the cartoon. These components could represent political friends, rivals, or emblems of certain principles or concerns. Jokowi's responses to or interactions with these factors

provided more background or remarks about his presidency. Political cartoons' visual cues varied depending on the cartoonist's perspective and desired effect.

### 3.4.3 Unpacking Critical Discourse in the Cartoons

#### 3.4.3.1 Satire as a Means of Criticism and Social Commentary

Satire is a powerful tool used in political cartoons featuring Jokowi in Indonesia to provide criticism and social commentary. Satirical elements in these cartoons can be analyzed to understand the underlying critiques and commentaries. For instance, in a cartoon that appeared in the first year of his second presidency in 2019 (Fig. 3.11), Jokowi's policy was satirized in Rachmadi's cartoon. President Jokowi was approved by a jury in the goods auction hall, holding a photograph with the word "ministers" (symbolizing that he is holding an auction for ministerial posts in the cabinet of his second presidency). Meanwhile, many other actors in the cartoon appear to be raising their hands and shouting for seats (symbolizing that many parties want to be part of Jokowi's cabinet). The cartoon satirizes Jokowi's leadership that can be very close to various external government interests. The biting satire is that there is no representation of common people in the cartoon (indicating that the public might never be involved as an important part of the cabinet).

Here is how satire is employed in political cartoons:

(1) *Exaggeration and Caricature*: Satirical cartoons often employ exaggeration and caricature to highlight specific characteristics or behaviors of political figures. Jokowi was portrayed exaggeratedly to emphasize particular aspects of his leadership style, policies, or personal traits.
(2) *Irony and Sarcasm*: Satire frequently utilizes irony and sarcasm to make pointed critiques, highlighting the gap between what the leaders say and what they do. Sarcasm can be employed to mock or ridicule their actions, decisions, or public statements. Using these rhetorical devices, cartoons challenged the sincerity or effectiveness of Jokowi's leadership.
(3) *Symbolism and Metaphor*: Satirical cartoons often use symbols and metaphors to convey deeper meanings and critiques. Symbols can represent specific policies, political ideologies, or societal issues associated with the leaders. Metaphors provide a figurative comparison that invites reflection regarding their actions or impact.
(4) *Critique of Policies and Actions*: Satirical cartoons frequently target specific policies or actions of political figures. Satire enabled cartoonists to draw attention to problematic aspects, challenge decision-making processes, or question the effectiveness of specific policies implemented by Jokowi.
(5) *Social Commentary and Public Sentiment*: Satirical cartoons reflect and comment on broader societal issues, public sentiment, and widespread concerns.

**Fig. 3.11** Proposal for ministerial seats. Benny Rachmadi, July 7, 2019 (Reproduced from *Kontan*, 2023)

By depicting Jokowi in specific scenarios or addressing topical issues, cartoons provided social commentary on governance, political climate, or socioeconomic challenges. They often resonated with public sentiment and contributed to public discussions. Using various satirical devices, cartoonists could challenge the actions and policies of Jokowi, provide commentary on his leadership and prompting critical reflection among the audience.

### 3.4.3.2 Reflection of Public Dissatisfaction or Unfulfilled Expectations

Political cartoons can reflect public dissatisfaction or unfulfilled expectations concerning political figures. Here are how political cartoons conveyed such public sentiments regarding Jokowi:

(1) *Criticism of Policies*: Political cartoons often critique specific policies or actions of political figures (e.g., Weydmann & Großmann, 2020). A cartoon portraying Jokowi negatively regarding their policies indicated public dissatisfaction with those policies.
(2) *Representation of Public Concerns*: Political cartoons depict public concerns and expectations regarding their leaders (e.g., Mahadian & Hasyim, 2022). When a cartoon portrayed Jokowi addressing popular issues or fulfilling public

expectations, this suggested that the cartoonist was reflecting the desires and hopes of the public.

(3) *Satirical Exaggeration*: Satire in political cartoons often amplifies or exaggerates specific characteristics or actions of political figures (e.g., Triputra & Sugita, 2016). If a cartoon portrays Jokowi exaggeratedly or caricatured, it might reflect public frustration or disappointment with their performance or perceived shortcomings.

(4) *Symbolic Representations*: Political cartoons frequently use symbols to represent broader societal issues or sentiments (e.g., Asidiky et al., 2022). For example, when a cartoon shows a broken promise symbolically represented by a shattered object associated with a specific leader, it indicates public disillusionment or unmet expectations.

(5) *Public Sentiment and Reactions*: Political cartoons can highlight public sentiment through their reception and reactions (e.g., Faliha & Putri, 2022). When a cartoon depicting Jokowi generated significant public discussion, sharing, or criticism, it suggested that it resonated with public sentiment, reflecting their dissatisfaction or expectations.

### 3.4.3.3 Examination of the Societal Impact of the Cartoons

Examining the societal impact of political cartoons featuring Jokowi entails an assessment of how these cartoons influenced public opinion, shaped public discourse, and contributed to social and political dynamics. Here are some aspects to consider:

(1) *Public Perception and Awareness*: Political cartoons can raise public awareness and shape perceptions of political figures (Putri, 2018). Cartoons criticizing or highlighting certain aspects of Jokowi's leadership could have influenced how the public perceived them.

(2) *Influencing Public Discourse*: Political cartoons often spark discussions and debates about political issues (Permana, 2020). They can visually represent complex ideas and stimulate conversations among the public. Cartoons that addressed controversial topics or critiqued specific policies of Jokowi shaped public discourse by setting the agenda and framing the discussion around those issues.

(3) *Satirical Critique and Accountability*: Political cartoons act as satire and criticism, holding political figures accountable for their actions (Rahman, 2022). This satire can contribute to public scrutiny and encourage a culture of accountability in the political sphere.

(4) *Mobilizing Social Movements*: Political cartoons can potentially mobilize social movements or drive collective action (Nuriarta & Sujayanthi, 2020). Cartoons that address societal issues or criticize the leaders can become symbols for collective action or demands for change.

(5) *Freedom of Expression and Democracy*: Political cartoons express freedom of speech and play a crucial role in democratic societies (Ritonga et al., 2019). Cartoons critical of Jokowi reflected a healthy democratic environment where

different opinions and dissenting voices were allowed. The impact of these cartoons on society highlighted the importance of freedom of expression and its role in shaping democratic processes.

## 3.5 Conclusion

This chapter has explored the vibrant realm of political cartoons to document and evaluate the political comedy that existed under SBY and Jokowi as presidents. It examined numerous topics, satirical depictions, and symbolic components of the cartoons through the perspective of CDA, illuminating the power relations, societal critique, and public attitudes that they contained. Some important conclusions emerged when examining the well-known political cartoons of SBY and Jokowi. This chapter exposed the satirical depictions of the presidents' physical characteristics and mannerisms, including caricatures and exaggerations. By analyzing the critical language embedded in the cartoons, power relations and societal critique were revealed. Overall, this chapter attempted to shed light on the complex interplay between politics, humor, and society in Indonesia, offering valuable insights for scholars, researchers, and readers interested in political communication, language studies, media studies, and Indonesian politics.

**Acknowledgements** I gratefully acknowledge the permission of Kontan to reproduce the cartoons presented in this chapter.

## References

Aragon, L. V., & Leach, J. (2008). Arts and owners: Intellectual property law and the politics of scale in Indonesian arts. *American Ethnologist, 35*(4), 607–631. https://doi.org/10.1111/j.1548-1425.2008.00101.x

Asidiky, Z., Sujatna, E. T. S., Sidiq, I. I., & Darmayanti, N. (2022). Multimodal portrayal of Joko Widodo on Tempo's cover story: A multimodal critical discourse analysis. *Jordan Journal of Modern Languages and Literatures, 14*(3), 479–493. https://doi.org/10.47012/jjmll.14.3.2

Attardo, S. (1994). *Linguistic theories of humour*. Mouton de Gruyter.

Attardo, S. (2001). *Humorous texts: A semantic and pragmatic analysis*. Mouton de Gruyter.

Balakrishnan, V., Venkat, V., & Manickam, M. (2019). Virality in the environment of political cartoons: When history intersects representation. *The European Journal of Humour Research, 7*(2), 137–152. https://doi.org/10.7592/EJHR2019.7.2.balakrishnan

Blommaert, J., & Bulcaen, C. (2000). Critical discourse analysis. *Annual Review of Anthropology, 29*(1), 447–466. https://doi.org/10.1146/annurev.anthro.29.1.447

Boukes, M., Boomgaarden, H. G., Moorman, M., & De Vreese, C. H. (2015). At odds: Laughing and thinking? The appreciation, processing, and persuasiveness of political satire. *Journal of Communication, 65*(5), 721–744. https://doi.org/10.1111/jcom.12173

Cohen, M. I. (2016). *Inventing the performing arts: Modernity and tradition in colonial Indonesia*. University of Hawaii Press.

Cohen, M. I. (2019). Three eras of Indonesian arts diplomacy. *Bijdragen Tot De Taal-, Land- En Volkenkunde/journal of the Humanities and Social Sciences of Southeast Asia, 175*(2–3), 253–283. https://doi.org/10.1163/22134379-17502022

Daniels, T. P. (2007). Liberals, moderates and jihadists: Protesting Danish cartoons in Indonesia. *Contemporary Islam, 1*, 231–246. https://doi.org/10.1007/s11562-007-0020-0

Djordjevic, N. (2014). The depiction of a (national) hero: Pangeran Diponegoro in paintings from the nineteenth century until today. *Doctoral dissertation*. Sebelas Maret University.

Dynel, M. (2013). Humorous phenomena in dramatic discourse. *The European Journal of Humour Research, 1*(1), 22–60. https://doi.org/10.7592/EJHR2013.1.1.dynel

Dynel, M., & Chovanec, J. (2021). Creating and sharing public humour across traditional and new media. *Journal of Pragmatics, 177*, 151–156. https://doi.org/10.1016/j.pragma.2021.02.020

Fairclough, N. (2013). Critical discourse analysis. In J. P. Gee & M. Handford (Eds.), *The Routledge handbook of discourse analysis* (pp. 9–20). Routledge.

Faliha, S., & Putri, K. Y. S. (2022). Semiotic analysis of Jokowi's political meme "the King of Lip Service" and "YNTKTS" as media for criticism in the digital age. *Persepsi: Communication Journal, 5*(2), 87–98. https://doi.org/10.30596/persepsi.v5i2.10183

Fein, O., Beni-Noked, S., & Giora, R. (2015). Under/standing cartoons: The suppression hypothesis revisited. *Journal of Pragmatics, 86*, 86–93. https://doi.org/10.1016/j.pragma.2015.05.016

Feldman, O. (1995). Political reality and editorial cartoons in Japan: How the national dailies illustrate the Japanese Prime Minister. *Journalism & Mass Communication Quarterly, 72*(3), 571–580. https://doi.org/10.1177/107769909507200308

Feldman, O. (2000). Non-oratorical discourse and political humor in Japan: Editorial cartoons, satire and attitudes toward authority. In C. De Landtsheer & O. Feldman (Eds.), *Beyond public speech and symbols: Explorations in the rhetoric of politicians and the media* (pp. 165–191). Praeger.

Harun, A., Razak, M. R. A., Ali, A., Nasir, M. N. F., & Radzuan, L. E. M. (2015). Anthropomorphism in political cartoons: Case study of the 1965 Malaysia-Indonesia confrontation. In O. Hassan, S. Abidin, R. Legino, R. Anwar & M. Kamaruzaman (Eds.), *International colloquium of art and design education research (i-CADER 2014)* (pp. 53–60). Springer. https://doi.org/10.1007/978-981-287-332-3_6

Hasanah, N., & Hidayat, D. N. (2020). A semiotic analysis of political cartoons on the first 100 days of the Anies Baswedan government. *EduLite: Journal of English Education, Literature and Culture, 5*(2), 322–333. https://doi.org/10.30659/e.5.2.322-333

Hill, M. R. (2013). Developing a normative approach to political satire: A critical perspective. *International Journal of Communication, 7*, 14. https://ijoc.org/index.php/ijoc/article/view/1934/856

Holbert, R. L., Hmielowski, J., Jain, P., Lather, J., & Morey, A. (2011). Adding nuance to the study of political humor effects: Experimental research on Juvenalian satire versus Horatian satire. *American Behavioral Scientist, 55*(3), 187–211. https://doi.org/10.1177/0002764210392156

*Kontan* (n.d.). Collection of cartoons by Benny Rachmadi. https://images.kontan.co.id/kartun_benny (in Indonesian).

Kreuz, R. J. (1997). Irony in context, by Katharina Barbe. *Journal of Pragmatics, 27*(2), 247–250. https://doi.org/10.1016/S0378-2166(97)80961-7

LaMarre, H. L., Landreville, K. D., Young, D., & Gilkerson, N. (2014). Humor works in funny ways: Examining satirical tone as a key determinant in political humor message processing. *Mass Communication and Society, 17*(3), 400–423. https://doi.org/10.1080/15205436.2014.891137

Landreville, K. D. (2015). Satire as uncertain territory: Uncertainty expression in discussion about political satire, opinion, and news. *Humor, 28*(4), 559–582. https://doi.org/10.1515/humor-2015-0105

Lent, J. A. (2014). Cartooning in Indonesia: An overview. In J. A. Lent (Ed.), *Southeast Asian cartoon art: History, trends and problems* (pp. pp. 6–38). McFarland.

Lis, M. (2014). Visual art in Indonesia. Introduction. *Art of the Orient, 3*, 208–221. https://doi.org/10.11588/ao.2014.0.8800

Mahadian, A. B., & Hashim, R. (2022). Political internet memes in Indonesia: Insulting the President in the 2019 presidential election Adi Bayu. *Journal of Contemporary Issues in Media & Communication (JCIMC), 2*, 27–57.

Meibauer, J. (2019). Irony, deception, and humour: Seeking the truth about overt and covert untruthfulness, by Marta Dynel. *Journal of Pragmatics, 147*, 17–21. https://doi.org/10.1016/j.pragma.2019.05.009

Morgan, M. (2010). The presentation of indirectness and power in everyday life. *Journal of Pragmatics, 42*(2), 283–291. https://doi.org/10.1016/j.pragma.2009.06.011

Nelson, R. (2019). *Modern art of Southeast Asia: Introductions from A to Z*. National Gallery Singapore.

Nugraha, D. S. (2020). The vlog register in Bahasa Indonesia: an Ethnolinguistics study. *International Journal on Language, Research and Education Studies, 4*(1), 92–103. https://doi.org/10.30575/2017/IJLRES-2020010408

Nugraha, D. S. (2022). On silent laughter: The political humour depicted in Indonesian cartoons. *VELES: Voices of English Language Education Society, 6*(1), 283–298. https://doi.org/10.29408/veles.v6i1.5022

Nuriarta, I. W., & Sujayanthi, N. W. M. (2020). Semiotics study of the 2019 Jawa Pos political cartoon. *Lekesan: Interdisciplinary Journal of Asia Pacific Arts, 3*(2), 41–47.

Ostrom, R. (2007). Risky business: Three political cartooning lessons from Indonesia during Suharto's authoritarian rule. *PS: Political Science & Politics, 40*(2), 297–301. https://doi.org/10.1017/S1049096507070473

Permana, Y. R. (2020). Analysis of political cartoons in Jakarta Post e-paper. *Journal of Languages and Language Teaching, 7*(1), 6–20. https://doi.org/10.33394/jollt.v7i1.1435

Piata, A. (2016). When metaphor becomes a joke: Metaphor journeys from political ads to internet memes. *Journal of Pragmatics, 106*, 39–56. https://doi.org/10.1016/j.pragma.2016.10.003

Pinar, M. J. (2020). Humour and intertextuality in Steve Bell's political cartoons. *The European Journal of Humour Research, 8*(3), 16–39. https://doi.org/10.7592/EJHR2020.8.3.Pinar-Sanz

Protschky, S. (2011). *Images of the tropics: Environment and visual culture in colonial Indonesia*. Brill.

Putri, S. A. (2018). A semiotic analysis of Joko Widodo political cartoons in the Jakarta Post e-paper. *Master's thesis*. Universitas Sumatera Utara.

Rahman, A. F. N. (2022). Multiliteracy in the Millennial Generation: A case study of political cartoons on Instagram Tempodotco. *PERSPEKTIF, 11*(4), 1291–1300. https://doi.org/10.31289/perspektif.v11i4.7312

Ritonga, R., Nugroho, E., & Handoko, D. (2019). Struggle of meaning and the Jokowi myth in the 2018 Asian games opening video. *Jurnal Komunikasi: Malaysian Journal of Communication, 35*(1), 137–155.

Rossen-Knill, D. F., & Henry, R. (1997). The pragmatics of verbal parody. *Journal of Pragmatics, 27*(6), 719–752. https://doi.org/10.1016/S0378-2166(96)00054-9

Sen, K., & Hill, D. T. (2007). *Media, culture and politics in Indonesia*. Equinox Publ.

Singh, R. K. (2012). Humour, irony and satire in literature. *International Journal of English and Literature, 3*(4), 63–72.

Spielmann, Y. (2017). *Contemporary Indonesian art: Artists, art spaces, and collectors* (Vol. 138). NUS Press.

Stewart, R. (2015). Breaking the mainstream mold: The birth of a local political cartoonist in post-3.11 Japan. *The European Journal of Humour Research, 2*(4), 74–94. https://doi.org/10.7592/EJHR2014.2.4.stewart

Streicher, L. H. (1967). On a theory of political caricature. *Comparative Studies in Society and History, 9*(4), 427–445. http://www.jstor.org/stable/177687

Susanto, M. (2018). *Soekarno's favorite painters*. PT Dwi Samapersada.

Susanto, M., Simatupang, G. R., & Haryono, T. (2018). Curating the painting collection of the presidential palace of the Republic of Indonesia. *Lekesan: Interdisciplinary Journal of Asia Pacific Arts, 1*(1), 19–29. https://doi.org/10.31091/lekesan.v1i1.342

Triputra, P., & Sugita, F. (2016). Culture jamming phenomenon in politics (the Jokowi's memes in TIME publication's cover and TokoBagus.com advertisement). *Journal of US-China Public Administration, 13*(6), 386–396. https://doi.org/10.17265/1548-6591/2016.06.002

Tsakona, V. (2009). Language and image interaction in cartoons: Towards a multimodal theory of humor. *Journal of Pragmatics, 41*(6), 1171–1188. https://doi.org/10.1016/j.pragma.2008.12.003

Vickers, A. (2020). *The impossibility of art history in Indonesia*. In: *International Conference on Aesthetics and the Sciences of Art*. Bandung Institute of Technology.

Wee, L. S. (Ed.). (2015). *Between declarations and dreams: Art of Southeast Asia since the 19th century*. National Gallery Singapore.

Weiss, G., & Wodak, R. (Eds.). (2007). *Critical discourse analysis*. Palgrave Macmillan.

Weydmann, N., & Großmann, K. (2020). Corona in Indonesian and German cartoons: Contested medical pluralism, distrust in the state and radicalization in times of crisis. *Philologie im Netz: PhiN; Beiheft, (24)*, 523–546. https://web.fu-berlin.de/phin/beiheft24/b24t33.pdf

Witek, M. (2022). Irony as a speech action. *Journal of Pragmatics, 190*, 76–90. https://doi.org/10.1016/j.pragma.2022.01.010

Young, D. G. (2017). Theories and effects of political humor: Discounting cues, gateways, and the impact of incongruities. In K. Kenski & K. H. Jamieson (Eds.), *The Oxford handbook of political communication* (pp. 881–884). Oxford University Press.

**Danang Satria Nugraha** is a Lecturer of Linguistics at the Department of Indonesian Language, Sanata Dharma University, Indonesia, and currently a PhD candidate at the Doctoral School in Linguistics, University of Szeged, Hungary. His research focuses on linguistic phenomena in Indonesia i.e., the relation between language and political communication, primarily based on theoretical linguistics. He has published journal articles, chapters, and books on issues related to Indonesian linguistics.

# Chapter 4
# Mocking the Inept: Brazilian Cartoons and Criticism of the Jair Bolsonaro Government

**Bruno Mendelski and Marco André Cadoná**

**Abstract** This chapter investigates representations of the Bolsonaro government in the cartoons of the influential and award-winning Brazilian cartoonist Laerte Coutinho. In the Brazilian case, political cartoons translate an important feature of the country's cultural tradition: humor. Brazilians value humor as a strategy to face the ills they confront in their daily relationships and in their socio-political coexistence. It is argued that through her cartoons, political humor was a form of denunciation and resistance to Bolsonaro's anti-democratic and anti-human rights agenda. By denouncing and mocking government actions, the cartoons raised awareness of key national questions, such as the Covid-19 pandemic, electoral system and democracy, conservative values, the environment, etc., contributing to a critical view and stance towards the Bolsonaro administration. In the context of a government aligned with authoritarian postures, humor emerges as a cultural trait of Brazilians and as a space for political socialization committed to strategies of resistance and construction of a critical political culture in the country. Methodologically, we used Documental Image Analysis, both in its qualitative approach to understanding cartoons based on the influence of their context, place, and author, as in their strategy of a three stage investigation: pre-iconographic, iconographic and iconological.

B. Mendelski (✉)
Department of Business Management and Communication, and Graduate Program in Regional Development (PPGDR) and Administration (PPGA), University of Santa Cruz do Sul (UNISC), Rio Grande do Sul, Brazil
e-mail: brunomendelskidesouza@gmail.com

M. A. Cadoná
Department of Science, Humanities, and Education, and Program in Regional Development (PPGDR), University of Santa Cruz do Sul (UNISC), Rio Grande do Sul, Brazil

© The Author(s), under exclusive license to Springer Nature Singapore Pte Ltd. 2024
O. Feldman (ed.), *Communicating Political Humor in the Media*,
The Language of Politics, https://doi.org/10.1007/978-981-97-0726-3_4

## 4.1 Introduction

Figure 4.1 sets the direction for this chapter: critical analysis of the Jair Messias Bolsonaro government (2019–2022) through cartoons. In the cartoon, Laerte Coutinho (known mainly as simply Laerte), a well-known and influential Brazilian cartoonist, depicts Bolsonaro's departure to the United States before the end of his government, from where he would not return before Luís Inácio Lula da Silva took over the presidency of Brazil in January 2023. From a time marked by destruction, represented by the lifeless tree, a new time is visualized, with the hope that favorable winds for the democratic regime will once again blow over Brazilian soil.

It is through cartoons like this that we here analyze how this expression of Brazilian humor contributed to the construction of perceptions and critical views about the government of Bolsonaro. The cartoon, while entertaining as a humorous and satirical representation, it also alerts, denounces, and provokes reflection. In the Brazilian case, the cartoon translates an important trait of the symbolic representation that is held of Brazilians: they value humor as a coping mechanism for daily struggles and an expression of resignation towards the social ills they face in their everyday lives and socio-political environments. For Brazilians, laughter and the numerous ways of interpreting facts and events indicate a way of playing even with facts considered serious, in addition to expressing forms of internalization of the social through which they produce their representations and their social and political positions.

The present chapter empirically references the work of Laerte, who represents a Brazilian cultural tradition of direct, ironic, sarcastic, and satirical humor concerning national governments in the country. By examining cartoons published by Laerte in a prominent national newspaper, *Folha de São Paulo*, we argue that political humor occupied a space of denunciation and resistance to the destructive agenda of the Bolsonaro government. By denouncing and mocking the government's actions,

**Fig. 4.1** The farewell. Laerte Coutinho, December 29, 2022 (Reproduced from Folha de São Paulo (2023))

the cartoons addressed important issues of the period in the country—such as the pandemic, the electoral system, fake news, gun control, the environment, and the rights of indigenous peoples—contributing to a critical stance towards that government. Especially considering that it was a government aligned with the authoritarian tradition present in Brazilian history, humor as a cultural trait of Brazilians contributed to political socialization committed to strategies of resistance and the construction of a critical culture in the country.

From a methodological point of view, we intend to analyze the representations present in the cartoons from the iconographic method proposed by Erwin Panofsky (2009): the object is investigated in its different meanings, including the influence of its context and author, according to its immanent or socially constructed characteristics (Silva, 2018). This is done by combining the following types of analyses: (i) *iconographic*: classification, description, study, identification, and interpretation of the meanings of the images, providing the bases for the subsequent interpretation; and (ii) *iconological*: interpretation of the symbolic values and the search for the ultimate meaning of the work, to explain its underlying rationale in the context of the culture and time in which it was created, regardless of its quality or its author (Casimiro, 2016).

As indicated, the research *corpus* consisted of cartoons by the cartoonist Laerte, published in *Folha de São Paulo*, during Jair Bolsonaro's presidency in Brazil. During this timeframe, Laerte published between one and two cartoons a week, all of which were available for free on the official website of *Folha de São Paulo*, one of the most influential newspapers in Brazil as the leader in paid subscriptions among the major Brazilian newspapers, in addition to having the largest circulation and audience on social networks (*Twitter* and *Instagram*). Laerte published approximately 218 cartoons during the period under study, 156 of which were directly related to the Bolsonaro government (71% of the total) (Folha de São Paulo, 2023). For this chapter, in addition to the above cartoon, five others were chosen, covering the five main axes of the Bolsonaro administration: (i) economic neoliberalism; (ii) political authoritarianism; (iii) moral conservatism; (iv) destructive environmentalism; (v) sanitary irresponsibility.

This chapter is organized in three sections including the conclusion. In the following section we discuss the role of cartoons in the Brazilian culture of humor, then examining the representation of the Bolsonaro government in Laerte's cartoons.

### *4.1.1 Situating the Cartoon in Brazil's Humor Culture*

The Portuguese word for cartoon, *charge*, comes from the French word *charger* and means "to charge," "exaggerate," and "attack violently" (as in a cavalry charge) (Fonseca, 1999, p. 26). Cartoons are humorous and satirical representations that possess a political nature and are inherently discursive and intertextual. In their political connotations and expression, cartoons can be seen as the contemporary successors of caricatures (Miani, 2010, p. 58). A cartoon consists of an image that might be accompanied by texts or words. In it, verbal and visual languages come together with an aesthetic experience related to the message that is intended to be transmitted, resulting in the need to be attentive to all the information that the visual brings, such as colors, figures, and graphic distribution (Santos, 2013).

A cartoon is not only intended to distract but also to alert, denounce, restrain, and prompt reflection (Agostinho, 1993, p. 229). Its informal nature is a significant factor in bringing politics into the popular sphere by simplifying complex topics through easily understandable resources or images, often referencing situations that readers experience in their daily lives (Silva, 2018).

Constituting a political and critical piece that is easy to understand (due to its exaggerated characteristics), the cartoon can also act as a mobilizing element in society. The cartoon, through the seduction of humor, can act as an instrument of persuasion within the scope of the process of political and ideological definitions of the receiver, thus creating an atmosphere of acceptability that allows a process of mobilization and reflection in the face of societal events (Santos, 2013). This occurs as the cartoon, through humor, brings news into conscious awareness (Liebel, 2017). It is worth noting that the cartoon mobilizes a common and effective strategy of political humor: the ridicule of reality. In this sense, the cartoons also aim to achieve comedic effects through distortions of human social actions, drawing attention to a specific theme or the behavior of a social actor (Silva, 2018).

In the Brazilian case, cartoons are expressions of a socio-cultural trait of great importance for Brazilians: humor (Saliba, 2002). Through humor, Brazilians reclaim, albeit briefly, public spaces almost always denied to them by institutionalized political power, given the historical socio-political exclusion that characterizes the country. But there is more: humor is a way for Brazilians to alleviate their frustrations stemming from significant social disparities. Throughout its history, Brazil has not succeeded in creating an authentic and lasting national identity. To the contrary, the country's history is marked by segregation and the isolation of different sectors of the population. In this context, laughter and good humor serve as compensators for such lack of identity in a not-very-cohesive society that always experienced domination and social exclusion (Saliba, 2002).

Laughter, therefore, is a socio-cultural phenomenon. Brazilians reinforce their solidarity through laughter and also through it can express rejection of strange elements (Goldenberg & Jablonski, 2011). Humor constitutes not only an integral part of social relations but also expresses political and social dispositions and orientations. This aspect is also evident in cartoons: the drawings and representations they contain reflect temporally delimited political and social themes and dynamics (Silva, 2018).

Laughter among Brazilians has emerged and developed as a strategy for coexistence and compensation for an emotional deficit in relation to the meaning of their own stories. As emphasized by Saliba (2002), humor allows Brazilians "in both everyday life and collective situations, to free themselves through irreverence from authorities and uncomfortable gestures, whether their own or others', giving individuals, for fleeting moments, a sense of belonging that the public sphere" subtracted from them and that they slowly try to regain (Saliba, 2002, p. 304). If changing history is not always possible, laughter is a way to resignify that history. Laughter and jokes are spaces and moments of altering meaning, of reversing significations.

The re-signification and alteration of the *status quo* through humor, in fact, is a historical activity of human beings in the West. Bremmer and Roodenburg (2000) argued that since ancient Greece and Rome, humor has been perceived as a potential catalyst for transgresing the social order. And when considering Brazilian reality, Saliba (2011) indicated that throughout the country's history, humor has also positioned itself as an important political tool for resistance and criticism against constant repressive and authoritarian periods. It can even be said that in the country, humor has become a "social weapon of the powerless" (Saliba, 2011).

It is important to note that humor has always been valued by the media in Brazil, especially since the nineteenth century, when the first cartoons and caricatures began to gain space in the written press. During the twentieth century, and especially in periods of authoritarian governments, cartoons also served as a way to criticize and denounce various governmental practices and the ruling classes. Therefore, since the beginning of print media in Brazil, cartoons have acted as a mechanism for transmitting political, social, and humanitarian ideals through criticism and denunciation of various issues in Brazilian society (Miani & Guimarães, 2018, p. 3).

During the military dictatorship (1964–85), the newspaper *O Pasquim* played an important role as an alternative press in Brazil, promoting an editorial, political, cultural, and ideological reaction to that dictatorial regime through caricatures and cartoons (Vieira, 2010). In the 1980s, amidst popular desire for "re-democratization," the cartoon contained inside the cartoon, the phrase *Diretas Já!* ("Direct Elections Now!") became synonymous with the social and political movement advocating for "re-democratization" (Miani & Guimarães, 2018).

In recent times, the Brazilian tradition of political criticism through cartoons has been kept alive in the work of authors such as Laerte, Carlos Latuff, Nando Motta, and Renato Aroeira, among others. Laerte stands out for her long career in Brazilian critical humor, as she was a member of *Pasquim*, having collaborated with social movements and several Brazilian newspapers with a wide readership, including *Gazeta Mercantil, Estado de São Paulo, Folha de São Paulo*. In *Folha de São Paulo*, Laerte has been publishing comic strips since 1991 and cartoons since 2014. Her cartoons have played a significant role in the Bolsonaro government era by contributing to the amplification of voices of denunciation and criticism against that government through the media (Coutinho, 2023).

Thus, the cartoon is an expression of the Brazilian way of being, in which humor becomes a means of transforming social, political, and economic woes into "boisterous laughter," but at the same time it serves as a form of denunciation and sociopolitical criticism, encompassing the desires for change and a less unequal and more just reality. As Brazilians themselves say: "Brazilians laugh at everything, even hairy things:" from politicians' underwear and socks filled with public money to sentimental woes, such as betrayals among family members. Therefore, we laugh at ourselves, seeking to make unbearable situations more bearable. But we laugh as an expression of the feeling that "the present is beyond repair," unable to bring joy, and we need to look ahead, nourishing the hope that something can change. Laughter, thus, comes to us as a possibility for liberation.

## 4.2 Cartoon Denunciations and Resistance to the Jair Bolsonaro Government's Destructive Agenda

Jair Bolsonaro was elected in 2018 to govern Brazil between 2019 and 2022. His election took place during a period of political crisis in Brazil, marking the end of the national governments led by the Workers' Party (PT) with the impeachment of President Dilma Rousseff in 2016. This period also witnessed the resurgence of a neoliberal agenda during Michel Temer's presidency (August 2016 to December 2018) and the rise of a right-wing and ultraconservative political front. Jair Bolsonaro, during his time in office, was committed to a political agenda broadly structured around several main political and ideological directions. These included the following: economically neoliberal, politically authoritarian, morally conservative, environmentally destructive, and sanitarily irresponsible.

### 4.2.1 Neoliberalism as the Orientation of Economic Policy

From the perspective of the political and ideological orientations of its *economic policy*, the Bolsonaro government dismantled important state intervention tools in the economy and adopted fiscal austerity (although it was compelled to create an emergency aid program to mitigate the effects of the Covid-19 pandemic), compromising public investments in almost all areas.

In its early stages, the Bolsonaro government created expectations of "economic recovery" and benefited from increasing confidence indices, mainly due to the broad support enjoyed by its Minister of Economy, Paulo Guedes, among market agents. However, the initial optimism turned into skepticism as early as 2019 when poor economic results were observed, exacerbated in 2020 with the shock of the Covid-19 pandemic. The economic recovery in 2022 was not sufficient to reverse a situation of economic stagnation, as reflected in some macroeconomic indicators: the GDP (Gross Domestic Product) had an average annual growth rate of only 0.65% between 2019 and 2022, an overall growth of only 2.6% in the period; investment rates remained low due to credit restrictions, high interest rates, stagnant wages, and permanent austerity reinforced by the introduction of a public spending ceiling; unemployment remained high (annual average of 13.4%), reducing workers' bargaining power and contributing to a decrease in purchasing power; and inflation by the end of the four year period reached 28% annually (Chernavsky, 2022).

The meager economic results had repercussions in the socioeconomic situation of the country, manifested through an increase in poverty and hunger for significant portions of the Brazilian population. For instance, poverty in metropolitan regions rose from 19.5% in 2019 to 23.7% in 2021 (FGV, 2023). In 2022, 33.1 million Brazilians did not have enough to eat, at a time when more than half of the population (58.7%) lived with some degree of food insecurity (mild, moderate, or severe) (Oxfam Brasil, 2022).

The neoliberal agenda of the Bolsonaro government, led by its Minister of Economy, Paulo Guedes, was a recurring theme in many of Laerte's cartoons. Among the issues emphasized by the cartoonist were the contradictions between the socio-economic needs of the Brazilian population and the economic policy orientation that favored the financial market. During the Covid-19 pandemic, for example, the prioritization of the financial market over the population was evident through "aid packages" implemented by the government to mitigate the economic effects of the pandemic.

In March 2020, the Central Bank allocated R$1.2 trillion to the country's banks in order to prevent a lack of resources and facilitate credit provision. Almost simultaneously, the government initiated the payment of emergency aid called *auxílio emergencial* (initially proposed at R$300.00, but later increased to R$600.00 per month) that by the end of 2020 represented an expenditure of approximately R$288 billion (Barbosa & Hessel, 2020; Brazil, 2020). In other words, the financial market received approximately four times more resources than the Brazilian population to create minimal conditions for mitigating the socio-economic effects of the pandemic. Figure 4.2 illustrates the relationship between neoliberalism and the necessary social care due to the pandemic.

The cartoon features two individuals, an adult, and a child: the first is represented by his hands and is holding a small bag of money; the second, with dark skin, wearing a mask and in a lower position than the first, carries a ragged sign written "2021."

**Fig. 4.2** Emergency aid and the spending ceiling. Laerte Coutinho, December 29, 2020 (Reproduced from Folha de São Paulo (2023))

The adult says: "Do not go hitting the ceiling, eh?" Also, on the left and top, it reads: "emergency aid" and "last installment."

The image shows a representative of the federal government, delivering a portion of the emergency aid to a boy, who by his features (torn clothing and black skin) symbolizes most of the Brazilian population (poor and black), in dire need of emergency aid. This criticizes the low amount of resources the Bolsonaro government allocated to the Brazilian population that needed to stop working because of social quarantining. The position of both characters is also not coincidental: above is the government, owner of the resources, and below are the people, waiting to receive emergency aid.

Laerte's message gains even more impact due to the irony embedded in the government member's speech: "Do not go hitting the ceiling, eh?" This can be seen as a critique of the fiscal adjustment policy that prioritizes respecting the debt ceiling over allocating sufficient resources to the population most affected by the pandemic, particularly when compared to the amount allocated to banks. In this context, the use of parody becomes evident in circumstances closely related to those expressed by Saliba (2002), who maintained that typical Brazilian humor is parodic because Brazilian life is so full of inconsistencies that to make humor they parody real life. Laerte's cartoon provides Brazilians with a common framework, shared by the majority of the population living in poverty: they see themselves in the image based on the historical oppression perpetuated by the elites.

### 4.2.2 An Agenda of Environmental Destruction

In relation to the *destruction of the environment* during the Bolsonaro government's tenure, in addition to the (denialist) narratives that sought to disqualify the debate on environmental issues in the country, it was possible to observe within the national executive and legislative spheres a clear movement towards deregulation, privatization, and flexibility regarding environmental norms and rules. The direction given by the Bolsonaro government to environmental issues can be exemplified by a significant statement made by the Minister of the Environment, Ricardo Salles, during a ministerial meeting in 2020. He suggested that the government should take advantage of society's attention being focused on the Covid-19 pandemic to "let the cattle run loose," meaning to swiftly and quietly promote extensive deregulation of the country's environmental legislation without public discussion.

Although the "agenda of environmental destruction" in Brazil had already occurred with changes in environmental legislation based on the assumption of "flexibilization," the Bolsonaro government intensified this process, emptying the public nature of the environmental agenda through "self-regulation" mechanisms, defined by the private agents (Barcelos, 2020).

The concrete results of environmental policy dismantling were visible even during the period corresponding to Bolsonaro's presidency. In the first three years of his government, for example, the deforested area in the Brazilian Amazon increased by

52.9% (PRODES/INPE, 2022). Additionally, Bolsonaro appointed a representative of the timber, mining, and civil construction sectors as the head of the Ministry of the Environment who while there sought to promote dismantling inspection bodies, deregulating environmental norms and rules, and reducing investments in environmental programs (Greenpeace Brasil, 2022). Bolsonaro's government also promoted policy offensives against indigenous peoples, emptying FUNAI (National Indigenous People Foundation) of its functions, opening legal possibilities for "invading" indigenous lands by mining and agribusiness, sharply reducing investments in indigenous health (Bolsonaro was denounced in the International Criminal Court for crimes against humanity and for inciting indigenous genocide) (Greenpeace Brasil, 2022). Moreover, inspection and control actions were disqualified, research in the environmental area was censored, scientists responsible for data related to deforestation were discredited, and budgets allocated to environmental agencies were strangled. The agenda of environmental destruction adopted by the Bolsonaro government did not go unnoticed internationally, eroding Brazil's credibility in the environmental debate. It is symbolic that several countries of the European Union began to demonstrate their opposition to the agreement between the bloc and Mercosur (Southern Common Market), pointing to the Brazilian government's lack of environmental commitment (Greenpeace Brasil, 2022).

The Bolsonaro government's agenda of environmental destruction was addressed in cartoons by Laerte, such as Fig. 4.3.

The critique presents a figure of a large insect (a grasshopper) with a human head. It is seated with utensils on its legs on a plate on top of a table. The character says: "Pass me the Amazon." Within the context of the Bolsonaro government and its policy of neglect towards the Amazon rainforest, the image of the insect represents the Minister of the Environment, Ricardo Salles. Two events that occurred shortly before the publication of the charge symbolize the minister's disregard for the Amazon rainforest: in April 2019, Salles dismissed the director of enforcement at IBAMA

**Fig. 4.3** The Amazon in the Bolsonaro administration. Laerte Coutinho, August 27, 2019 (Reproduced from Folha de São Paulo (2023))

(Brazilian Institute of the Environment and Renewable Natural Resources) after a report by the Brazilian press on a large-scale operation against illegal mining in the Amazon; in May of the same year, Salles attempted to change the rules of the Amazon Fund so that the money raised could be used to compensate landowners (G1, 2020).

The allegory of the minister as a grasshopper, points to Salles' and the Bolsonaro government's predatory stance towards the environment, as evidenced by his phrase: "Pass me the Amazon." The charge's straightforward and clear content aligns with Cagnin's premise (1975), suggesting that the cartoonist aims to draw critical attention to a fact based on their ideological positions. The comical and easily understandable image serves the political role of spreading the discussion of environmental destruction to all social strata. In other words, the easy association of the grasshopper as an environmental pest disseminates criticism of the government's positions on the issue. The representation of Salles as a grasshopper itself highlights the use of ridicule as a mechanism. Thus, exaggeration and distortion act as warnings regarding the Bolsonaro government's careless stance towards the environment.

### 4.2.3 Irresponsibility and Denialism in the Face of the Pandemic

Another political and ideological direction of the Bolsonaro government was manifested in the *irresponsible approach to the Covid-19 pandemic*. It is crucial to acknowledge that in Brazil, from February 2020 to mid-September 2022, there were 34,568,833 confirmed cases of the disease, with a total of 685,203 deaths directly attributed to the Covid-19 pandemic, figures that positioned Brazil among the countries with the highest death tolls from Covid-19 worldwide (Greenpeace Brasil, 2022). During this period, particularly in 2020 and 2021, the policies implemented by the government, influenced by President Bolsonaro's consistently irresponsible remarks, demonstrated a lack of ability to effectively manage the spread of the disease and mitigate its impact on people's lives. The unwillingness of the government, especially at the federal level, to assume broader commitments to control the pandemic, through policies to structure health strategies and to protect economic activities, work, and income, imposed significant costs on the lives of the Brazilian population.

Surveys conducted in 2021 indicated that Brazil could have potentially prevented at least 400,000 deaths if the government had taken proactive measures to control the spread of the disease. These measures would have included promoting the use of masks, implementing social distancing measures, conducting public awareness campaigns, and prioritizing the timely acquisition and distribution of vaccines (Senado Notícias, 2021). Instead, President Bolsonaro himself preferred to make fun of the pandemic, question data on the spread of the disease in the country, deny scientific guidelines, and boost a denialist sentiment in the population. Furthermore, he encouraged the use of strategies with no scientific evidence (as was the case with the so-called "early treatment," based on the use of hydroxychloroquine).

4 Mocking the Inept: Brazilian Cartoons and Criticism of the Jair … 83

**Fig. 4.4** Bolsonaro, the pandemic, and anti-science. Laerte Coutinho, May 19, 2022 (Reproduced from Folha de São Paulo (2023))

The management of the Covid-19 pandemic represented, therefore, the most destructive policy of the Bolsonaro government. The wide defense of medications without scientific evidence was one of the elements of this process, as shown in Fig. 4.4.

The figure features two characters: the first one is a man wearing the Brazilian presidential sash, and the second one is a medicine package with arms and legs. On the front of the package it says "chloroquine," and below it "generic minister." The second character is signing a paper on a table with the emblem of Brazil, under the gaze of the first character. The first character represents Bolsonaro, and the second represents the former Minister of Health, Eduardo Pazuello (a military general with no academic background in the health field). This is due to the extensive defense by Bolsonaro of the use of chloroquine (without scientific evidence).

Furthermore, the period of the cartoon's publication coincides with Pazuello's appointment as Minister of Health. The disagreement over the use of chloroquine and other unproven drugs (such as Azithromycin) against the Coronavirus led to the departure of the two previous ministers (both doctors) (Idoeta, 2021). There is also a double entendre joke involving the traditional inscription on medications in Brazil (generic), with Pazuello's and Bolsonaro's denialist attitude. This point refers to the tradition of double entendre jokes in Brazilian society, dating back to the late nineteenth century, aimed at protest and laughter (Martins, 2017). We can also infer that through exaggeration the cartoon seeks to draw the public's attention to Bolsonaro's policies regarding the pandemic. As argued by Liebel (2017), it is through humor that the cartoon transforms the news into public awareness. Moreover, the humor employed by Laerte enables the Brazilian audience to ridicule the national political elite, as well as their disastrous actions in combating the pandemic.

### 4.2.4 The Government's Political Orientation: Authoritarianism

Regarding the *political orientation* of his government, it is important to highlight that Jair Bolsonaro is a retired army officer, having served as a federal deputy for the state of Rio de Janeiro from 1991 to 2018. Throughout this period, Bolsonaro became known for his defense of the dictatorship regime that existed in Brazil from 1964 to 1985, including praising political persecution, torture, and the use of other forms of violence during that period. His presidential candidacy in 2018 brought together political and social forces that in the republican history of Brazil have cultivated political behavior averse to democracy, always advocating authoritarian solutions and not hesitating to defend the use of violence to prevent the advancement of sentiments and values associated with the expansion of democratic rights.

Consistent with this tradition, during his tenure as the national executive Bolsonaro spared no effort to praise authoritarian solutions, promote a culture of violence, and discredit democratic institutions. Symbolically, in this regard is the distrust he himself spread throughout the country regarding elections, electronic voting machines, and electoral results. One of the most emblematic effects of this systematic attack on the country's democratic institutions were the events of January 8, 2023, when supporters of Jair Bolsonaro carried out a series of acts of vandalism, invasions, and destruction in buildings of the executive, legislative, and judicial branches in the capital city of Brasília. Their objective was to incite a military coup against the elected government of Lula da Silva and reinstate Bolsonaro as the president of the Republic.

The attacks on the democratic regime were not limited to mere bravado and expressions against democratic institutions. While in power, Bolsonaro launched an offensive against social movements and various spaces of societal participation in state decision-making bodies. In 2021, for instance, the national press reported that since the beginning of his government's tenure until that year, 75% of national councils and committees had been abolished or significantly weakened by the Bolsonaro government (O Globo, 2021).

In addition to flirting with the armed forces and the possibility of a military coup, Bolsonaro's political orientation prioritized rejecting democratic rules and tolerance, encouraging violence, undermining important judicial institutions, denying the legitimacy of political rivals, and discrediting broad sectors of society that opposed his government, including influential media outlets in the country. The Bolsonarism movement and his government, therefore, represented the instantiation of contemporary authoritarianism in Brazil. This was extensively depicted in the cartoons of Laerte, as illustrated in Fig. 4.5.

The Figure features three groups of characters: in the center, a middle-aged man wearing a suit and tie with aggressive facial expressions; to his left, three men in military attire; and to his right, a blindfolded woman holding a sword and a balance in her hands. The central character (President Bolsonaro) exclaims "Catch!" and looking at the individuals to his left (representatives of the Brazilian armed forces: white Navy, blue Air Force, and green rmy), points with his arm towards the character

**Fig. 4.5** Bolsonaro and the coup essays. Laerte Coutinho, May 5, 2020 (Reproduced from Folha de São Paulo (2023))

on the right. On the right, given the characteristics previously mentioned, Justice is represented.

Figure 4.5 points to an attempt to restrict the Brazilian judiciary's power and consequently weaken the country's democracy. Throughout his term, Bolsonaro was involved in several crises with the Brazilian judiciary, especially with the Supreme Federal Court (Bublitz, 2021). Referring to the period when the cartoon was published, it likely alludes to the Supreme Court's decision granting autonomy to Brazilian municipalities and states to determine restrictions on people's movement in the context of Covid-19 social isolation measures (Freire, 2020). This contradicted Bolsonaro's policy, opposed to the need for social isolation since the beginning of the pandemic.

Laerte's visual and aesthetic framing in the cartoon indicates Bolsonaro's rude and simplistic posture (expressed in the colloquial term "catch" and his angry features) and the danger to Brazilian democracy from the massive presence of military personnel in his government. Among them, several generals openly flirted with coup tendencies (Araujo & Sales, 2022). However, it also highlights how the military forces showed themselves to be submissive to the government; it is symbolic that the generals are shown in a position of respect towards a retired military officer who was even expelled from the army for misconduct. Thus, Laerte's work fulfills the political role of the cartoon in generating civic awareness through humor, universalizing high-level political issues for all Brazilian social segments.

## 4.2.5 Within the "Moral Agenda," Interest in Attacking Rights

From a *moral point of view*, it is important to note that in Brazil significant changes (considered progressive) have taken place in terms of reproductive and sexual rights since the democratization process. These advances, led by important social movements such as feminism and the LGBTQI+ community, have sparked a conservative backlash in the country with strong repercussions in different religious expressions, particularly those linked to the Christian tradition. At the core of this conservative reaction, from a moral point of view, various concepts associated with the patriarchal family have always been made primary, aiming to guide public debate on body, sexuality, family, primary bonds in society, and the socialization of children, teenagers, and young people.

The progressive changes observed from the 1990s onwards that gained significant political ground during the period when the Workers' Party (PT) led a political coalition in national executive leadership, propelled social and religious sectors defending conservative moral traditions to directly engage in the state's sphere. They provided political support to candidates committed to their causes, in the legislative and executive branches. In 2018, Bolsonaro received broad support from these social and religious sectors, and once in power he opened up positions in his government for them to pursue important public policies. This included the creation of the Ministry of Women, Family, and Human Rights, led by evangelical pastor Damares Alves. She became known for her criticism of feminist movements, the LGBTQI+ community, the so-called "gender ideology," abortion rights, and education disconnected from Christian values.

During his tenure, Bolsonaro insisted on what became known as the "moral agenda." This label aimed to shift the discussion towards individual customs and moral values to be upheld in society. However, it had a direct interest in launching an offensive against a "rights agenda" that encompassed gender equality, racial equality, LGBTQI+ rights, civil rights, sexual and reproductive rights, and the recognition of the sociocultural diversity that characterizes Brazilian society.

The defense of conservative agendas, such as the affirmation of the patriarchal family as the desired model for family arrangements, opposition to abortion, and binary sexuality, became strategic in Bolsonaro's government's critical stance towards the agendas of different social movements (Barbosa, 2022). Figure 4.6 exposes part of this conservative agenda defended by the Bolsonaro government.

The image has three stages. In the first stage, there is a sculpture of a woman with two men holding large scissors. They say, "We won't censor… just preserve Christian values." In the second panel, the men with the scissors cut the sculpture into several pieces. Finally, the piece takes on a newly diminished form, and the men walk away.

Analysis of the cartoon indicates that based on features and appearance the sculpture represents Rio de Janeiro councilwoman Marielle Franco, a human rights activist who was assassinated in 2018. Marielle became a symbol of the struggle

**Fig. 4.6** Bolsonaro and the censorship of diversity. Laerte Coutinho, October 8, 2019 (Reproduced from Folha de São Paulo (2023))

for rights in the periphery, often clashing with Bolsonaro and his political group in the state he represented in the Brazilian Congress. In 2018, a few months after her death (remaining unsolved by the Brazilian police), two politicians aligned with Bolsonaro—Daniel Silveira and Rodrigo Amorim—gained notoriety by destroying a street sign that paid tribute to Marielle Franco. At the time, Amorim was even wearing a shirt with Jair Bolsonaro's face (Marques, 2018). It is noteworthy that Marielle identified with identities and positions that are clearly opposed to those advocated by Bolsonaro, namely historically marginalized categories in Brazil: women, blacks, those from the periphery, LGBT, and leftist.

In addition, another event that occurred in 2019 helps establish the context of the cartoon. In April 2019, Bolsonaro ordered the removal of an advertising campaign by Banco do Brasil (a Brazilian, public, financial institution). The commercial featured young actors, including black men, women, and transgender people. Some of them had colored hair and tattoos. The director of marketing at Banco do Brasil, Delano Valentim, was also fired at Bolsonaro's request (Wiziack & Uribe, 2019).

Given the described context, it can be assumed that the two men holding scissors represent members of Bolsonaro's government. The new image formed seems to resemble the character from the children's animated film franchise "Despicable Me," known as minions. They are characterized by their childish behavior and act as henchmen to the villains in the cartoon.

The arrangement and order of the cartoon serve to satirize Bolsonaro's ultraconservative agenda. The transformation of Marielle Franco's image into a character associated with immature behavior highlights the emotional and rational fragility of the Bolsonarism movement. Moreover, the ridicule of government agents in a scenario of significant civilizational setbacks seems to align with the notion of humor as a defensive tool for Brazilians (Saliba, 2002). In other words, given the impossibility of changing their actual history, Brazilians attempt to modify its meaning through political humor, in this case by mocking the reactionary actions of the Bolsonaro government.

Indeed, these five cartoon's political and ideological directions do not define the entirety of Bolsonaro's government for Brazil and its population. However, they are sufficient to indicate the destructive nature of his administration. It was a government that actively worked to dismantle the already fragile Brazilian democratic regime, using acts and actions with cumulative effects to degrade the political order, destroy mechanisms of representation, undermine the judicial system and the media, and erode democratic institutions. This government's tenure occurred precisely during a time when humanity faced a pandemic that caused hundreds of thousands of deaths in Brazil, many of which were a result of the genocidal approach adopted in the country—since the strategies employed to address the crisis were not even minimally aligned with those shown to be effective by the global scientific community.

Bolsonaro, despite the destructive nature of his government, ran for reelection in 2022. In the first round of those elections, he received a total of 51,072,345 votes (43.20% of valid votes), which qualified him to compete in the second round, where he garnered 58,206,354 votes (49.10% of valid votes), slightly less than the winning candidate, Lula da Silva, who received 60,345,999 votes (50.90% of valid votes) (TSE, 2022). His resilience, in this sense, raises questions that will undoubtedly persist for a long time: how to explain the electoral success of a candidate who was even nicknamed the "knight of death"? Brazilians' serious need to answer this question certainly requires a critical reflection committed to unveiling the contradictions present in the country's sociopolitical, cultural, and economic formation. However, the need for critical reflection does not exclude the different languages through which it can be constructed, including those stemming from "our daily humor."

## 4.3 Conclusions

This chapter discussed the representation of the Bolsonaro government in the cartoons of Brazilian cartoonist Laerte, published in *Folha de São Paulo*, the largest circulating newspaper in Brazil. To do so, in addition to the opening illustration of the study, five illustrations were selected that encompassed the main axes of Bolsonaro's political agenda: (1) Economic Neoliberalism; (2) Political Authoritarianism; (3) Neglect of the Environment; (4) Management of the Covid-19 Pandemic; and (5) Moral Conservatism. This *corpus* was methodologically investigated through Erwin Panofsky's Iconographic approach (2009) and conceptually through Saliba's (2002) conception of humor as a Brazilian cultural trait.

Through the analysis, it was observed that Laerte relied on the Brazilian tradition of critically mocking politicians. Besides the inherent humor of this medium, her cartoons had in common the subjectivity with which major themes of Brazilian politics were addressed. This characteristic points to the essence of political cartoons:

drawing attention in original fashion to an important issue through humor. Additionally, the clarity of the author's strokes contributed to disseminating political awareness about topics that have a significant impact on the lives of Brazilians. Embedded in the perspective that humor is a cultural trait of Brazilians, Laerte fulfills her role as an intellectual of humor and presents to Brazil in a simple, funny, and critical way, a powerful interpretation capable of generating socio-political engagement in Brazilian society.

As laughter and good humor are unifying mechanisms for Brazilians, Laerte's work warned about the contradictions and injustices of economic policies through parody. Regarding the omission in the face of the destruction of the Amazon rainforest and the environment in Brazil, Laerte employed the strategy of ridicule to draw attention to Bolsonaro's reckless management of the issue. Exaggeration and double-entendre jokes were the graphic mechanisms used to highlight the government's denialist approach to the Covid-19 pandemic. The close connection between the military and civilian government, as well as Bolsonaro's impulsive and childish demeanor, were the focus of the cartoon that pointed to the authoritarian tendencies of his administration. Lastly, the agenda of values and customs was portrayed through mockery.

Therefore, the study provided evidence for the argument that Laerte's graphic humor work was a form of denunciation and resistance to the regressive agenda of the Bolsonaro government, contributing to a critical stance towards that government. As limitations of the study, the impossibility of increasing the quantitative analysis of the examined object i.e., the cartoons, due to the scope of the work, is acknowledged. Six cartoons were studied out of approximately 156 produced by Laerte regarding the Bolsonaro government. The inherent difficulty of quantitatively measuring the impact of Laerte's work on the Brazilian audience is also recognized. In this regard, as a suggestion for further research, conducting interviews with readers of newspapers that publish cartoons could generate interesting data and insights.

## References

Araujo, R., & Sales, J. (2022). Political activity of the Armed Forces and the Bolsonarist phenomenon in Brazil (2013–2022). *Notebooks of the Present Time, 13*(01), 26–42 (in Portuguese).

Agostinho, A. (1993) *A cartoon*. University of São Paulo (Doctoral thesis). (in Portuguese).

Barbosa, C. (2022). From myth to barbarism: Bolsonarism and the resurgence of the conservative right in Brazil. University of São Paulo (Doctoral thesis). (in Portuguese).

Bublitz, J. (2021). Three cases in which the STF and the Bolsonaro government came into conflict. GZH Portal, November 8, 2021 (in Portuguese). https://gauchazh.clicrbs.com.br/politica/noticia/2021/11/tres-casos-em-que-stf-e-governo-bolsonaro-entraram-em-conflito-ckvr3e11m0001017f93k6ira6.html

Barbosa, M., & Hessel, R. (2020, March 24). Emergency aid has already paid more than R$288 billion to guarantee social protection for Brazilians. *Correio Braziliense*. https://www.correiobraziliense.com.br/app/noticia/economia/2020/03/24/internas_economia,836224/pacote-anunciado-pelo-governo-deve-liberar-r-1-2-trillion-to-banks.shtml. (in Portuguese).

Barcelos, E. (2020). Environmental deregulation and political disputes: A brief retrospective of the dismantling of environmental licensing in Brazil. *Ambientes–Revista de Geografia e Ecologia Política, 2*(2). (in Portuguese).

Brazil. (2020). Emergency aid has already paid more than R$288 billion to guarantee social protection for Brazilians. *Serviços e Informações do Brasil.* https://www.gov.br/pt-br/noticias/assistencia-social/2020/12/auxilio-emergencial-ja-pagou-mais-de-r-288-bilhoes-para-garantir-protecao-social-aos-brasileiros-1. (in Portuguese).

Brazil. (2022). Ministry of health. *Covid data in Brazil.* https://infoms.saude.gov.br/extensions/covid-19_html/covid-19_html.html. (in Portuguese).

Bremmer, J., & Roodenburg, H. (Eds.). (2000). *A cultural history of humour.* Records.

Cagnin, A. (1975). The comics. Atica. (in Portuguese)

Casimiro, L. (2016). The iconographic method and its application in the analysis of the façade of the church of Madre de Deus in Macau. In M. Hernández & E. Lins (Eds.), *Iconography: Research and application in studies of visual arts, architecture and design* (pp. 18–39). EDUFBA.

Chernavsky, E. (2022, May 5) Among the worst in the world: An assessment of the Brazilian economy under Bolsonaro. *Carta Capital.* https://www.cartacapital.com.br/blogs/observatorio-da-economia-contemporanea/entre-as-piores-do-mundo-um-balanco-da-economia-brasileira-no-governo-bolsonaro/. (in Portuguese).

Coutinho, L. (2023). Official site. https://laerte.art.br. (in Portuguese).

Folha de São Paulo. (2023). *Cartoons.* https://fotografia.folha.uol.com.br/charges. (in Portuguese).

Fonseca, J. (1999). *Caricature: The graphic image of humor.* Artes e Ofícios. (in Portuguese).

Freire, S. (2020, March 24). STF decides against Bolsonaro and frees governors to restrictive mobility. *Poder 360.* https://www.poder360.com.br/justica/stf-decide-contra-bolsonaro-e-libera-governadores-a-restringirem-locomocao/. (in Portuguese).

FGV (Fundação Getúlio Vargas). (2023, June 25). *Retrospective 2022: New poverty map reveals that 29.6% of Brazilians have a family income of less than R$497 per month.* https://portal.fgv.br/noticias/retrospectiva-2022-mapa-nova-pobreza-revela-296-brasileiros-tem-renda-familiar-inferior-r. (in Portuguese).

G1. (2020, May 25). Minister of the Environment defends passing "the cattle" and "changing" rules while media attention is focused on Covid-19. https://g1.globo.com/politica/noticia/2020/05/22/ministro-do-meio-ambiente-defende-passar-a-boiada-e-mudar-regramento-e-simplificar-normas.ghtml. (in Portuguese).

Goldenberg, M., & Jablonski, B. (2011). The genre of laughter. *Clinical Psychology, 2*(2). (in Portuguese).

Greenpeace Brasil. (2022, October 28). *The truth about the Amazon under Bolsonaro.* https://www.greenpeace.org/brasil/blog/a-verdade-sobre-a-amazonia-sob-o-governo-bolsonaro/. (in Portuguese).

Idoeta, P. (2021, May 21). Bolsonaro's story with hydroxychloroquine in 6 points: From Trump's tweets to the Covid CPI. *BBC News Brasil.* https://www.bbc.com/portuguese/brasil-57166743. (in Portuguese).

Liebel, V. (2017). Charges. In R. Rodrigues (Ed.), *Possibilities for research in history.* Contexto. (in Portuguese).

Marques, J. (2018, October 3). Candidates from Bolsonaro's party break a plaque honoring Marielle in Rio. *Estado de Minas.* https://www.em.com.br/app/noticia/politica/2018/10/03/interna_politica,994042/correligionarios-de-bolsonaro-quebram-placa-que-homage-marielle.shtml. (in Portuguese).

Martins, P. (2017). Christianity and humor: Laughter in Brazil until the days of the internet. *Revista de Literatura, História e Memória, 12*(22). (in Portuguese).

Miani, R. (2010). Iconography in the Brazilian alternative press at the end of the 20th century: The presence of caricatures in the newspaper *Brazil. Patrimônio e Memória, 6*(1). (in Portuguese).

Miani, R., & Guimarães, V. (2018). Humor taken seriously: The use of cartoons by Carlos Latuff as a discursive and ideological tool in social manifestations. *Revista de História e Estudos Culturais, 15*(1). (in Portuguese).

O Globo. (2021, October 25). *Research shows that 75% of national councils and committees were extinguished or emptied in the Bolsonaro government*. https://g1.globo.com/jornal-nacional/noticia/2021/10/25/pesquisa-mostra-que-75percent-dos-conselhos-e-comites-nacionais-foram-extintos-ou-esvaziados-no-governo-bolsonaro.ghtml. (in Portuguese).

Oxfam Brasil. (2022, June 8). *Hunger advances in Brazil in 2022 and reaches 33.1 million people*. https://www.oxfam.org.br/noticias/fome-avanca-no-brasil-em-2022-e-atinge-331-milhoes-de-pessoas/. (in Portuguese).

Panofsky, E. (2009). *Iconography and iconology: An introduction to the study of Renaissance art*. Editora Perspectiva S.A. (in Portuguese).

PRODEST/INPE. (2022, November 30) *The Amazon lost 11,500 km$^2$ of forest in 2022*. https://oeco.org.br/noticias/amazonia-perdeu-115-mil-km%C2%B2-de-floresta-em-2022-aponta-inpe. (in Portuguese).

Saliba, E. (2002). *Roots of laughter: Humorous representation in Brazilian history from the Belle Époque to the early days of radio*. Companhia das Letras. (in Portuguese).

Saliba, E. (2011). The roots of laughter and Brazilian emotional ethics. Interview for Marcia Junges. *Revista do Instituto Humanitas Unisinos*. (in Portuguese)

Santos, F. (2013). Political cartoons as ethical language. *II Encontro de Estudos Bakhtinianos*, Juiz de Fora, Brasil. (in Portuguese).

Senado Notícias. (2021, June 24). *Research points out that 400,000 deaths could be avoided; Government supporters question*. https://www12.senado.leg.br/noticias/materias/2021/06/24/pesquisas-apontam-que-400-mil-mortes-poderiam-ser-evitadas-governistas-questionam#:~:text=%E2%80%94%20Quatro%20de%20cada%20cinco%20mortes,no%20entanto%2C%20criticaram%20essa%20estimativa. (in Portuguese).

Silva, S. (2018). *Caricato gegê: Comic representations of Getúlio Vargas in the cartoons of Careta magazine (1929–1934)*. Federal University of Juiz de Fora, Juiz de Fora (Doctoral thesis). (in Portuguese).

TSE (Tribunal Superior Eleitoral). (2022). *Disclosure of the results of the 2022 Elections*. https://www.tse.jus.br/eleicoes/eleicoes-2022/divulgacao-dos-resultados-das-eleicoes-2022. (in Portuguese).

Vieira, A. (2010). *Guerrilla of paintbrushes: Graphic humor in the newspaper O Pasquim as cultural and political resistance to military dictatorship* (1969–1970). Federal University of Ceara (Master Dissertation). (in Portuguese).

Wiziack, J., & Uribe, G. (2019, April 25). BB president meets Bolsonaro, dismisses director and takes commercials with "cool" young people off the air. *Folha de São Paulo*. (in Portuguese).

**Bruno Mendelski** is Assistant Professor of International Relations at the Department of Business Management and Communication, and Collaborator Professor at the Graduate Program in Regional Development (PPGDR) of University of Santa Cruz do Sul (UNISC), Brazil. He is the author of journal articles and book chapters in the fields of IR, with focus on identity and politics, migration, Middle East IR, Brazilian foreign policy, and IR theories.

**Marco André Cadoná** is Assistant Professor at the Department of Sciences, Humanities and Education, and Permanent Professor at the Graduate Program in Regional Development (PPGDR) of University of Santa Cruz do Sul (UNISC), Brazil. He is the author of journal articles and book chapters in the fields of Regional Dynamics of Labor Markets in Medium Cities, Social Classes and Collective Action, and Class Formation of the Industrial Bourgeoisie in Brazil.

# Chapter 5
# How Political Cartoons Reveal Türkiye's Cultural Dynamics: An Analysis of Three Satirical Magazines

Ayşe Deniz Ünan Göktan

**Abstract** This study elaborates on the characteristics of Turkish political humor through satirical magazines *Bayan Yanı*, *Uykusuz* and the *Misvak* platform. Magazines are examined for a thirteen month period to understand how cultural dynamics operate through political humor. Accordingly, cultural characteristics are incorporated as a supportive element to the narrative structures of *Uykusuz* covers, but also challenged. Political authority is criticized by adopting elements of black humor, concern, and despair as prominent themes. On the other hand, *Bayan Yanı*, a pro-feminist magazine, inspires readers with hope, prompting them to take action despite the recent decline in gender equality policies and the ongoing issue of violence against women, thus activating alternative editorial strategies that refer to a culture of struggle. Lastly, the pro-government platform *Misvak*'s cartoons are heavily based on populist dualities, seeking to construct an alternative historical narrative. *Misvak* instrumentalizes cultural characteristics in the process of a neo-conservatist, political Islamist, cultural hegemony project, undermining the genre potential of Islamic humor.

## 5.1 Introduction

Political cartoons in the Republic of Türkiye (hereafter, Türkiye; previously Turkey) trace their origins back to Anatolia's oral folk satire (Apaydın, 2005, p. 135) that voiced social criticism through historical figures like Nasreddin Hodja and Bektashi.[1] Political humor was incorporated in the traditional improvised shadow theatre that took place in coffeehouses, through the dialogues of its leading characters Karagöz

---

[1] Nasreddin Hodja is a legendary, humorous character, living in thirteenth century Anatolia under Seljuk Rule. Famous for being smart and quick at repartee, he is also known by different names throughout the Muslim world (Mir, 2014). Bektashi, on the other hand, refers to those who follow the Hadji Bektas Veli order, identified with Alevism-Sufism. Their origins also date back to the thirteenth century. Bektashis have been the main characters of jokes involving social criticism.

A. D. Ü. Göktan (✉)
Kadir Has University, Istanbul, Türkiye
e-mail: deniz.goktan@khas.edu.tr

© The Author(s), under exclusive license to Springer Nature Singapore Pte Ltd. 2024
O. Feldman (ed.), *Communicating Political Humor in the Media*,
The Language of Politics, https://doi.org/10.1007/978-981-97-0726-3_5

and Hacivat (Öztürk, 2006). While Karagöz represented ordinary people, Hacivat stood for the elite, and tensions between the high and low cultures, between the ruling and the ruled, were voiced through their interaction. Thus, the satirical press of the late Ottoman period was influenced by the dialogical structure of the shadow theatre (Brummett, 1995), Stylistically, early examples of political cartoons dating back to nineteenth century were inspired by Western techniques, especially French and then German influences being prominent (Cantek & Gönenç, 2017). The early cartoons' main topics were modernization and critiques of modernization (Şengül, 2018).

Political humor, by nature, is identified with being in political opposition, on the side of the oppressed, revealing dominant discourse contradictions. The majority of cartoonists in Türkiye define political humor as a tool to challenge authority in a witty manner, as an anti-depressant, helping to build a common language, encouraging tolerance (Eğilmezler Boylan, 2015, pp. 190–199), and contributing to the culture of democracy. When brought to the legal arena under various accusations, court decisions protecting the right to journalism and freedom of expression set examples for future artists (Tunç, 2002).

Political humor is shaped by pressures and censorship. The Tanzimat Period, and the rule of Sultan Abdulhamid II, are associated with press censorship, causing intellectuals and journalists to go abroad and publish periodicals from there (Şahin, 2017). Limitations of press freedom were loosened from time to time; yet lack of tolerance for criticism and official pressures against the press remain contemporary problems. Today, the pressure on freedom of expression and criticism makes political satire a sensitive topic, leaving practitioners feeling on edge. No longer only those whose profession is to inform the public but individuals in general are reluctant to express themselves, practicing self-censorship (Kocer & Bozdağ, 2020). On the other hand, oppression, authoritarian rule, and social upheavals like the Gezi Protests cause new forms of humor to emerge (Yavuz Görkem, 2015).

This study elaborates on the characteristics of Turkish political humor by examining three satirical magazines, to explore culture's role in shaping political humorous content. Three magazines with diverse backgrounds are analyzed: *Bayan Yanı* (2011-) is produced by mostly female writers and cartoonists, emphasizing gender equality and revealing patriarchal discourses. *Uykusuz* (2007–2023), on the other hand, was a best-selling satirical magazine, representing the political opposition, that recently closed down. Third, *Misvak* (2015-) is a pro-government platform that supports President Edoğan, advocating religious doctrines promoted by political Islam, as well as a nationalism framed by political Islam, populism, neo-conservatism (Altunok, 2016), and Erdoğanism.

How do these magazines differ in their approaches to current news and developments? What are the main cultural elements that stand out in cartoons? What clues do they provide regarding Türkiye's political humor culture? An overview of Türkiye's ongoing political atmosphere and how it affects political humor are discussed. Afterwards, the three magazines' contents are examined.

## 5.2 Politics and Humor in Türkiye: An Overview

The Justice and Development Party (JDP: *Adalet ve Kalkınma Partisi*) is the longest ruling party in the republic's history, having won every election since its inception. Yet, along with still having ongoing public support, JDP policies that undermine democracy and the separation of powers principle have been escalating, drifting the country towards competitive authoritarianism (Esen & Gumuscu, 2016). Concerns were raised with the constitutional referendum in 2010 that changed the structure of the judiciary, and also after the 2017 referendum confirming the transition to the presidential system from parliamentary democracy. However, pro-government sources define the transition as a step to end the "bureaucratic oligarchy" (Altınok, 2018). JDP advocates undermining checks and balances in the political system as triumphs of the periphery over center (Ünan Göktan, 2021), with its increasing authoritarianism accompanied by populist rhetoric. Research on world leaders' speeches demonstrates that Erdoğan's populist rhetoric has escalated over the years (Lewis et al., 2019), built on an us-them, elite-public dichotomy, fostering political polarization (McCoy et al., 2018).

JDP discourse has been transformed in light of major events over the last decade. In 2013, the largest anti-government protests (Gezi) took place. That same year the government was shaken by a massive bribery and corruption operation. It eventually emerged that this operation, and the failed coup attempt of 2016, were organized by Gülenists, a religious cult headed by Fethullah Gülen that had been infiltrating state institutions for years. Once framed as a civil society organization and the government's unofficial partner, it is today officially a terrorist organization. On July 15, 2016 a failed coup attempt took place. People were called to the streets by President Erdoğan to defend the state. The attempt was suppressed with the help of mass participation that poured out on streets that evening, with the death of more than two hundred citizens.

Although political polarization and intolerance have become more pronounced in recent years, the government was intolerant towards criticism through political humor from the start. There is an ongoing clash between the government and oppositional journalists and cartoonists, with cases often taken to court by Erdoğan and cabinet members, opening cultural fault lines in the public debate regarding political humor and freedom of expression. The first major case was Musa Kart, sued by Erdoğan for drawing him with a cat body in 2005. Penguen cartoonists drew Erdoğan in many animal forms on the cover to show solidarity with Kart, and they were also prosecuted but the case was dismissed. In 2014, a cartoon in Penguen Magazine, depicting Erdoğan and bureaucrats in front of the presidential mansion, was again taken to court. The cartoon criticized the systematic targeting of journalists, drawing an analogy between them and a sacrificial lamb. A citizen filed an official complaint to the Prime Minister's Communication Center (BİMER), arguing that one of the bureaucrats was making an "insulting" hand gesture to Erdoğan. Actually, he had misunderstood the gesture. The prosecutor opened the case anyway with the court ultimately deciding that the cartoon insulted Erdoğan, if not by a hand gesture, then by the cartoon's general content. A pro-government source (Demir, 2016) argues that these indictments are the result of being unjustly targeted. Cartoonists are deliberately creating Tayip-phobic satire to gain popularity among their audience.

As part of "the neoliberal restructuration of the communication sector" (Çelik, 2020, p. 352), the JDP eventually reshaped the media. Today, numerous newspapers and TV channels are owned by holding companies that invest in non-media sectors like construction and energy, with close ties to the government. Some have grown symbiotically along with the JDP. Thus, the majority of media channels are under government control (Yanardağoğlu, 2021). Being one of the world's most TV viewing countries, it is of crucial importance to control Türkiye's television channels (Çelik, 2020). Intense propaganda is produced through discussion and news programs as part of election campaigns, based on political fear, equating Erdogan's election loss with the country's loss of security and stability, villainizing enemy figures, and attacking them (Çelik, 2020).

Productions belonging to political comedy genre, such as the 1990s TV shows *Olacak o Kadar* and *Plastip Show*, can no longer find their place on TV (De Cramer, 2021). The reasons behind the decline of TV comedy is manifold. First, financial concerns divert channels to cover as much time possible with a single production, so they invest in dramas in which an episode can last for hours. Second, political humor on TV is risky as channels can be sanctioned by the government in formal and informal ways. Very rarely, political leaders (not the president himself but members of the cabinet) are mocked in popular sketch comedy shows such as *Güldür Güldür*, leading to discussions of whether scenes that are in the trailer will be shown uncut on prime time TV (*Independent* Türkçe, 2022). Youtube view counts of these sketches and program ratings in general, show that political humor is popular. On the other hand, magazines and newspapers are far from their previous high circulation rates. Through the 1970s, visual humor culture was led by the best-selling humor magazine *Gırgır*, and before that by periodicals like *Akbaba* and *Marko Paşa* (Cantek & Gönenç, 2017). Cantek and Gönenç state that today humor magazines lag behind the public; especially in Gezi, the style of the humorous content that protesters created spontaneously was different than what people found in magazines.

Pro-government discourse relies heavily on the idea that Türkiye has been liberated. Past grievances of conservative-religious people, especially of women wearing headscarves, have ben eliminated during the JDP era (Özkan, 2022). "Religious defense" was an important pillar of JDP's populist discourse. However, the government becoming the establishment and the policy changes it made could have rendered its populist rhetoric unnecessary (Altınordu, 2021, p. 84). Within the framework of the inclusion-moderation hypothesis, religious or radical left political groups are expected to moderate their discourse by accepting the outcome of the democratic election process. Unfortunately, this is not the case in Türkiye where political parties heavily engage in identity politics, class conflict is not settled, and the secularization process is not completed (Kaya, 2019). Over its long governmental rule, the JDP government abandoned its more inclusive-moderate stance from the early periods, modified its discourse to be anti-elite, raised threats of "external powers," and in general its approach became more uncivil (Altınordu, 2021).

In addition, violence against women, child abuse, and violence against animals became prominent issues. Embedded in the ruling ideology, gender politics constitutes a base for populist discourse, creating an us (national, authentic group that protects traditions, family values) vs. them (anti-national) dichotomy (Kandiyoti, 2016). Anti-gender and LGBT phobic discourse has been voiced more strongly, based on protecting the family, culture & values; claiming that gender equality is not compatible with nature [*fıtrat*], criticizing modernity, and labelling an international convention against gender-based violence and promoting gender equality as a "cultural invasion" (Kaya et al., 2021). Kandiyoti (2016) stated that the increasing anti-gender rhetoric and violence against women refer to a crisis in the patriarchal order in a changing social environment where women demand autonomous decision making. In 2021, the government announced its withdrawal from The Istanbul Convention. Interestingly, before this rejection by the JDP, Türkiye was the first country to ratify it in 2011. This repositioning process is in line with the sectarian camp's demands of political Islam that the JDP feels compelled to lean on for votes.

Among recent developments in Türkiye the Gezi Protests stand out as an exceptional case: a large-scale protest against authoritarian politics, characterized by creativity and humor. Magazines like *Penguen* and *Uykusuz* supported protests, and symbols, images, and materials were at play. Gezi is associated with a Bakhtinian carnivalesque humor, where the ruling authority is ridiculed, and equality accompanied by limitless freedom is experienced for a limited time period (Öğün Emre et al., 2014; Dağtaş, 2016). Gezi slogans incorporated features of incongruity, relief, and superiority over the police and Erdoğan (Tekinalp, 2016). At the same time, some slogans emerged during that period feeding the already existing secular/religious divide (Dağtaş 2016, p. 27). The government attempted to frame these protests as a center-periphery issue, reducing the protests as religious/secular tension, or degrading protesters by defining them as looters. It brought forward allegations that the protesters were drinking ("were disrespectful to religion") at a Mosque in Beşiktaş, and attacking a headscarfed woman with a baby in Kabataş ("protesters were attacking a citizen who seems to be a JDP supporter"). Both allegations eventually turned out to be false. Nonetheless, the discontent expressed through protests was not reflected at the ballot box and the JDP won a victory in the 2014 elections.

Nevertheless, although JDP's public support prevails, Türkiye is still experiencing political turmoil, to which one can add exhaustion of the middle class and the recent economic crisis. Although this led to criticism of the government, and the 2023 elections were touted by the opposition bloc as Türkiye's last chance to eliminate the threat of authoritarian rule, the elections again ended with JDP-NAP coalition victory.

We might have expect that the political atmosphere and difficult economic conditions would provide a rich hub for political humorous content, and yet satirical magazines are stagnating. *Penguen*, one of the leading humor magazines closed in 2017, listing the reasons as the print media and journalism's shrinkage in the world as reflected in Türkiye, a political environment making it difficult for humorists to make humor, and their inability to receive royalties due to uncontrolled digitalization (Bianet, 2017). In addition, printing paper is imported, so that the cost of publishing increased as foreign exchange rates rose, making it hard for independent magazines, not sponsored by a holding company, to survive (Çalışkan, 2023). Other factors: the changing habits of readers, different forms of humor emerging in social media, and the aging of artists (Çelebi, 2017). *Uykusuz*, founded by artists who left *Penguen*, was closed in 2023 for similar reasons. Interestingly, Islamic humor magazines that support the government are going through a similar process. *Hacamat* (2015–2016) and *Cafcaf* (2007–2015), published during the JDP period, were eventually closed. *Misvak*, examined in the present study, exists only digitally. The political atmosphere and living conditions framed above are reflected in these magazines' contents, each with its own unique cultural references, revealing the variegated cultural dynamics of Türkiye's political humor.

## 5.3 Methodology

This study focuses on the covers of magazines to examine the topics they emphasize. Given that *Misvak* is not a print magazine but a site on a social media platform, all cartoons *Misvak* has published are included in the research. Cartoons and covers were examined over a 13-month period (all of 2022 through January 2023), providing an up-to-date view. 18 cartoons from *Bayan Yanı* and 55 from *Uykusuz* were included. Additionally, 240 posts from *Misvak* were examined, excluding irrelevant posts (announcements or ads).

First, content analysis was carried out to identify the main themes, people, and items – each categorized accordingly (Stokes, 2003, p. 62). Then cartoons were examined via a qualitative discourse analysis approach, to obtain a deeper understanding of their messages, discursive styles, the emotions they excite, and how cultural dynamics operate through political humor.

### 5.3.1 Mapping Political Culture Through Misvak, Uykusuz and Bayan Yanı

#### 5.3.1.1 Uykusuz

*Uykusuz* was published for 16 years until 2023, ceasing publication due to increasing expenditures (Çalışkan, 2023). It belonged to the tradition of the *Gırgır* magazine (Tellan, 2015). Directed by a team that left *Penguen* in 2007, *Uykusuz* was an alternative information source covering topics from everyday life along with political news (Tellan, 2015). The media's reporting of events and the hegemonic language adopted by politicians, were made visible and challenged by the magazine (Şimşek, 2021).

*Uykusuz* covers mainly criticized the government (42 of 55), focusing on its economic and foreign policies, polarizing language, and its pressuring the judiciary. Five covers related to the economic crisis and price hikes without directly targeting the government. Also covered were the decrease in public support for the JDP, the dangerousness of blue collar jobs confronting the capitalist boss and the worker, with a critique of neo-liberal policies disregarding human life.

Overall, 25 covers related to the economic crisis i.e., price inflation and the JDP government's economic policies. Nureddin Nebati's statements, as Minister of Treasury and Finance, are quoted in eight covers, himself appearing there six times. During that period, Nebati became an antihero who provided cartoonists with much fodder for humorous content based on his contradictory statements.

In Fig. 5.1, Nebati's speech on the government's desire to formally include under-the-mattress savings of gold to the economic system, was combined with a tradition: gold day [*altın günü*]. A traditional event among women, friends gather in each other's house once a month, eating and socializing. In addition, each brings a gold to the hostess, so that gold accumulates in each household periodically, creating a source of alternative income for group members. In the cartoon, Nebati is portrayed as a guest on gold day, emphasizing the government's desperate attempts to find new sources of income. Here, humor is created in the cartoon through the presence of the hero (a government officer, male, formal) in an environment that does not match his position (an informal, private area, for females only).

Political criticism is also pointed at Erdoğan and his polarizing discourse, underlining the fact that political authority no longer understands the wishes and problems of the people. In a cover, Erdogan doesn't understand a citizen's complaint "We are suffering from poverty!" thinking that he's saying "slut" instead, a phrase Erdogan used for those who participated in the Gezi Protests. Thus, Erdogan's claim to be an ordinary person, speaking the same common language, and the success of his populist discourse, are challenged (Uykusuz, 2022d). Another topic is criticism towards the justice system and the (non)independence of judiciary. In the Gezi trial decision, the verdicts are covered with the argument that the judiciary cannot make decisions independently of the government. The trial scene is drawn on the cover. The judge, smiling, asks: "guess what I will decide?" – indicating that it's already clear the Gezi trial defendants will be found guilty and sentenced (Uykusuz, 2022c).

The government's framing of malpractice, negligence, and policy failures, as outcomes of divine fate is also attacked on the covers: the Minister of Finance's request from the public to pray for economic policy success; a minister asking for forgiveness and blessings after a citizen froze to death at his home during power cuts; following the Amasra mine explosion, the government's definition of the disaster as "destiny," was a reminder of a similar statement made in the Soma disaster in 2014 when Erdoğan stated that "these accidents are in the nature [*fıtrat*] of such occupational fields" (CNNTürk, 2014). Statements that mask the responsibility of government and mining companies in these accidents, are unveiled, as can be seen in Fig. 5.2.

In Fig. 5.2, mine workers who died in the disaster are depicted with safety helmets and angel wings. New victims encounter other workers who died in previous disasters,

**Fig. 5.1** Nebati Attends "Gold Day". So you are organizing a "gold day," let golds be collected first at me. *Source Uykusuz*, February 16, 2022

asking each other how the political authority defines these accidents and deaths. The magazine cover criticized such cultural fatalism as instrumentalized by the government. Explaining government malpractice as a matter of faith or of a divine nature, overlaps with the neo-liberal structuring of governmental policies, referring to the impoverishment of state institutions, getting away with official responsibility, and undermining laicism.

**Fig. 5.2** Amasra mine disaster. Did they also say that yours is natural disposition [fıtrat]? They said ours was destiny…
*Source Uykusuz*, October 19, 2022

Bans on youth entertainment-art activities such as concerts and music festivals (1 cover), media censorship (3), brain drain (1), the greediness of government supported conglomerates (1), are other topics. Two covers directly criticized Erdoğan's contradictory statements on foreign policy, and one attacks his son, Bilal Erdoğan, for trying to censor news about a friend being awarded a tender. Lastly, one cover criticized government officials and pro-government media for targeting celebrities (here, *Sezen Aksu*).

The last thirteen months of *Uykusuz* incorporated elements of black humor. A cover about the economic crisis pointed to the increase in people who considered selling their kidneys (Uykusuz, 2022b). Cartoons in general, register feelings like hopelessness or fatigue. The financial crisis, economic policies, irrational statements of cabinet members, social and legal injustice, oppression and censorship, deterioration of legal institutions, are all prominent topics.

Cultural elements are adopted to set a background scene for the narrative, as seen in Fig. 5.1. Alternatively, the magazine criticizes elements of culture such as fatalism, and how they are used by the government (Fig. 5.2), as well as how companies further transfer it abusively to the workplace (Uykusuz, 2022a). Finally, *Mahsa Amini* protests, covered by all the magazines, is also represented in *Uykusuz*. A young Iranian woman's death in police custody for violating the rule of wearing Hijab, led to mass protests and raised further fears of violent governmental counterattacks. *Uykusuz* provides background information, reporting that 41 women were killed in the protests.

As Fig. 5.3 shows, *Uykusuz* uses the European tale Rapunzel to create its narrative, contrasted with the ongoing violence in Iran.[2] Two characters from different cultural backgrounds confront each other, meeting in the same fairy tale. Here, humor is created by drawing a character in an absurd situation (an Iranian woman locked in a tower as Rapunzel). Yet the woman depicted in the story is in despair, oppressed by a violent, conservative, patriarchal authority. That cover, while criticizing the Iranian events, also reproduces a stereotypical west–east dichotomy.

Finally, the man with the white undershirt [*beyaz atletli*], who says "goodbye" in the farewell cover, originates from *Kıllanan Adam* by Ahmet Yılmaz, from the *Leman* magazine (Tetik, 2020, p. 121). He also represents the magazine's logo, this version drawn by Yiğit Özgür. He is a archetype of an ordinary Turkish man, representing an elite view of ordinary people (Tetik, 2020, p. 122). *Misvak*, reframing his prominent characteristics, portrays the man with the white undershirt as a hero, referring to his struggle on the 15 July coup attempt to defend the nation.

### 5.3.1.2 Bayan Yanı

*Bayan Yanı* has been publishing since 2011. The editorial team worked in other popular magazines for a long time, eventually establishing a periodical predominantly on women's issues, emphasizing characters that can be followed, like Granny Fethiye, Bad Girl Berna, Life Coach Afet, and Sıdıka,[3] expressing political messages. *Bayan Yanı* provides informative content on the women's movement, praising its gains.

---

[2] As opposed to the classic Rapunzel story, in Iran the protests don't have a happy ending. Women who want to take part in the public sphere with their hair uncovered are subjected to violence and the authorities have a say over their appearance.

[3] Fethiye, drawn by İpek Özsüslü, draws a profile that challenges stereotypes of being an old woman. Berna, by Ramize Erer, is a character who says and does things that are not considered "appropriate"

**Fig. 5.3** Mahsa amini protests. Rapunzel!
I can't help you
*Source Uykusuz*, September 28, 2022

The magazine supports the Istanbul Convention, with the popular slogan "İstanbul Convention keeps us alive." In her analysis on the magazine, Mızrak (2022) stated that *Bayan Yanı* caricatures create an area of resistance for women. Fear and death are prominent themes, given that femicide and violence against women are current

---

for women. Feyhan Güver's Afet gives wise advice to people. Finally, Atilla Atalay's Sıdıka is an intelligent, intellectual woman who stands up to traditional family roles and norms.

social problems. Yet, inconsistencies between the written and visual text at times leads heterosexist discourses to be reproduced e.g., female characters doing housework. The magazine is cautious in its approach to the modest clothing style. There are no headscarf wearing women in cartoons where women appear collectively (Mızrak, 2022). However, in the website cartoon by Ramize Erer supporting the Istanbul Convention, a woman with modest clothing is also represented along with other characters. The magazine did not cover the General Elections of May 2023, yet it openly supported the Nation Alliance and its candidate Kemal Kılıçdaroğlu.

The core themes of *Bayan Yanı* appear as solidarity and activism, along with challenging patriarchal norms. It differs from *Uykusuz* and *Misvak* in its open support of groups that face injustices: street animals, women in Iran, people who are convicted of organizing Gezi Protests, university students struggling with lack of accommodation facilities. Slogans and hashtags are frequently used, encouraging readers to take action on social media. Seven out of eighteen magazine covers involve criticism of government policies – two on the economic crisis and how it affects everyday life. Others include: the government eliminating retirement age requirements, freedom of expression, inefficient university student dorms, the public figure Zehra Ana, and trials of Gezi protests. Above all, solidarity is a common theme. For instance, as seen in Fig. 5.4, blocking the commercial activities of street vendor Zehra Ana, who became famous for her anti-government statements in a street interview, is on the cover. The injustice she faced was criticized in reference to the government's appointing trustees to municipalities won by the People' Democratic Party (HDP) in local elections, stating that the government doesn't even tolerate Zehra Ana's political criticism.

The claim "Germany is jealous of us," mentioned in Fig. 5.4, reflects a political strategy of the government and is used more broadly as "Europe is jealous of us." JDP officials argue that Europeans envy the success of the government's infrastructure investments. Here, humorous content is first produced through exaggeration; the government appoints a trustee even for a street vendor. Second, she repeats the well known sentences attributed to people defending the government, like a tape recording loop, referring to a stereotypical JDP supporter. *Bayan Yanı* also focused on violence against animals, twice carrying them on its cover. In November 2022, images of workers torturing animals in the Konya Animal Shelter caused a public backlash. This issue has Granny Fethiye on the cover, offering a message of solidarity and support, seen in Fig. 5.5. The headline is an arabesque song: "If this world is to be burned one day, it will be burned by the poor !" In the cartoon, Fethiye protects a street dog. Humor arises from a contrast: Fethiye's behavior would not be expected of an old woman as a protester who sets places on fire.

*Mahsa Amini* protests against Iran; its message of unity and solidarity with Iranian women appear on various covers. As depicted in Fig. 5.6, we see a group of angry ladies, with hair blowing, protesting and shouting, and carrying a flag made of hair. *Bayan Yanı* highlights the protesters and their struggle, condemning the government's exercise of power over the female body. It adopts an empowering discourse emphasizing the freedom and solidarity of women, with a perspective differing from *Uykusuz*.

**Fig. 5.4** Zehra Ana. There was a wise, revolutionary auntie who was selling bath puff here, we are looking for her!
Zehra Ana!
The government has appointed me on her place, as a trustee! I also have a way with words! We have everything, nothing is missing! Germany is jealous of us!
*Source Bayan Yanı*, January 2022

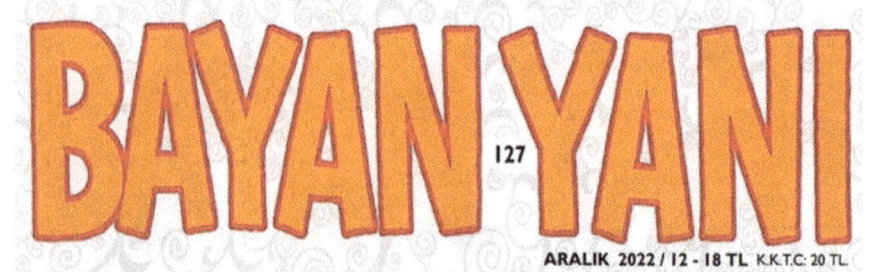

**Fig. 5.5** Granny Fethiye and the Street Dog I set the shelter on fire because you are afraid of the dark!
*Source Bayan Yanı*, December 2022

**Fig. 5.6** Mahsa Amini Protests You can't forcefully take us to your heaven!
*Source Bayan Yanı*, October 2022

The magazine focuses as well on topics not covered by *Uykusuz* and *Misvak*; such as the joy of spring, people fed up with contaminating diseases, solidarity with female celebrities who speak up against male violence and receive backlash. In addition, the prime minister of Finland Sanna Marin, whose partying videos on social media caused a backlash, is also covered. The editorial carried the news on the cover with life coach Afet dancing to show solidarity with Sanna Marin.

Overall, freedom, activism, solidarity, and struggle are prominent themes in *Bayan Yanı*. The magazine instills hope in the readers, encouraging them to be vocal against injustice. This attempts to foment social change and cultural transformation, as patriarchal norms are challenged. *Bayan Yanı* is published in an atmosphere where substantial gains of the women's movement are under threat, as authorities try to position women primarily within the family, as mothers. Despite the anti-abortion and anti-caesarean rhetoric of the government, the increase in violence and female homicides, acceleration of the anti-gender movement, and the annulment of the Istanbul Convention, the magazine informs its audience about the history of the women's movement, emphasizing solidarity, hope and activism, coming out of the closet, as original struggle strategies. This editorial line also harks back to an established protest culture of women's movement in Türkiye.

### 5.3.1.3 Misvak

*Misvak* is not a magazine but a social media site since 2015 that mostly shares political cartoons. This enables it to post content on a daily basis in line with its political agenda, also sharing animations and news video clips, enriching its visual material. It represents some religious values and customs, yet it is hard to say that *Misvak* is an Islamic humor platform given its heavy emphasis on praising the government and Erdoğan.

In a speech delivered in 2017, President Erdoğan stated that his movement has successfully established dominance in the political arena, but deficiencies in the social and cultural field remain (Hurriyet Daily News, 2017). Accordingly, Islamic humor magazines established during JDP rule can be considered as serving the purpose of forging cultural power (Gürgen, 2019; Keten, 2017). There are reservations as to whether Islam is compatible with or suitable for humor (Cantek & Gönenç, 2017). However, humor has even been produced on Qur'anic verses and prayers (Uz, 2017). Nonetheless, in Türkiye during the JDP period, "humor itself is sacrificed for the sake of giving a political message" in the Islamic popular culture magazines (Keten, 2017).

Religion, nationalism, anti-Westernism, criticism of modernity, sexism or traditional gender roles stand out as cultural references in Islamic humor (Gürgen, 2019). These elements are also found in *Misvak*. Yet current politics and the opposition created along the good/bad axis dominates. Previous research on other Islamic humor magazines (Çolak, 2016; Gürgen, 2019; Şengül, 2018) show that they include criticisms of the political authority, albeit very rarely. In *Misvak*, however, criticizing the government is nonexistent. So much so, that the economic crisis and rising prices are linked to international developments, grocery store chains are blamed, or no background information is provided at all.

*Misvak* differs from its antecedent *Cafcaf* that served as a bridge between the secular lifestyle and the new Islamic generation (Özgür, 2012). The readers of political humor in Türkiye, and cartoonists that produce cultural material, are associated with secularity (Özgür, 2012). In addition, political humor is identified with taking an oppositional stance. Therefore, the emergence of Islamic humor in the 1990s aimed to express an alternative culture and to criticize the dominant discourse (Şengül, 2018). This genre was also a reaction to the depiction of women as sexual objects, eroticism, and the use of swear words in cartoons (Çolak, 2016). Nonetheless, the idea of political humor being in opposition by nature is challenged (Dinç, 2012). Faruk Günindi, Executive Editor of *Hacamat*, argued that the belief "humor must challenge and criticize authority" is a cliche; targeting the government is making the easy way out (Saruhan, 2015).

Departing from earlier Islamic humor magazines like *Cıngar*, *Ustura* or *Cafcaf*, *Misvak* is produced by a small group of people, who have alternate careers not necessarily related to the press. Its aggressive language brings it closer to the line of the Akit newspaper. Tetik (2020) states that utilizing the center-periphery paradigm to make sense of the platform's discourse (Nas, 2018, p. 82) is not fully explanatory. *Misvak* aims to challenge the secular left's cultural hegemony (Nas, 2018). Misogyny, anti-westernism, and speciesism emerge as representations of the "cultural other" in *Misvak*. However, its cartoonists' ideological stance and worldview are not clearly defined. They were once positioned in the periphery, but today identify themselves with the ruling party and Erdoğan. However, rather than describing their worldview through narrative structures, its cartoons establish and condemn political enemies. According to Nas (2018), this highlights a cultural crisis.

Tetik (2020) further argues that the all-embracing language in the first years of the political authorities was gradually abandoned. Especially after Gezi, the tendency to appeal to all social segments, as a hegemony project, is in decline. Today *Misvak* carries a narrow hegemony project that serves to consolidate the JDP' already existing political support (Tetik, 2020). This is parallel to JDP's uncivil populism (Altınordu, 2021) and neo-conservatism, all about "reinventing and re-engineering the social-cultural fabric" rather than protecting old and new values (Altunok, 2016, p. 6).

JDP emphasizes protecting and disseminating "a national culture" [*milli kültür*]; a culture that "transcends the nation state ideal" (National Culture Council Report, 2017), based on an "ummah" perspective and cultural pluralism, referring to the Ottoman past. According to this view, Turkish culture is also under attack by external forces and social institutions need to be protected from this threat. The emphasis on dark forces and external enemies is also found in *Misvak*. The threat is constantly emphasized through cartoons that defend government actions, like withdrawal from the Istanbul Convention. JDP has not been republican-nationalist; during the Kurdish opening period and when Syrian civil war broke out, the government often vocalized its neo-Ottoman ideals, envisaging a form of federalism (CNN Türk,

2013). Yet, in line with its coalition with the Nationalist Action Party (NAP), nationalistic discourses were increasingly activated, a phenomenon also represented in *Misvak*, emphasizing the military and its operations.

Unlike the other two magazines, *Misvak* predominantly focuses on upcoming elections, with its cartoons based on binary oppositions. On one side there are external enemies and the political opposition, in contact with or dependent on those external enemies – people and symbols that once belonged to "center" i.e., elites, often corrupt and undermining the state; supporters of the political opposition, irreligious, sassy and vociferous; social media that "poison the youth," marketing chains that raise prices disproportionately. On the other side: Erdoğan, along with some selected government officials, depicted as heroes; ordinary people; Ottoman rulers and commanders; government projects; and the military. JDP policies and Erdoğan (heavily identified with Sultan Abdulhamid II) are framed as images that belong to authentic culture, sincerely defending the country against external enemies. Antiwesternism and *setting forth an alternative historiography*, as a reflection of neoconservatism (Altunok, 2016), stand out as important causes. While cultural tensions and identities are heavily underlined, no class perspective is seen in the magazine.

To understand how cultural elements are reconstructed and instrumentalized to build binary oppositions, the depiction of "monşer" in *Misvak* constitutes a relevant case. Monşer refers to elites who connect Turkish society to the international world, mainly bureaucrats, diplomats, and ambassadors. Officials or diplomats that criticize how JDP handles foreign affairs are called monşer by Erdoğan. They belong to the upper class, and blamed for being estranged from the public.

In Fig. 5.7, two men are talking to each other about the upcoming elections. They are portrayed among books, and especially Nutuk, Atatürk' speech on the establishment of the modern Turkish Republic. These people are old, giving that they belong to the pre-JDP era, which government officials refer to as "old Türkiye" (Gürgen, 2019). All the empty rakı bottles and rakı glasses tell us that they are heavy drinkers (secularism is identified with drinking). One of them has a pipe, a symbol of being pro-western and intellectual. They read the opposition opinion newspaper, labelled as "mud." The conversation identifies the People's Democratic Party that advocates for Kurdish political autonomy, along with the main opposition Republican People's Party (RPP) and Good Party. As PDP is further identified with PKK, a separatist terrorist organization, the cartoon actually blames the opposition for being related to terrorism, showing how the authentic us vs. them (cultural other) discourse is built. The platform tries to deconstruct the "modern intellectual bureaucrat" of the early Republic period, and rebuild it as a cultural other by creating a stereotypical monşer. Heavy drinking, Atatürk, being intellectual and pro-western are negated, these features further associated with the political opposition and PKK.

Another example of how the populist discourse is built involves one of the JDP's founders and former president, Abdullah Gül. As seen in Fig. 5.8, he is the neighbor of the man with the white undershirt. Gül is framed as an elite and a stranger to the Turkish public, influenced by British culture. This negative depiction is a result of his moving closer to the political opposition over the years. In the cartoon, Gül is wearing a bow-tie, a symbol of western-style clothing, has (probably) tea in a ceramic

**Fig. 5.7** Monşers. Monşer I am saying that: Lets directly vote for PDP (HDP) instead of Good Party or RPP."
Why is that?
At least we wouldn't let the brokers win
*Source Misvak*, September 7, 2022

cup, reading the Times. His neighbor, the man with the white undershirt, is drinking tea with a glass, a Turkish custom, and displaying the Turkish flag on the window. The fact that these are neighbors gives the impression that Gül once belonged to that group but later became a cultural other.

Among the cartoons on political criticism, Istanbul Mayor Ekrem İmamoğlu and Republican People's Party leader Kemal Kılıçdaroğlu are the most targeted figures. İmamoğlu is depicted as a politician who constantly plans vacations, unable to act on his own (a mysterious hand is constantly drawn on his shoulder. It is understood that this hand belongs to his adviser, Murat Ongun), trying to appropriate the success of the government. He is portrayed as a liar, untrustworthy, unable to manage the mayorship. His connection with foreign powers and terrorism is emphasized by employing individuals in the municipality who are accused of being connected to the PKK, and having dinner with the British Ambassador on a snowy day, where people needed instead to see him providing information and updates in Istanbul.

İmamoğlu was claimed to have Greek origins going back to 2019, when he was running for the Istanbul mayorship. Figure 5.9 shows these allegations that he has a secret agenda and will potentially work for "external powers" instead of the people of

**Fig. 5.8** Abdullah Gül and the Man with the White Undershirt. Shhh…My condolences. The Queen passed
*Source Misvak* September 8, 2022

Istanbul. In addition, İmamoğlu does not want to work, and people of İzmir don't ask for any public service because their political views are fixed (they will vote for the political opposition RPP no matter what). Here the cartoon carries multiple messages and symbols, framing İmamoğlu, RPP voters, İzmir Mayorship, and having Greek origins, in a negative way. What all cartoons have in common here is the denigration of those who are in political opposition and attributing to them too many negative messages. This represents an aggressive sense of humor that can harm the other person who is marked as the other, while attributing feelings of superiority to the producers and their audience.

After all, *Misvak* follows the government's populism strategy, building its discourse on binary oppositions. It incorporates cultural characteristics like nationalism or religiosity, but serving to praise the JDP and demonize the opposition. Similarly, anti-Westernism has turned into a tool used to denigrate the opposition while praising the JDP. Whoever challenges JDP's power and authority is framed as evil, in line with the limited hegemony approach (Tetik, 2020). A structural pattern emerges, condemning a person/institution in an overly direct way, or using a single cartoon with several symbols and negative messages. In this sense, cartoons exhaust their technical features and limits, so much so that it is difficult for an individual who

**Fig. 5.9** Ekrem İmamoğlu on Vacation. I am saying…Shall I become the İzmir Mayor next elections? No need to work at all. People don't ask for service as well. Every day is off. Besides, it is also closer to my hometown
*Source* Misvak, July 13, 2022

doesn't read the news through pro-government newspapers/platforms to make sense of these cartoons. This is an indicator of political polarization, with pro-government media feeding each other in their attempt to set the agenda.

## 5.4 Conclusion

This study examined how culture operates in forming humorous political content. An analysis of three satirical magazines reveals ongoing political culture having diverse effects on their editorial style. The research reveals pro-government sources dramatically differing in their news coverage, compared to publications in the political opposition. *Uykusuz* and *Bayan Yanı* at times meet on common ground: the Animal Shelter scandal and animal cruelty news are in both magazines, yet not mentioned in *Misvak*. The three magazines also differ in their approach to economic crises. Where *Uykusuz* and *Bayan Yanı* refer to the government's responsibility for rising prices, *Misvak* depicts the issue differently, decontextualizing the situation and thus blaming grocery store chains.

Taken together, *Bayan Yanı* promotes themes of activism, protest and resistance, representing a culture of struggle and movement, protest and solidarity. *Uykusuz* mostly highlights pessimistic feelings while criticizing the dominant discourse and governmental policies. *Misvak*, on the other hand, adopts JDP's populist discourse as the backbone of a cultural hegemony project with an aggressive editorial approach. This world of images envisioned by the JDP and constructed by *Misvak* aims at sustaining political power rather than reflecting an emerging subculture or referring to cultural tensions. The JDP is offered as a reliable option to the citizen surrounded by enemy figures. Here, cultural values such as religiosity, nationalism, and traditions are used rather superficially or as a means to consolidate audience support for the JDP and President Erdoğan.

One can state that the political criticism in these magazines contains relatively few humorous elements. This situation constitutes an important basis for future studies. It can be a side effect of the increasing political polarization and pressure, or can be explained by a shift of humorous political elements to other social media platforms. Political authoritarianism and economic problems in the country put pressure on the *Uykusuz* team, pushing them to emphasizing black humor, hopelessness, and fatigue. The magazine relates to cultural elements, often incorporating them but at times criticizing them. These pressures cause the feminist movement, with novel editorial strategies, to instill hope, encourage activism, and to establish solidarity with all living beings and segments harmed by government policies. On the other hand, it locks conservative-Islamic humor in the ruling party's agenda, undermines its potential to contribute to this genre. Pro-government, neo-conservative political humor, instrumentalizes cultural values in an effort to promote a new culture with a new historic narrative, yet itself is a caricature.

## References

Altınok, M. (2018). The collapse of Turkey's bureaucratic oligarchy. *Daily Sabah*. https://www.dailysabah.com/columns/melih-altinok/2018/07/12/the-collapse-of-turkeys-bureaucratic-oligarchy

Altınordu, A. (2021). Uncivil populism in power: The case of Erdoğanism. In J. C. Alexander, P. Kivisto, & G. Sciortino (Eds.), *Populism in the civil sphere* (pp. 74–95). Polity.

Altunok, G. (2016). Neo-conservatism, sovereign power and bio-power: Female subjectivity in contemporary Turkey. *Research and Policy on Turkey, 1*(2), 132–146. https://doi.org/10.1080/23760818.2016.1201244

Apaydın, G. E. (2005). Modernity as masquerade: Representations of modernity and identity in Turkish humour magazines. *Identities, 12*(1), 107–142. https://doi.org/10.1080/10702890590914339

Bianet. (2017). Penguen: We wish a magazine could be published with "Likes" on Facebook. https://m.bianet.org/bianet/medya/185929-penguen-keske-facebook-taki-like-larla-dergi-cikabilse (in Turkish).

Brummett, P. (1995). Dogs, women, cholera, and other menaces in the streets: Cartoon satire in the Ottoman revolutionary press, 1908–11. *International Journal of Middle East Studies, 27*(4), 433–460.

Cantek, L., & Gönenç, L. (2017). *Opposition's notebook: Humor magazines and culture in Turkey.* Yapı Kredi. (in Turkish).

CNNTürk. (2013). "Strong Turkey shouldn't be afraid of the canton system" [Video]. YouTube. https://www.youtube.com/watch?v=_gjf9pHl-2o (in Turkish).

CNNTürk. (2014). Erdoğan spoken at Soma: These are ordinary things. https://www.cnnturk.com/turkiye/erdogan-somada-konustu-bunlar-olagan-seylerdir (in Turkish).

Çalışkan, I. (2023). Humor can't be eradicated. *Birgün.* https://www.birgun.net/haber/mizah-yok-edilemez-418959 (in Turkish).

Çelebi, A. (2017). Cantek and Gönenç: "Humor magazines have always been the most talked about magazines." *Edebiyathaber.* https://www.edebiyathaber.net/cantek-ve-gonenc-mizah-dergileri-her-zaman-cok-konusulan-dergiler-oldular/ (in Turkish).

Çelik, B. (2020). Screening for Erdoğanism: Television, post truth and political fear. *European Journal of Communication, 35*(4), 339–354. https://doi.org/10.1177/0267323120903680

Çolak, E. (2016). Islam and visual humor: Transformation of the Islamic humor magazine publishing in Turkey. *Moment Dergi, 3*(1), 228–247. https://doi.org/10.17572/mj2016.1.228247 (in Turkish).

De Cramer, A. (2021). The strange death of Turkish satire. *New Lines.* https://newlinesmag.com/reportage/the-strange-death-of-turkish-satire/

Dinç, E. (2012). On the limits of oppositional humor: The Turkish political context. *Middle East Journal of Culture and Communication, 5*(3), 322–337.https://doi.org/10.1163/18739865-00503012

Demir, S. T. (2016). *Humor magazines in Turkey: Cultural hegemony and the opposition.* SETA. https://setav.org/assets/uploads/2016/10/20161011162019_turkiyede-mizah-dergileri-pdf.pdf (in Turkish).

Eğilmezler Boylan, M. (2015). Humorists' narratives on the social role of humor in Turkey in a historical perspective [Unpublished doctoral dissertation]. Middle East Technical University.

Erdoğan, M. (2022). *Syrians Barometer 2021.* https://www.unhcr.org/tr/wp-content/uploads/sites/14/2022/12/SB-2021-English-01122022.pdf

Esen, B., & Gumuscu, Ş. (2016). Rising competitive authoritarianism in Turkey. *Third World Quarterly, 37*(9), 1581–1606. https://doi.org/10.1080/01436597.2015.1135732

Gürgen, M. (2019). *The place of humor magazines in the cultural power struggle: The example of Hacamat magazine* [Unpublished doctoral dissertation]. Istanbul University. (in Turkish).

*Hurriyet Daily News.* (2017, May 29). We still have problems in social and cultural rule: President Erdoğan. https://www.hurriyetdailynews.com/we-still-have-problems-in-social-and-cultural-rule-president-erdogan-113644 (in Turkish).

*Independent Türkçe.* (2022, May 8). Güldür Güldür Show's sketch on Nureddin Nebati has not been aired. https://www.indyturk.com/node/506851/haber/güldür-güldürün-nureddin-nebati-skeci-yayınlanmadı (in Turkish).

Kandiyoti, D. (2016). Locating the politics of gender: Patriarchy, neo-liberal governance and violence in Turkey. *Research and Policy on Turkey, 1*(2), 103–118. https://doi.org/10.1080/23760818.2016.1201242

Kaya, A. (2019). The inclusion-moderation thesis: Turkey's AKP, from conservative democracy to conservatism. In P. Djupe (Ed.), *Oxford encyclopedia of politics and religion.* Oxford University Press. https://doi.org/10.1093/acrefore/9780190228637.013.661

Kaya, E., Yılmaz, S.B., & Türkmen-Yılmaz, S. (2021). *A new paradigm to family and women politics.* Memur-Sen Akademi. (in Turkish).

Keten, E.T. (2017). Government's culture warriors: Islamic political culture magazines. *Academia. Edu.* https://www.academia.edu/34753828/İktidarın_kültür_savaşçıları_İslamcı_popüler_kültür_dergileri (in Turkish).

Kocer, S., & Bozdağ, Ç. (2020). News-sharing repertoires on social media in the context of networked authoritarianism: The case of Turkey. *International Journal of Communication, 14*, 5292–5310.

Lewis, P., Barr, C., Clarke, S., Voce, A., Levett, C., & Gutiérrez, P. (2019, March 6). Revealed: The rise and rise of populist rhetoric. *The Guardian.* https://www.theguardian.com/world/ng-interactive/2019/mar/06/revealed-the-rise-and-rise-of-populist-rhetoric.

McCoy, J., Rahman, T., & Somer, M. (2018). Polarization and the global crisis of democracy: Common patterns, dynamics, and pernicious consequences for democratic polities. *American Behavioral Scientist, 62*(1), 16–42. https://doi.org/10.1177/0002764218759576

Mızrak, C. (2022). *Signifying practices of gender images in caricature as a product of popular culture: Case study of Bayan Yanı caricature magazine* [Unpublished doctoral dissertation]. Yeditepe University.

Mir, M. (2014). Mullah Nasreddin. In S. Attardo (Ed.), *Eyncyclopedia of humor studies* (pp. 405–406). Sage.

*National culture council report.* (2017). Turkish republic ministry of culture and tourism. https://kultursurasi.ktb.gov.tr/Eklenti/50571,raporsurasonucpdf.pdf (in Turkish).

Nas, A. (2018). *Media representations of the cultural other in Turkey.* Palgrave Macmillan.

Öğün Emre, P., Çoban, B., & Şener, G. (2014). Humorous form of protest: Disproportionate use of intelligence in Gezi Park's resistance. In E. Z. Güler (Ed.), *New opportunities and impasses: Theorizing and experiencing politics: POLITSCI' 13 political sciences conference proceedings* (pp. 430–447). Dakam Publishing.

Özgür, I. (2012). Cafcaf: An Islamic humor magazine, no joke! *Contemporary Islam, 6*(1), 1–27.

Özkan, F. (2022). The silent but essential revolution of JDP: Women policies and social policies. *Kriter, 70.* https://kriterdergi.com/dosya-ak-parti/ak-partinin-sessiz-ama-esasli-devrimi-kadin-politikalari-ve-sosyal-politikalar (in Turkish).

Öztürk, S. (2006). Karagöz co-opted: Turkish shadow theatre of the early republic (1923–1945). *Asian Theater Journal, 23*(2), 292–313.

Şahin, E. (2017). Humor press from Tanzimat to secondary constitution. *Düzce Üniversitesi Sosyal Bilimler Enstitüsü Dergisi, 7*(2), 20–43. https://dergipark.org.tr/tr/pub/dusbed/issue/33302/370681 (in Turkish).

Saruhan, E. (2015). We came to fix the one that broke down. *Yeni Şafak.* https://www.yenisafak.com/hayat/bozulana-ayar-vermeye-geldik-2107731 (in Turkish).

Şengül, T. (2018). *Islamist humour, power and hegemony in Turkey: Cafcaf and Hacamat magazines.* [Unpublished doctoral dissertation]. Hacettepe University. (in Turkish).

Şimşek, B.Ş. (2021). *The place of counter-hegemony initiatives in media representation and democracy relationship: Uykusuz journal example.* [Unpublished doctoral dissertation]. Sakarya University. (in Turkish).

Stokes, J. (2003). *How to do media and cultural studies.* Sage.

Tekinalp, S. (2016). Value priority and humor as a defense to cultural schism: Analysis of the Istanbul Gezi Park protest. *International Journal of Communication, 10,* 2346–2376.

Tellan, B. (2015). Sleepless newsmaking: Satirical magazines as an alternative media. In B. Çoban & V. Ataman (Eds.), *Alternative media in Turkey in the age of disobedience.* (pp. 449–475). Kafka. (in Turkish).

Tetik, N.H. (2020). *The ideological discourse of the Islamist humor magazines in Turkey: The case of Misvak* [Unpublished doctoral dissertation]. Middle East Technical University.

Tunç, A. (2002). Pushing the limits of tolerance: Functions of political cartoonists in the democratization process: The case of Turkey. *Gazette (Leiden, Netherlands), 64*(1), 47–62. https://doi.org/10.1177/17480485020640010301

Uykusuz. (2022a, February 23) Twitter [Cartoon]. https://twitter.com/UykusuzDergi/status/1496168008007536640 (in Turkish).

Uykusuz. (2022b, March 23) Twitter [Cartoon]. https://twitter.com/uykusuzdergi/status/1506547482330816515?lang=he (in Turkish).

Uykusuz. (2022c, April 27). Twitter [Cartoon]. https://twitter.com/UykusuzDergi/status/1519239468951252992 (in Turkish).

Uykusuz. (2022d, June 8). Twitter [Cartoon]. https://twitter.com/UykusuzDergi/status/1534481810310168577 (in Turkish).

Uz, E. (2017). Perceptions of humor in Islam and colorful figures of religious life. In R. Uçkun, K. Doğan, D. Ersöz & N.S. Derdiçok (Eds.), *International young academics culture conference proceedings book* (pp. 95–104). İzmir (in Turkish).

Ünan Göktan, A. D. (2021). The role of culture in Turkish political discourse: President Recep Tayyip Erdoğan and the Justice and Development Party. In O. Feldman (Ed.), *When politicians talk: The cultural dynamics of public speaking* (pp. 53–72). Springer. https://doi.org/10.1007/978-981-16-3579-3_4.

Yanardağoğlu, E. (2021). *The transformation of the media system in Turkey: Citizenship, communication and convergence.* Palgrave Macmillan.

Yavuz Görkem, Ş. (2015). The only thing not known how to be dealt with: Political humor as a weapon during Gezi Park Protests. *Humor, 28*(4), 583–609. https://doi.org/10.1515/humor-2015-0094

**Ayşe Deniz Ünan Göktan** is a visiting lecturer at Kadir Has University, Department of New Media. She holds a Ph.D. in Sociology from the University of Essex. She is the author of the book *Hate Crime in Turkey: Implications of Collective Action, Media Representations and Policymaking* (2017). Media studies, discourse studies, political culture and sociology of consumption are among her research interests.

# Chapter 6
# Spanish Humor and Political Culture Through Cartoons: Multimodal Discursive Analysis of *Forges*'s Socio-political, Graphic Universe

**María del Mar Rivas-Carmona**

**Abstract** Humor and political culture have always gone hand in hand in contemporary Spain to the extent that the satirical press has not only been a faithful portraitist of political and social concerns, but also humor itself has managed to shape diverse political cultures throughout human history. For more than two centuries, Spain's satirical press has served as a loudspeaker and reference for such transcendental issues as the Franco dictatorship, the democratic transition, territoriality, and anticlericalism. One of the most popular sections of the daily press in Spain is graphic humor. Some of the cartoonists have become individuals of prestige and relevance, as is the case of Antonio Fraguas i.e., *Forges*, who portrayed Spanish social and political reality over the past 50 years in such a way that politicians of all ideologies, journalists, and citizens, agree that Spain cannot be conceived without his cartoons. This paper aims to analyze the relationship between political culture and humor in a selection of cartoons by *Forges* in present-day Spain. For this purpose, considering the importance of the relationship between verbal and non-verbal communicative elements, this study is carried out following the Relevance Theory approach to multimodal texts.

## 6.1 Introduction

Cartoons and graphic humor are one of the most popular genres within the media, which through a multimodal form of narrative, employ humor that leads us to reflect on relevant current issues. As Reig and Mancinas-Chávez (2018, p. 505) point out, "humor is a special way of 'sneaking in' issues and approaches that the usual journalistic text either cannot or does not want to adopt." Because of their combination of text and image, and the brevity and speed of accessibility and transmission, they

---

M. M. Rivas-Carmona (✉)
Faculty of Philosophy and Letters, University of Córdoba, Córdoba, Spain
e-mail: mmrivas@uco.es

© The Author(s), under exclusive license to Springer Nature Singapore Pte Ltd. 2024
O. Feldman (ed.), *Communicating Political Humor in the Media*,
The Language of Politics, https://doi.org/10.1007/978-981-97-0726-3_6

have a greater impact and reach than other genres used for political and social criticism. Political cartoons that are usually present in the daily press in print and digital versions, arise in specific contexts shaping relevant issues and establish a dialogue with viewers who will have to decipher their content to interpret the message. In the media, "the graphic humor of the daily press picks up the comments, prejudices and concerns existing among the sector of the population identified with the ideological and social profile that makes up the bulk of its readers" (Segado-Boj, 2009, p. 479).

Caricatures are, without a doubt, a very quick and striking means of drawing attention to far-reaching social issues. Their expressiveness comes not only from the text, but especially from the rest of the non-verbal visual elements that manage to transmit messages of great relevance even without words. Therefore, as Tsakonaa (2009) pointed out, it is not always easy to deduce all the communicative baggage that they contain, since the meaning is derived from a set of multimodal elements.

The decoding and interpretation of vignettes, especially those with an often vindictive component, as in the case of political vignettes, depends to a large extent on the prior beliefs and assumptions of the recipients (Sperber & Wilson, 1986; Wilson & Sperber, 2004), as it is the shared background knowledge and the previous cognitive context that serves as a basis for comprehension, helping to process the new incoming information. In this chapter, following the postulates of Relevance Theory (Sperber & Wilson, 1986, 1987, 1995), I will focus on the way Forges encodes the message through verbal and nonverbal elements, as well as on the strategies involved in the encoding–decoding process and on the humorous effects of verbal and nonverbal stimuli on readers. Since cartooning has a high visual component, I will focus primarily on the multimodal nature of cartooning, to address discourse as well as visual metaphors.

## 6.2 Graphic Humor in Spain: Forges as the Dominant Figure

Throughout history, graphic humor has served such diverse and vital functions as criticizing and ridiculing certain social events, raising readers' awareness of relevant issues, helping to shape ideas, and even creating a political culture on the margins of the establishment. Its jocular and "apparently less serious" character than that of the generalist or opinion press has also served to enable it to circumvent the bonds of censorship more skillfully (Gómez Mompart et al., 2019).

In Spain, from the mid-nineteenth century until the fall of the Second Republic with the military uprising of General Franco, graphic humor had a marked combative character railing against the political and clerical establishment. The satirical press had great relevance thanks to its visual strength in forging the ideas of the popular and poorly educated classes, thanks to magazines such as *La Traca* (1884–1939).[1]

---

[1] As can be seen, it disappeared with the victory of the Francoist rebels almost at the end of the Civil War in 1939 and was maintained even during the war.

In those decades, the satirical press that dealt with nationalist territorial issues also stood out, such as *Campana de Gràcia* (1870–1934), *La Esquella de la Torratxa* (1872–1932), *Cu-Cut!* (1902–1912) or *Papitu* (1908–1937). Apart from Madrid, the Catalan, Basque, and Galician press were important sources of satire dealing with state and identity questions.

The graphic cartoons that appeared in the satirical press in the last years of Francoism helped to create a political culture that could deconstruct the ideology of "*sociological Francoism*," along the thin line that separates seriousness from jokes. Humor served to demystify Francoist clichés to create a true democratic culture.

The four most important satirical magazines since the last years of Franco's regime, the transition, and the return of democracy, have been *Hermano Lobo* (1972–1976), *El Papus* (1973–1987), *Por favor* (1974–1978) and *El Jueves* (1977-present). The need to overcome the aftermath of the fascist dictatorship led all of them to a cultural framework of progressive, left-wing, and anti-Francoist tendencies.

There have been important graphic cartoonists in Spain, but the greatest icon of graphic humor of all has been Antonio Fraguas (1942–2018), known as "Forges," "the genius of graphic humor of social criticism" (El Periódico, 2022). Such has been the impact of his figure in the country that even the Google platform paid tribute to him with a visible doodle in Spain on what would have been his 80th anniversary. Stamps have also been dedicated to him and well-known singers such as Luis Eduardo Aute made albums inspired by him.

Forges was one of the best interpreters of society, and of the convulsed, changing world. He has been praised for his intelligent humor, his irony, acidity, sarcasm, but also for his *costumbrismo*,[2] his political criticism, his permanent commitment to the underprivileged, and his fight against social injustice. As for his style, Forges' work had an original and unique design. With an extensive iconography of comic characters and situations, what he named his "*forgendros*" (from the fusion of the words 'Forges' and 'engendros,' Forges' creations), he satirically reflected through them the idiosyncrasy and sociology of contemporary Spain.

His vignettes are in everyone's mind: in black and white, with thick, black line speech bubbles expressing words in capital letters, and a very popular style taken directly from the street. He invented words that all Spaniards use today on a regular basis, "[a] particular vocabulary that already belongs to everyone" (Grijelmo, 2018), such as "*bocata*" for "*bocadillo*" (sandwich), "*tocata*" for "*tocadiscos*" (record player), "*muslamen*" for "*muslos*" (thighs), which are used as much as, or even more, than the original words; also expressions like "*tontérrimos*" instead or "*tontísimos*" (very silly), "*gurtélidos*" (a made up word for people of the corrupt plot Gurtel), "*cuñadings*" for "*cuñados*" (brothers-in-law), "*gensanta*", an invented word shortening the expression "¡*Virgen Santa!*" (Holy Mother of God!), "*nefecto!*" for "¡*en efecto!*" (indeed!), or "*stupendo*" for "*estupendo*" (great!);" he also used swear words, but they appeared crossed out in his texts, which attenuated them, thus allowing him to use them.

---

[2] It is a literary and pictorial trend that portrayed local everyday life, manners, and customs, primarily in nineteenth century Spain, but has since become generalized to any particular social milieu.

Forges published his daily cartoons for 50 years, the last 23 in the newspaper *El País*. This newspaper describes him as "the humorist who has best portrayed the last half century of Spanish history," because "he knew how to capture with tenderness and irony the evolution of a society that went from the Francoist developmentalism of his first drawings to the hyper-technological world of his last stage" (Marín, 2018).

His first drawing dates from 1964 and, from that moment onwards his cartoons have helped many readers to understand and process the evolution of Spanish society. He published more than thirty cartoon books, many of them about his vision of Spain, such as *Historia Forgesporánea* (Forgesporary history), but he also made novels, cartoon books, TV scripts and even directed films. Although he never wanted to be a candidate for awards, he received many award recognitions, such as the Freedom of Expression Award of the Union of Journalists of Spain, and the Ibero-American Graphic Humor Award. He was also a Professor of Humor at the University of Alcalá de Henares (since 1997) and given Doctor Honoris Causa by the same center. Although he died in February 2018, several generations of readers continue to recognize his characters, and his work will remain eternal for Spanish people.

## 6.3 Political Cartoons as Powerful, Multimodal, Humorous-Vindictive Texts

Multimodal texts employ different modes or vehicles of semiotic communication (words, sounds, gestures, images, music, paralinguistic elements) to produce meaning (Kress & van Leeuwen, 2001, p. 92). In fact, any form of human communication is intrinsically multimodal. Face-to-face dialogue i.e., oral language is accompanied by paralanguage and kinesics, and even a written message communicates beyond its words, by the typeface, the signs, or the layout of the page.

Although there are numerous studies on nonverbal communication, linguistics has neglected the nonverbal component in multimodal, communicative situations until relatively recently, focusing on multimodal texts, such as comics or cartoons, with high verbal density. However, new approaches have emerged such as Multimodal Discourse Analysis (MDA) (Baldry & Thibault, 2006; Kaindl, 2004; Kress, 2010; Kress & van Leeuwen, 2001, 2006; van Leeuwen, 2005)—focusing on "intersemiosis" i.e., the relevant combination of semiotic modes like verbal language and visual language.

Also, from the field of cognitive pragmatics, work has emerged that employs Sperber and Wilson's (1986, 2004) Relevance Theory (RT) for the study of multimodal texts. This approach is traditionally related to the study of verbal language, but it can be extended to nonverbal messages too, as it is based on the principle that the receivers of a (non)verbal message interpret or deduce the meaning that carries more interest (greater cognitive effects) with the least mental effort, something valid for any type of message (Yus Ramos, 1998).

In the case at hand, cartoonists create their message from the combination of different semiotic modes that not only add up, but multiply their significant potential (Lemke, 1998, p. 92). Indeed, vignettes combine verbal and visual elements (drawing, illustration, design, color, signs, typography) that become quick and powerful stimuli for the receivers. Moreover, in political cartoons the sender usually has two interrelated purposes; on the one hand, a humorous effect is pursued, and on the other, criticism or vindication is intended to be transmitted. On many occasions, cartoonists and caricaturists also resort to satire, albeit surreptitiously, to ridicule certain phenomena (Olowu et al., 2014).

Successful collaborations between editors and cartoonists began to occur from the late nineteenth century (Hoff, 1976), thanks to the powerful and rapid effect of humorous cartoons. Undoubtedly, the influence of visual media in contemporary society and the growing need for quick and compressed information contributed to this success. A cartoon is a simplified artistic form with the power to transmit an opinion, to expose a social, historical, economic or political criticism, and even to have transcendence in the course of events. In other words, cartoons are "a visual editorial, an interpretive picture which makes use of symbolism and bold and humorous exaggeration to present a message or point of view concerning people, events, or situations" (Steinfirst, 1995, p. 63).

The power of cartoons is such that on several occasions they have played a relevant role in historical processes of democratization or pacification (Lent, 2001, p. 54). Many countries have cartoonists who have captured in their drawings and words the social–historical evolution of that territory or who have influenced it, becoming part of its history. This is the case of the Spanish humorist Forges, whose cartoons have become an integral part of the Spanish national heritage.

Each cartoonist expresses his/her vision of the country in a humorous way, more or less politically correct or proactive, and even aggressive (Riffe et al., 1987). But cartoonists have to strike a balance between being humorously critical and not offending any group, given that unlike decades ago their messages now reach a very wide audience through mass and social media (Donnelly, 2013). This ability to reach a broad audience, together with the fact that non-verbal elements are usually less explicit than verbal ones, implies that not all recipients will reach the same interpretation, as they will follow different inferential processes depending on their own cognitive schemes and the spatio-temporal context in which they access the cartoon (Dines & Humez, [1995] 2010); Forceville, 2005).

In her study El Refaie (2009, p. 181) concluded that many cultural factors come into play when interpreting them, as it requires "a broad knowledge of past and current events, a familiarity with the cartoon genre, a vast repertoire of cultural symbols, and experience of thinking analytically about real-world events and circumstances."

## 6.4 Research Methodology

In this chapter I analyze a selection of vignettes by the great cartoonist Forges, all of them published in the newspaper *El País*. The analysis focuses on the combination of verbal and non-verbal elements for the configuration of the humorous and critical message, typical of the author. For this purpose, we follow the precepts of the Relevance Theory applied to humorous multimodal texts.

### 6.4.1 Relevance Theory

Cognitive science affirms that thought is much more complex and informative than what can be expressed in words, hence interpreters use all their faculties to deduce the meaning intended by the sender by means of all the explicit and implicit verbal and non-verbal clues (Pinker, 2008).

This is the starting point of Relevance Theory (Sperber & Wilson, 1986, 1995; Wilson & Sperber, 2004), whose pragmatic premise is that to deduce meaning one must not only decode the code, but also interpret by means of inferences based on linguistic and non-linguistic clues that are in the context of the utterance.

According to the communicative principle of relevance, the addresser (in this case, the cartoonist) makes his/her communicative intention apparent or *ostensive* by means of explicit verbal and non-verbal (graphic, kinetic, paralinguistic) clues; these contextual clues help the addressees infer the intended meaning. This interpretative model thus entails mutual knowledge or 'manifestness' between addresser and addressee.

The addressees interpret the message by establishing hypotheses of meaning about the explicit content (*explications*), about the intended contextual assumptions (*implicated premises*), and the intended contextual implications (*implicated conclusions*) (Wilson & Sperber, 2004, p. 261).

Evidently, the addresser, in this case the cartoonist, will deliberately "exploit" the possible explicit and implicit procedures to achieve the greatest contextual effects. The main contextual effect in cartoons is humor (Yus Ramos, 2003, p. 1300).

## 6.5 Analysis of the Cartoons

### 6.5.1 On the Political Administrative System and State Bureaucracy

As can be seen in Fig. 6.1, in this vignette text and image complement each other in the construction of the message to be interpreted by the reader. Two typical characters in many of Forges' cartoons are the married couple Concha and Mariano. They represent average Spaniards; she is an intelligent and inquisitive housewife and her husband is a clerk in a public organization who usually appears in many vignettes sitting in front of the TV watching football or reading the newspaper. In this cartoon they reflect with their dialogue the problem of excessive bureaucracy and the huge number of advisors and positions that politicians appoint as soon as they come to power. In Spain, the public administration is the country's largest employer.

In the vignette, Concha asks her husband if the new appointment at work will mean an improvement in his CV, to which he replies that being "deputy supervisor to the chief delegate of the integrated service of civilian agencies for administrative simplification is an amazing job." Such a bombastic name will most likely hide a job of little relevance and remuneration. Moreover, we are faced with the humorous

**Fig. 6.1** On politicians' excessive appointment of officials and advisers.
WIFE: But is that remodeling appointment going to improve your resumé? I wonder.
HUSBAND: Woman, deputy supervisor to the chief delegate of the integrated service of civilian agencies for administrative simplification is an amazing job.
WIFE: … By the way, you are shaving with the coffee pot.
HUSBAND: Because of my nerves. WIFE: Yeah. *Source Pinterest* (n.d.a)

paradox of how it can be a position to simplify the administration if it is a new link in the chain of innumerable positions that advise and supervise other positions; in other words, it is hardly a "*cargazo*" (an amazing job), since it is the umpteenth subordinate of a superior.

They are in the bathroom, Mariano is still in his underwear, probably getting ready for work. Concha notices something that is a new rupture of expectations that also provokes humor: "by the way, you are shaving with the coffee pot." The nerves before the appointment have made Mariano a man who is neither physically nor emotionally strong, but rather totally absent-minded.

### 6.5.2 On the Spanish Labor System: Employers, Scholars, and Labor Precariousness

The Spanish labor system suffered from an excessive amount of precarious and temporary jobs that the labor reform, recently approved in February 2022, has tried to correct, advocating indefinite hiring.

In the cartoon shown in Fig. 6.2, Forges criticizes the Spanish labor system, specifically the internship contracts for trainees in companies, which often have low or no pay, but many hidden hours of work. The labor reform of the current socialist government has tried to regulate this type of situation, promoting permanent jobs instead of temporary and exploitative ones.

In the cartoon, Forges presents some of his usual characters, such as the exploitative businessman and the waiter. The exploitative businessman represents all those who in their companies seek profitability without conscience and relate to extremely conservative and neoliberal capitalist positions. He is a character that is immediately recognizable visually, with an almost mafia-like appearance, dressed in a black suit and tie, black glasses, a thick complexion due to good eating, bald and with a black moustache. There are many graphic elements that help readers to interpret this situation; we all have a mental scheme of what is done and said in a restaurant, and in this case the protagonists are choosing the menu in a luxurious restaurant, as can be deduced by the type of chairs, the flowers or the waiter's bow tie.

The discourse is also typical of this situation, as the waiter is asked how one of the dishes is prepared. Nevertheless, the humorous effect comes again from the rupture of the usual expectations for this particular context; here the diner does not ask for a typical or expected meal, such as meat or fish; on the contrary, the expectations are broken when the man asks "How do you serve the trainee?" to which the waiter responds with curious and astonishing naturalness as if it were a roast, using the typical culinary terminology of a haute cuisine restaurant: "Roast in its juice…, with a garnish… and a deconstructed foam…". The resulting text is a hybridization of a logical dialog structure in a restaurant context, completed by absolutely absurd complements for this context that belong to the semantic field of work: against all logic, what accompanies the main meal is a juice of "12 h of work" (much more than

**Fig. 6.2** How do you serve the trainee?
BUSINESSMAN: How do you serve the trainee?
WAITER: Roast him in 12-h juice, with a garnish of €280 a month and a deconstructed foam of "that's the way it is." *Source* Patricialuceno (2013)

allowed to an intern), the garnish is a paltry salary of "280€ per month," and all of this is adorned by a "deconstructed foam" of "this is what you get" or "that's the way it is" (the conditions are set by the company and there is no possible negotiation).

Faced with this dish, the businessmen are laughing with pleasure, expressed with the onomatopoeic interjection, invented by Forges, "Slurp." In the background at another table there are other characters typical of his vignettes that due to their unexpected appearance in the context of a restaurant, and even more so dressed in such an incongruous way, produce humor. They are a bishop with his miter, a nun with her headdress, and someone with horns who looks like a devil—clothing that clashes even more with the two religious characters.

Forges presented another masterful vignette on the Spanish labor system exactly on Labor Day, May 1, 1972, being reproduced on different occasions.

As shown in Fig. 6.3, two adult men are walking along in winter clothes with work briefcases. One of them is singing a well-known tune that the reader will easily recognize from the first words "*Si yo fuera fijo* (If I were a permanent worker), dubidubidubidubidubiduuuu...", rhyming with "*Si yo fuera rico* (If I were a rich man...)", recalling the 1964 musical *Fiddler on the Roof*). When the other man answers in surprise: "Don't tell me you're still interim!" he replies that he is not only telling him, but he is also singing it to him.

As sad as it is that such old people talk about job instability, the humorous effect comes from the play on words with the well-known song ("*fijo/rico*," permanent/rich); the very fact that he is recounting his serious employment situation by singing

**Fig. 6.3** Happy 1st of May, Labor Day.
MAN 1: If I were permanent... Dubidúbidubiduu Tralalalálalalalá Lálalalálalalalaluuuu-uaá...a...a...a... If I were permanent...
MAN 2: Don't tell me you're still an interim...!
MAN 1: I'm not only telling you, I'm singing it to you! *Source Pinterest* (n.d.b)

and humming, which is not what one would expect; the actual amusing and curious transcription of what the man is humming ("Dubidúbidubiduu Tralalalálalalalá Lálalalálalalalaluuuuuaá"); and the literalness with which he takes the indirect speech act "Don't tell me...," clearly not a request but an indirect exclamation of astonishment, similar to "I can't believe that...."

6 Spanish Humor and Political Culture Through Cartoons: Multimodal … 129

## *6.5.3 On Political Corruption*

Unfortunately, as of March 2023, more than 90% of Spaniards thought that corruption was linked to politics, to a greater or lesser extent. As Casos Aislados (2023) points out, practically half of the corruption cases (48.8%) among 43 parties and institutions correspond to the right-wing Popular Party.

Taking advantage of the celebration in Spain of the Mobile World Congress (MWC), Forges published a cartoon inspired by the novelties in the world of mobile telephony, directly attacking the corrupt (see Fig. 6.4).

In the cartoon, located at a mobile phone sales stand at the WMC (in imitation of the acronym MWC), the mobile phone salesman offers the corrupt politician a new model of phone, the *"listófono"* ("smart-arse-phone") that "has a special alarm to attend trials as a defendant and also has a digital (money) envelope counter." Readers will easily associate this with the black money that the corrupt received in envelopes, especially the envelopes of the Popular Party's black accounting that in those years were known to have been collected, costing them the elections. For this reason, too, many politicians have had, and still have, to stand trial as defendants.

The special humor of this cartoon comes not only from the witty invention of such a "smart" phone with all its incredible functions (serving to introduce the critique), but also from the ingenious puns, such as "smart-arse-phone," or the adverts *"Meñophone"* (Cress phone) and *"Norula phone"* (Not-work phone), which appear on the counter.

**Fig. 6.4** Smart phones for smart politicians.
SALESMAN: It is the latest model of smart(ass)phone: It has a special alarm to attend trials as a defendant and it also has a digital (money)envelope counter. *Source* El País (2014a)

Forges mocks and criticizes political corruption in many of his cartoons. For instance, another amusing vignette (El País, 2016a) reproduces the outline of a kind of pastime in which you have to sharpen your eyes in order to find the answer to a proposed riddle. On this occasion, by means of the explication i.e., the text of the enigma, the reader is asked to find out in five seconds the name of a political party whose advisors are preparing anti-corruption sentences for the electoral speeches of their candidates:

> VISUAL ACUITY. Find out, in less than five seconds, to which political party these advisers belong, who prepare sentences for their candidate's electoral speeches on the fight against corruption carried out by their party

> (SOLUTION: Yes, indeed. [written upside-down])

One would expect, therefore, to find the necessary clues encrypted in some way in the image below the text, supposedly of advisors preparing anti-corruption phrases; however, the readers find an image of four advisors crying with laughter (tears of laughter are visible), covering their mouths with their hands and tapping each other's shoulders ("pow, pow"), while pointing in the air at the deluded who will be looking for these non-existent phrases. Readers of this cartoon will be able to identify the meaning intended by the humorist thanks to their background knowledge. Evidently, the implication is that there are no such phrases, because not only do they not care about fighting corruption but they also do not plan to fight it at all, because they are going to work corruptly. Therefore, the author of the cartoon, in a totally indirect way, is providing us with the answer: the political party that does "not" have advisors who look for anti-corruption phrases, because it does not intend to fight it as it is populated by corrupt people, is the Popular Party—the first political party in the history of Spanish democracy to be condemned as a legal entity in a corruption case (*El Plural.com*, 2018).

In imitation of these pastime games, in the bottom right-hand corner we read "Solution" and facing down we find the answer that confirms that our hypothesis is right: "Yes, indeed." Thus, the strategy of imitating a riddle from pastimes becomes a very useful, indirect way to accuse a party of corruption without naming it, and in addition it becomes a source of humor because of the apparent but strategic incoherence between what the riddle proposes and what the image implies.

In another cartoon on corruption (Fig. 6.5), a corrupt politician is in the street and addresses a citizen while putting his left hand in the citizen's pocket. Humorously,

**Fig. 6.5** Direct contact with citizens.
POLITICIAN: Don't be surprised; our renewed electoral program commits us to direct, unmediated dealings with citizens. *Source* El País (2015)

the arm is extremely long and stretches out to "rob" the citizen. When the citizen reacts in astonishment, the politician asks him not to be surprised, for his electoral program commits him to "dealing directly, without intermediaries, with the citizens." Thus, when he refers to a "direct deal," he implies straightforwardly that he will not use subterfuge to obtain economic commissions through intermediaries but will rob the citizen directly.

The comic effect is rounded off with small corrupt businessmen with bat-like wings fluttering around the corrupt politician, like vampires sucking the blood of the citizen, and a surrealistic bishop with glasses and a black mustache carrying a football under his arm.

Corruption was so worrying during the previous Popular Party legislature, leading them to lose power in a motion of censure won by the Socialist Party currently in power, that many cartoons dealt with the subject. The plots and cases of corruption were innumerable and were given names that identified them, many learned by the public.

Forges placed another cartoon (El País, 2014b) in the office of the UDEF, the Central Unit for Economic and Fiscal Crime, a unit attached to the General Commissariat of the Judicial Police.

UDEF Central Unit for Economic and Fiscal Offences

> CHIEF OFFICER: Well, wasn't the "shrunken plover bird" plot before the "Saharan leaf litter" plot?

> AGENT 1: No, no; it was before the "When you wear a miniskirt" plot

> AGENT 2: Noooo…

> AGENT 3: Yeeesss, it was…

> AGENT 4: Gee whiz; what a real pain

The chief officer asks his collaborators about the order in which corruption cases are being filed, deduced from their comments. What is particularly amusing for a Spanish reader is the name given to the plots in this cartoon. Normally, key words alluding to some elements of the plots are used, and on this occasion they are "*chorlito gurrumío*" (something like "shrunken plover bird," "*gurrumío*" being an adjective invented from other similar-sounding adjectives), "hojarasca sahariana" ("Saharan leaf litter"), and "*te pongas la minifarda*" ("when you wear the miniskirt," which is particularly funny as it is a syntactically odd excerpt from a very well-known Spanish *copla*). From the linguistic expressions of the other characters, para-linguistically elongated ("*Que nooooo*" (Noooo), "*Que síiiiiiiiiiiii*" (Yeeees)) or simply invented ("*Jofestes, qué sinvivir*" [something like "Gee whiz, what a real pain"]) and their gestures of being overwhelmed, it is easy to infer that they cannot cope with filing and alphabetizing the cases due to their enormous number.

### 6.5.4 On Social Policy and the Rule of Law in Spain

As shown in Fig. 6.6, Forges uses carnival costumes to clearly criticize the supposed "social policy and rule of law" of Mariano Rajoy's right-wing neoliberal government (December 2011–June 2018). The humorous effect depends largely on the

6 Spanish Humor and Political Culture Through Cartoons: Multimodal … 133

visual metaphor represented by a character disguised as an ax and another character disguised as a "middle finger"; it also comes from the contradiction or antonymy between what is expressed in the text and the drawing.

The character disguised as an ax claims to be the "neoliberal social policy" and leads to the implication to be inferred by the reader that neoliberal social measures are carried out on the basis of budget cuts and axes; in short, that public, social outlays for ordinary citizens are reduced. The character disguised as a "middle finger" claims to be the "social state and the rule of law," but the gesture of the finger indicates mockery and the inference is clear: neoliberalism does not care about the society and the rule of law, that is, it does not care about the welfare of citizens but only its own profits. The character also emphasizes "above all, […] of law" in allusion to the lax application of certain legal norms by some politicians and businessmen.

To support this criticism, on both sides of the cartoon we can see two buildings corresponding to "TENERSUS QUIETOS que sus echamos AGRUPACIÓN ULTRAPATRONAL" and "GALEOT@S empresa de trabajo temporal fugaz." In colloquial language, the former represents a paradoxical parody of a trade union, but of employers, an "ultra-employer grouping" called "stay still or we'll throw you out." The second represents a temporary employment agency that given the low quality

**Fig. 6.6** Carnival Tuesday.
CARNIVAL TUESDAY…
AX-MAN: I'm going as the neo-liberal social policy, and you?
MIDDLE FINGER-MAN: I'm going as the socialist state and the rule of law.
…above all, of the law. *Source Pinterest* (n.d.c)

and very short duration of the jobs, instead of being "temporary" (word which has been crossed out) has become a "fleeting" agency.

The following cartoon also relates to the welfare state and the right to housing in Spain (see Fig. 6.7). Taking advantage of Human Rights Day, the cartoonist criticizes the number of evictions of people who have been unable to continue paying their mortgages due to the economic crisis and the rise in interest rates, and how politicians and banks have failed to articulate measures to help them, putting banking prerogatives before the right to housing.

**Fig. 6.7** What to do on a long weekend.
WHAT TO DO ON A LONG LOOOOOONG WEEKEND?
Remember, and don't forget, that today is Human Rights Day, in which one reports the number of evictions in Spain so far this year: ±30,000.
CITIZEN: I think... ...therefore no one understands this. *Source Pinterest* (n.d.d)

Despite the fact that in recent years the number of evictions has been decreasing, this issue is also ideologized in Spain and it is curious how the right-wing media and politicians create social alarm about squatting, when it is unjustified due to its very small number (Herrera, 2020), and do not worry about evictions, whose number is significant.

Forges took advantage of a holiday break to reflect on what to do on such a "looooong weekend" and suggested in the narrator's text to remember Human Rights Day, and that 30,000 evictions of vulnerable families had been carried out that year, up to the date of the cartoon. The cartoonist's desired effect is evident: by recalling both events, he aims to awaken in the reader a critical feeling towards the inhumanity of evictions that constitute an attack on the right of many people in distress to have a decent home.

The central character in the cartoon, who reads the newspaper and represents the readers, carries out this reflection as an example of what the author intends. His thought is made visible through a sentence that begins "I think, therefore...," similar to Descartes's aphorism "I think, therefore I am"; but on this occasion the conclusion is unexpected: "I think, therefore no one understands this," because it is humanly incomprehensible that the rights of human beings are lower than those of bank profitability.

The humorous effect that accompanies this serious theme comes from the headline and the exaggeratedly long spelling of "*laaaaaaaaaargooooo*" (looooooong), as well as the name of the buildings surrounding the reader who is the protagonist of the cartoon walking down the street. Forges once again plays with language and calls them, metaphorically, "LATROCINING Investment Funds" (LARCENYING Investment Funds), "*Fabada's flatulences of design*" (Design bean stew flatulence), "hands up! BANK" (*sic*) and "*Soplachickens* coaching" ("*soplachickens*" is a compound word which is an insult in Spanish, but which Forges softens by translating the second word of the compound into English, which has a humorous effect in Spanish); it is, therefore, a mixture of invented linguistic constructions and anglicisms that in Spanish have the meaning of stealing and swindling, but which are humorously critical because of the lexical and morphosyntactic creativity.

### 6.5.5 *On Hate Speech and the Hardening of Political Discourse*

Since the recent arrival of the far right in political life, there has been a drift towards a hardening of political language that has also dragged the main opposition party, the conservative Popular Party, along with it. Their strategy is to oppose everything, trying to block the approval of many progressive measures. Right and ultra-right have traditionally appropriated the discourse of saviors of the country, establishing the discursive strategy of the opposition between "them vs. us," together with a long list of discursive fallacies.

For example, in one of the cartoons dedicated to ultraright discourse (El País, 2017b), Forges presents the typical right-wing candidate dressed in a perfect suit in the context of an election rally in front of a large audience.

LAST ELECTION RALLIES

POLITICIAN: It's either us or chaos…!

AUDIENCE: Chaos!

POLITICIAN: Stupendous

The politician introduces himself firmly with the dilemma "It's either us or chaos," to which the audience surprisingly responds with the same firmness and in unison: "Chaos!"—humorous and surprising as they have attended this candidate's rally, so that one would have expected them to be sympathetic to that party. The audience in the cartoon is conveying to the reading public the message that they unhesitatingly prefer even chaos to such a candidate.

The candidate's comic and ironic apostille is a "*stupendo*" (for "*estupendo*" (great, stupendous), in Forgian spelling.

In the face of the degradation of political language and the politics of hatred that certain parties are carrying out, Forges does not remain impassive and draws numerous vignettes on this subject.

As shown in Fig. 6.8, Forges presents a new married couple sitting at home. The husband, like many of the husbands in his vignettes, is sitting reading the newspaper and comments to his wife: "You look tense," and then explains why: "You vote what you vote and what happens, happens."

Merging this information with the amusing drawing of the contorted wife completes the meaning of the cartoon. The woman appears as a real "*forgendro*" (Forges' spawn), deformed, with a misshapen face, stiff hair, bulging eyes, fangs, wild animal nails, legs rolled up in knots. It is, then, understood that voting for hate parties turns people into deformed beasts.

6  Spanish Humor and Political Culture Through Cartoons: Multimodal … 137

**Fig. 6.8** Political tension.
HUSBAND: You seem tense, María Jesús…
…You vote for what you vote and, then what happens, happens. *Source Pinterest* (n.d.e)

## *6.5.6 Overview of Politics by Politicians and Citizens*

In numerous cartoons, Forges represents the opinion generated by "political and media noise" among citizens. In one of these vignettes published in *El País* on December 5, 2017 (*Pinterest* n.d.f), Concha and Mariano, a married couple who are regulars in his vignettes and well-known to readers, represent the average Spaniard. Concha, who is always busy doing things, asks her husband, Mariano, who almost always appears seated watching television, why those on the TV are all talking at the same time.

> CONCHA: Why are they all yelling at the same time?

> MARIANO: Because they're not right

She may be alluding to both the parliamentary debates and the political talk shows on television. Mariano's curious and unexpected response is both humorous and critical, "because they are not right." One might logically assume that if someone raises their voice emphatically in a conversation it is because they want to assert their rightness; however, in this case, in politics and on talk shows, the appearance of rightness may be more important even if it is not there.

The feeling of many citizens that they are being cheated by politicians is confirmed by the attitude of some politicians who seem to mock and exploit these citizens. In one of Forges's cartoons (El País, 2016b), two politicians walk down the street dressed casually in order to approach citizens; one, looking surprised, asks the other why he is wearing a T-shirt that says "*Votadnos, gilipollas*" (Vote for us, assholes) (where the insult is crossed out, as Forges always does, in order to tone it down and include it), to which the other replies: "*Porque funciona*" (Because it works).

> MAN: Why are you wearing a "Vote for us, assholes" T-shirt?

> POLITICIAN: Because it works

The humorous effect is, once again, caused by the rupture of expectations; it is not to be expected that someone would vote for someone who takes them for a fool, nor is it to be expected that someone would confess to doing so, just like that.

I conclude with the following vignette (see Fig. 6.9), in which, once again, two citizens walk while reflecting on various questions, this time in a rural rather than a city environment, as we can see the small village with the church in the background and the unpaved country road. One of them, wearing a typical village beret, comments on the cultural fact that "in literature we Spaniards are the creators of the picaresque genre." As readers know from their background knowledge, the picaresque novel is a literary narrative, sub-genre that emerged in Spain in the sixteenth century. It is an autobiographical novel starring the "picaro," a shrewd and shameless antihero who narrates the tricks he plays to survive. The humorous effect comes from the response of the other traveler: "if it were only in literature…," a clear allusion to the fact that

**Fig. 6.9** Picaresque.
MAN 1: …And in literature we are the creators of the picaresque.
MAN 2: If only it were in literature. *Source* El País (2017a)

the Spanish rogue character is also typically found in politics and other social and economic spheres, as the reader will infer.

## 6.6 Conclusions

The history of Spain, its political and social life, has not only been reflected in a palpable way through graphic humor, but it has also accompanied and formed part of many processes experienced by Spanish society. Magazines like *Hermano lobo* or *El jueves*, and humorists like Mingote, Chumy Chúmez or El Roto have been and are the portrait artists of Spanish society and politics that through humor, irony, and sarcasm, provide a reflective and critical vision, sometimes fierce, sometimes kind. Without a doubt, one of the most important exponents has been the humorist Antonio Fraguas, Forges, who created characters and a language that form part of the collective Spanish heritage.

The above analysis of a selection of cartoons related to Forges' vision of Spanish politics and society has revealed how his cartoons combine linguistic, paralinguistic, and visual elements with the aim of providing clues that awaken in his readers the desired cognitive effects, processing them in order to interpret their meaning.

The application of Relevance Theory has revealed how the interpretation of cartoons is also related to the addressees' prior cognitive schemas i.e., their prior knowledge, beliefs, and assumptions (Sperber & Wilson, 1986). Cartoonists, and in this case Forges, deliberately exploit the procedures their audience goes through when interpreting the cartoons, in order to provoke a humorous effect that will serve as an effective and rapid vehicle for reflection and vindication.

On a daily basis, Forges was able to portray Spanish political and social life in such a way for 50 years that his legacy has also become part of Spanish history. The editorial of *El País* on February 22, 2018 noted that he was a daily chronicler and analyst of "our political, social, economic, domestic and even intimate life," penetrating the reality he presented to us every day "taking flight, sinking his teeth in, sharpening his stiletto, ruminating on the episode to delve into its deepest secrets… and drawing (and filling the balloons with words) undressing us all…. In these times in which the political struggle seems to be reduced to the squalid battle of intransigent positions, Forges was admired for the intelligence with which he pronounced himself on everything…that happened in Spain, and in the lives of Spaniards. *He made great politics with humor*" (El País, 2018a). For Jiménez (2018), Forges "taught us to laugh at ourselves and to reflect."

Rilova Jericó (2018) emphasizes one of Forges' most important achievements. Thanks to him, a generation of Spaniards frightened by their dramatic history, began to approach it: "Forges, for half a long century, wrote down with his drawings the Spanish society of the late Francoism and the long and changing Transition that has reached our days… [H]e knew how to keep the fear of reading Spanish history books at bay; many Spaniards had become truly terrified of it thanks to the ineffable teachings of the National Catholic school of the Franco dictatorship."

As the editorial of Entreletras (2018) pointed out, "His contribution to the settlement of values for democratic coexistence during and after the Transition, as well as his commitment to the emancipation of women, to environmentalism and to solidarity causes in prostrate countries of the Third World, have been some constants of his creations." His cartoons became daily companions for readers, educating them in history, culture, and values—not limiting himself to verbally and visually "narrating" reality, but as a solidarity activist he included messages that appealed directly to citizens and rulers through his "Don't forget" notes: "The cartoonist, FAO award winner in 2012, constantly urged to take into account refugees, the hungry, women, the poor…" ("The unforgettable Forges's 'Don't forget's", El País, 2018b).

Perhaps the secret of his unanimous acceptance was that Forges knew how to perceive the common sense of good people and use it as a powerful ethical weapon to erode autocratic powers and democratize them, always generating a smile. His harsh criticisms were accepted because they brimmed with the storytelling talent and intelligent tenderness of a good man, always committed to Spanish society.

As a legacy, in addition to drawing 250,000 cartoons or writing dozens of publications, his activism was demonstrated in initiatives he led as technical director of the Quevedo Institute of the Arts of Humor, the first university center on humor studies in Spain. Among other initiatives, he achieved the support of cartoonists from all over the world for the UN Millennium Goals on the occasion of the United Nations

Assembly in October 2008, presenting the book *Humorists for the Millenium Goals. Eradicate Hunger and Poverty* at the Cervantes Institute in New York. Cartoonists from around the world continue to support the SDGs (Sustainable Development Goals) and the 2030 Agenda in subsequent editions.

The legacy of all his works is part of the National Library of Spain and there are monuments dedicated to the humorist in different places of our geography. He never applied for any award, but nevertheless he obtained more than two hundred!

In his books he reviewed the history of Spain and the world, science, and literature, inventing a particular language that permeated Spanish society itself and many of his new or re-signified words are part of the *Dictionary of the Royal Spanish Academy* and of our daily life. He was a strong advocate for science funding in Spain; for this reason, in November 2019 the Spanish National Research Council held the exhibition "Science according to Forges," given his struggle to raise awareness in society and political authorities of the importance of science. He also promoted digital journalism congresses and awards.

Forges was one of the most popular Spaniards of the last half century. Kings, all the political parties, and citizens of all ages spontaneously expressed their sincere condolences upon his death; his image was projected from soccer stadiums such as San Mamés (Bilbao) to the bibs of the Spanish runners of the Tokyo marathon (February 25, 2018).

Forges has been the subject of countless academic publications, communications in conferences and seminars, academic and journalistic interviews. He also served as a referee for teaching and pedagogical proposals, and inspired publications on literature, veterinary medicine, bioethics, statistics, economics, and law—some of which he illustrated. Dr. Blanco Mercadé was inspired by Forges' philosophy of life in one of his scientific articles on ethics and medicine: "It is good that life is long, but it is more important that it is *wide*" (2018, p. 151).

As his friend and colleague Cruz (2018) pointed out, of this enormous legacy, perhaps the most important, was his uninterrupted daily effort for five long decades "to bring out, in a benevolent, respectful, critical, funny, transversal and always intelligent way, the most human entrails of life in society: *Humor*."

# References

Baldry, A., & Thibault, P. J. (2006). *Multimodal transcription and text*. Equinox.
Blanco Mercadé, A. (2018). The remaining days: Living to the end. *Eidon, 49*, 151–155. (in Spanish).
CasosAislados.com. (2023). List of corruption cases in Spain. *Isolated cases of systemic corruption*. https://casos-aislados.com/tramas.php. (in Spanish).
Cruz, J. (2018, February 23). Farewell to a genius of graphic humor. But don't forget Forges. *El País*. https://elpais.com/cultura/2018/02/22/actualidad/1519330555_058805.html. (in Spanish).
Dines, G., & Humez, J. (Eds.). ([1995] 2010). *Gender, race and class in media: A critical reader* (3rd ed.). Sage Publications.
Donnelly, L. (2013). *Women deliver, the world receives: Cartoons for and about every woman*. http://www.womendeliver.org/assets/Cartoon_Book.pdf

*El Periódico*. (2022, January 17). Antonio Fraguas, "Forges", the genius of social criticism graphic humor. *El Periódico*. https://www.elperiodico.com/es/tecnologia/20220117/antonio-fraguas-forges-13106536. (in Spanish).

El Refaie, E. (2009). Multiliteracies: How readers interpret political cartoons. *Visual Communication, 8*, 181–205.

*El País*. (2014a, February 25). Smart phones for smart politicians. (Cartoon). https://elpais.com/elpais/2014/02/25/vinetas/1393344686_920468.html. (in Spanish).

*El País*. (2014b, November 13). At the central unit for economic and fiscal offences. (Cartoon). https://elpais.com/elpais/2014/11/13/vinetas/1415895880_590905.html. (in Spanish).

*El País*. (2015, April 22). Direct contact with citizens. (Cartoon). https://elpais.com/elpais/2015/04/22/vinetas/1429713907_131927.html. (in Spanish).

*El País*. (2016a, June 6). Visual acuity. (Cartoon). https://elpais.com/elpais/2016/06/06/opinion/1465229751_688116.html. (in Spanish).

*El País*. (2016b, June 24). Political mockery. (Cartoon). https://elpais.com/elpais/2016/06/23/opinion/1466701725_104350.html. (in Spanish).

*El País*. (2017a, September 7). Picaresque. (Cartoon). https://elpais.com/elpais/2016/06/23/opinion/1466701725_104350.html. (in Spanish).

*El País*. (2017b, September 23). Last rallies. (Cartoon). https://elpais.com/elpais/2017/09/22/opinion/1506090301_648138.html (in Spanish).

*El País*. (2018a, February 22). Farewell, Forges. Antonio Fraguas turned humor into the best way to portray half a century of Spain. *El País*. https://elpais.com/elpais/2018/02/22/opinion/1519328448_021808.html (in Spanish).

*El País*. (2018b, February 22). The unforgettable Forges's 'Don't forget's'. *El País*. https://elpais.com/elpais/2018/02/22/album/1519285038_555092.html (in Spanish).

*El Plural.com*. (2018, May 24). PP, the first party to be convicted of corruption in democracy. *El Plural.com*. https://www.elplural.com/politica/pp-el-primer-partido-condenado-por-corrupcion-en-democracia_128474102. (in Spanish).

*Entreletras*. (2018, Feberuary 26). Editorial: Forges, a democratic common sense. *Entreletras.eu*. https://www.entreletras.eu/tribuna/forges-un-sentido-comun-democratico/. (in Spanish).

Forceville, C. (2005). Addressing an audience: Time, place and genre in Peter van Straaten's calendar cartoons. *Humour: International Journal of Humour Research, 18*, 247–278.

García Cerrada, J., et al. (Coords.) (2008/2011). *Humorists for the millenium goals. Eradicate hunger and poverty*. Universidad de Alcalá. (in Spanish).

Gómez Mompart, J. L., Martínez Gallego, F. A., & Bordería Ortiz, E. (Eds.) (2019). *Humor and political culture in contemporary Spain*. Hacer Any. (in Spanish).

Grijelmo, A. (2018, February, 22). Forges dies: A particular vocabulary that now belongs to everyone. *El País*. https://elpais.com/cultura. (in Spanish).

Herrera, E. (2020, August 31) The false alarm of squatting. *ElDiario.es*. https://www.eldiario.es/politica/falsa-alarma-okupaciones-ley-garantiza-desalojo-expres-allanamientos-residencia-habitual-segunda-vivienda_1_6187271.html. (in Spanish).

Hoff, S. (1976). *Editorial and political cartooning: From earliest times to the present, with over 700 examples from the works of the world's greatest cartoonists*. Stravon Educational Press.

Jiménez, J. (2018, February 22). Forges, the humorist who taught us to laugh at ourselves. *RTVE.es*. https://www.rtve.es/noticias/20180222/forges-humorista-enseno-reirnos-nosotros-mismos/1682321.shtml. (in Spanish).

Kaindl, K. (2004). Multimodality in the translation of humour in comics. In E. Ventola, C. Cassily, & M. Kaltenbacher (Eds.), *Perspectives on multimodality* (pp. 173–192). John Benjamins.

Kress, G. (2010). *Multimodality: A social semiotic approach to contemporary communication*. Routledge.

Kress, G., & van Leeuwen, T. (2001). *Multimodal discourse. The modes and media of contemporary communication*. Arnold.

Kress, G., & van Leeuwen, T. (2006). *Reading images. The grammar of visual design*. (2nd ed.). Routledge.

Lemke, J. L. (1998). Multiplying meaning: Visual and verbal semiotics in scientific texts. In J. R. Martin & R. Veel (Eds.). *Reading science*. Routledge.

Lent, J. A. (2001). Cartooning and democratization world-wide. *Media Development, 48*(2), 54–58.

Marín, B. (2018, February 22). Forges, the brilliant cartoonist of half a century of Spanish history, dies. *El País*. https://elpais.com/cultura/2018/02/22/actualidad/1519268111_985350.html. (in Spanish).

Olowu, A., Kayode, M. B., & Egbuwalo, L. (2014). Satirising the Nigeria police force: A multimodal discourse analytical study of selected cartoons of TELL newsmagazines. *Research on Humanities and Social Sciences, 4*(2), 119–127.

*Patricialuceno*. (2013, 20 May). "How do you serve the intern?" (Cartoon). *Humor for interns I. Forges Special*. https://preperiodistas.wordpress.com/2013/05/20/humor-para-becarios-i-especial-forges/. (in Spanish).

Pinker, S. A. (2008). *The stuff of thought*. Penguin Books.

*Pinterest*. (n.d.a) On politicians' excessive appointment of officials and advisers. (Cartoon). *Pinterest*. https://www.pinterest.es/pin/633387436797429/. (in Spanish).

*Pinterest*. (n.d.b). Happy 1st of May Labor Day. (Cartoon). *Pinterest*. https://www.pinterest.es/pin/21532904453489305/. (in Spanish).

*Pinterest*. (n.d.c). Tuesday of carnival. (Cartoon). *Pinterest*. https://www.pinterest.es/pin/633387437039483/. (in Spanish).

*Pinterest*. (n.d.d). What to do on a long weekend. (Cartoon). *Pinterest*. https://www.pinterest.es/pin/443604632051964398/. (in Spanish).

*Pinterest*. (n.d.e). Political tension. (Cartoon). *Pinterest*. https://www.pinterest.es/pin/633387436797338/. (in Spanish).

*Pinterest*. (n.d.f). Political and media noise. (Cartoon). *Pinterest*. https://www.pinterest.es/pin/653303489721108657/. (in Spanish).

Reig, R., & Mancinas-Chávez, R. (2018). Transgression and critique of the system: The journalistic cartoon. *Revista Latina De Comunicación Social, 73*, 504–530. https://doi.org/10.4185/RLCS-2018-1267(inSpanish)

Riffe, D., Sneed, D., & van Ommeren, R. (1987). Deciding the limits of taste in editorial cartooning. *Journalism Quarterly, 64*(2–3), 607–610. https://doi.org/10.1177/107769908706400252

Rilova Jericó, C. (2018). A remembrance for the author of "History of Here". *Diariovasco.com*. https://blogs.diariovasco.com/correo-historia/2018/02/26/un-recuerdo-para-el-autor-de-historia-de-aqui-forges-en-san-sebastian/. (in Spanish).

Segado-Boj, F. (2009). The road to the 1977 elections: The first government of Adolfo Suárez in the daily press. *HISPANIA. Revista Española de Historia, LXIX, 232*, 477–512. https://doi.org/10.3989/hispania.2009.v69.i232.112. (in Spanish).

Sperber, D., & Wilson, D. (1986). *Relevance: Communication and cognition*. Blackwell.

Sperber, D., & Wilson, D. (1987). Précis of relevance: Communication and cognition. *Behavioural and Brain Sciences, 10*, 697–710.

Sperber, D., & Wilson, D. (1995). *Relevance: Communication and cognition*. (2nd expanded ed.). Blackwell.

Steinfirst, S. (1995). Using editorial cartoons in the curriculum to enhance visual (and political) literacy. In *Literacy: Traditional, cultural, technological. Selected papers from the Annual Conference of the International Association of School Librarianship* (pp. 63–69). Pittsburgh Press.

Tsakonaa, V. (2009). Language and image interaction in cartoons: Towards a multimodal theory of humor. *Journal of Pragmatics, 41*(6), 1171–1188.

Van Leeuwen, T. (2005). *Introducing social semiotics*. Routledge.

Wilson, D., & Sperber, D. (2004). Relevance theory. In L. R. Horn & G. L. Ward (Eds.), *The handbook of pragmatics* (pp. 607–632). Blackwell.

Yus Ramos, F. (1998). Relevance theory and media discourse: A verbal-visual model of communication. *Poetics, 25*, 293–309.
Yus Ramos, F. (2003). Humor and the search for relevance. *Journal of Pragmatics, 35*, 1295–1331.


**María del Mar Rivas-Carmona** is a Senior Lecturer at the University of Cordoba, Spain. She has previously taught at Harvard University, USA, and the University of Seville, Spain. Her classes focus on Translation, Discourse and Pragmatics, and her research interests include discourse analysis and specialized translation. Standing out among her recent publications are two international co-editions on the discursive aspects of translation, published by Peter Lang (2013) and Narr Verlag (2013).

# Chapter 7
# Far-Right Political Humor in Australia: Culture, Coloniality, and Exclusion

**Kurt Sengul and Jordan McSwiney**

**Abstract** This chapter examines the use of political humor in the communicative and discursive repertoire of the Australian far right. Specifically, this chapter critically analyzes the co-constitutive and mutually informing relationship between far right political humor and Australian culture. Existing research has demonstrated the effective use of humor and comedy in mainstreaming the far right and softening the exclusionary and ideological content of their messages. The purpose of this chapter then is to understand how far-right humor is articulated, shaped, and transformed by the cultural context in which it takes place. Australian culture is shaped by several factors, including its settler colonial reality, its strong multicultural legacy, its proximity to Asia, and cultural, social, and political ties to the United States and United Kingdom. Through a Critical Discourse Analysis and Thematic Analysis of far-right political humor, including memes and animations, this chapter will demonstrate how Australian far-right humor maintains a distinctly "Australian" lens. At the same time, this chapter will argue that far-right political humor works to shape culture by stretching the boundaries of socially acceptable behavior by cueing participants that it is acceptable to express contempt and hostility towards ridiculed out-groups.

## 7.1 Introduction

The strategic role of humor in the communicative repertoire of the contemporary far-right has come under increasing focus within the literature (Matamoros-Fernández et al., 2022; Meyer, 2000; Pérez, 2017). It is widely accepted that contemporary far-right movements are savvy media performers who employ a range of innovative communication strategies to exploit the highly mediatized and hybridized political

---

K. Sengul (✉)
Department of Media and Communications, The University of Sydney, Camperdown, Australia
e-mail: kurt.sengul@uon.edu.au

J. McSwiney
Centre for Deliberative Democracy and Global Governance at the University of Canberra, Canberra, Australia
e-mail: Jordan.McSwiney@canberra.edu.au

© The Author(s), under exclusive license to Springer Nature Singapore Pte Ltd. 2024
O. Feldman (ed.), *Communicating Political Humor in the Media*, The Language of Politics, https://doi.org/10.1007/978-981-97-0726-3_7

landscape. A key feature of this communication and media strategy is the effective use of satire, comedy, humor, and irony across a variety of digital and traditional media. As the far-right becomes more mainstream, it has tended to employ a range of euphemistic and covert strategies (Sengul, 2022a, 2022b, 2023) to conceal the exclusionary and supremacist nature of its messages in order to broaden its appeal to mainstream audiences (Wodak, 2021).

Our aim in this chapter is to deepen our cultural understanding of far-right political humor by critically analyzing the mutually informing and co-constitutive relationship between culture and political humor. We employ Critical Discourse Analysis (CDA) and Thematic Analysis (TA) to analyze a diverse range of far-right humor across digital and traditional media, including an online animated series, internet memes, and political cartoons, to explore how culture works to shape, and in-turn, is shaped by Australian culture. Adopting a critical perspective, we demonstrate how far-right political humor (re)produces racialized and colonial discourses that are heavily influenced by Australia's settler colonial past and present. We argue that far-right political humor is highly contingent and cannot be holistically understood without grasping the cultural context in which it takes place. As such, this chapter, along with the others in this volume, helps to advance our understanding of the mutually informing dynamics of political humor and culture.

## 7.2 'Australian Culture' and the *Colonial Fantasy*

To understand the interplay of culture and far-right political humor, it is important to critically unpack and interrogate the myths and realities associated with "Australian culture." Discussions and explanations of Australian political culture are abounding with mythologized references to ideas of *mateship, egalitarianism, authenticity, optimism, humility, common sense,* and *humor* (e.g., Evanson, 2016). Hegemonic understandings of Australian culture are heavily embedded in dominant discourses, symbolism, myths, and legends of a tolerant, multicultural, and egalitarian nation built on the idea of a "fair go" that is distinctly "Australian" (Bromfield et al., 2021). As suggested by McAllister (1997, p. 6), "the notion of equality in Australian society has its origins in the frontier tradition which emerged in the early years of white settlement."

The harsh environment and life on the frontier inspired a particular imaginary of Australian nationalism (Piccini, 2020) and masculinity. The image of the Aussie bushman typifies unique Australian tropes: "the 'typical Australian' is a practical man [note the masculine nature of the bush myth], rough and ready in his manners and quick to decry and appearance of affection in others" (Ward, 1977, pp. 1–2). The Australian characteristics of practicality and "larrikin" irreverence, mischievousness, and disrespect of authority (see Seal, 2004, p. 3) that evolved on the frontier were thus characteristics necessary to the conquest (and destruction) of the environment. Indeed, the white heteronormative trope of the Australian man is further articulated by Waling as "a White working-class, Australian male who is typified by his loyalty, his able-bodiedness, his belief and practice of mateship and egalitarianism […] his hard-working ethic, and his pride in being Australian" (2019, p. 26).

The centrality of egalitarianism to Australia's cultural identity and sense of nationhood were cemented with the rise of multiculturalism in the 1970s following the abolition of the *White Australia Policy* which prevented non-whites from immigrating to Australia until its formal repeal in 1973. Australia's embrace of multiculturalism in the 1970s "[…] has been viewed as an integral component of the Australian national identity, which emphasizes normatively the overarching goal of achieving a just society that is inclusive of culturally diverse groups" (Elias et al., 2021, p. 79).

Indeed, it is the multiculturalism and multiracialism of contemporary Australia that is offered as proof of a modern, tolerant, forward thinking, egalitarian, and diverse nation. We argue, however, that while these popular articulations of Australian culture are hegemonic, they are replete with contradictions and erasure, and belie an ongoing history of colonization, dispossession, and racialized discrimination. Our aim is not to discount these pervasive and dominant expressions of Australian culture, as they are important in understanding the articulation of far-right humor and culture, but rather to present a more holistic and critical account of Australia's cultural identity formation.

Australia is a white settler colonial state (Wolfe, 2006). It was founded on the violent usurpation, colonization, and dispossession of sovereign Aboriginal and Torres Strait Islander lands (Moreton-Robinson, 2015). The establishment of white sovereignty, attempted erasure of First Nations sovereignties, and the ongoing exclusion/conditional inclusion of Indigenous peoples into Australian national identity, reproduces white material and discursive possessiveness over First Nations people, the state, and political culture (Moreton-Robinson, 2015). The optimistic revisionism and erasure of this colonial history and *present* in dominant understandings of Australian culture reflect what Sarah Maddison (2019) refers to as a *colonial fantasy*. Ghassan Hage suggests that in stark contrast to the relaxed, open, and proud multicultural nation painted in popular cultural depictions, Australia is a nation riddled with paranoia, fear, anxiety, and worry (Hage, 1998, p. 10):

White Australians who think they have a monopoly over 'worrying' about the shape of the future of Australia. They are constantly finding a source of concern: look at how many migrants there are, look at crime, look at ghettos, look at tourists. Such a pathological worry is that of people who use worrying to try and construct themselves as the most worthy Australians in the land.

The racialized discomfort of white Australians, as articulated by Hage (1998) and convincingly argued by Moreton-Robinson (2015), can be traced back to the founding of the Australian colonial state: "The founding white fathers of Australia's federation feared that nonwhite races would want to invade the country. They were concerned with white racial usurpation and dispossession and took action to ensure that Australia would be a nation controlled by and for whites" (Moreton-Robinson, 2015, p. xxi). This white anxiety accelerated with the rise of multiculturalism that despite rhetoric to the contrary, "[…] has never sat comfortably in the national imaginary" (Papastergiadis, 2004, p. 9).

We can therefore see a clear contradiction between the myth and reality of Australian cultural understandings. Indeed, we argue that the dominance of the egalitarian view of Australian culture is, in fact, a product of colonial hegemony. As we demonstrate in this chapter, far-right political humor leans heavily into the popular tropes of Australian culture, while being underpinned by colonial, imperial, and racial logics. In the following section we discuss the characteristics and function of right-wing political humor.

## 7.3 Far-Right Political Humor

Comedy is a double-edged sword. On the one hand, it can be pro-social, engendering feelings of enjoyment through shared laughter (Meyer, 2000). It can persuade or align audiences (Billig, 2005), engendering social cooperation by uniting interlocutors (Meyer, 2000; Pérez, 2017), thereby encouraging group cohesion and solidarity (Ziv, 2009). On the other hand, comedy can be used to discipline and marginalize those considered the "Other." Ridicule and mockery can be used to reinforce outgroup status and alienate minorities (Billig, 2005; Pérez, 2017), playing an active role in the construction and maintenance of social boundaries (Meyer, 2000). Exclusionary practices of comedy, such as racist joking, serves to reproduce and normalize racial categories and hierarchies by casting the other as buffoonish, dangerous, inferior, and so on (Pérez, 2022; Weaver, 2011).

The mainstreaming of internet communications, and in particular social media and associated digital cultures, has seen increased attention paid to the use of humor by the far right, particularly in the wake of Donald Trump's successful 2016 campaign for the U.S. presidency and the proliferation of far-right memes surrounding it. Much has been written since then regarding the use of memes and the critical role of humor within them to make far-right content more palatable to wider audiences (Greene, 2019; Hakoköngäs et al., 2020; McSwiney et al., 2021). Far-right comedy has internal uses also. It works to facilitate and structure interactions within the far right, providing a means of political resistance to those perceived as outsiders, while reinforcing a shared sense of identity within the movement (Windisch & Simi, 2022).

However, the kinds of exclusionary humor circulating within the far right, whether it be racist jokes, mockery of trans people, and so on, is not limited to far-right actors. Rather, exclusionary humor forms part of the everyday construction and maintenance of social inequalities, even (or especially) within multicultural societies like Australia. For example, the circulation of racist cartoons in Australian newspapers (e.g., Ata, 2010; Cunneen & Russell, 2017), the use of racial minstrelsy (Sharpe & Hynes, 2016), and the continued circulation of racist jokes within Australian workplaces, schools, and police (Dunn et al., 2011; Grigg & Manderson, 2015; Pérez & Ward, 2019). The circulation of exclusionary humor beyond the confines of the far right legitimizes the far right's exclusionary humor. It also highlights the paucity of a fixed conceptual distinction between the far right and the mainstream, where in reality the borders are often blurry (Brown et al., 2023; Mondon & Winter, 2020).

Critically, the kinds of exclusionary humor engaged by the far right (and the mainstream), are couched in a meta-discourse justifying and excusing such humor as "just a joke" (Billig, 2001). This seeks to recast such exclusionary humor as merely (or at least primarily) a form of harmless enjoyment, shielding joke teller from accusations of racism. Rather than the joke teller and listener participating in an act of racism, homophobia, and so on, it is the critic who is (indirectly accused of being) at fault for being humorless. This allows the joke teller to test the waters of the political culture, by saying things that might otherwise be considered inappropriate. At the same time, it co-constitutes the political culture by normalizing such speech acts and the sentiments underlying them by signaling to audiences that such expressions are acceptable (Pérez, 2022).

## 7.4 Research Approach, Data, and Methods

In order to holistically understand the complexity and culturally contingent nature of far-right political humor in Australia, we draw on the analytical tools of Critical Discourse Analysis (CDA) (Wodak & Meyer, 2009) and Thematic Analysis (TA) (Clarke & Braun, 2017). Critical Discourse Analysis is concerned with "[…] the way social power-abuse and inequality are enacted, reproduced, legitimates and resisted by talk and text in the political context" (van Dijk, 2015, p. 466). As previously established, far-right political humor is inherently exclusionary and frequently employs a range of coded semiotic and discursive practices, and strategies to conceal the discriminatory and supremacist nature of their messages to broaden their appeal to mainstream audiences (McSwiney & Sengul, forthcoming). Critical Discourse Analysis has particular utility in researching this kind of euphemistic, covert, and coded political rhetoric due to its capacity to "[…] expose strategies that appear normal on the surface, but which may, in fact, be ideological and seek to shape the representation of events and persons for particular ends" (Machin & Mayr, 2012, p. 5). Importantly, we see an alignment in how CDA conceptualizes discourse and the co-constitutive nature of political humor. We follow Ruth Wodak in understanding discourse as "[…] a set of context-dependent practices that are simultaneously socially constituted and socially constitutive" (2021, p. 73). In other words, as suggested by Bhatia (2013, p. 2):

Discursive events share a co-constitutive relationship with the social, institutional and professional contexts within which they take place. They are socially conditioned by the local and macro contexts in which they occur, but at the same time the discursive events shape the social identities and relationships of the participants engaged in these events themselves.

This understanding of discourse as co-constitutive aligns with our understanding of far-right political humor as being shaped by the socio-cultural context in which it takes place, while simultaneously also working to shape culture. Moreover, in attempting to understand the mutually informing relationship between far-right political humor and culture, CDA's sensitivity to the contextual nature of language and discourse further strengthened our decision to adopt a critical discourse-oriented framework. As noted by Filardo-Llamas and Boyd (2018, pp. 312–313), it is vital to "[…] consider the immediate and wider contexts which define the text. This includes the co-text, situational context as well as the socio-cultural and historical context." We found that CDA's attentiveness to the socio-cultural and historical context of discourse and text was vital in understanding the contingent and mutually informing nature of far-right political humor and Australian culture (Sengul, 2022b).

We combined Critical Discourse Analysis with Thematic Analysis (TA) which we use to identify and code broad themes in the data before applying a closer analysis using CDA. Thematic Analysis was particularly useful in identifying patterns with and across the diverse multimodal data collected for this study (Clarke & Braun, 2017, p. 297). We found that the flexibility of TA complemented the theoretically rich framework of Critical Discourse Analysis. As explained by Braun et al. (2016, p. 191, emphasis in original), "It is not *tied to* a particular theoretical framework, and it does not come with methodological stipulations about, for example, how to sample, or collect data." The analytical toolkits associated with CDA and TA allowed us to identify, code, and critically analyze a range of multimodal semiotic messages, strategies, and practices embedded in far-right political humor. These included intertextuality and interdiscursivity, metaphors, framing, euphemisms, caricatures, props, presuppositions, as well as a range of linguistic and rhetorical devices (Wodak, 2021).

To capture the diverse ways that far-right humor manifests itself in the highly mediatized and hybridized Australian political landscape, we drew from a multifaceted dataset, including an online animated series, political memes, political cartoons, and social media posts. We adopted a purposive sampling strategy which is widely used in qualitative research and "[…] involves selecting data cases (participants, texts) on the basis that they will be able to provide information rich data to analyse…with the aim of generating insight and in-depth understanding" (Braun & Clarke, 2013, p. 56). Our purposive sampling strategy enabled us to identify rich illustrative examples to holistically capture the interplay of culture and far-right political humor in the Australian context. Finally, we take a constructivist approach to our understanding of humor. That is, we see humor as indicated by the claim of the participants, not the aesthetic preferences of the analysts (Billig, 2001).

## 7.5 Findings and Analysis

### 7.5.1 *Political Cartoons*

The irony underpinning satire in political cartoons is a function of the incongruity between the written and visual components of the image, and typically requires a certain degree of the viewer's cultural and political contextual knowledge to understand (Moloney, 2007). For a cartoon to convey satirical comment, the images need to be "instantly and irrefutably recognizable" to audiences, and so must resonate with how viewers perceive an individual or group (Moloney et al., 2013). This can have negative and demeaning effects for minorities (Moloney, 2007). Essentializing minority groups to make them "recognizable" can, deliberately or unwittingly, foster exclusion and marginalization. Here, we explore the interplay between the moving images of *Please Explain,* an online cartoon produced by Australian far-right party Pauline Hanson's One Nation (PHON), the editorial cartoons published in Australia's only national broadsheet newspaper *The Australian,* and mainstream political culture in Australia. Rather than an aberration, we argue that the far-right humor of *Please Explain* constitutes a radicalization of mainstream political humor, and Australian politics more broadly.

Though the party's electoral impact has been relatively small compared to similar parties in say, Western Europe, PHON and its founder Pauline Hanson have enjoyed a media presence well beyond their size and influence. Since its founding in 1997, the party has been a lightning rod for issues of immigration, multiculturalism, and Aboriginal reconciliation in Australia (Mondon, 2013). The series reimagines the 46th Parliament of (2019–2022) as a school classroom, with PHON leader Pauline Hanson cast as the teacher of an unruly class of students made up of her parliamentary peers, such as the then Coalition Prime Minister Scott Morrison, ALP leader Anthony Albanese, and Greens leader Adam Bandt. The series was conceived primarily as a piece of political comedy, with the party describing the aims of the program to "deliver a humorous yet sobering glimpse into the Australian political arena" (Pauline Hanson's Please Explain, n.d.). However, it is through its use of humor that the *Please Explain* series is able to disseminate highly ideological and exclusionary far-right content to wider audiences, shielding the party from claims of racism by claiming it is "just a joke."

This can be seen in the various "jokes" made at the expense of Aboriginal and Torres Strait Islander people. Throughout the series, Acknowledgements of Country—statements that recognize the Traditional Custodians of the land and their long and continuing relationship with it—are repeatedly mocked. So too is the 2008 Apology to Australia's Indigenous Peoples, reframing the push to redress historical and ongoing injustices perpetrated against Aboriginal and Torres Strait Islander people as a kind of daily humiliation and self-flagellation for white Australia (PHON, 2022e [00:30–00:37]). There is also an implication that the votes of Aboriginal and Torres Strait Islander people can be "bought" through symbolic gestures, with the character of Coalition PM Scott Morrison claiming that "I've just bought the Aboriginal flag and a bunch of votes" (PHON, 2022a [00:09–00:12]). In another episode, efforts to provide Covid-19 public health messaging in the state of Western Australia in Australian Kriol, an English-based creole language spoken in some remote Aboriginal Communities, is ridiculed, mocking speakers as just poor English speakers, rather than speakers of a distinct language (PHON, 2022b [01:38–01:43]).

Anti-Indigenous racism intersects with misogyny in the way the series portrays First Nations women—in particular, independent Senator Lydia Thorpe. Thorpe, whose anti-colonial and anti-racist rhetoric is ridiculed throughout the series, is almost exclusively depicted as angry, erratic, and destructive. In one episode, she wields a flamethrower and burns down a building with her parliamentary colleagues inside (PHON, 2022d [01:04–01:10]). In another, while participating in an Easter egg hunt, Thorpe is depicted throwing a tantrum after opening an egg to find that it is white, jumping up and down yelling: "White chocolate? I hate white chocolate! I hate it! I hate it! I hate it!" (PHON, 2022c [01:12–01:21])—the "joke" being that as a staunchly anti-colonial and anti-racist Aboriginal woman, Thorpe allegedly hates everything white. These characterizations lean heavily on the racist "angry Black woman" trope (Ashley, 2014).

By articulating far-right messages through political satire and parody, the *Please Explain* miniseries constitutes a novel form of political party campaigning in the Australian context. Importantly, the series was extremely successful in generating coverage, albeit often negative, in traditional news media, with the cartoon covered in at least 55 different media articles, across publications like *The Guardian Australia*, *The Daily Mail*, and the *Sydney Morning Herald*. In generating such extensive mainstream media coverage, the *Please Explain* series has played a role in shaping, albeit for a limited time, mainstream news agendas and in turn increasing mainstream attention to the far right's preferred issues, like anti-Indigenous racism and criticism of multiculturalism. As well as a feeding back into it, the videos are themselves a reflection of Australian political culture. Perhaps the clearest example of this is the intersections between the mocking of Aboriginal and Torres Strait Islander people in the *Please Explain* series, and the negative stereotypes of "angry Black women" and Australian editorial cartoons, two of which, we discuss below.

Perhaps the most infamous recent example is a drawing published by editorial cartoonist Bill Leak in the national broadsheet *The Australian* entitled "Dear Old Dad" (Leak, 2016a). The image depicts an Aboriginal man, beer can in hand, unable to recall the name of his son, who a police officer holds by the scruff of his neck. The cartoon was condemned by several Aboriginal and Torres Strait Islander organizations, labelled racist by Coalition Indigenous Affairs Minister Nigel Scullion, and was the subject of more than 700 complaints to the Australian Press Council as well as a complaint to the Human Rights Commission under the Racial Discrimination Act. According to Leak and *The Australian*, the cartoon was satirizing Aboriginal parenting in response to revelations regarding the treatment of detainees at the Northern Territory's Don Dale Youth Detention Centre that. had recently been the subject of an investigative report, showing teenage boys being assaulted, stripped naked, and teargassed. As Leak wrote the day after the cartoon's publication, "if you think things are pretty crook for the children locked up in the Northern Territory's Don Dale Youth Detention Centre, you should have a look at the homes they came from" (Leak, 2016b).

Beyond the plainly racist thrust of the satire, that Aboriginal parents are too drunk and disorderly to even know the names of their children, the rendering of the characters draws on well-trod anti-black caricatures, like exaggerated big red lips, and protruding brows. Not an isolated incident, the cartoon was but the latest in a series of racist, anti-Aboriginal cartoons by Leak. Consider two other infamous examples, published in *The Australian* in 2006, one of which depicted intimate-partner violence in Aboriginal communities as "an enriching cultural experience," while in another an Aboriginal man claimed that "rape's out, bashing's out—this could set our culture back by 2000 years!" (Media Watch, 2016).

The intersection of anti-black racism and misogyny can be seen in the example of a drawing by editorial cartoonist Mark Knight in the Melbourne daily newspaper, the *Herald Sun*. The cartoon, published on September 11, 2018, sought to satirize and mock heated exchanges between the tennis champion Serena Williams and the chair umpire during the 2018 U.S. Women's Open finals. In the cartoon, Williams is caricatured as an angry, tantrum-throwing child, jumping her racquet with a baby's dummy (Tate, 2022). She is drawn with dehumanizing facial features, reminiscent of the racial caricatures of Afro-American people during Jim Crow, most notably the oversized mouth and large, red lips. In a complaint to the Australian Press Council, William's pose, leaning forward with arms jutting out to the side, was further described as "ape-like" (Tate, 2022). The newspaper responded to accusations of racism by defending the cartoon and its author, with a front-page montage of Knight cartoons the next day that warning that "self-appointed censors" were going to ruin satire, and that "our new politically correct life will be very dull indeed" (in ABC, 2018). Fortunately for Knight and the *Herald Sun*, in 2019 the Press Council ruled in their favor, declaring the cartoon was "non-racist," simply a caricature of someone who is angry (Tate, 2022)—just another "angry Black woman."

## 7.5.2 Internet Memes

Internet memes are groups of digital items that share common characteristics constituting a template, created, and circulated with awareness of each other (Shifman, 2014). Memes have become an important tool in the far right's communications arsenal, popularized by the rise of the so-called "alt-right" in the U.S. Memes are generally humorous in tone, providing them with great virality. Among the Australian far-right, memes have been a prominent part of the digital visual culture of far-right alternative media (McSwiney et al., 2021). Thanks to their virality, humorous, and ironic tone, and remixing of popular culture iconography, memes help the far right to broaden their appeal by deactivating social boundaries and softening the ideological content (Askanius, 2021). Memes have been used directly as part of the recruitment strategy of Australian far right groups, with their humorous and ironic memes employed "as a mechanism of (self-radicalization)" (Zhang & Davis, 2022, p. 10). At the same time, memes can also be used as part of an antagonistic communication strategy to mock and ridicule minorities and political opponents (Tuters & Hagen, 2020), by targeting them for harassment.

The circulation of memes in Australian political culture has not been limited to the far right. There has been an increased use of memes by both political parties in election campaigns (Leon, 2020) and among social movements in campaigns for social justice (Frazer & Carlson, 2017). However, there are also instances where explicitly far-right memes have penetrated mainstream political culture. Most notably, in the online content shared by Clive Palmer, an Australian mining magnate and leader of the right-wing, small United Australia Party (UAP). In the lead up to the 2019 federal election, Palmer began posting far-right memes on his verified Facebook and Twitter pages. This included memetic elements like Pepe the Frog, Trash Bird, as well as gestures to the anti-Semitic "happy merchant" meme (McSwiney, 2018)|. The far-right pivot in UAP and Palmer memes first came to public attention with the establishment of the "Palmy Army" Facebook group. The group, set up and moderated by Palmer's official Facebook page and so directly linked to the party, was soon flooded with racist, sexist, and homophobic content, including Palmer in a Nazi SS uniform and a several political opponents in a gas chamber (Esposito, 2018).

Despite a pledge to moderate the group (Caccamo, 2018), Clive Palmer's personal social media accounts continued to post far-right content up to the 2019 federal election. Though electorally marginal, Palmer and by extension the UAP, is able to command significant media attention in Australia. As such, the (re)production of far-right iconography and themes in the party's memes is a worrying instance of far-right political humor influencing mainstream Australian political culture.

Below, we examine two such examples in depth. The first, posted to Clive Palmer's verified Facebook and Twitter accounts, depicts Palmer himself appearing in a cartoon rendition of the military uniform worn by Adolf Hitler, though the swastika armband and Iron Cross medal of the original have been left out (Fig. 7.1).

Palmer's hands have been colored green in reference to Pepe the Frog. Present also is the Facebook sticker-cum-meme Trash Bird. Both were popular memes among the so-called alt-right. At the top of the image is the text "Do you want meme war," which echoes the "Great Meme War" of the 2016 U.S. presidential campaign, an online culture war predominantly between Trump's far-right supporters and supporters of the Sanders and Clinton Democratic campaigns.

The second image, in true memetic tradition, is a remix of a remix. The original cartoon was drawn by American far-right political cartoonist Ben Garrison, and was commissioned by Mike Cernovich, an American Men's Rights activist best known for his involvement in the "Pizzagate" conspiracy, a direct precursor to QAnon (McSwiney, 2018). The initial remix that circulated on image boards like 4chan and 8chan, inserted the antisemitic "happy merchant" holding a copy of the Protocols of the Elders of Zion, a fabricated antisemitic text outlining a conspiracy for Jewish world domination. The version that appeared on Clive Palmer's Facebook page includes some edits (Fig. 7.2).

It replaces the antisemitic "happy merchant" figure with then-leader of the ALP Bill Shorten. It also includes a minor change in the title of the book from the "Protocols of the Elders of Zion" to the "Protocols of the Globalist World Bankers," another euphemism for Jews in far-right circles. It also incorporates the logos of several Australian trade unions, and the face of the Greens then-leader Richard Di Natale, as contributors to "social degeneracy."

These two examples are a startling indication of the ease at which even the most explicit far-right content can seep into mainstream political culture through the cover of edgy political humor and satire. Despite the explicit, far-right content in both

7  Far-Right Political Humor in Australia: Culture, Coloniality, and Exclusion         155

**Fig. 7.1** Far-right meme depicting Clive Palmer as Hitler-Pepe. April 1, 2018 (Reproduced from Facebook, 2023)

examples, the genre conventions of internet memes, namely ironic distance and a humorous tone, allowed Palmer and the UAP to play them off as "just a joke."

## 7.6  Discussion and Conclusion

Our analysis of Australian far-right internet memes, political cartoons, and digital animations reveals the interconnected, co-constitutive, and mutually informing relationship between political humor and culture. Through the findings of our Critical Discourse Analysis and Thematic Analysis, we argue that Australian far-right humor

**Fig. 7.2** Far-right meme decrying race mixing, same sex marriage, feminism, drug decriminalization, and trans rights as 'social degeneracy'. September 14, 2018 (Reproduced from Facebook, 2023)

does not reflect the egalitarian ideals found in mythologized imaginaries of Australian culture, but rather they reflect and (re)produce the colonial realities of Australian society. That is, a white hegemonic nation defined by the ongoing colonial dispossession of Indigenous Peoples and a racialized unease with the multicultural fabric of Australia. This reflects what Ghassan Hage (1998, p. 21) refers to as the pervasive discourse of Anglo-decline, defined as:

A discourse which bemoans what it sees as the attack on the core British values of traditional white Australia and where the figure of the ordinary 'mainstream' Australian, the 'traditional Aussie battler' is perceived as a victim of a conspiracy to change the very nature of the country.

In this sense, it can be argued that they capture the *true* essence of Australian political culture. The three cultural products analyzed in this chapter demonstrate how political humor is shaped by the cultural context in which it takes place. We found that the *Please Explain* miniseries leans heavily on *intertextuality and interdiscursivity*, requiring a strong understanding of Australian political, social, and popular culture to holistically comprehend the references made throughout the series. Likewise, while the far-right memes did reproduce international far-right iconography and themes, these were frequently articulated alongside Australian cultural references. Thus, while there is a clear and consistent thread to international far-right discourses and cultures, reflecting the global and interconnected nature of political communication (Chadwick, 2017), we argue that Australian far-right humor maintains a *distinctly Australian lens*.

We found the use of cartoons and animations by the Australian far-right to be particularly noteworthy given the key role of cartoons in translating, (re)producing, and shaping Australian cultural history. As argued by Phiddan (2014, p. 83), "[...] cartoons have been one of the most prominent ways in which artists have tried to articulate a distinctive colonial or Australian voice and stance; in particular, they have played a crucial role in the development of the larrikin myth within Australian media and culture." Moreover, Phiddan notes the importance of political cartoons in shaping Australian culture: "Cartoons have seldom, if ever, changed the course of history, but this body of work certainly played a substantial role in the making of a distinctive cultural identity" (Phiddan, 2014, p. 84). Thus, we can see the far-right clearly engaged in cultural production work through the use of memetic and animated political communication.

However, while we argue that Australian far-right humor reflects a more accurate picture of white Australian colonial culture, we also found that it frequently contradicted the fantastical mythologies of Australian culture as rooted in egalitarianism, fairness, and multiculturalism. Our sample of far-right humor was replete with exclusionary, offensive, and discriminatory jokes that served to essentialize and stereotype minorities. In particular, we found a strong current of anti-Indigenous racism present in the *Please Explain* series and among the political cartoons published in the *Australian* newspaper. This, we argue, can only be explained through the lens of a white, racial settler, colonial politics articulated through the medium of satire and comedy. The function of this exclusionary and racialized humor is, as Pérez (2017, p. 985) suggests, to "[...] target, discipline, marginalize, and alienate groups and individuals who are othered."

The effect of far-right political humor is to simultaneously foster greater social affiliation with an in-group and create greater social distance against out-groups (Pérez, 2017). In this respect, we argue that far-right political humor is a consequential form of political communication and should not be dismissed as frivolous and unserious due to its comedic and ironic genre. We agree with Basu and Zekavat (2021, p. 1, emphasis added) that political humor represents "*substantial* political action conducted through amusing means." In this context, we see the use of humor by the Australian far right as playing an important role in mainstreaming and normalizing their political project. By employing genres such as cartoons and caricatures, the Australian far-right "[...] cleverly play with the fictionalization of politics" (Wodak, 2021, p. 5) to expand their exclusionary agenda while minimizing accusations of racism and sexism with claims that it is "just a joke" (Pérez, 2022). We argue that far-right political humor works to extend the boundaries of the sayable (Wodak, 2021), and through its use of humorous popular culture references has the potential to reach a more mainstream audience. Therefore, we view far-right political humor as certainly being shaped by Australian settler colonial culture, but also working to shape culture through the mainstreaming and normalization of far-right discourses. This co-constitutive dynamic between political humor and culture is noted by McAllister (1997, p. 5):

The activities that are generally considered to be political within a society are moulded by the culture of the society within which they take place. Political culture, in turn, represents the accumulation of all the shared experiences and historical events that have occurred within a society, and which have evolved to shape that society's character and outlook on the world.

In summary, the findings of this chapter demonstrate that far-right political humor is heavily embedded in the cultural context in which it takes place. While there are clear connections to international far-right cultures, Australian reactionary humor maintains a distinctly "Australian" flavor. It is hoped that this chapter, along with the others in the volume, will advance our understanding of not only the culturally contingent and co-constitutive nature of political humor, but also its strategic function in our highly mediatized and hybridized political landscape.

## References

ABC. (2018). *Serena Williams cartoon: Herald Sun publishes defiant front page defending Mark Knight*. https://www.abc.net.au/news/2018-09-12/serena-williams-herald-sun-republishes-mark-knight-cartoon/10235886

Ashley, W. (2014). The angry black woman: The impact of pejorative stereotypes on psychotherapy with black women. *Social Work in Public Health, 29*(1), 27–34. https://doi.org/10.1080/19371918.2011.619449

Askanius, T. (2021). On frogs, monkeys, and execution memes: Exploring the humor-hate nexus at the intersection of neo-Nazi and alt-right movements in Sweden. *Television & New Media, 22*(2), 147–165. https://doi.org/10.1177/1527476420982234

Ata, A. W. (2010). Entrapping Christian and Muslim Arabs in racial cartoons in Australia: The other anti-Semitism. *Journal of Muslim Minority Affairs, 30*(4), 457–462. https://doi.org/10.1080/13602004.2010.533438

Basu, S., & Zekavat, M. (2021). Contingent dynamics of political humor. *The European Journal of Humor Research, 9*(3), 1–8. https://doi.org/10.7592/EJHR2021.9.3.635

Billig, M. (2001). Humor and hatred: The racist jokes of the Ku Klux Klan. *Discourse & Society, 12*(3), 267–289. https://doi.org/10.1177/0957926501012003001

Billig, M. (2005). *Laughter and ridicule: Towards a social critique of humor*. SAGE.

Braun, V., Clarke, V. & Weate, P. (2016). Using thematic analysis in sport and exercise research. In B. Smith & A. C. Sparkes (Eds.), *Routledge handbook of qualitative research in sport and exercise* (pp. 191–205). London: Routledge.

Braun, V., & Clarke, V. (2013). *Successful qualitative research: A practical guide for beginners*. Sage.

Bhatia, A. (2013). Critical discourse analysis: History and new developments. In C. A Chappelle (Eds.), *The encyclopedia of applied linguistics* (pp. 1–8). Oxford: Wiley-Blackwell.

Bromfield, N., Page, A., & Sengul, K. (2021). Rhetoric, culture, and climate wars: A discursive analysis of Australian political leaders' responses to the black summer bushfire crisis. In O. Feldman (Ed.), *When politicians talk* (pp. 149–167). Springer. https://doi.org/10.1007/978-981-16-3579-3_9

Brown, K., Mondon, A., & Winter, A. (2023). The far right, the mainstream and mainstreaming: Towards a heuristic framework. *Journal of Political Ideologies, 28*(2), 162–179. https://doi.org/10.1080/13569317.2021.1949829

Caccamo, C. (2018). Clive Palmer is locked in a battle with the alt-right for control of his own Facebook meme page. *Junkee.* https://junkee.com/clive-palmer-facebook-memes/148917

Chadwick, A. (2017). *The hybrid media system: Politics and power (2nd Edition).* Oxford University Press.

Clarke, V., & Braun, V. (2017). Thematic analysis. *The Journal of Positive Psychology, 12*(3), 297–298. https://doi.org/10.1080/17439760.2016.1262613

Cunneen, C., & Russell, S. (2017). Social media, vigilantism and indigenous people in Australia. In *The Oxford encyclopedia of crime, media, and popular culture.* Oxford University Press.

van Dijk, T. A. (2015). Critical discourse analysis. In D. Tannen, H. Hamilton, & D. Schiffrin (Eds.), *The handbook of discourse analysis* (2nd ed., pp. 352–371). Wiley-Blackwell.

Dunn, K., Loosemore, M., Phua, F., & Ozguc, U. (2011). Everyday ethnic diversity and racism on Australian construction sites. *International Journal of Diversity in Organizations, Communities, and Nations, 10*(6), 129–148. https://doi.org/10.18848/1447-9532/CGP/v10i06/38939

Elias, A., Mansouri, F., & Paradies, Y. (2021). *Racism in Australia today.* Springer. https://doi.org/10.1007/978-981-16-2137-6

Esposito, B. (2018). I regret to inform you the Clive Palmer meme page has turned into a racist alt-right cesspit. *BuzzFeed.* https://www.buzzfeed.com/bradesposito/palmy-army

Evason, N. (2016). Australian culture: Core concepts. *SBS Cultural Atlas.* https://culturalatlas.sbs.com.au/australian-culture/australian-culture-core-concepts

Frazer, R., & Carlson, B. (2017). Indigenous memes and the invention of a people. *Social Media + Society, 3*(4). https://doi.org/10.1177/2056305117738993

Filardo-Llamas, L., & Boyd, M. S. (2018). Critical discourse analysis and politics. In J. Flowerdew & J. E. Richardson (Eds.), *The Routledge handbook of critical discourse studies* (pp. 312–327). Routledge.

Greene, V. S. (2019). "Deplorable" satire: Alt-right memes, white genocide tweets, and redpilling normies. *Studies in American Humor, 5*(1), 31–69.

Grigg, K., & Manderson, L. (2015). "Just a joke": Young Australian understandings of racism. *International Journal of Intercultural Relations, 47,* 195–208. https://doi.org/10.1016/j.ijintrel.2015.06.006

Hage, G. (1998). *White nation: Fantasies of white supremacy in a multicultural society.* Routledge.

Hakoköngäs, E., Halmesvaara, O., & Sakki, I. (2020). Persuasion through bitter humor: Multimodal discourse analysis of rhetoric in internet memes of two far-right groups in Finland. *Social Media + Society, 6*(2). https://doi.org/10.1177/2056305120921575

Leak, B. (2016a). Dear old dad. *The Australian.* https://www.theaustralian.com.au/commentary/cartoons/bleak-gallery/image-gallery/ee8a4ef1032a9da5a37c87ecb7f34c5c

Leak, B. (2016b). *What are you tweeting about? I listen to indigenous truth tellers.* https://theaustralian.com.au/opinion/another-twitter-feed-tantrum-about-my-cartoons/news-story/e4a2db48aa81424c6daf54a4497330e6

Leon, L. (2020). Cartoons, memes and videos. In A. Gauja, M. Sawer & M. Simms (Eds.), *Morrison's miracle: The 2019 Australian federal election* (1st edn, pp. 473–498). ANU Press. https://doi.org/10.22459/MM.2020.24

Machin, D., & Mayr, A. (2012). *How to do critical discourse analysis: A multimodal introduction.* Sage.

Maddison, S. (2019). *The colonial fantasy: Why white Australia can't solve black problems.* Allen & Unwin.

Matamoros-Fernández, A., Rodriguez, A., & Wikström, P. (2022). Humor that harms? Examining racist audio-visual memetic media on TikTok during Covid-19. *Media and Communication, 10*(2), 180–191. https://doi.org/10.17645/mac.v10i2.5154

McAllister, I. (1997). Political culture and national identity. In B. Galligan, I. McAllister, & J. Ravenhill (Eds.), *New developments in Australian politics* (pp. 3–21). MacMillan.

McSwiney, J., Vaughan, M., Heft, A., & Hoffman, M. (2021). Sharing the hate? Memes and transnationality in the far right's digital visual culture. *Information, Communication & Society, 24*(16), 2502–2521. https://doi.org/10.1080/1369118X.2021.1961006

McSwiney, J., & Sengul, K. (2023). Humor, ridicule, and the far right: mainstreaming exclusion through online animation. Television & New Media. https://doi.org/10.1177/15274764 2331213816

McSwiney, J. (2018). Alt-right memes and Clive Palmer's return to politics. *PoP Politics Australia.* https://poppoliticsaus.wordpress.com/2018/09/27/alt-right-memes-and-clive-palmers-return-to-politics/

Media Watch. (2016). Fear, loathing and the right to offend. *ABC.* https://www.abc.net.au/mediawatch/episodes/fear-loathing-and-the-right-to-offend/9972908

Meyer, J. C. (2000). Humor as a double-edged sword: Four functions of humor in Communication. *Communication Theory, 10*(3), 310–331.

Moffitt, B., & Sengul, K. (2023). The populist radical right in Australia: Pauline Hanson's one nation. *Journal of Language and Politics, 22*(3), 306–323. https://doi.org/10.1075/jlp.22132.mof

Moloney, G., Holtz, P., & Wagner, W. (2013). Editorial political cartoons in Australia: Social representations & and the visual depiction of essentialism. *Integrative Psychological and Behavioral Science, 47*(2), 284–298. https://doi.org/10.1007/s12124-013-9236-0

Moloney, G. (2007). Social representations and the politically satirical cartoon. In G. Moloney & I. Walker (Eds.), *Social representations and identity: Content, process, and power* (pp. 61–84). Palgrave Macmillan. https://doi.org/10.1057/9780230609181_5

Mondon, A. (2013). *The mainstreaming of the extreme right in France and Australia: A populist hegemony?* Ashgate.

Mondon, A., & Winter, A. (2020). *Reactionary democracy: How racism and the populist far right became mainstream.* Verso.

Moreton-Robinson, A. (2015). *The white possessive: Property, power, and indigenous sovereignty.* University of Minnesota Press.

Papastergiadis, N. (2004). The invasion complex in Australian political culture. *Thesis Eleven, 78*(1), 8–27. https://doi.org/10.1177/0725513604044544

Pauline Hanson's *Please Explain.* (n.d.). https://www.youtube.com/watch?v=QIUefMHjoKQ&ab_channel=PaulineHanson%27sPleaseExplain

Pérez, R. (2017). Racism without hatred? Racist humor and the myth of "colorblindness." *Sociological Perspectives, 60*(5), 956–974. https://doi.org/10.1177/0731121417719699

Pérez, R., & Ward, G. (2019). From insult to estrangement and injury: The violence of racist police jokes. *American Behavioral Scientist, 63*(13), 1810–1829. https://doi.org/10.1177/0002764219842617

Pérez, R. (2022). *The souls of white jokes: How racist humor fuels white supremacy.* Stanford University Press.

Phiddan, R. (2014). Cartoons and cartoonists. In B. Griffen-Foley (Ed.), *A companion to the Australian media* (pp. 83–85). Australian Scholarly.

PHON. (2022a). Australia day (No. 11). In *please explain.* https://www.youtube.com/watch?v=jwxRyOIzVhM&ab_channel=PaulineHanson%27sPleaseExplain

PHON. (2022b). How to pass the buck (No. 14). In *Please explain.* https://www.youtube.com/watch?v=IpWuMF5LOkY&embeds_referring_euri=https%3A%2F%2F. https://www.onenation.org.au%2F&embeds_referring_origin=https%3A%2F%2F. https://www.onenation.org.au&source_ve_path=Mjg2NjY&feature=emb_logo&ab_channel=PaulineHanson%27sPleaseExplain

PHON. (2022c). Campaign Easter special (No. 22). In *Please explain.* https://www.youtube.com/watch?v=YgjmTqky7cQ&ab_channel=PaulineHanson%27sPleaseExplain

PHON. (2022d). Immigration numbers (No. 9). In *Please explain.* https://www.youtube.com/watch?v=YgjmTqky7cQ&ab_channel=PaulineHanson%27sPleaseExplain

PHON. (2022e). The progressive dream (No. 16). In *Please explain.* https://www.youtube.com/watch?v=fHspovdUld4&ab_channel=LesPat

Piccini, J. (2020). Myth and myth-making. In J. M. Lewis & A. Tiernan (Eds.), *The Oxford handbook of Australian politics*. Oxford University Press. https://doi.org/10.1093/oxfordhb/9780198805465.013.3

Seal, G. (2004). *Inventing ANZAC: The digger and national mythology*. University of Queensland Press in association with the API Network and Curtin University of Technology.

Sengul, K. (2022a). The role of political interviews in mainstreaming and normalizing the far-right: A view from Australia. In O. Feldman (Ed.), *Adversarial political interviewing* (pp. 357–375). Springer. https://doi.org/10.1007/978-981-19-0576-6_18

Sengul, K. (2022b). 'I cop this shit all the time and I'm sick of it': Pauline Hanson, the far-right and the politics of victimhood in Australia. In E. Smith, J. Persian & V. J. Fox (Eds.), *Histories of fascism and anti-fascism in Australia* (1st edn, pp. 199–217). Routledge. https://doi.org/10.4324/9781003120964-11

Sengul, K. (2023). The shameless normalization of debasement performance: A critical discourse analysis of Pauline Hanson's Australian, far-right, populist communication. In O. Feldman (Ed.), *Debasing political rhetoric* (pp. 107–123). Springer. https://doi.org/10.1007/978-981-99-0894-3_7

Sharpe, S., & Hynes, M. (2016). Black-faced, red faces: The potentials of humour for anti-racist action. *Ethnic and Racial Studies, 39*(1), 87–104. https://doi.org/10.1080/01419870.2016.1096405

Shifman, L. (2014). *Memes in digital culture*. MIT Press.

Tate, S. A. (2022). Serena Williams and anti-black woman hate: Contempt, love, friendship, shame. In *The Routledge companion to gender and affect* (pp. 70–78). Routledge.

Tuters, M., & Hagen, S. (2020). (((They))) rule: Memetic antagonism and nebulous othering on 4chan. *New Media & Society, 22*(12), 2218–2237. https://doi.org/10.1177/1461444819888746

Waling, A. (2019). *White masculinity in contemporary Australia: The good ol' aussie bloke* (1st ed.). Routledge. https://doi.org/10.4324/9781315207766

Ward, R. (1977). *The Australian legend*. Oxford University Press.

Weaver, S. (2011). Jokes, rhetoric and embodied racism: A rhetorical discourse analysis of the logics of racist jokes on the internet. *Ethnicities, 11*(4), 413–435. https://doi.org/10.1177/1468796811407755

Windisch, S., & Simi, P. (2022). More than a joke: White supremacist humor as a daily form of resistance. *Deviant Behavior*. 1–17. https://doi.org/10.1080/01639625.2022.2048216

Wolfe, P. (2006). Settler colonialism and the elimination of the native. *Journal of Genocide Research, 8*(4), 387–409. https://doi.org/10.1080/14623520601056240

Wodak, R. (2021). *The politics of fear: The shameless normalization of far-right discourse* (2nd ed.). Sage.

Wodak, R., & Meyer, M. (Eds.). (2009). *Methods of critical discourse analysis* (2nd ed.). Sage.

Zhang, X., & Davis, M. (2022). E-extremism: A conceptual framework for studying the online far right. *New Media & Society*, 1–17. https://doi.org/10.1177/14614448221098366

Ziv, A. (2009). The social function of humor in interpersonal relationships. *Society, 47*(1), 11–18. https://doi.org/10.1007/s12115-009-9283-9

**Kurt Sengul** is a Postdoctoral Research Fellow (MQRF) in the Department of Media, Communications, Creative Arts, Language, and Literature at Macquarie University, Australia. His research interests include the communicative and discursive strategies of the contemporary far-right. He has published widely in journals such as Critical Discourse Studies, The Journal of Language and Politics, Media International Australia, and Communication Research and Practice

**Jordan McSwiney** is a Postdoctoral Research Fellow at the Centre for Deliberative Democracy and Global Governance at the University of Canberra. His research focuses on the far right, with an interest in their ideology, organizing practices, and use of the internet. His work has been published in Information, Communication & Society, New Media & Society, and Patterns of Prejudice, among others.

# Part II
# Political Humor in the Broadcast Media

# Chapter 8
# Televised Political Satire in Poland: Historical Roots and Social Implications of Stereotypical Representations of Politicians and Politics

**Agnieszka Kampka and Katarzyna Molek-Kozakowska**

**Abstract** Since the fall of communist rule in Poland in 1989, political imagery has diversified due to new media technologies and a variety of content providers abolishing a monopoly over official representations of Polish governance and politics. Parallel to this, traditional cabaret and political satire moved from club stages and festivals to television stations and streaming platforms. In this study, we trace the evolution of televised satire through three case studies of popular televised parody programs. We explore how historical references are recontextualized for comic effect, and how stereotypes are reproduced to satirize ruling elites or expose personal vices and incompetence. However, rather than explaining the instantiations of satire in specific episodes, we focus on the narrative devices and construction of characters to capture the cumulative functions of humor. We show how the analyzed productions draw on cultural schemes and metaphors of governance, power, and partisan politics, especially harshly ridiculing autocracy and corruption. The study exposes the ambivalence of political satire: its role in cultivating citizenship by demystifying the processes behind the exercise of power on the one hand, and in diminishing trust in politicians and depoliticizing the citizens on the other hand.

---

A. Kampka (✉)
Department of Sociology, Institute of Sociological Sciences and Pedagogy, Warsaw University of Life Sciences, Warsaw, Poland
e-mail: agnieszka_kampka@sggw.edu.pl

K. Molek-Kozakowska
Department of English, Institute of Linguistics, University of Opole, Opole, Poland

Department of Creative Communication, Vilnius Gediminas Technical University, Vilnius, Lithuania

K. Molek-Kozakowska
e-mail: molekk@uni.opole.pl

© The Author(s), under exclusive license to Springer Nature Singapore Pte Ltd. 2024
O. Feldman (ed.), *Communicating Political Humor in the Media*,
The Language of Politics, https://doi.org/10.1007/978-981-97-0726-3_8

## 8.1 Introduction

This chapter presents political satire from the perspective of a diachronic comparative overview of three selected Polish televised productions that were popular with audiences at different times following 1989 that marked the fall of communism in Poland. Through a contextual, genre-based, thematic analysis, we trace the main devices through which changing media affordances and cultural patterns have shaped the content and humor of political satire. We look especially at cases where the target of satire is a political issue, governmental decision, or leader persona that deserves to be ridiculed. The examples of satirical productions studied here are parodist in nature and draw on the tradition of Polish cabaret, presented via a wider cultural background of politicized artistic performance.

As national culture is likely to influence, even determine, the most popular types of humor, we focus on episodes, narrative devices, or satirical sketches that include historical references, ethnic stereotypes, and representations of individual political leaders. While these references constitute common knowledge for most Poles, in satirical productions they are recontextualized for comic effect, mainly through metaphor, irony, or the absurd. As it is usually futile to try to explain a humorous statement without losing much in translation, we approach selected examples of Polish satirical productions in a synthetic way by focusing on identifying salient cultural schemes and metaphors representing governance, power, and partisan politics that are satirized. We also posit some cultural explanations of the fact that a substantial part of Polish satire depends on relatively negative associations with corruption or oppressiveness. It also produces humor by exaggerating personal vices and the incompetence of political leaders.

The chapter's Sect. 8.2 provides a historical overview of post-1989 Poland, focusing on its cabaret tradition, and reviews the literature on Polish political satire. Section 8.3 offers a description, analysis, and interpretation of three landmark satirical productions: (1) Marcin Wolski's "Polish Zoo" [*Polskie zoo*] (1991–1994) that captured the uncanny processes of democratic institutional formation in Poland; (2) a series of sketches by a group called The Cabaret of Moral Anxiety [*Kabaret Moralnego Niepokoju*] on "Government in Session" [*Posiedzenie rządu*] that satirized Prime Minister Donald Tusk's administration (2011–2014); and (3) a comedy series by Robert Górski—"The Chairman's Ear" [*Ucho prezesa*] (2017–2019). The latter portrayed behind-the-scenes politics by the ruling party, as imagined from the perspective of Jarosław Kaczyński, the chairman of Law and Justice Party. In Sect. 8.4, we explain the functions of political satire of the kind described in the study, and the social implications of such forms of political humor that are based on parody, stereotype, and the absurd.

## 8.2 Polish Political Humor

Since the fall of communism in Poland in 1989, scholars who trace the evolution of Polish political discourse point to the historical and ideological meta-narratives that shaped Polish political expression, including political humor (e.g., Kampka, 2009). They note that the main historical determinants of Polish politics have been rather serious, even tragic: from Polish Romanticism's yearnings for nationhood, to the World War II resistance to Nazi and Soviet occupation, and from the oppressive Stalinist regime to the bloody suppressions of the workers' Solidarity movement and the persecutions of the Polish Catholic Church. By the 1990s, the Polish political sphere was divided ideologically into left-wing (post-communist) parties and democratic (post-Solidarity) parties with new political voices that sometimes brought an influx of colloquial language or coarse humor into the public arena (Kampka & Molek-Kozakowska, 2023, pp. 192–193). In recent decades, the Polish party system has been characterized by ideological fluidity and a transitory and pragmatic nature of political affiliations and coalitions.

In the 2000s the fragmentation of the Polish political scene intensified, with the renewed struggle between various visions of political reality, given Poland's joining the EU (Cap, 2021). This time the biggest wedge was driven between pro-European liberals, as represented by Civic Platform [*Platforma Obywatelska*], together with other progressive parties on the one hand, and conservatives, nationalists, and populists represented by Law and Justice [*Prawo i Sprawiedliwość*, L&J henceforth] on the other hand. Meanwhile, politicians' attempts to exploit the media to increase political capital gave rise to various scandals, blunders, and absurdities that were hard to pass up for Polish comedy authors and cabaret artists. For example, one of the recurrent allegations is related to the politicians' inclination to dispatch secret services to spy on and discredit their political opponents. Even though the motives of conspiring and abusing power are invoked in cabaret sketches in humorous ways, they are exposed as an actual threat to democracy (cf. Molek-Kozakowska & Kampka, 2021).

The Polish cabaret tradition encompasses club and festival genres of mostly political humor that predominantly draws on longer stand-up sketches. Adamczyk (2012, pp. 24–25) reviews examples of humor of top Polish cabaret groups and concludes that most contents have been heavily commercialized in the 2000s. The witty and avant-garde humor of traditional cabaret has been scaled down to be consumable by mass (TV) audiences, and good political satire is relatively rare.

It is noted that much humor derives from recontextualization of Polish history, or the excessive reliance on ridiculing social conventions and manners. For example, comic effect is created when historical names (e.g., of heroic leaders, won battles, significant events) are used in conversational contexts to satirize current issues or politicians e.g., by comparing their ineptitude to the heroism of past leaders. Moreover, since the advent of the mass and streaming media, diverse Polish cabaret festivals and club life were being replaced by live or filmed productions, with anything from a puppet show to satirical news/interview mock-ups and filmed situational comedy (Fox, 2011).

Some of the most memorable earlier televised productions include "Olga Lipińska's Cabaret" [*Kabaret Olgi Lipińskiej*] 1990–2010, parodying the incompetence and scheming of politicians (vis-à-vis the naiveté of the voters) by means of intelligent artistic performances. "TV Daily News Bulletin" [*Dziennik telewizyjny*] 1995–2005 by Jacek Fedorowicz, for example, cited prominent politicians in doctored interviews, or in edited statements, so that the message became absurd or hilarious, while making conspicuous all the linguistic puns and blunders imaginable.

Political satire regarding the transition from the communist to the capitalist system and mentality was taken up in Wojciech Mann and Krzysztof Materna's "Program to Be Continued Soon" [*Za chwilę dalszy ciąg programu*] 1988–1994. The sketches chastised Polish stereotypical vices, including the poor work ethic and defiance of leadership. Political entertainment was at the core of "What a Shame" [*Ale plama*] 1998–2004, a weekly satirical "current affairs" program created by Krzysztof Piasecki and Janusz Rewiński for the commercial TVN station. The two "anchors" would comment on the events of each passing week by focusing on parliamentary bickering, or inept political PR maneuvering. They would wittily, but sometimes controversially, attack historical heroism and religious traditions, or debase political visions by alluding to the drunken haziness of their originators. Later on a distinctly parodist tone was exploited in Szymon Majewski Show's "Chatting in the crowd" [*Rozmowy w tłoku*] 2005–2011, where made-up actors impersonated prominent politicians and imitated their speech and behavior mannerisms while discussing current political decisions in a ridiculous re-framing of the talk-show format.

The politically tinted humor in Polish satirical productions has relied on subverting what is culturally decent, interpersonally polite, and politically correct (Adamczyk, 2012; Błąd, 2013; Fox, 2011). It also grounds the comic effect in the evocations of ethnic stereotypes. The performers routinely engage in stylizations that tend to be very crass in the case of accent and garb, especially as regards Polish historical "others": Germans, Russians, Americans, Czechs, Arabs, Jews. It is not uncommon to exaggerate a given stereotypical trait to the point of absurd. However, it is far from unique to have political satire as a means of embodying and performing international relations in Poland, as various forms of satirical stereotyping are very often involved in national identity production and contestation in the dense geopolitical context of Europe (Saunders & Bruun, 2021).

The Polish scholarly literature on entertainment through satirical outputs finds multiple ways in which the Polish are also self-stereotyped (Adamczyk, 2012; Brzozowska & Chłopicki, 2015; Burzyński, 2012; Piwowarczyk, 2021). In political sketches, Poles are often represented as undisciplined, drunk, overtly patriotic, miserly, thieving, complaining, religious, intolerant, or xenophobic. All these qualities have some historical roots and cultural bases. For example, the unruly and self-interested behavior of Polish nobles in the eighteenth century (undisciplined), the influence of the Catholic Church and faith during the nineteenth century oppression (religious), the military resistance movements of the WWII period (patriotic), and the social resistance of the political and economic regime of the post-war communist state where it was an act of courage to steal from, or sabotage, the industrial plants that provided profits to the communists (thieving).

The historical turbulence and oppressive existence in much of the twentieth century left some trace on cultural norms of Polish behavior. According to social psychologists who explore Polish humor in social interactions, Poles do not tend to smile or laugh as an expression of the default norm of cheerfulness, in contrast to, for example, Americans (Wojciszke & Baryła, 2005). In fact, being very friendly to strangers seems odd and suspicious, because it may mask insincerity or ulterior motives. For most Poles, routine interpersonal interactions are expected to at least start off from a neutral or serious baseline. It is typical to engage in mutually reinforced complaining (about well-publicized political issues), and to express cautious pessimism rather than unbridled optimism.

Laughter and humor tend to be eagerly embraced in closer relationships and often sparked by unusually funny situations or jokes. Self-directed humor is not very common, while other-directed humor (even if sexist or racist) is traditionally, and often unreflexively, reproduced (Szarota, 2006). In addition, Poles' performance of everyday humor, and particularly its ironic expression, involve much negativity. This is manifested in the default assumption that the social world is marked by unfairness and exploitation, and the self is a victim of powerful institutions of evil leaders (Wojciszke & Baryła, 2005, p. 39). This "norm of negativity" might be diminishing with globalization, but it is still likely to underpin the pessimistic, absurdist, or surreal strands in Polish televised political satire.

## 8.3 Case Studies

According to Dynel (2021), political satire often implies negativity, aggressiveness, or at least an incisive commentary directed at a specific target. One subtype of satire is parody, where performers, through acted characters or puppets, recontextualize a fragment of political action, a situational encounter or a speech, for comic effect. Sometimes this involves verbalizing what could potentially be uttered by a parodied person. This is usually accompanied by voice quality, speech mannerisms, and gesticulation or facial expressions typical of the parodied politician. The impersonation that is required in political satire is usually well received, as the parodied persons are well known public figures. Nevertheless, parody, be it in internet memes, video shorts, stand-up comedy, or televised satirical entertainment, requires knowledge of the political issue in contention, recognition of a political figure, and activation of various linguistic and cultural references. While mainly entertaining, Polish parody is sometimes seen as debasing (Kampka & Molek-Kozakowska, 2023). It might offer illuminating social criticism but it can also breed political cynicism.

The following case studies have been selected to trace the evolution not only of stereotypical representations of politics and politicians over time, but also of the changes in the use of satirical devices and modes of parodic expression. The analysis focuses on specific thematic and formal characteristics of humor in three popular televised productions. The latest one receives the most attention due to the build-up of narrative and expressional devices that are deployed in contemporary cabaret performance that creatively draws on stand-up comedy, pop-culture, and mediatized political confrontainment.

### 8.3.1 "Polish Zoo"—Musical Cabaret on TV

"Polish Zoo" [*Polskie zoo,* PZ henceforth] was a weekly satirical magazine broadcast by public TV between 1991 and 1994, created by Marcin Wolski and two popular comedic actors Jerzy Kryszak and Andrzej Zaorski (Wolski, 1991, 2003). Apart from them, the characters on screen were animal puppets (hence the zoo metaphor) representing the most recognizable public figures of the time, mainly politicians. The great popularity of the program was attributed to its light-weight music-infused humor comprehended even by youngsters (Kończak, 2008, p. 253), caricature-based parody, and nuanced intertextual references to what was happening on the Polish political scene (Fox, 2011, p. 113).

The puppet show convention draws on theatrical performances of the carniva-lesque, where puppets embodied easily identifiable leaders, the plotlines were based on current rivalries, and entertainment was derived from transgression, absurdist humor, rhyming, and music. This televised form of cabaret is considered typically Polish, as it is based on a long tradition of poets and artists who were politically engaged but had to dodge censorship and suppression of free speech (Błąd, 2013, pp. 130–131). In this manner, PZ was notable for bridging serious topics and buffoon-like staging, politics and circus, public sphere folklore, engagement, and distancing (Nabiałek, 2022, pp. 113, 117). Needless to say, PZ characters were mainly flat, stereotypical personas (a typical manual worker, a journalist, a voter) played by the two actors put into encounters with individual politicians impersonated by animal puppets with a capacity to show emotional states with facial expressions—inspired by Jim Henson's Muppets, as well as its French political counterpart Le Bébête Show.

PZ's main character was the lion as the king of the zoo that represented Poland's first democratically elected President Lech Wałęsa. The match between animals and politicians was based partly on physical appearance and partly on their well-known behavioral mannerisms. It exploited both the biological affordances (predator/prey, large/small, animal/bird) and the symbolic meanings of the animal in (popular) culture. In this vein, the first Polish Prime Minister after 1989, Tadeusz Mazowiecki, was rather phlegmatic, so he was represented by a tortoise; the twin politicians Lech and Jarosław Kaczyński were two inseparable but destructive hamsters (a possible reference to cartoonish Chip and Dale squirrels); the politician Donald Tusk was cast as a duck (on the immediate phonic association with the American icon of Donald Duck). Interestingly, in spin-off fashion, prominent politicians of the next administration were also given animal alter egos in press caricatures and TV satire: the post-communist President Aleksander Kwaśniewski was a wild boar, a left-wing

PM Włodzimierz Cimoszewicz—a pitiful jackal, and Andrzej Lepper (the leader of a peasant party)—a pig (Błąd, 2013).

In episode 75 relating to an international summit, international leaders are also brought on stage: UK's John Major as a unicorn (in reference to the British coats of arms symbol), Bill Clinton as an American buffalo (by origin and stature), Germany's Helmut Kohl as a walrus, France's François Mitterrand as a rooster, and Russia's Boris Yeltsin as a bear. While the puppets activated both physical and cultural associations with particular, anthropomorphized animals, the voice providers additionally made fun of accented speech and individual tonality characteristic of those leaders. Needless to say, the characters' dramatic interactions on screen can be interpreted at least on two levels: in terms of the divided political world as well as the hierarchical animal kingdom, strengthening the parodic effect.

PZ episodes are typically composed of a playful theme tune and a recited song that summarizes the major developments of the week with intermittent flashes of TV footage from news agencies. Selected issues of political importance or social currency are then elaborated into a few sketches featuring animals and actors before the episode closes with another musical piece. The theme song is an anchoring element that explores the zoo metaphor through visuals and lyrics—after the "zookeepers are gone" (the end of Soviet control of Poland), the animals have to arrange some system where they live freely (political transformation from communism to liberal democracy), but being animals they are not up to it (political leaders are not competent enough) and the zoo turns into a mess (party rivalry displaces common good, not much is done). The bittersweet tone of the lyrics implies the general disappointment with political elites, particularly the lack of speedy economic or political progress. The overall focus of the program is often on exploiting Polish leaders' political ineptness and blunders.

PZ uses not only animal-related connotations but also ethnic stereotypes and historical references, as for example in episode 75 devoted to a hypothetical political summit between Western and Eastern leaders. While the French delegation brings along their own cheese, the Americans want more hot-dogs, and the British check tabloid coverage of the royal family. At some point all the delegations, including the Russians, whose rail system is crippled by a strike, meet in Warsaw at what appears to be an international replica of "the round table" (historic 1989 talks between Polish communists and the Solidarity movement) arranged by the lion Lech Wałęsa. Unfortunately, the table itself is by then eaten by mold and woodworm, and needs to be covered by a tablecloth made of the Polish flag.

The symbolic summit—halfway between Paris and Moscow—is to enable closer international cooperation. To this end, funny interviews are screened featuring inhabitants of East and West Germany after the fall of Berlin Wall, in fact highlighting their disparities rather than mitigating their differences. It becomes apparent that Western leaders are not very open to helping post-communist countries financially, instead promising to send experts and managers to give guidance and advice, provided the easterners contain the migration. This is accompanied by a scene of poor-looking people demanding to be "granted asylum in Disneyland." All the worst fears of the other side are raised: Italian mobsters are afraid of eastern criminal gangs, while

Poles are worried that land and businesses will be bought up by wealthier foreigners. To mitigate the differences, all the delegations agree to put on a good show, just to cover up the fact that nothing useful could be agreed on.

This episode is but one example of a variety of humor types, themes, and enactments, based on (1) playing with parodic convention by exaggerating the problematic issues to the point of absurdity; (2) recontextualizing historical events and decisions, and (3) exploiting the stereotypes and myths of the other. The storylines are relatively complex, and conflicts tend to be overrepresented. The overall message of the episode reinforces the negative perception of international politics, which is based on appearances and propagandistic tricks. Other episodes present Polish politics as inefficient, chaotic, even dishonest and exploitative at times, and use metaphors of laundry making, cheating at card games, bazaar bargaining, drunken partying, children's play, mental institution. For example, episode 39 castigates parliamentary debates as inane babbling that does not allow anything to be done, episode 100 criticizes illogical and inconsistent law-making, and episode 24 points to one common trait of all politicians—hunger for power.

To conclude, when PZ was made, political rivalry was at its highest in Poland and the transition was in full swing, so there were many disagreements about legal and political concepts, economic priorities, and ways of approaching historical aspects of the communist period. However, PZ may not have been able to help the viewers deal with the new challenges; instead, it perpetuated negative stereotypes of politics as an absurd circus of animalistic characters, or as a vision of reality taken straight from a drunken party. Perhaps in the chaotic reality of post-communist transformation, any reason for laughter was appreciated, but PZ lacked constructive ways of dealing with this chaos, and the metaphor of the zoo, albeit entertaining, cannot be considered as productive in building social capital for responsible citizenship and civic society.

### 8.3.2 The Cabaret of Moral Anxiety and "Government in Session" Sketches

The Cabaret of Moral Anxiety [*Kabaret Moralnego Niepokoju*, KMN henceforth] is a well-known Polish group of four core stand-up comedians who started performing in 1996 and who have occasionally invited other actors, musicians, and performers to their shows or televised sketches. The group has been enormously popular in Poland over the last decades and is frequently invited to either outdoor cabaret festivals or studio shows, while the video clips of their sketches are available on streaming platforms, CDs, and YouTube. The members of the group include Robert Górski, Przemysław Borkowski, Mikołaj Cieślak and Rafał Zbieć.

The group is known for a series of sketches called "Government in Session" [*Posiedzenie rządu*], initially produced by TVP (Polish Public Television), and distributed between 2008 and 2014. The sketches were intended to satirize the inept behaviors and decisions taken by the ruling liberal government of Civic Platform, and the Prime Minister of the time, Donald Tusk, impersonated by the leader of the comedy group Robert Górski (Cieślik & Górski, 2012). The overall frame of the sketch series sees the cabinet ministers convening at a table, unprepared and disorganized because they are in a hurry to play their next soccer match (an allusion to Donald Tusk being an avid amateur soccer player). The football metaphors and, more generally, sports references such as UEFA Euro 2012, FIFA World Cup 2014, resonated with the public, but at the same time normalized the trivialization of politics as a sport or a match with extended scenarios of sports-related pathologies, such as doping, unfair play, and corrupt refereeing.

The government politicians were often ridiculed by KMN as ignorant of the specifics of political strategy, and mainly motivated to please the leader or ready to do any outrageous thing to defeat the opponents—especially the conservative L&J. They were also shown to be corruptible when it comes to using public funds for personal gratification. For example, when the question about the time to close the meeting is asked, allusions are made to a junior minister who was caught wearing expensive wristwatches that he had failed to declare as personal assets. A few sketches were based on the conceit of showing how power and privilege lead to political arrogance, particularly how the politicians in their own circle expressed disdain for the idea of "serving for the good of the common people"—their voters. The sketches reinforced the image of one's joining politics as an opportunity to enrich oneself, not serve.

Some other sketches referred to well-entrenched ethnic and national stereotypes, as when portraying Polish politicians embarrassing themselves amongst the world leaders of the time: U.S.A.'s Barack Obama, U.K.'s David Cameron, Germany's Angela Merkel, and France's Francois Hollande. Needless to say, much of the malicious satire was targeted at Vladimir Putin and the Russians that support his regime, especially after the annexation of Crimea and attacks on eastern Ukraine. For example, in an episode entitled "Sanctions" [*Sankcje*], the faux cabinet is trying to come up with ideas how Poland could harm Russia by imposing economic and trade sanctions, always ending up with a solution that actually harms Poland and Poles' interests even more than Russia's economy. KMN satirically attacked the politicians who like to act before they think, who are swayed by pride more than reason, and who do not seek advice from experts, but insist that "they know better" and have a mandate to act as they please because they were elected.

The satirical humor of many "Government in Session" sketches was based on the following generally accepted preconceptions about politics: politicians will appear to call for efficiency and austerity during crises, but they will not economize on their own salaries and expenses (episode entitled "Plumbers" [*Hydraulicy*]); politicians will appear to be educated, hard-working and well-informed, whereas in fact most of the time they make wild guesses and emotion-driven decisions (episode "Government Reshuffle" [*Rekonstrukcja rządu*]); politicians will try to ingratiate themselves with the public by appearing to have high moral values, whereas in fact they are deeply self-interested, even corrupt, and use all sorts of manipulative propaganda (episode "JPII Generation" [*Pokolenie JPII*], which demystifies the appearances of the moral upper ground reintroduced into the Polish public sphere during Pope John Paul II's beautification proceedings).

Apart from KMN's hilarious and acerbic comic devices deployed with the aim to expose the preconceptions about politicians in Poland, the show was appreciated for its parodic acting, props, and actors' bodily expressivity. The showrunners established their names for replicating exaggerated speech mannerisms of political figures and creatively exploiting linguistic puns and double entendre.

### 8.3.3 *"the Chairman's Ear" Comedy Series*

"The Chairmam's Ear" [*Ucho prezesa*, UP henceforth] is a political satire comedy series broadcast in 2017–2018 (special episodes also in 2019) available on YouTube, streaming platforms, and cable TV. Robert Górski from KMN is the showrunner and has the lead role along with a cast made up of Polish comedic actors as supporting actors. The series showcases the chairman of the ruling L&J party—Jarosław Kaczyński—and his closest collaborators and government ministers who seek an audience in his party headquarters' office. It is worth noting that Robert Górski has been able to impersonate two radically different political figures—not attributable only to his acting skills but rather to the Polish audience's ability to follow cabaret conventions of political satire. After all, each political figure is an actor, even in real life.

All of UP's characters are parodies of well-known persons, who however are not recognized by their physical likeness or name dropping, but by speech and behavior mannerisms and functional dependence on the chairman for party decision-making. One of the rather pitiful characters is the impersonation of President of Poland Andrzej Duda, who represents the same conservative political orientation. Despite being the head of state, he is portrayed as subordinate to the chairman, politically ineffective and dependent on the party talking points for his official stances on domestic and international issues. To ridicule his irrelevance, the showrunners make other characters mispronounce his name, or forget who he is.

The series was enormously popular in 2017, when it was the third most trending topic and the most searched Polish series title on Google. It has remained popular since then and is often re-watched, even though some political references have lost their currency. Nevertheless, the cumulative humor, metaphorical images of governing, and stereotypes of politicians are appealing and continue to shape perceptions of politics in Poland. Each episode is based on an interaction between the chairman Jarosław Kaczyński and a few other characters in relation to a specific issue of political relevance. The figure of the chairman is ambivalent: on the one hand, he is presented as totally in control of his political party and ruthless with the opposition; on the other hand, he is shown to be devoted to his closest advisors, his female secretary—Basia—who acts as his gatekeeper and loyal advocate, and his cat. The figure of the chairman can also be interpreted as a metaphor of any leader—a person who grows to be addicted to power, and the manipulations that come with it. Shown to be suspicious, scheming, disdainful, and prone to humiliating even his closest collaborators in order to control them, the chairman is able to resort to strategic lying, preemptive personal attacks, spin-doctoring, and playing with human vanity and greed to get what he needs.

The comic effect in UP is often achieved by contrasting the mannerisms of a jolly elderly man with the aura of a larger-than-life political strategist. In the visual domain, the representation of the secluded office setting where strategic decisions are taken might remind many viewers of the scenes with Vito Corleone from "The Godfather." At times, this setting overlays the storyline with additional connotations of politics resembling mob-like arrangements. Alternatively, the interpretative frame for political interactions can be sourced from the medieval feudal system, with loyal servants given estates and positions, or from the intrigue-ridden royal court, where courtiers compete for favor, and constant compliments and proofs of loyalty are expected from them (Kananowicz, 2020, pp. 170–171).

The narrative of many episodes is driven by individual politicians (the Prime Minister, senior MPs, ministers, heads of executive agencies that are under media scrutiny for corruption) coming to the chairman for advice or called in to be reprimanded. Each of them is deferential, confused, shown to be incompetent, or ignorant. In addition, the motif of Polish patriotism is an important narrative device of the series: everything the chairman does is driven to strengthening Poland and making the nation more recognizable worldwide. UP parodies such extreme patriotic zeal and exposes the xenophobic or chauvinistic elements of the conservative party's leadership (with the iconic "globe of Poland" model sitting on the side table).

The chairman's trusted advisor is Mariusz—a party crony and political figure with many functions bestowed upon him over time due to his unwavering loyalty, even servility. With exaggerated mannerisms and lack of wit, the character is created to make fun of public figures who never show any initiative, free will, or personal stance, but who embody blind obedience to authority. This could be a powerful critique of autocratic governance and party discipline but for the fact that Mariusz is a funny simpleton—a Sancho Panza to a Don Quixote (Górski & Sobień, 2019).

Basia, the chairman's helpful and attentive secretary, provides a down-to-earth outlook on politics and represents a typical conservative Pole and L&J party loyalist. The conversations she conducts just outside of the chairman's office, mainly with visitors eager to secure an audience with "the boss," complement the political narrative with comments that touch on the absurdities of some everyday lifestyle aspects in contemporary Poland. For example, she praises her own daughter for standing up to bullies of a new pupil but tells her to stop doing so when she learns that the new pupil is a Muslim immigrant. This is because L&J politicians are known for demonizing Muslim immigrants as a threat to Polishness.

A recurrent theme in UP are Polish-American diplomatic relations and the need to maintain a friendly personal relationship with President Donald Trump by keeping up appearances of agreeing with American agendas, while trying to push party interests. At some point, the chairman refuses to take a call from the White House and talk to the American president, because "he is not of sufficiently high rank." This is how the showrunners ridicule the megalomaniac scale of self-importance assumed by a party leader who has been elevated to a position of the Poland's "savior" by a very loud minority of enthusiastic supporters. The chairman's obvious blunder and diplomatic crisis is not even pointed out to him by his cronies, because "obviously he knows best."

In other episodes, the videoconferences the chairman conducts with President Trump are used to indicate that despite claiming to make the world a safer and better place, especially when it comes to containing Russian imperialism, their autocratic personalities, persistent ignoring of advice, and a penchant for lying make the situation in both countries even more precarious. In an ironic twist, at some point President Trump is addressing Mr. Kaczyński as Putinsky. The irony of such episodes is that the character representing Poland's President Duda, who is actually authorized by the Polish constitution to take defense-related decisions, is still patiently waiting outside of the chairman's office, with a collection of magnets he brought from his diplomatic visits, hoping to get further instructions.

One of the episodes is devoted to another diplomatic crisis, this time between Poland and Israel (as well as the U.S.A. and Ukraine). The tensions were aggravated by a bill accepted by the L&J-controlled parliament that decreed it a punishable crime to attribute Nazi crimes to Polish nationals or the Polish state, which would likely threaten freedom of speech and academic research on the responsibility for the Shoah or on other controversial or complex cases of aiding and abetting. While the Prime Minister is defending the law despite the protests from the Israeli ambassador, outside the office the director of the state foundation for the promotion of Poland abroad is displaying kitschy gadgetry subsidized by a sizable governmental grant. New ideas on how to remedy the stereotype of Poles as anti-Semites abroad reveal the director's deeply rooted prejudices: He will not invest in a movie production about heroic Poles because "the Jews in Hollywood will not have it"; neither will he authorize a film about how the Polish people have been helping the refugees because "that could attract more of the so-called refugees" and the government does not want that.

Back in the chairman's office, the Prime Minister emphasizes how he cares about "Polish-Israeli dialogue," but he makes offensive comments when the Israeli ambassador tries to speak in Polish. UP shows clearly that the party establishment's claim to want dialogue is just an empty gesture, because in truth they are hardliners who will never engage in negotiations. Instead, the ruling party will come up with all kinds of false claims and faulty generalizations, for example by arguing that "people who aided or abetted crimes against the Jewish people simply could not have been true Poles." The chairman's lesson to the Prime Minister is "to never apologize," "always deny," "say what people want to hear, not what you want to say." Such a cynical and duplicitous image of politics pervades many episodes, pointing to the ugly reality behind the public pomp and propaganda of ministerial success stories.

A range of metaphorical clichés is used in UP to activate specific ways of thinking about autocratic politics and to infuse the relatively serious narrative with comedic humor. One is the overarching schema in the title "The ball of the dummies" [*Bal manekinów*], the opening episode of UP's season four, which calls out the ridiculously fake identities of many political figures and their habit of dressing up, and staging performances. The characters are told to never speak their mind, but rather follow the party's talking points. However, in other episodes the chairman is also represented as a "dog-tamer" who keeps even senior politicians on a leash, since he can withhold rewards or act on the threat of removing them. In this scenario, the politicians can be represented as different breeds of dogs with various anthropomorphized properties. In yet another metaphorical script, the issues of (lack of) control are portrayed in colloquial Polish terminology of a "mad house" [*dom wariatów*], or a "negotiating table" [*stół negocjacyjny*], whose setup can obviously be orchestrated and managed by the chairman. The historical reference to the Round Table negotiations [*obrady Okrągłego Stołu*], where post-communists and the Solidarity movement had to discuss the peaceful transition to a democratic free-market statehood, is deconstructed by UP showrunners. There is no longer any need for negotiations because "the party is always right" with this chairman. Sitting at the "right side of the table" also enables the party members to reach out for the best resources and to profit from their lucrative positions.

The issue of corruption is taken up in several episodes that touch on the uneasy relations Poland has had with the European Commission under L&J rule. The European Union represents for L&J an adversary (because it requires the government to follow EU directives), as well as a patron (because its funding schemes allow poorer countries, such as Poland, to develop faster). Needless to say, the series shows that Poland's representatives to EU institutions tend to be the chairman's most servile political cronies, who plead with him to obtain these lucrative posts in order "to save for retirement," or "to arrange for their children to get jobs there." The candidates for European posts are not only instructed by the chairman to resist EU policy and endorse traditional Polish values, but also are given the green light to lie if necessary, or even to defraud, provided they do not get caught. Ironically, the characters that visit the chairman resemble delegates that have been caught lying about their official expenditures. Despite being aware of their inclination for cheating, the chairman rewards them for their blind loyalty, and downplays the damage they do—after all they cheat the EU (not us).

Keeping up double moral standards, dealing with European institutions or elsewhere, is exposed in UP as the actual backbone of L&J's political strategy. The chairman's decisions are rarely predictable, because the rules of the political game shift depending on the scope of the crisis at hand. In addition, party propaganda is made to be more convincing and believable than the reality. UP creators tend to use the conceit of blurring fact and fiction, or right and wrong, to play with the viewers who also can no longer be certain to what extent the absurdist script coincides with Polish political reality. For example, the last episode shows the chairman, Mariusz, and Basia leaving the office and walking into a Warsaw street gradually falling out of their character roles and becoming regular people wondering where to have lunch.

With its varied narrative devices, ambivalent representations of the ruling elites, and complex satirical humor, UP has been subjected to many reviews in the Polish blogosphere, some focusing on the ideological dimension, and others on the resonance of ridicule regarding any hierarchically organized institution plagued by incompetence and ignorance or fawning and favoritism.[1]

## 8.4 Conclusion: Functions of Satirical Humor and Implications for Citizenship

The parodic case studies presented above exploit the entertaining potential of historical references and stereotypes for popular consumption. Admittedly, the fictitious scenes presented in the sketches, the verbalizations attributed to parodied politicians, and the use of recontextualization of political decisions may offer comic relief in relatively serious contexts. Satirical humor techniques identified here include irony, hyperbole, metaphor, pun, anthropomorphism, and absurdism. As is the case with similar types of Polish cabaret outputs, these productions rely on the following devices: (1) animal characteristics for a humorous experience, (2) the ambiguity of ethnic and national stereotypes (both exploited and critiqued), and (3) comic effects of presenting high-ranking public figures with their flaws and vices, "just like us."

In the analyzed cases, satire tends to act as the Polish audience's buffer against negative sentiments and disenchantment, when either incompetent or wicked individuals are called out, and self-serving motivations of political decision-makers are brought to light. The examples also show how the culturally validated expressions of the Polish "norm of negativity" have been incorporated into satirical televised productions. The studied sketches testify to how freedom of speech and democratic entitlements to critique the vices of people in power are exercised by comedians and artists (Piwowarczyk, 2021). It can only be applauded that the mature and sophisticated forms of political humor have been created for entertainment purposes, rather than being the only way to bypass censorship in an illiberal state, as it used to be in the past, before 1989 (Wolski, 2003).

Following the claims made by Adamczyk (2012) about the Polish cabaret tradition, it is possible to observe that in the three productions presented and analyzed here, humor can be appreciated on two levels. For the general public, the funny songs (PZ), crude jokes, and crass references to Polish vices (KMN), or flat characters used to ridicule current top politicians (UP), are the basis for comic effects leading to popular entertainment. However, for politically savvy viewers, the witty puns and recontextualized historical or diplomatic references can offer another layer of satirical content and spectators' pleasure. It would seem that the intellectual traditions and rhetorical characteristics of the anti-authoritarian streak of Polish cabaret are

---

[1] For example, positive reviews and analyses by the liberal *Oko Press* https://oko.press/komedia-dworsko-polityczno-biurowa-nas-smieszy-uchu-prezesa, mixed or positive by centrist *Rzeczpospolita* https://www.rp.pl/plus-minus/art9501651-jan-boncza-szablowski-scheda-czyli-ucho-prezesa-pelne-niespodzianek, and negative in the conservative *Fronda* https://www.fronda.pl/a/ucho-prezesa-analiza-polityczna-tresci-serialu,100229.html.

still resorted to. For example, the romantic Polish yearnings for strong national leadership and international recognition can be discerned in PZ's lion figure, and the hierarchical organization of the allegorical zoo. The notion of leadership also informs both KMN's blatant criticism of the government as an inane amateurish soccer team, and very acutely, UP's depiction of the chairman's persona, who is capable of single-handedly bearing responsibility for decision-making on all political issues (Kananowicz, 2020).

Contemporary Polish televised political satire cannot be described fully without commenting on its stylistic alignment with pop culture, with its entrenched clichés, preoccupation with kitsch and debasing humor. For some scholars of the Polish cabaret tradition, the televised productions tend to reinforce stereotypes, even though the showrunners were aiming to deconstruct them (Adamczyk, 2012, p. 25). This is because demystifying cultural schemas requires more subtlety and sophistication than is needed in the cases of the blunt reproductions of stereotypes. For example, not all politicians are corrupt, not all Poles are anti-Semites, not all Germans have Nazi connections, and not all Russians are evil. However, harmful stereotypes and sweeping generalizations have to be presupposed for the comic effect to work in a given sketch. Also, the frequency of comedians' resorting to ridiculing speech mannerisms, lampooning physical appearances, and relying on exaggeration and crude metaphors, or double entendres with sexual innuendos, demonstrates an increasing popular demand for such humor devices (Brzozowska & Chłopicki, 2015; Burzyński, 2012).

In the Polish cabaret tradition, political humor serves as a coping strategy or reaction against negativity of some cultural schemas and strenuous processes of political transformation (Wojciszke & Baryła, 2005). Witty political jokes might make it easier to comprehend ambiguous political realities or might provide a new perspective to understand political processes, particularly the nature of political conflict. For example, PZ tames the fears related to a rapid post-communist transition, KMN introduces Poles to the techniques of modern political marketing, and UP unveils the power play behind party politics in the state's institutions and media.

Related to such "mental hygiene" functions of political humor are its educational and community-building functions, particularly mobilization and solidarity building (Saunders & Bruun, 2021). This is notably the case with humor that pervades alternative public spheres in the blogosphere and enables communing around exclusively satirical content, absurdly fake news, and meme factories. These supposedly aim to ease the psychological burden of having to endure living in the world of permacrisis (Dynel, 2021). It is not uncommon, as shown by Feldman and Borum Chattoo (2019), that satirical humor exposing hypocrisy and bigotry can also be a useful tool for changing social attitudes, deconstructing negative stereotypes (e.g., of refugees), and providing new ways of expression for social movement activism.

However, there is also scholarship contending that political humor that is overwhelmingly and crudely parodist tends to lower citizens' trust in politicians by taking away their dignity (Holm, 2017). Since dignity is a prerequisite of a functioning public sphere, and is mandatory for respectful deliberation and reasoning, deploying overtly satirical humor could be counterproductive to public engagement.

According to Holm (2017), even when humor is not explicitly critical, the satirical comic effects potentially threaten leaders' ethos and their ability to productively contribute to policymaking. While parody might be entertaining for increasingly desensitized audiences, it is important to consider the unwanted cumulative byproducts of ever-present ridicule, and to keep in check commercial enterprises that profit from debasing politicians (Kampka & Molek-Kozakowska, 2023).

As pointed out by Koivukoski (2022), humor is used in the construction of identities, and to set agendas, frame issues, and legitimize or delegitimize political ideas and people. The recontextualization of stereotypes to expose the bigotry of those who accept them is seen as a pathway to their critique. In the contemporary Polish cabaret, political satirists create public controversies for certain provocative or aggressive forms of humor to resurface in the media and spark reflection. The case studies presented above illustrate that the potential effects of political humor are gradual rather than instant. While parody might not be able to radically change political attitudes, it can nevertheless encourage people to become more aware of their own entrenched perceptions of political conflicts and public issues.

# References

Adamczyk, M. (2012). The linguistic picture of the Polish history in the sketches of contemporary cabaret groups. *Acta Universitatis Lodziensis. Folia Linguistica, 46*, 7–27. http://hdl.handle.net/11089/5930. (in Polish).
Błąd, Ł. (2013). *Political satire in festival and television programs of cabaret groups in 1989–2007.* University of Warsaw (Doctoral dissertation). (in Polish).
Brzozowska, D., & Chłopicki, W. (2015). *Polish humor.* Tertium. (in Polish).
Burzyński, R. (2012). *Metaphors as a tool of cognizing politics and exerting political influence.* University of Warsaw (Doctoral dissertation). (in Polish).
Cap, P. (2021). *The discourse of conflict and crisis.* Bloomsbury.
Cieślik, M., & Górski, R. (2012). *How I became a prime minister: Conversations full of moral anxiety.* Znak. (in Polish).
Dynel, M. (2021). COVID-19 memes going viral: On the multiple multimodal voices behind face masks. *Discourse & Society, 32*(2), 175–195. https://doi.org/10.1177/0957926520970385
Feldman, L., & Borum Chattoo, C. (2019). Comedy as a route to social change: The effects of satire and news on persuasion about Syrian refugees. *Mass Communication and Society, 22*(3), 277–300. https://doi.org/10.1080/15205436.2018.1545035
Fox, D. (2011). Polish cabaret—tradition and contemporaneity. *Postscriptum Polonistyczne, 2*, 123–141. (in Polish). https://www.journals.us.edu.pl/index.php/PPol/article/view/10707
Górski, R., & Sobień, M. (2019). *How I became the chairman.* Czerwone i Czarne. (in Polish).
Holm, N. (2017). *Humor as politics: The political aesthetics of contemporary comedy.* Springer. https://doi.org/10.1007/978-3-319-50950-1
Kampka, A., & Molek-Kozakowska, K. (2023). Incivility in the language of the powerful: Debasing and derisive discourse in Polish politics. In O. Feldman (Ed.), *Debasement and dumping: Cynicism and irony in parliamentary discourse* (pp. 191–208). Springer.
Kampka, A. (2009). *Persuasion in political language.* Wydawnictwo Naukowe Scholar. (in Polish).
Kananowicz, T. (2020). The image of Jarosław Kaczyński in the TV series "The Chairman's Ear." In A. Kiklewicz (Ed.), *Image as a category in communication theory, cultural anthropology and textual semiotics* (pp. 167–177). Uniwersytet Warmińsko-Mazurski. (in Polish).

Koivukoski, J. (2022). *Political humor in the hybrid media environment: Studies on journalistic satire and amusing advocacy.* University of Helsinki (Doctoral dissertation).

Kończak, J. (2008). *From Tele-echo to Polish Zoo: The evolution of TVP programming.* Wydawnictwa Akademickie i Profesjonalne. (in Polish).

Molek-Kozakowska, K., & Kampka, A. (2021). Talking politics: The influence of historical and cultural transformations on Polish political rhetoric. In Feldman, O. (Ed.) *When politicians talk: The cultural dynamics of public speaking* (pp. 111–127). Springer. https://doi.org/10.1007/978-981-16-3579-3

Nabiałek, M. (2022). Nativity play—between sacrum and profanum. The genealogy of the show. *Tematy i konteksty, 12*(17), 102–121. https://doi.org/10.15584/tik.2022.7. (in Polish).

Piwowarczyk, K. (2021). The increasing potential of comical political satire as an element of activity and political activism in the world. In M. Mikołajczyk & A. Tasak (Eds.), *The generational potential of politics* (pp. 473–489). Instytut Wydawniczy Książka i Prasa. http://hdl.handle.net/11716/10849. (in Polish).

Saunders, R. A., & Bruun, H. (2021). "Radio Free Sweden": Satire, national identity, and the un-PC (geo)politics of Jonatan Spang. *Global Society, 35*(1), 84–101. https://doi.org/10.1080/13600826.2020.1828297

Szarota P. (2006). *The psychology of smiling: A cultural analysis.* Gdańskie Wydawnictwo Psychologiczne. (in Polish).

Wojciszke, B., & Baryła, W. (2005). The culture of complaining, or the psychological traps of expressing discontent. In M. Drogosz (Ed.), *How do the Poles lose? How do the Poles win?* (pp. 35–52). Gdańskie Wydawnictwo Psychologiczne. (in Polish).

Wolski, M. (1991). *From Yalta to Magdalenka or the political sketch in a provincial place.* Tommy. (in Polish).

Wolski, M. (2003). *The third funniest part of cabaret supereditor's picks: Polish Zoo, Cabaret Sixty, Extra-Marital Counselling, Polish Sketches.* Zsyp. (in Polish).


**Agnieszka Kampka** is Assistant Professor at the Department of Sociology at Institute of Sociological Sciences and Pedagogy, Warsaw University of Life Sciences, Poland. She is the author of journal articles and book chapters in the fields of political and visual rhetoric, and the author, editor, and co-editor of 10 books and monographs, including *Persuasion in Political Language* [in Polish] 2009; *Public Debate: Changes in Social Communication Standards* [in Polish] 2014; and *Rhetoric, Knowledge, and the Public Sphere*, 2016. She is the chief editor of the journal Res Rhetorica (https://resrhetorica.com).

**Katarzyna Molek-Kozakowska** is Associate Professor and Head of the Department of English at the Institute of Linguistics, University of Opole, Poland, and Senior Research Fellow at Department of Creative Communication, Vilnius Gediminas Technical University, Lithuania. With over 80 published articles and chapters, and seven authored or co-edited monographs, she specializes in political discourse, journalism and mediated communication, rhetoric, and critical literacy. She co-edits the journal Res *Rhetorica* (https://resrhetorica.com).

# Chapter 9
# Sexist Humor in Public Facebook Comments Delegitimizing Female Politicians Within Montenegro's Patriarchal Culture

**Milica Vuković-Stamatović**

**Abstract** Despite its recent formal steps taken to ensure more gender equality, Montenegro still has a rather patriarchal culture. A United Nations Development Program (UNDP) supported study (2021) found that 90% of Montenegrin female politicians have experienced discrimination due to their gender, and 70% have experienced violence during their political work. Against such a background, this study explores sexist humor targeting female Montenegrin politicians in public Facebook comments. Comments that elicited humorous reactions were considered humorous, whereas those that reduced female politicians to sexual objects, presented them as caricatures conforming to traditional gender roles in Montenegrin society, or played on the stereotype of women's inferiority, were regarded as sexist. Although a significant share of the commentary was sexist, most often such comments were not recognized as humorous. In those that were recognized as humorous, the most prevalent themes included women's bodies and appearance, the sexual objectification of female politicians, personality flaws stereotypically associated with women (such as lacking intelligence or being evil), and encouraging women to prioritize family over politics.

## 9.1 Introduction

Patriarchal cultures favor men as sources of primary power and moral authority, as well as holding dominant roles of political leadership, social privilege, and property. While virtually all cultures are patriarchal to some extent and prescribe gendered roles for women and men (James, 2010), some cultures are much more patriarchal than others. This has consequences regarding the position and opportunities women have within such cultures, including the political realm.

---

M. Vuković-Stamatović (✉)
Faculty of Philology, University of Montenegro, Podgorica, Montenegro
e-mail: vmilica@ucg.ac.me

Montenegro is one of the countries that has traditionally been seen as very patriarchal, the remnants of which are still present to a large extent in modern-day, Montenegrin society (Rakonjac, 2020). Misogyny towards women in Montenegro's public, particularly political, sphere is becoming increasingly common (UNDP, 2021). This is also valid for political communication in social media, having become true political fora. *Inter alia*, Facebook has become a forum for discussing politics, with the risk of incidental exposure to political stances while on Facebook rising considerably (Funk & Coker, 2016). Facebook users' comments on politicians might have a significant offline impact on political attitudes, political knowledge, and political engagement (cf. Funk & Coker, 2016), as well as on the credibility of politicians (Housholder & LaMarre, 2014). Humorous, sexist comments are among the tactics attempting to silence the voices of female politicians, sending them the message that the internet and politics are a place where they do not belong (Southern & Harmer, 2019).

Sexist humor is a form of disparaging humor, that under superiority theory assumes that amusement is the result of a feeling of superiority evoked when recognizing the misfortunes or the infirmities of the other (Ferguson & Ford, 2008). Critical discourse approaches to humor urge researchers to study the negative aspects and potential consequences of such humor (Drakett et al., 2018). This form of humor is typically directed at women, playing on cultural stereotypes that see women as weak, less intelligent than men, overly emotional, dishonest, or which focus on their physical appearance. As such, its use may lead to further marginalization of women in society (Bemiller & Schneider, 2010).

In the context of social networks, many factors favor the expression of sexism (including humorous sexism) against female politicians—among them certainly is the anonymity of online interaction, an insufficient legal framework for supervising it, as well as the policies of online platforms (Southern & Harmer, 2019, p. 191). However, "it is crucial not to lose sight of the deeply embedded social and cultural factors that legitimate the denigration of women," Southern and Harmer warn (ibid.). With this in mind, in this chapter I study sexist humor that Facebook users have recently directed at female Montenegrin politicians in connection with the country's patriarchal culture. The corpus analyzed here consists of commentary responding to 24 Facebook posts of various Montenegrin news outlets, relaying the statements issued by twelve Montenegrin female politicians with their photographs. The study is corpus-based, and the general perspective is that of Critical Discourse Analysis.

## 9.2 Theoretical Background and Literature Review

In this section of the chapter, the focus is first on Montenegro's patriarchal culture. Attention is then shifted onto sexist humor, especially when directed at female politicians, and finally onto the discourse strategy of delegitimization connected to such disparaging humor.

## 9.2.1 Montenegrin Patriarchal Culture

As noted above, Montenegro is a rather patriarchal society, despite recent formal steps taken to ensure more gender equality. Throughout Montenegro's complex history patriarchal culture has been its defining feature, shaping the roles and the expectations of men and women, reinforced by the country's historical experience of foreign domination and occupation that often saw men taking on a leadership role in the resistance against these external threats (Erdeljanović, 1981). In the country's traditional patriarchal culture, the woman is socialized to be a self-sacrificing, steadfast, loyal, and obedient mother and wife from her early childhood, but also to raise her children in the spirit of patriarchy (Rakonjac, 2020, p. 63). Furthermore, "in this culture, woman is taught that man has unquestionable precedence, that he is 'head of the family' and the condition for its survival" (Mašnić, 2011, p. 86).

Despite the significant social changes that have occurred in Montenegro over the past century, such patriarchal attitudes continue to be prevalent in contemporary Montenegrin culture. Because of this, women in Montenegro continue to face significant barriers to achieving gender equality, including discrimination in the workplace and limited political representation. Thus, almost half of Montenegrin citizens believe that businesswomen with successful careers and in high positions in society are neglecting their families, with as many as 60% of them believing that for the sake of family's well-being and a better quality of the life of children it is preferable that men work and that women devote their time to the household and family instead (UNDP, 2021). Furthermore, many Montenegrin citizens think that women have no place in public and political life, a view supported not just by a substantial proportion of men but also of women, especially in rural and less developed parts of Montenegro (Vujović & Vujović, 2022, p. 136). About 90% of Montenegrin female politicians have experienced discrimination on account of their gender, while 70% of them have experienced violence during their political work (UNDP, 2021).

Montenegro is still a country of "patriarchal political culture in whose political space men dominate, while women in the Montenegrin society are still on the political margins" (Tomović et al., 2014, p. 3). Patriarchal attitudes remain deeply ingrained in Montenegrin culture and continue to play a significant role in shaping women's experiences in the workplace, politics, and their personal lives.

## 9.2.2 Sexist Humor as a Type of Disparaging Humor

Disparaging humor has "an aggressive element relevant to putting down others and establishing superiority" (Hodson & MacInnis, 2016, p. 65). As a specific type of such humor, sexist humor is directed against one gender, usually women, and it "demeans, insults, stereotypes, victimizes, and/or objectifies a person on the basis of his or her gender" (LaFrance & Woodzicka, 1998). Though seemingly harmless and entertaining, it might have real-world consequences and contribute to the marginalization of women in society (Bemiller & Schneider, 2010). In fact, studies show that sexist humor allows for the expression of negative attitudes and may lead to the tolerance of violence against women (Argüello-Gutiérrez et al., 2022).

One of the most significant characteristics of sexist humor is that it plays upon negative cultural stereotypes, such as women are weak, overly emotional, or incapable. Sexist jokes may refer to their physical appearance (with a focus on certain parts of their bodies e.g., breasts, legs, etc., their figure, weight, and so on), personality characteristics (such as their intelligence or emotionality), their place in the private sphere (jokes about cleaning, cooking, childcare, etc.), while some might even be openly violent against women (suggesting abuse of women) (Bemiller & Schneider, 2010). Based on these themes and subthemes, Bemiller and Schneider (2010) classified sexist humor as follows:

(1) Devaluation of personal characteristics ([im]perfect body, personality/character, intelligence/ability);
(2) Women's place in the private sphere (division of labor, marriage);
(3) Backlash against feminism;
(4) Sexual objectification of women;
(5) Violence against women.

Sexist humor could reinforce and perpetuate the said harmful stereotypes (Ford et al., 2008). Consequently, this can make it more challenging for women to succeed in male-dominated industries or to be taken seriously in personal and especially in professional and public settings, such as that of politics.

Sexist humor can also contribute to the objectification of women (Ford et al., 2015). By reducing women to their physical appearance, sexist jokes perpetuate a culture that devalues women and reduces them to sexual objects. Furthermore, sexist humor can also create an environment that is hostile to women (Glick & Fiske, 1997)—when women are made to feel unwelcome or uncomfortable in a social or professional setting, they are less likely to participate or succeed in that environment. This can have a ripple effect, leading to fewer women in leadership roles and a perpetuation of gender inequality.

The described "othering" of women conveyed through sexist humor can lead to inequality of women in various social spheres, the political realm included (Connell, 2002). Sexist humor is an expression of sexism, and online sexism "regardless of tone […] is pernicious and reinforces and normalizes the idea that people are entitled to belittle and demean women" (Southern & Harmer, 2019, p. 191). Some evidence from Australia, the U.K., Sweden, and Bolivia even suggests that sexist hostility has driven some female politicians out of politics (Southern & Harmer, 2019), which is why this phenomenon deserves special attention by critical discourse analysts, among others.

## 9.2.3 Delegitimization and Disparaging Humor

Various directions can be taken in Critical Discourse Analysis (CDA). Here, however, the focus will be on just one—the framework of discourse strategies proposed by Teun van Dijk in his socio-cognitive method of analyzing ideological discourse (van Dijk, 1993a, 1993b, 2000, 2001, 2002, 2006). A major discourse strategy employed in ideological discourse is that of *delegitimization*—of particular interest for this chapter.

Delegitimization as a discourse strategy has been extensively researched regarding political discourse (Ross & Rivers, 2017). It is typically defined relative to its counterpart—the discourse strategy of legitimization. Whereas legitimization refers to the defense of institutionalized behaviors and procedures (cf. Ristić, 2016), delegitimization refers to discursively creating and transmitting a negative image of the Other (Screti, 2013).

Hodson and MacInnis (2016) argue that targets can be delegitimized in everyday, mundane ways, through disparaging humor—for instance, a male boss using chauvinistic jokes at work denigrating his female co-workers. They further recognize three key aspects of delegitimization: dehumanization, disparaging humor, and status-quo support. Dehumanization reduces targets to animals or to machines, relieving them of the protection mechanisms typically afforded to people. In this way, they are *ruled out* of consideration and rights-based protection, whereas, conversely, disparaging humor *rules* targets *in* as acceptable for denigration. Status-quo support entrenches these two categorization processes. The three aspects of delegitimization are interconnected and can be simultaneously present in the delegitimization of certain targets.

Disparagement, including sexist humor, might play a key role in the process of delegitimizing certain targets, trivializing their rights and their credibility, as well as their right to protection (cf. Hodson & MacInnis, 2016). The interplay of disparaging humor, dehumanization, and status-quo support, is understudied and warrants future research, the authors conclude.

## 9.3 Research Aim and Questions

With this background, the aim of this chapter is to study sexist humor in the online Facebook commentary on Montenegrin female politicians, as a reflection and a perpetuator of this society's patriarchal culture. The following research questions are addressed:

(1) How common is sexist humor on Montenegrin female politicians in online Facebook commentary?
(2) What categories of sexist humor on Montenegrin female politicians in online Facebook commentary can be identified and which ones are the most prominent?
(3) How are Montenegrin female politicians delegitimized in sexist humor within Facebook commentary?

(4) How does the Montenegrin patriarchal culture relate to the *frequency* of sexist humor on Montenegrin female politicians in online Facebook commentary?
(5) How does the Montenegrin patriarchal culture relate to the *prominence* of the categories of sexist humor on Montenegrin female politicians in online Facebook commentary?

To answer these questions, the following corpus and the analytical steps are employed.

## 9.4 Corpus and Analytical Steps

In this study, the commentary responding to 24 Facebook posts from various Montenegrin news outlets is examined. These posts conveyed statements issued by 12 Montenegrin female politicians and included their photographs. They were all current or former (but still politically active) ministers or members of parliament, representing various positions and opposition political parties in Montenegro. Two media texts posted on Facebook for each female politician from the period 2021–2022 were randomly chosen, resulting in a total of 3,992 comments initially considered.

Methodologically, the most difficult question when studying humor is how to identify it objectively. Most researchers have used laughter as the decisive criterion to establish whether an utterance is humorous (Attardo, 2015, p. 182). The present study opted for the methodology of analyzing audience reactions, specifically the reactions of Facebook users. Thus, comments were considered humorous if they received a laughing emoji or a "ha-ha" (or similar) reply ("hahaja," "ahahah," "xaxa," "LOL," and laughing GIFs of various kinds).

On the one hand, this methodology risks underreporting humor due to the high number of comments generated by the media texts, making it unlikely for the average reader to read and react to all of them. Consequently, many comments did not receive any reaction. On the other hand, there may also be some false positives, as what one reader finds humorous might not be the same for another; however, this is almost always the case with any type of humor. Thus, the chosen methodology, being the most commonly used in humor studies, should be sufficient for the purpose of this chapter.

The comments were then read to establish whether they contained sexism—the comments were considered sexist if they reduced female politicians to sexual objects, presented them as caricatures of the traditional gender role assigned to women in Montenegrin society, or if they played on the stereotype of female inferiority. A total of 125 such comments were found, and these make the final corpus analyzed in this chapter.

The details of the initial and the final corpus, as well as the breakdown of the number of comments per each female politician, are presented in the following section, responding to research question number 1.

The comments were then categorized according to their themes and subthemes, most following the Bemiller and Schneider model (2010), presented in Sect. 9.2.2. above, to answer research question no. 2, and analyzed through critical discourse analysis to answer research question no. 3. In this analysis, the corpus is investigated against the backdrop of Montenegrin patriarchal culture (in response to research questions 4 and 5).

## 9.5 Analysis

### 9.5.1 Political Sexist Humor Frequency in Montenegrin Facebook Comments

Table 9.1 presents the breakdown of the number of sexist humorous comments relative to the number of total comments, and the number of the humorous comments per each female politician encompassed in this study.

As can be seen in Table 9.1, a total of 125 sexist humorous comments were identified using the methods described in Sect. 9.4. These make up 3.13% of all comments replying to the chosen media texts on Montenegrin female politicians.

**Table 9.1** Breakdown of the number of Facebook comments per female politician

| Woman politician | Total number of comments | Number of comments with a laughing emoji or "ha-ha" etc. reply | Number of comments with a laughing emoji or "ha-ha" etc. reply containing sexism |
|---|---|---|---|
| Aleksandra Vuković | 514 | 208 | 31 |
| Draginja Vuksanović-Stanković | 734 | 205 | 26 |
| Vesna Bratić | 810 | 349 | 13 |
| Jelena Borovinić-Bojović | 484 | 190 | 13 |
| Jelena Božović | 112 | 55 | 9 |
| Olivera Injac | 357 | 182 | 9 |
| Suada Zoronjić | 192 | 76 | 5 |
| Snežana Jonica | 31 | 14 | 5 |
| Branka Bošnjak | 73 | 21 | 4 |
| Božena Jelušić | 403 | 129 | 4 |
| Danijela Đurović | 182 | 78 | 4 |
| Daliborka Pejović | 100 | 38 | 2 |
| Total | 3,992 | 1,545 | 125 |

Furthermore, these 125 sexist humorous comments made up 8.09% of all humorous comments here considered i.e., one of every 12 humorous comments was sexist.

## 9.5.2 Identifying Prominent Categories of Sexist Humor in Montenegrin Facebook Political Commentary

The starting point for categorizing sexist humorous commentary is the model of classification by themes and subthemes proposed by Bemiller and Schneider (2010), presented in Sect. 9.2.2. The model used here is somewhat modified as it does not include the theme "backlash against feminism," because the corpus did not feature it; the theme "devaluation of personal characteristics" is here subdivided into two themes: "devaluation of personal characteristics" and "devaluation of physical characteristics"; and some additional subthemes were also introduced, to reflect the present data: "age," "styling," and "moral character." The results are shown in Table 9.2 below. It should be noted that whereas most of the comments contained just one subtheme (given their relative brevity), some comments in the corpus contained two subthemes; these are shown twice in the Table, in both of their respective categories.

**Table 9.2** Themes and subthemes in Facebook sexist humorous comments on female politicians

| Themes | Subtheme | Comments containing a theme/subtheme | Percentage of all sexist humorous comments (%) |
|---|---|---|---|
| Devaluation of physical characteristics | (IM)perfect body | 25 | 20 |
| | Poor styling | 23 | 18.4 |
| | Too young/too old of age | 6 | 4.8 |
| Devaluation of personal characteristics | Low intelligence | 20 | 16 |
| | Inability | 9 | 7.2 |
| | Evil moral character | 3 | 2.4 |
| Place of women in the private sphere | Division of labor (should stay at home; should stay away from politics as a men's affair) | 3 | 2.4 |
| | Marriage (should get married; devaluation because of being a spinster or a divorcee) | 8 | 6.4 |
| Sexual objectification of women | | 38 | 30.4 |
| Violence against women | | 2 | 1.6 |

The most prominent themes in the corpus were: devaluation of physical characteristics of women (present in 43.2% of the sexist comments); sexual objectification of women (featured in 30.4%); and devaluation of personal characteristics of women (found in 25.6%). The place of women in the private sphere motivated 8.8% of the sexist comments, while comments calling for violence against women were rarer (1.6%).

### 9.5.3 How Are Montenegrin Female Politicians Delegitimized in Sexist Humorous Facebook Comments?

This section critically analyzes how each of the categories of sexist humorous comments delegitimizes Montenegrin female politicians.

Almost half the sexist humorous comments devalued the physical characteristics of female politicians. Most commonly, this was on account of their "(im)perfect" bodies, as in the following examples (including the original emojis), all made by Facebook users:

**Example 1** Ohhh, ugly, what's wrong with you 😅
[*Auu grdna što ti je* 😅] (comment to Crnogorski Vremeplov,[1] 2023).

**Example 2** Hey beauty, you've been gone for a while, can anyone tell me what she said, I don't feel like reading it
[*dje si lepoto, odavno te nije bilo, jel moze ko da mi kaze sto je rekla, mrzi me da citam*] (comment to RTCG[2], 2022, June 5).

**Example 3** Imagine if she cut all her hair, she would look like a man. 😅😅 (…)
[*zamisli da se osisa do glave, izgledala bi kao* muskarac. 😅😅 (…)] (comment to RTCG, 2020, August 15).

**Example 4** Wish she would never take the mask off […]
[*Kamo sreće da masku ne skida* […]] (comment to RTCG, 2022, November 20)

Most of the Facebook users employing sexist humorous comments foregrounded the imperfect bodies of female politicians—thus, in Examples 1, 3 and 4, they were said to be *ugly*, resembling a *man*, and that they looked better covered by a *mask*. The references to perfect bodies were often ironic—thus, in Example 2, the use of the vocative *beauty* was most probably used ironically, given that it referred to the oldest female Montenegrin MP and that it was given in the Ekavian form[3] that in Montenegro is frequently used to convey irony. The humor in these comments rests

---

[1] Crnogorski Vremeplov (Montenegrin Timemachine) is a Facebook news portal from Montenegro.
[2] RTCG stands for Radio-televizija Crne Gore (Radio and Television of Montenegro), the national broadcasting company of Montenegro.
[3] One of the three isoglosses of Bosnian/Croatian/Montenegrin/Serbian (BCMS), chiefly spoken in Serbia. The standard isogloss used in Montenegro is Ijekavian.

on the incongruity of the idealized female appearance and the looks of the female politicians as perceived by the commentators (ugly vs. beautiful, and the looks of a man vs. the looks of a woman).

Comments 1 through 4 and others from this category reduce female politicians to just their physical bodies and do not even discuss their political statements i.e., their political "bodies." For instance, in Example 2 the Facebook user literally says: "can anyone tell me what she said, I don't feel like reading it." Similarly, when the female politicians are called out on account of their poor appearance i.e., choice of clothes, hairstyles, and similar accoutrements:

**Example 5** Common, get that hair done already and continue presiding over the sitting [...]
[*Ajde više sredi tu frizuru i nastavi onu sjednicu.* [...]] (comment to RTCG, 2022, September 25)

**Example 6** You will be longer remembered by your hat than your intelligence
[*Mnogi će te duže pamtit po kapi, nego po pameti*] (comment to RTCG, 2022, November 13)

**Example 7** She started using hair balm 😂 and combing her hair
[*Počela je da koristi balsam* 😂 *i da se češlja*] (comment to RTCG, 2022, November 13)

As can be seen, the comments do not just refer to the poor style of women but are downright offensive. Example 7 contains a presupposition that the female politician did not use to comb her hair, and Example 5 presupposes that the Deputy Speaker of the Parliament is disheveled. In other examples, it is a particular fashion style that is the target—as in Example 6, where the member of parliament is called out for wearing hats. This particular comment also insults the female member of parliament's intelligence, drawn from the patriarchal stereotype that women are of lower intelligence than men. Again, what is foregrounded is the outward, physical appearance, to which female politicians are reduced. Their political stances are not commented on at all by these Facebook users. In this way, these women are delegitimized as political agents and professionals.

Some of the comments foregrounded the age of female politicians instead of commenting on their political stance:

**Example 8** You, little one, started doing politics early
[*Ti mala rano si se dala ypolitiky*] (comment to RTCG, 2022, January 10)

**Example 9** User 1: Are you eating[4] anything, grandma?
User 2: Very little, she has no appetite and there is no interest. Gone with the wind! 😀

---

[4] *J(ed)eš* is used as a word play. The form *jedeš* is the 2nd person singular present verb form of *to eat*; however, a change of one letter in it results in the verb with the meaning of *to have sex*—the use of the brackets suggests that the verb should not be understood literally; the latter verb is not written explicitly probably to avoid being automatically filtered out for use of profanity words.

User 3: Very little, she is being paid badly.
[*J(ed)eš li što bako./slabo, nema apetit a ni interesovanja. Prohujalo sa vihorom!/ Slabo lose je placena*] (comment to RTCG, 2022, June 5)

In Example 8 a then 38-year-old female politician is referred to as the *little one* i.e., as a child. In Example 9, one of the older MPs is referred to as *grandma*, which is also offensive. The incongruity on which the humor draws is that between some idealized age for a professional woman and the actual ages of the female politicians here discussed (either too young or too old relative to that idealized age). Facebook user 1 in Example 9 uses wordplay with a sexual allusion, recognized and picked up in the replies to this comment, two of which are given above for illustration. Again, these are offensive, especially the second reply suggesting that the female politician is paid badly for her services, alluding to sex work. Given that in these comments a woman is valued by her physical characteristics if she is not in her (sexual) prime, especially if she is past it, she is delegitimized as a woman and consequently as a politician. This is clearly seen in the following:

**Example 10** User 1: This little cow is so stupid 😂😂😂 your milk-producing ability is falling and your expiration date is passing, you cowwww 😂😂😂😂 what's the horse doing 😂😂 [*Toliko je glupa ova kravica 😂😂😂 opada ti mlječnost i rok upotrebe 😂😂😂😂 sto radi konj 😂😂*]

User 2: she is now in her prime, she needs a good stallion now 😂😂😂
[*Od najljepše je ruke sad, trebanjoj dobar dorot 😂😂😂*] (comment to RTCG, 2021, December 25)

The comment given in Example 10 delegitimizes the female politician at several levels: "the expiration date" is clearly equated with the sexual prime of the woman, she is sexually objectified, and in addition her intelligence is equated to that of a cow—an animal which in Montenegrin culture is associated with low intelligence and an ungainly appearance (Vujković, 2019). Similar examples of targeting the intelligence of female politicians are given below:

**Example 11** And under the hat, there is nothing 🐔
[*A pod kapu nema ništa 🐔*] (comment to RTCG, 2022, November 13)

**Example 12** User 1: Goat with horns still staring at nothing.
[*Koza roguša i dalje bjeli u prazno*], and
User 2: Jovan, haha. Please do not insult the Alpina goats with horns good sweetie
[*Jovane ha ha nemoj da mi vređaš kozu rogušu alpina dušiicaa dobraa*] (comments to Crnogorski vremeplov, 2023)

Chicken, goats, and cows are the animals most frequently likened to female politicians in the comments, with a view to insulting their intelligence. These metaphors are not just verbal; for instance, in Example 11 an emoji visually representing a chicken is used and similar emojis as well as memes with pictures of the three said animals are used frequently. The invoked images of animals acting as humans involve the unexpected and, therefore, can be perceived as comic.

Similarly, several sexist humorous comments target the ability of female politicians. The Facebook users see them as unskilled for doing politics and this certainly rests on the patriarchal stereotype that men are more skilled than women so that the former should be in charge of making decisions also in the household as well as in society. A few such comments are given below:

**Example 13** You're better at getting implants than politics! 😅
[*Bolje ti idu implantanti od politike*] (comment to Portal Analitika,[5] 2022)

**Example 14** You were born to do politics 😂😂😂😂
[*Ti si za politiku rođena* 😂😂😂😂] (comment to RTCG, 2022, November 20)

The ironic and humorous intent is frequently marked by the laughing emojis in many of the comments, as can be seen in the above examples.

In the category of personal devaluation are also comments delegitimizing the moral character of women and depicting them as evil:

**Example 15** Say, old woman, are you really a witch????
[*Kazuj, babo, jesi li vještica????*] (comment to RTCG, 2022, August 17)

The comment given in Example 15 is actually derived from the most quoted, 19th-century Montenegrin poet Njegoš, who is known for poetry heavily imbued with cultural references. In Montenegrin culture, evil women are often equated with witches. The comment also devalued the female politician on account of her age.

About 8.8% of sexist comments used the theme of the place of women in the private sphere. Some of the comments suggested that women should stay at home and take care of their families instead of delving into men's affair such as politics, whereas others commented on their marital status, whereby those who are not married are frowned upon, as in the following example:

**Example 16** User 1: Is there anything new? Did this spinster get married, I am asking for a friend? 😂😂😂😂
[*Šta ima novo? udade li se ova usedelica, pitam za druga?* 😂😂😂😂]
User 2: You're not going to set up a friend with her, are you 😅 […] ask for an enemy
[*a nećeš je valjda drugu utrapit* 😅[…] *pitaj za (ne)prijatelja*] (comment to Fos Media,[6] 2021).

These comments certainly arise from the patriarchal culture that sees a perfect woman as a married one, taking care of her household, as will be commented upon later.

Most comments sexually objectify female politicians. Sexual allusions were present in examples 9 and 10, and some further examples follow:

---

[5] Portal Analitika (Analytics Portal) is a news outlet from Montenegro.

[6] FOS Media (FOS is short for *infos*) is an online news portal from Montenegro.

**Example 17** This one always turned me on ughh 😖😖
[*Ova me vazda palila uff* 😖😖] (comment to RTCG, 2022, April 14)

**Example 18** Ask Milutin if electricity will be cheaper. whisper into his ear, bite his ear!!!!
[*Pitaj Milutina hoće li biti struja jeftinija šapni mu ugrizi ga za uvo!!!!*] (comment to RTCG, 2022, January 10)

**Example 19** She hasn't had sex for a while so she\s nervous 😖😖
[*Odavno se nije prčila pa u nervozu udarila* 😖😖] (comment to Crnogorski Vremeplov, 2023)

As can be seen, the female politicians are sexually objectified, reduced to their sexual aspect, while their political agency is not even backgrounded—it is not even noted to exist. And this is not the case just with some female politicians but in fact with all of them, no matter their age, looks, or style. All the comments foreground the characteristics of these women—comments that have nothing to do with politics but have everything to do with their gender that fully defines them in the eyes of the commenters. For them, it is hard to see these women past their gender and their physical looks; their personal characteristics, that the commenters could hardly assess as they do not know these women personally, are devalued by default. Thus, these women are robbed of the qualities expected of a politician and delegitimized as professionals.

### 9.5.4 *Montenegrin Patriarchal Culture and the Frequency of Sexist Humor in Online Facebook Commentary*

In the introduction, Montenegro's culture was portrayed as a modern patriarchy that was expected to impact the perception of female politicians in the public eye.

In Sect. 9.5.1, it was established that 3.13% of the comments in relation to the total number were sexist humorous comments. It should be noted that there were additional sexist humorous comments in the initial corpus not included here based on this study's strict definition that only counted comments with humorous reactions from readers. As a result, the 3.13% represents the minimum presence of such comments in the corpus. Additionally, it was observed that every twelfth comment with a humorous reaction was sexist. The percentages reported here do not seem that high in light of Montenegro's strongly patriarchal culture. Two possible conclusions might be drawn—either there really was not that much sexism in the comments or the sexist comments were not often recognized as humorous.

To establish the average presence of sexism in the comments, five randomly selected media texts taken from a subsection of the corpus were closely inspected. The results:

(1) Two texts about the MP Branka Bošnjak (RTCG, 25 September 2022 and RTCG, 14 April 2022) generated a total of 73 comments, 15 of which were sexist (20.55%);
(2) A text about MP Aleksandra Vuković (RTCG, 22 November 2022) generated 186 comments in total, 42 of which were sexist (22.58%);
(3) A text about then Minister Vesna Bratić (Portal Analitika, 16 March 2022) generated a total of 221 comments, 60 of which contained sexism (27.15%);
(4) A text about the MP Draginja Vuksanović-Stanković (RTCG, 25 December 2021) generated a total of 317 comments, 62 of which were sexist (19.56%).

These five texts generated a total of 797 comments, 179 of which were sexist (22.46%). Therefore, every 4th or 5th comment contained sexism, a significant portion, especially taking into account the fact that most of the commentators were not anonymous and that some comments might have been reported as offensive and removed prior to collecting the corpus. It should also be added that one particular category of comments, replies to comments, were counted in this methodology but that many of these were, in fact, off-topic—they typically did not discuss the female politicians themselves but most often contained arguments amongst the commentators on general politics and issues related to nationalism. Had the replies to comments been excluded, the share of sexist comments would have been even larger.

From the results above, it can be concluded that sexism was significantly present in the comments but that it frequently was not recognized as "funny." There is, indeed, a link between Montenegrin patriarchal culture and the relatively notable presence of sexism in comments regarding Montenegrin female politicians. However, there is not a strong link between Montenegrin patriarchal culture and sexism which is perceived as humorous, an interesting result.

The literature finds that sexist humor is more enjoyed by men (as the out-group), is more acceptable when used by women (as the in-group) and, most important, is more likely to be appreciated by those who use it themselves (Parrott & Hopp, 2020). In other words, it takes a strongly patriarchal commentator and a strongly patriarchal reader for this kind of humor to work. The relatively low presence of this kind of humor in overall commentary humor indicates that despite the high presence of sexism in the comments most often these are not appreciated by the Facebook audience. This should be a good sign for Montenegrin society, given that a lack of humorous reception is likely to discourage use of such "humor" in the future.

### 9.5.5 Montenegrin Patriarchal Culture and Sexist Humor Category Prominence in Online Facebook Commentary?

"Sexist humor has been an integral part of many patriarchal cultures for centuries," as Knyazyan (2015, p. 26) notes, and all its categories i.e., themes and subthemes found in the corpus, can be directly sourced to Montenegrin patriarchal culture.

In patriarchal cultures, the devaluation of women's physical characteristics is commonplace. Nasreen (2021) suggests that body-shaming women serves as a means of imposing patriarchal bodily control over them. Controlling women is a fundamental principle of patriarchal cultures, encompassing not only their behavior but also their appearance. As observed, the comments featured an excessive focus on the female body as an object to be observed, judged, modified, or rejected by the commenters. Simultaneously, the "political body" of these women remained invisible. The Montenegrin patriarchy has established a cultural norm dictating how an ideal woman should look, dress, and even what age she should be. Departing from this norm, as evident in the comments, subjects a woman to sexist humor that devalues her, given that solely the conforming, silent, and uncomplaining woman is "the ideal of patriarchal culture" (Bordo, 1993, p. 177).

Even when the commenters go past the physical and into the realm of the personal, their judgment of the female politicians is again imbued with their patriarchal culture. Namely, the stereotype of women being subordinate to men i.e., of the inferiority of women, includes the perception of their being less intelligent and less skilled than men, and therefore not fit for politics—decisions, in the household and society, should be made by men, in the view of Montenegrin patriarchal culture. Cultural influence was also evident in the metaphorical representation of women's intelligence, likened to certain animals perceived in Montenegrin culture as representative of low intelligence (chicken, cows, and goats), as has already been noted in the literature (Vujković & Vuković-Stamatović, 2021). There is a degree of cultural specificity in the choice of these animals, as in various cultures different animals represent intelligence or lack thereof. Seen as irrational and sometimes as evil, women threaten "to erupt and challenge the patriarchal order" (Bordo, 1993, p. 206), the reason that female politicians were devalued on the plane of the personal in addition to the plane of the physical.

In the Balkan modern patriarchies that Montenegro is part of, the two most frequent "patriarchal constructs" are that of representing women as sexual objects and that of seeing women as ideal housekeepers/wives/mothers (Nenić, 2012). The former was the most frequent theme found in the comments. The latter was certainly present, but not as much as could have been expected—it seems that this historical patriarchal ideal regarding the role(s) of a woman in society has lost priority over the patriarchal ideal of controlling the female body and sexualizing it, at least when the perception of female politicians is in question. Still, women were given the message that politics is a realm for men, which is certainly due to the patriarchal culture.

## 9.6 Conclusion

In this chapter, the focus was on sexist humorous comments posted on Facebook as reactions to media texts on Montenegrin female politicians. In answering the five research questions posed in the study, the following was found: sexist humorous comments were found in one of every twelve humorous comments; the most prominent themes included the sexual objectification of women politicians and the devaluation of their physical and personal characteristics; all sexist humorous comments delegitimized female politicians as political professionals; and finally, all the themes featured in the sexist humorous comments can be directly linked to Montenegrin patriarchal culture. While sexism featured in almost a quarter of the comments, most often the comments containing it were not recognized as "funny," a good sign for Montenegrin society, given that a lack of humorous reception is likely to discourage the use of such "humor" in the future.

The results of this study are in line with the conclusion reached by Bemiller and Schneider (2010, p. 476), who noted that sexist humor is not humor at all but "a form of power that is used to oppress and subordinate." Thus, sexist humor in Montenegrin Facebook comments made its target, female politicians, less fit for politics and redirected attention elsewhere—into domains not particularly relevant for doing politics—those of physical looks, personality and sexuality. What was foregrounded in the comments were the different bodily aspects and this was certainly engendered by the "patriarchal ideology of the female body as an object to be dominated and managed" (Ponterotto, 2016, p. 139). Recognition and deconstruction of this patriarchal design that excludes women from real political power should be a step to bettering their position in patriarchal cultures.

# References

Argüello-Gutiérrez, C., Cubero, A., Fumero, F., Montealegre, D., Sandoval, P., & Smith-Castro, V. (2022). I'm just joking! Perceptions of sexist humor and sexist beliefs in a Latin American context. *International Journal of Psychology,* Online first. https://doi.org/10.1002/ijop.12884

Attardo, S. (2015). Humor and laughter. In D. Tannen, H. E. Hamilton, & D. Schiffrin (Eds.), *The handbook of discourse analysis* (pp. 168–188). Wiley. https://doi.org/10.1002/9781118584194.ch8

Bemiller, M. L., & Schneider, R. Z. (2010). It's not just a joke. *Sociological Spectrum, 30*(4), 459–479. https://doi.org/10.1080/02732171003641040

Bordo, S. (1993). *Unbearable weight: Feminism, western culture and the body.* University of California Press.

Connell, R. (2002). *Gender.* Blackwell Publishers.

Crnogorski Vremeplov. (2023, January 9). *The Republic of Srpska is not and will never be a state* [Image and link attached] [Status update]. Facebook. https://m.facebook.com/story.php?story_fbid=647966910462412&id=100057473258451. (in BCMS).

Drakett, J., Rickett, B., Day, K., & Milnes, K. (2018). Old jokes, new media—online sexism and constructions of gender in internet memes. *Feminism & Psychology, 28*(1), 109–127. https://doi.org/10.1177/0959353517727560

Erdeljanović, J. (1981). *The Clans of Kuči, Bratonožići and Piperi.* Slovo Ljubve. (in BCMS).

Ferguson, M. A., & Ford, T. E. (2008). Disparagement humor: A theoretical and empirical review of psychoanalytic, superiority, and social identity theories. *Humor—International Journal of Humor Research, 21*(3), 283–312. https://doi.org/10.1515/HUMOR.2008.014

Ford, T. E., Boxer, C. F., Armstrong, J., & Edel, J. R. (2008). More than "just a joke": The prejudice-releasing function of sexist humor. *Personality and Social Psychology Bulletin, 34*(2), 159–170. https://doi.org/10.1177/0146167207310022

Ford, T. E., Woodzicka, J. A., Petit, W. E., Richardson, K., & Lappi, S. K. (2015). Sexist humor as a trigger of state self-objectification in women. *Humor—International Journal of Humor Research, 28*(2), 253–269. https://doi.org/10.1515/humor-2015-0018

Fos Media. (2021, 21 March). *Congratulations also from Bratić: Lionesses, you are the pride of our country* [Image and link attached] [Status update]. Facebook. https://m.facebook.com/story.php?story_fbid=2967814300207610&id=1821253298197055. (in BCMS).

Funk, M. E., & Coker, C. R. (2016). She's hot, for a politician: The impact of objectifying commentary on perceived credibility of female candidates. *Communication Studies, 67*(4), 455–473. https://doi.org/10.1080/10510974.2016.1196380

Glick, P., & Fiske, S. T. (1997). Hostile and benevolent sexism: Measuring ambivalent sexist attitudes toward women. *Psychology of Women Quarterly, 21*, 119–135. https://doi.org/10.1111/j.1471-6402.1997.tb00104.x

Hodson, G., & MacInnis, C. C. (2016). Derogating humor as a delegitimization strategy in intergroup contexts. *Translational Issues in Psychological Science, 2*, 63–74. https://doi.org/10.1037/tps0000052

Housholder, E. E., & LaMarre, H. L. (2014). Facebook politics: Toward a process model for achieving political source credibility through social media. *Journal of Information Technology & Politics, 11*(4), 368–382. https://doi.org/10.1080/19331681.2014.951753

James, K. (2010). Domestic violence within refugee families: Intersecting patriarchal culture and the refugee experience. *Australian and New Zealand Journal of Family Therapy, 31*(3), 275–284. https://doi.org/10.1375/anft.31.3.275

Knyazyan, A. (2015). Gender and disparaging humour. *Armenian Folia Anglistika, 11*(2/14), 25–32. https://doi.org/10.46991/AFA/2015.11.2.025

LaFrance, M., & Woodzicka, J. A. (1998). No laughing matter: Women's verbal and nonverbal reactions to sexist humor. In J. Swim & C. Stangor (Eds.), *Prejudice: The target's perspective* (pp. 61–80). Academic Press. https://doi.org/10.1016/B978-012679130-3/50038-7

Mašnić, J. (2011). Personality traits as determinants of the attitude towards women leaders in Montenegrin society. *Psihološka Istraživanja, 14*(1), 85–98. https://doi.org/10.5937/PsIstra1101085M

Nasreen, Z. (2021). 'Have you not got a sense of humour?': Unpacking masculinity through online sexist jokes during the COVID-19 pandemic. *Society and Culture in South Asia, 7*(1), 148–154. https://doi.org/10.1177/2393861720977632

Nenić, I. (2012). A promising matrix? In A. Zaharijević, S. Gavrić & E. Bošnjak (Eds.), *Did someone say feminism? How did feminism affect 20$^{th}$ century women?* (pp. 333–343). Sarajevo Open Centre. (in BCMS).

Parrott, S., & Hopp, T. (2020). Reasons people enjoy sexist humor and accept it as inoffensive. *Atlantic Journal of Communication, 28*(2), 115–124. https://doi.org/10.1080/15456870.2019.1616737

Ponterotto, D. (2016). Resisting the male gaze: Feminist responses to the "normatization" of the female body in Western culture. *Journal of International Women's Studies, 17*(1), 133–151.

Portal Analitika. (2022, 16 March). *When you try to do something and you see that you can do it, you want to continue doing it* [Image and link attached] [Status update]. Facebook. https://m.facebook.com/story.php?story_fbid=1811071749098557&id=211681129037635. (in BCMS).

Rakonjac, M. (2020). Under the auspices of patriarchy: The social identity of women in the patriarchal culture of Montenegrin society. *Sociološka Luča, 14*(1), 58–70. (in BCMS).

Ristić, D. (2016). (De)Legitimization as the discursive strategy of ideology. *Facta Universitatis, Series: Philosophy, Sociology, Psychology and History, 14*(3), 155–166.

Ross, A. S., & Rivers, D. J. (2017). Digital cultures of political participation: Internet memes and the discursive delegitimization of the 2016 U.S Presidential candidates. *Discourse, Context & Media, 16*, 1–11. https://doi.org/10.1016/j.dcm.2017.01.001

RTCG. (2020, August 15). *The shame of the State Electoral Commission and the Constitutional Court will live forever* [Image and link attached] [Status update]. https://m.facebook.com/story.php?story_fbid=4235332963204743&id=434618853276192. (in BCMS).

RTCG. (2021, December 25). *The Government of Montenegro is falling and that is certain* [Image and link attached] [Status update]. Facebook. https://m.facebook.com/story.php?story_fbid=6731299296941418&id=434618853276192. (in BCMS).
RTCG. (2022, January 10). *The Prime Minister should be hiding behind his ministers* [Image and link attached] [Status update]. Facebook. https://m.facebook.com/story.php?story_fbid=6822164701188210&id=434618853276192. (in BCMS).
RTCG. (2022, April 14). *The first point of the session must be the election of the President of the Parliament* [Image and link attached] [Status update]. Facebook. https://m.facebook.com/story.php?story_fbid=7331057833632225&id=434618853276192. (in BCMS).
RTCG. (2022, June 5). *As soon as I have a conflict with my conscience, I will pack my bags* [Image and link attached] [Status update]. Facebook. https://m.facebook.com/story.php?story_fbid=7579930845411588&id=434618853276192. (in BCMS).
RTCG. (2022, August 17). *No that everyone can be in coalition with everyone else, I wish for an election* [Image and link attached] [Status update]. Facebook. https://m.facebook.com/story.php?story_fbid=7925155337555802&id=434618853276192. (in BCMS).
RTCG. (2022, September 25). *I believe that the Board of Inquiry will find out whether there was any corruption in the Možur affair* [Image and link attached] [Status update]. Facebook. https://m.facebook.com/story.php?story_fbid=8107363906001610&id=434618853276192. (in BCMS).
RTCG. (2022, November 13). *As long as the hate concentrates on my hat, I don't care about it* [Image and link attached] [Status update]. Facebook. https://m.facebook.com/story.php?story_fbid=8339735229431142&id=434618853276192. (in BCMS).
RTCG. (2022, November 20). *Borovinić Bojović will be the President of the Assembly of the capital* [Image and link attached] [Status update]. Facebook. https://m.facebook.com/story.php?story_fbid=8373770142694317&id=434618853276192. (in BCMS).
Screti, F. (2013). Defending joy against the popular revolution: Legitimation and delegitimation through songs. *Critical Discourse Studies, 10*(2), 205–222. https://doi.org/10.1080/17405904.2013.764614
Southern, R., & Harmer, E. (2019). Othering political women: Online misogyny, racism and ableism towards women in public life. In K. Lumsden & E. Harmer (Eds.), *Online othering* (pp. 187–210). Springer. https://doi.org/10.1007/978-3-030-12633-9_8
Tomović, N., Selić, A., Vujović, I., Popović, D., Mijanović, M., Dedović, V., & Vujović, Z. (2014). *Political activism of women in Montenegro*. CEMI. https://cemi.org.me/wp-content/uploads/2018/02/Politicki_aktivizam_zena_u_Crnoj_Gori.pdf. (in BCMS).
UNDP. (2021). *Gender mainstreaming: Attitudes and perception of employees in the public administration regarding gender equality and assessment of the application of the principle of gender equality in institutions of public authority*. Ipsos Public Affairs. https://rodnamapa.me/assets/documents/stavovi-2021.pdf. (in BCMS).
van Dijk, T. A. (1993a). Discourse and cognition in society. In D. Crowley & D. Mitchell (Eds.), *Communication theory today* (pp. 107–126). Pergamon Press.
van Dijk, T. A. (1993b). Principles of critical discourse analysis. *Discourse & Society, 4*(2), 249–283. https://doi.org/10.1177/0957926593004002006
van Dijk, T. A. (2000). *Ideology and discourse: A multidisciplinary introduction*. Pompeu Fabra University.
van Dijk, T. A. (2001). Critical discourse analysis. In D. Schriffin, D. Tannen, & H. Hamilton (Eds.), *Handbook of discourse analysis* (pp. 352–371). Blackwell.
van Dijk, T. A. (2002). Political discourse and political cognition. In P. Chilton & C. Schäffner (Eds.), *Discourse approaches to politics, society and culture* (Vol. 4, pp. 203–237). John Benjamins. https://doi.org/10.1075/dapsac.4.11dij
van Dijk, T. A. (2006). Discourse and manipulation. *Discourse & Society, 17*(3), 359–383. https://doi.org/10.1177/0957926506060250
Vujković, V. (2019). The conceptual metaphor WOMAN IS AN ANIMAL in Montenegrin webpages. *Logos et Littera, 6*(1), 67–80. https://doi.org/10.31902/LL.2019.6.1.4

Vujković, V., & Vuković-Stamatović, M. (2021). "What a kitty!": Women's physical appearance and animal metaphors in Montenegro. *Slovo, 34*(1), 1–22. https://doi.org/10.14324/111.444.0954-6839.1239

Vujović, S., & Vujović, T. (2022). The gender gap as an obstacle to the development of female entrepreneurship in Montenegro. *BizInfo (Blace) Journal of Economics, Management and Informatics, 13*(2), 133–144. https://doi.org/10.5937/bizinfo2202133V. (in BCMS).

**Milica Vuković-Stamatović** is Associate Professor in English Linguistics at the University of Montenegro, Montenegro. She has published two books, as well as numerous articles and book chapters on English and Montenegrin media and political discourse. Her articles have appeared in *Discourse & Society, Journal of Language and Politics, Pragmatics & Society, Zeitschrift für Slawistik, Gender & Language,* among others. The genres which she has studied the most include political interviews, parliamentary debates, online media articles and news article comments.

# Chapter 10
# Exploring Attitudinal Meaning in Iranian Political Humor Targets as Distributed Through Social Networks

**Alireza Jalilifar and Yousef Savaedi**

**Abstract** In order to be incongruously informative, safely aggressive, and provide psychological relief, political discourse relies considerably on humor. Whereas political humor outwardly looks to elicit laughter in a culture-bound context, it also strives to cast judgment on its targets. Attitudinal markers are among the linguistic techniques used to show how religious, economic, and historical events shape political humor and consequently judge politicians effectively. Despite the many functions attitudinal markers can play in humor, there aren't many studies that address the role of these markers in presenting their targets and the socio-political considerations that affect them in evaluating their targets. This chapter analyzes a corpus of Iranian political humor distributed through social networks, in order to identify how the targets or the stereotypical victims are culturally addressed in this context. Through the Appraisal Model, the study attempts to further our knowledge regarding how social status, economic conditions, and religious views form political humor within the Iranian socio-political context. The study is expected to reveal how attitudes are presented in sets of context-bound, target-value patterns. Finally, we show that the closed socio-political context affects the selection of the targets and the tone of the humor.

## 10.1 Introduction

Even though matching humorous discourse with serious politics seems far from feasible, a close exploration reveals their longtime tangled bonds throughout the history of politics (Speier, 1998). In fact, as a mode of persuasive discourse, political humor dates back to ancient Greece and Rome. For centuries, politicians and elites have been afraid of the strong impact on public opinion of combining politics and

A. Jalilifar (✉)
Shahid Chamran University of Ahvaz, Ahvaz, Iran
e-mail: a.jalilifar@scu.ac.ir

Y. Savaedi
Farhangian University of Ahvaz, Ahvaz, Iran

humor (Caufield, 2008; Test, 1991). As long as there have been people in power, there have always been complainants who used political humor to mock them and persuade others to protest against them or their decisions.

While political humor outwardly looks to elicit laughter, as an umbrella that encompasses any humorous text dealing with targets such as *political issues, people, events, processes, or institutions* (Young, 2014) it simultaneously strives for objecting to and casting judgments on its targets. Most humor is about what people find undesirable, wicked, and disturbing (Brottman, 2004); nevertheless, attributing unfavorable qualities to different targets cannot be so easy. It is presumed that the selection of the targets and the variety of the qualities pinned to them are highly affected by the socio-political and cultural context that might be unique for each society, and according to Kuipers (2006) its investigation can inevitably become something of an ethnography of that society.

Political humor is also capable of revealing the openness of different political systems. The constitution, the span of the president's authority, government type, political parties, and the constitutionally approved freedom of speech are just a few instances of issues worth considering while trying to understand humor and show how religious, economic, and historical events shape political humor and consequently judge politicians effectively. Above and beyond this, according to Mietusch (2013), *the way people perceive, produce, and appreciate humor is determined by cultural considerations.*

To understand the mechanism of how these issues affect political discourse, it seems essential to study political humor as an informative, entertaining channel of hard news communication in relation to different socio-political contexts. Thus, by analyzing a corpus of humor from the Iranian political context, this chapter seeks to show how cultural norms and patterns can provide grounds for evaluating the target of humor.

Due to its nature, political humor calls for the frequent use of attitudinal devices that are used to effectively take politicians to task in the guise of banter, derision, and mockery. Nevertheless, although this area has extensively been researched from different aspects, including its themes, targets, and multi-features (Jalilifar et al., 2021; Naghdipour, 2014; Pearce & Hajizada, 2014; Shehata, 1992; Zlobin, 1996), studies that might depict the ways political humor evaluates specific targets by employing evaluative meanings and the sociological elements leading to such evaluation seem to be inconspicuous or limited, considering the great potential that attitudinal markers might have on featuring meanings in humor. For instance, Shehata (1992) studied political humor on the assumption that political jokes reflect popular feelings and opinions. Likewise, Naghdipour (2014), Pearce and Hajizada (2014), and Zolbin (1996) attempted to show how the targets of political humor are judged and represented.

Nevertheless, none of these studies introduced a specific attitudinal framework for their analysis. Therefore, as a part of a wider research project, this study attempted to identify the targets or the stereotypical victims in this context, and through the framework suggested by the Appraisal model (Martin & White, 2005) the present study sought to develop knowledge regarding the linguistic strategies employed in this genre by scrutinizing both inscribed (explicit) and invoked (implicit) attitudinal values, in order to evaluate specific targets of political humor within the Iranian sociopolitical context. Furthermore, by developing a sociopolitical model of humor, clues were provided that might help researchers unveil the socio-political openness of different contexts. Hence the following questions stand out:

(1) How are attitudes realized in Iranian political humor to shape the targets of these texts?
(2) How does the Iranian socio-political context affect the type of attitudes used to evaluate its targets?

## 10.2 Iran's Socio-Political Context

Before the Islamic Revolution, according to Fazeli (2006) the Shah's state was a totalitarian dictatorship and hardly tolerated any criticism. SAVAK, the regime's frightening intelligence agency, stopped all objectors from expressing their opinions. Fazeli (2006, pp. 79–80) added that:

The regime did not allow any democratic process to develop. On the other hand, thanks to the increase in oil income and rapid growth in higher education and urbanization, the middle class and the intelligentsia expanded—as did the demand for political and social participation. By excluding these social groups from political participation, the state undermined the formation of the institutions of civil society, exacerbated the regime's crisis of legitimacy and, in particular, drove the middle class and intelligentsia towards creation of dissident social movements and political cultures.

As Fazeli noted (2006), like his father the Shah wanted to secularize and modernize Iranian society without modernizing the political system. By 1979, tremendous changes had taken place in the ideology of the state. Islamism became the dominant ideology of the 1979 revolution. The new state had a strong enthusiasm to Islamize everything. The socio-political context remained like this up to the 1990s when Iran began to undergo fundamental political, cultural, and economic changes. These changes included the cessation of the 8-year war between Iran and Iraq, the death of the Islamic Revolution founder, Ayat-Allah Khomeini, the decline of revolutionary anti-nationalism ideology, the birth of a new Islamic nationalism, the "explosion of youth and, as a corollary, the social demand for higher education," failure to meet the people's social, political, and economic expectations despite a reformist movement (Fazeli, 2006, pp. 165–166), and finally the dominance of the conservative, authoritarian, and traditional view of the state.

### 10.2.1 Freedom of Speech in the Iranian Constitution

According to the 1979 Iranian constitution with amendments through 1989 (Chapter III, Articles 23, 24, 25), investigation of individuals' beliefs is forbidden, and every Iranian can have every belief he/she chooses. In addition, the constitution explicitly states that the press and publications are free to express their opinions. The constitution also permits all political activities that do not threaten the principles of independence and national unity (Article 26). Radio and television (Chapter XII, Article 175) enjoy conditional freedom of expression and dissemination of thoughts. However, this freedom must be guaranteed to keep within Islamic criteria and the best interests of the country.

The Iranian constitution (Article 3), in accordance with the Islamic form of government, emphasizes the basis of participation by all members of society at all stages. The Article states the necessity of "the participation of the general public in determining its own political, economic, social, and cultural destiny" (ibid, p. 166). This way, each individual will be involved in and responsible for the development of the society toward perfection.

However, since the Constitution of the Islamic Republic of Iran, on the other hand, does not explicitly refer to freedom of expression and thought (Rezvani, 2016), and due to the ambiguity in stating the special categories of expression that may be restricted under Article 24, this right is liable to different temporal and local interpretations. Thus, the Iranian context sometimes witnessed a lot of ups and downs in this respect e.g., based on a report by ISNA (2014), during two governments Ahmadinejad's government suspended or closed 46 publications., whereas based on a report by Abdoli (2015), the more moderate government of Rouhani also suspended seven newspapers, four of which resumed publishing after a period of suspension.

### 10.2.2 The Sociological Model (Openness Model)

Communication that is shared in social interactions enjoys a variety of forms, one of which is humor—by nature a social phenomenon or at least implying a social relationship (Fine, 1983; Owen, 2002). Social, because a person can hardly fool or tell him/herself a joke. Besides, social and cultural factors, and sometimes temporal and local influencers, are the ones that help shape humorous utterances. The themes and topics of these humorous utterances usually revolve around social, cultural, moral, and political issues.

Although humor is a social aspect of interaction, only in the twentieth century did sociology concern itself with humor. As a result, humor came into focus when it was found to be concerned with important social issues like political conflicts and social resistance (Kuipers, 2008). In this regard, some perspectives and approaches have been propounded. Functional analyses, for example, interpret political humor as a safety valve or social corrective; phenomenological and symbolic interactionist approaches stress humor's ambiguous and manifold meanings, and its role in negotiating meanings and worldviews; comparative-historical studies tend to stress humor's connection with larger social and cultural concerns; and finally, conflict theories see humor as an expression of conflict, struggle, or antagonism (Kuipers, 2008).

According to conflict theories, humor is interpreted not as venting off—and hence avoidance or reduction—but as an expression or correlate of social conflict: humor as a weapon, a form of attack, a means of defense (Speier, 1998). In conceptualizing jokes as weapons, Speier (1998) emphasized that both the strong who use humor from above, and the weak who joke from below, employ humor for aggressive and defensive purposes, and that power relations shape the conception and the reception of humor.

On the other hand, and from an anti-theoretical point of view, Davies (2008) found unsolved problems with the great theories of humor in the social sciences. As he argued, the problem with the functionalist theory and the conflict approach theory lies in the fact that their object of study, humor, is so slippery and ambiguous that it ends up casting doubt on their proposals. These theories also have numerous exceptions, so that they are forced to make extravagant interpretations to justify themselves. Nevertheless, criticism of such theories does not mean that we cannot construct models for analyzing humor (Moreno, 2013). Having reached this point, we developed a model inspired basically by the studies of Davies (1990, 1991, 2002).

Every sociological or linguistic model is usually developed to assess a specific aspect of the targeted text, context, or society. The model developed for the analysis of the data in the current study is intended to exclusively locate meanings that might reflect freedom of speech. Other meanings have not been considered in developing our sociological model.

To avoid forcing the jokes to fit into an arbitrary and unsophisticated explanation, the analysis was based on large aggregates of jokes in the Iranian context. The massive number of jokes, according to Davies (2011), constitutes a facet of a particular social world that calls for an explanation.

Our reading of the data suggests that the ways in which political issues and targets have been treated indicate different degrees of directness. Some humor, instead of blaming high-ranking personalities, mocked the nation in a mild, non-aggressive way, as evidenced by Example 1 (bounded, placate, neutral).

**Example 1** A new discovery of early human history!!!!!!

Iranian nationality of Adam and Eve was proved:

One day, a disciple asked: O Sheikh (master), has the nationality of Adam and Eve been investigated? Some consider them English and some French?!!!!

The Sheikh said: When they had no clothes to wear and no house to live in, and their only food was an apple, which was considered "haram" (forbidden) to eat, and despite all these troubles, they still thought they were in "heaven," they were definitely.

"Iranian"!

This joke, through non-aggressive, non-insulting language, expressed the hardships the common people suffer in the form of a humorous short story.

Some other jokes targeted politicians and political issues in a mild, non-aggressive manner, as shown by example 2 (conservative).

**Example 2** Although the dust is bothering the people of Khuzestan, we are happy that the "person in question" is crying for us in Tehran...

This piece of conservative humor puts forward the negligence and false concerns of the government, especially the president (the person crying for us in Tehran) in dealing with the dust problem of Khuzestan province in a gentle and non-offensive manner.

A third group targeted the nation, including the tellers themselves, using harsh incendiary language, as evinced by example 3 (provoker).

**Example 3** We are a nation that only in the heavy traffic keep behind each other (watch each other's back...).

With an insulting tone, the creators and broadcasters of such provocative humor accuse the nation of not supporting each other, fearing solidarity in the face of officials and betrayal. Accordingly, such humor tries to incite the nation into solidarity against the officials.

A fourth set of humor feels free in belittling politicians and political issues in an open and aggressive way, as represented by example 4 (unbounded).

**Example 4** The career future according to the GPA in Iran;

GPA 20 = doctor

GPA 17–19 = engineer or university professor

Grade 16 = teacher

GPA 14–15 = employee

Grade 12–14 = CEO

GPA 5–11 = MP

Rejected = billionaire

Running away from school = President

Roughneck (rabble) of the school = Minister

Snitch (talebearer) of the school = Governor

These last ones destroyed me!!!

This piece of aggressive unbounded humor, with a very insulting tone, tries to depict the government officials as uneducated, liars, irresponsible, and incompetent

**Table 10.1** Socio-political categories of political humor

|  | Non-aggressive | Aggressive |
|---|---|---|
| Self-mocking | Bounded (neutral) | Unbounded (provoker) |
| Other-mocking | Bounded (conservative) | Highly unbounded (conflictive) |

people. At the same time, this humor claims that none of the educated, knowledgeable, and capable people are in positions of authority and the educated ones are separate from the ruling group.

Some rare types of humor followed other themes including amusement and retaliation (Note example 5). These themes were left intentionally uncategorized for their paucity in our data.

**Example 5** It is said that when Ahmadinejad and Baghai were going to register (for the presidential candidacy), they told Mohsen Rezaei, "Don't come, we are going to get an injection and come back."

This kind of humor deals with other less significant issues. For example, the above piece of humor ridiculed Mohsen Rezaei's repeated candidacy issue. Mohsen Rezaei nominated himself for several presidential elections in which he always received minimum votes. Nevertheless, it seems that he wants to be a permanent candidate for all elections. This kind of humor has both an entertainment and a retaliation aspect. The retaliation aspect is mostly satisfied by mocking (sometimes for no particular reason) the heads and special personalities in the system.

Using these themes and following the terminology suggested by Davies (1990, 2002) (self/other-mocking, non/aggressive), we devised a model of categorization depicted in Table 10.1.

## 10.3 The Study

### 10.3.1 The Appraisal Model

Humor, by nature, cannot be understood apart from the feeling that underlies it (Chafe, 2009) and this feeling can be realized in the evaluative meanings employed in this specific genre. The Appraisal model, "opening a new area of interpersonal meaning" (Liu, 2010, p. 133), promises to equip practitioners with analytical tools which might help them better understand evaluative meanings and the negotiation of inter-subjective positions. Evaluative devices intend to enrich a narrative and grab and hold attention (Chen, 2004, p. 677). This model allows the analyst to systematically categorize attitudinal meanings in texts (Wan, 2008). Evaluative meanings show the nature and kind of relationship that speakers, writers, listeners, or readers have. They also reveal the interlocutors' expectations and perceptions of each other (Chen,

2004). Hence, an analysis of evaluative meanings embedded in political humor can reveal humorists' political expectations and how they appraise their targets.

The Appraisal framework, as presented by Martin and Rose (2003), identifies three interacting categories of evaluative meaning-making: Attitude, dealing with meanings related to positive/negative assessments or responses; Engagement, targeted at dialogistic positioning of the author in relation to other voices, viewpoints, and potential respondents; and Graduation, whereby the author adjusts the force of utterances or of the boundaries of semantic categories (Don, 2016).

As the main concern of this study, Attitude provides different options for its taxonomy of attitudinal sub-types. It helps the analyst determine whether the attitudinal value under scrutiny (in a piece of humor) is an example of Affect, dealing with the expression of emotions (happiness, fear, etc.), Judgment, dealing with moral assessments of human behavior (honesty, kindness, etc.), or Appreciation, dealing with aesthetic assessments of artifacts, natural objects, and products (subtlety, beauty, etc.)—and whether the orientation is positive or negative (Don, 2016). As Don (2016) noted, Attitude can be conveyed through nouns (e.g., triumph, catastrophe), verbs (e.g., love, hate), and especially through adjectives. These wide categories, in turn, are manifested in more delicate taxonomies of sub-types, each of which reflects a specific aspect of attitude. The main categories of Affect are encapsulated as Happiness/unhappiness, Security/insecurity, Satisfaction/dissatisfaction, and Inclination/disinclination (see Martin & Rose, 2003; Martin & White, 2005).

The Attitude sub-system of Judgment encompasses norms about how people should (not) behave. Like Affect, this taxonomy has positive and negative dimensions corresponding to positive and negative Judgments about behavior. The main categories of Judgment are *Social Esteem* (Normality: fate, Is s/he special? Capacity: Is s/he capable? Tenacity: Is s/he dependable?) and *Social Sanction* (Veracity: Is s/he honest? and Propriety: Is s/he beyond reproach?).

Like Affect and Judgment sub-systems, the Appreciation sub-system encompasses positive and negative dimensions corresponding to a positive and negative evaluation of texts, objects, processes, and natural phenomena encapsulated as *Reaction*: Did it grab me, did I like it? *Composition*: Did it hang together, was it hard to follow? *Valuation*: Was it worthwhile?

This study particularly explored the meanings related to positive/negative assessments of the political humor targets, and not the dialogistic positioning of the writer/speaker in relation to other voices (Engagement) or the adjustments of the force of utterances (Graduation). Rather than touching the surface, our concern was to delve deeply into the Attitude category of evaluative meaning making and leave Engagement and Graduation to be studied in separate research projects.

## 10.3.2 Methodology

The current study is qualitative and quantitative. The qualitative content analysis of the study aimed to provide in-depth insights into political humor by detecting the popular themes in Iranian political humor and identifying the social causes that lead to forming political humor. The quantitative analysis, on the other hand, helped draw numerical conclusions.

### 10.3.2.1 Data

The present study concerned itself only with verbal jokes, leaving performance comedy and other forms of humor aside. The studied jokes were targeted at Iranian readers. Due to their abundance on the Net, jokes in printed venues were not added to the corpus. It is also assumed that on-line jokes are more available to a vast spectrum of readers. The jokes were taken from various net-based platforms (*Facebook, Instagram, Telegram, Twitter, WhatsApp*, and online comment sections). The data were collected by downloading the most recent political jokes and moving backward in time, for as Kuipers noted (2006, p. 23): "jokes are recycled more often than new jokes are invented." This continued until we made sure no new themes could be located. More than 351 fit the determined criterion. As one of the main objectives of this research is to provide a completely unbiased sample that includes all sections and strata of the society, we collected jokes told by people involved in political issues as well as jokes formed and shared by lay people.

### 10.3.2.2 Procedure

Having saved the jokes in Rich Text Format (RTF), we conducted an initial pilot on 30 percent of the jokes randomly selected to verify the dependability of the adapted sociological model and to see what attitudinal values were instantiated. Care was exercised to include jokes around diverse topics. The targets of the jokes (phenomena, people, and their behavior) were then traced, and drawing on the formulations of the Appraisal framework (Martin & White, 2005) the attitudinal markers employed to evaluate targets in the jokes were subsequently identified and counted by the second author of this chapter. Locating and categorizing evaluative markers inside political humor is not always straightforward. The markers sometimes fit more than one category; in such cases, the double-faced markers were classified after the authors discussed and agreed on their most appropriate categories. The raters held a number of online and face-to-face meetings in which all disagreements were resolved. Furthermore, from a sociological point of view, the researchers had a second reading of the whole sample focusing on aspects other than attitude.

This time the researchers sought to evaluate whether the jokes mocked local people (self) or t political personalities (others), and whether the target identity was invoked or explicit. In addition, the analysis aimed to uncover whether the tone of the jokes was harsh and insulting (aggressive) or mild and conservative (non-aggressive). Accordingly, we classified humor into four possibilities. Following the terminology used by Davies (1990, 1991, 2002), the categories were titled as non/aggressive and self/other-mocking. Then, the distribution of jokes was compared to see if the jokes focused more on mocking self or others and if that mocking was aggressive or restrained. In addition, to find out if the socio-political context affects the target-attitude patterns, the findings of both models (the Appraisal model and the Socio-Political model) were juxtaposed. This combination helped the researchers to see if the socio-political, economic, and cultural considerations could affect the selection of evaluative markers.

As anthropological research into humor shows a clear connection between humor and culture (Apte, 1985), and because jokes efficiently exploit indirect language (Dascal, 1985), and the attitudinal values tend to be implicit, seeking help from professionals was inevitable. To this end, our data and the relevant analysis were emailed and discussed in a step-by-step routine with an experienced Socio-Political and Appraisal researcher who was a lecturer at the University of New South Wales, Australia, to be double-checked. The data were then examined by one of the researchers of this study to guarantee coding reliability. Coding reliability was measured using the Kappa coefficient (0.995). The differences, due to differences in interpretation, were negotiated and an agreement was reached on the method of analysis.

## 10.3.3 Findings and Discussion

Our findings suggest that in their quest for safe and persuasive objections and criticism, political activists and local people always tested different ways to express their dissatisfactions. Depending on the socio-political conditions of the context, the status of the targets, the ruling ideology, and above all, the cultural conventions of the country, humor took different forms: either expressed frankly while targeting explicitly named political personalities or conveyed behind a shroud of implicitness directed toward unspoken targets. This was exercised by means of different strategies including socio-politically implied meanings (openness) and the inscribed or invoked attitudinal markers. In what follows we shall report the findings and discuss the target selection, the preferred attitudinal patterns, and the effect of the social context on shaping humor.

### 10.3.3.1 The Targets of Political Humor

In order to locate the attitudinal markers used by humorists to shape their targets, discover the probable patterns used to shape those targets, and find the ways in which the socio-political contexts and cultural considerations affect their evaluative choices, first and foremost the targets of humor had to be identified. Table 10.2 depicts the most targeted individuals and political structures in the Iranian humor dataset. Logically, people blame their targets as the sole explanation for their problems and misery.

**Table 10.2** Targets of Iranian political humor

| Targets | Sub-targets (examples) |
|---|---|
| Politicians and political parties | The reformists, the conservatives…. |
| Religious leaders | The Leader, Jannati, Makarem, Raeisi, Friday preachers, clergymen, inept authorities in general |
| The government—the executive power | The president, the ministers, governors, etc |
| Despotic forces | The *Basij* i.e., nonuniformed forces, the intelligence forces, parallel powers, security forces, the Islamic Republic of Iran Broadcasting (IRIB) |
| Candidates | Parliament members, presidential election candidates such as Ahmadinejad, Raeisi, Jahangiri, Karrobi, Mousavi, Rezaei… |
| Aristocrats (highborn) | Ministers' and high-ranking personalities' children and family members |
| High-level Individuals | e.g., Rouhani, Raeisi, Ahmadinejad, Qalibaf, Jannati, Makarem, Zangeneh, Nobakht, Mirsalim, Larijanis, Rezaei |
| The nation | Teachers, workers, lay people |
| The tripartite powers | The judicial power, the legislative power, the executive power… |
| American Presidents | Bush, Trump, Obama, Clintons… |

As the table shows, the main targets of Iranian humor at the time that the data were collected were triple forces: candidates, the nation, politicians' children, and infrequently the supreme leader. The study also found that high-ranking targets within this context tended to be selected cautiously and disparaged implicitly. This careful selection and vigilant introduction of the targets in Iranian humor can have different explanations. First, punishments assigned by law for what is called insulting or ridiculing of dignity. The defense of dignity is dealt with in Articles 102 and 39 of the Islamic Republic of Iran's Constitution, stating that it is forbidden to ridicule and denigrate others. The constitution does not consider any excuse to be admissible (even for true and fair causes). Accordingly, the Islamic Penal Code has imposed different penalties for what it calls denigrating or ridiculing the Supreme Leader, religion, and government officials. According to Article 513 of the Islamic Penal Code, insulting (ridiculing or denigrating) Islamic values justifies a person's punishment by execution or one to five years of imprisonment (Zahedi, 2019). Also, according to Article 514, any kind of insulting (ridiculing or denigrating) Ayatollah Khomeini or the Supreme Leader leads to punishment of six to twenty-four months imprisonment (Zahedi, 2019).

The Islamic Penal Code also states that under Article 609, anyone who insults (ridicules or denigrates) the president, one of heads of the triple forces, parliamentarians, or government officials, is punished by three to six months' imprisonment, or flogging (Zahedi, 2019). Other forces for this type of watchful target selection in Iranian humor are the deep religious and cultural beliefs of the Iranian nation.

Adhering to polite speech is one of the strongest ethical recommendations in Islam and Iranian culture. While religion, and hence its culture, respect freedom of expression, opinion, and thought (The Quran Alnahl verse 125; Aala verse 9), it restricts the right to criticize subjects through strict principles and regulations (The Quran, Alnesa verse 148; Aal-Omran verse 66).

Digging for more popular targets, the study found that Iranians felt free to sneer at ex-presidents and the political wing they belong to, especially people who were outraged by the supreme leader and the ruling system. The findings also showed that clergymen, Friday preachers, and divine leaders are popular targets in Iranian humor. Note examples 6 and 7:

**Example 6** (Iran) Ahmadinejad after 4 years of the presidency: My work is over. Does anyone want to go to the bathroom?

Ahmadinejad (ex-president for two terms) is the explicit target of this piece of humor who is blatantly presented as an incapable president.

**Example 7** (Iran) Makarem's new decree!

Death is forbidden in Iran because it causes freedom from hardships and leads to the joy of the soul!

The above short example of conservative humor presents multiple targets simultaneously. The main target is the clergymen (symbolized by Makarem) who, according to this piece of humor, abused religion to adjudicate decrees[1] for the benefit of the ruling system. Example 8 below is a clear instance of humor that attacks ex-governments or former presidents by targeting them and their achievements.

**Example 8** Among the achievements of this government in terms of dispelling Iran-phobia and increasing its global popularity, it is enough that Real Madrid wore purple in the final tournament. After all, this is said by one of the statesmen.

Due to problems that are rooted in the power structure on the one hand, and the nature of political actors in the Islamic Republic on the other hand, the political arena in Iran does not have the necessary transparency to demonstrate the major political parties and their tendencies and differentiate them one from the other. However, what the common people know is that the executive president and the legislative president were exchanged between the two parties of fundamentalists and reformists in certain periods of time since 1998 when after years of fundamentalist power, Seyyed Mohammad Khatami obtained his office through a decisive majority, with the official slogan of political reforms. From that time onward, whenever a party lost its political status and handed over the government to a rival party, people plucked up their courage to make various jokes about the losing party. Forgery, incompetence, and even betrayal, are among the attributes that are ascribed to the losing party as the main target of political humor.

---

[1] Adjudicating a decree or issuing a Fatwa is a ruling on a point of Islamic law given by a recognized authority.

## 10.3.3.2 Types of Evaluation and Their Patterns in Iranian Humor

This section reports the attitudinal markers that Iranian political humor utilizes to attack its targets. In addition, it sets to answer the question about the probable availability of particular patterns of attitude used in shaping the targets of these texts. The findings show that Iranian political humorists utilized different types of attitudinal values to evaluate their targets. The attitudinal expressions utilized in the web-based social networks dealing with this genre were identified and calculated. The results are displayed as follows.

As depicted in Table 10.3, Iranian humor opted for Veracity, Capacity, Propriety, and Normality in evaluating its targets. Veracity (30.6%) in Iranian political humor was the most favored resource to which humorists resorted. The study also found some repeatedly utilized target-value patterns (see Table 10.4). Iranian humor consistently employed nation-Tenacity/Normality, politicians-Propriety, and government officials/clergymen-Veracity. Furthermore, as shown in Table 10.3, although all types of attitudinal resources were applied to evaluate targets, the Judgment subcategory constituted the greatest share among the other two. This is reasonable, as political dissatisfaction would undoubtedly originate from the malfunction of some personalities.

Table 10.3 Types and percentages of evaluation in Iranian political humor

| Attitude types | (%) |
| --- | --- |
| Normality | 40 (11.6) |
| Capacity | 78 (22.7) |
| Tenacity | 6 (1.7) |
| Veracity | 105 (30.6) |
| Propriety | 63 (18.3) |
| Reaction-impact | 1 (0.3) |
| Reaction-quality | 28 (8.1) |
| Composition-balance | 18 (5.2) |
| Composition-complexity | 1 (0.3) |
| Valuation | 1 (0.3) |
| Affect | 2 (0.6) |
| | 351 (100) |

Table 10.4 Types of repeated target-value patterns in Iranian political humor

| Pattern | Implied meanings |
| --- | --- |
| Nation–tenacity | Cowardice, Gutlessness |
| Nation–normality | Quality of life, economic problems of the nation |
| Politicians—propriety | Corruption, immorality, meanness |
| Government officials/clergymen—veracity | Deceit (religious abuse), manipulation (sophistry) |

The target-value patterns and the meanings they imply follow ideological, cultural, and economic considerations. Example 9, constituting a sample of the veracity-politicians pattern through symbolic use of chess as a game well-known for its fixed principles and rules (similar to fixed principles of cultures), suggested that the governments have distorted the Iranian culture through political means and for political ends.

**Example 9** New rules of chess.

Ajmedinejad became the head of the chess federation and issued these orders.

(1) From now on, the horse (knight) must become a donkey.
(2) From now on, no one has the right to close the door of the castle (rook).
(3) From now on, instead of a king, we have a Faghih (jurisconsult). If someone checkmates a Faghih, he will be arrested. The Faghih moves in any direction he wants and knocks every piece he wants.
(4) From now on, the Sayyids (the clergymen with a black turban) will only play with black pieces and the common people will play with white pieces. And to respect Sadat (descendants of Prophet Mohammad), from now on the black piece will start the game.
(5) From now on, if the Faghih is in danger, the pawns can go to the opponent's last square and become the president instead of becoming a minister (queen). (Value: veracity, Target: government officials)

Another popular pattern, as mentioned in Table 4 above, deals with Normality-nation humor. By way of example 10, the Normality category, when accompanied with the nation as its target in the Iranian context, usually refers to the economic problems people suffer:

**Example 10** (Iran): The year 1396 [2017] has been named:

"No matter how much you poove up (trade your derriere), you cannot manage your family bread." (Value: Normality, target: Iranian nation)

Such humor, by showing how hapless the nation is, tried to depict the complicated economic problems Iranians experience nowadays. The targets (including the humorist him/herself) have been judged as a negative Normality value.

Due to the sanctions imposed by American allies, Iran is facing loads of economic, social, and political problems (Erdbrink, 2019). Although the government and the mass media have always attempted to depict the sanctions as ineffective, everyday humor proves the opposite. People's life standards have worsened, their purchasing power and their income have declined, and their health has deteriorated since the beginning of the sanctions (Erdbrink, 2019; Sepehrifar, 2019). In addition, as the above-mentioned humor shows, because of their excessive worries about the future and their unsatisfactory financial situation, people have to work in as many jobs as possible.

Similar to example 10, example 11 shows how implanting wrong policies not only affected the people's life standards but also manipulated Iranian pure culture by normalizing unfamiliar phenomena such as embezzlement and disloyalty, planting them in the society's daily lexicon.

**Example 11** It is said that Iranian mathematicians discovered a new numerical position after *yekkan* (single numbers), *dahgan* (tens), and *sadgan* (hundreds)..., called *akhtlasgan* (embezzlement numbers). It's out of our knowledge but all that we know is that it has a lot of zeros!!! (Value: Propriety/Veracity; Target: Politicians).

Another category of propriety humor can be seen in the following example, representing value-target, context-bound patterns.

**Example 12** Fourteen types of *Halal* things to eat which do not invalidate fasting;

1. *Bayt-al- mal* (public property)
2. Assets of banks
3. People's personal property
4. My property
5. Your property
6. Minors' property
7. The poor's property
8. The orphans' property
9. Three Thousand billions
10. Twenty five thousand billions
11. Sixty thousand billions
12. 100 trillions
13. Four tankers full of fuel
14. Oil drilling rigs

[It should be noted that drinking water, eating bread, and even smoking a cigarette leads to fast cancellation (*haram*)...]

As example 12 shows, the usual Propriety-target patterns (targeting politicians) in Iranian humor deal with economic corruption, not other types of corruption. Certainly the absence of humor scandalizing other types of corruption such as sex affairs in this category of humor does not suggest the absolute absence of such incidents, but rather that this absence might be due to the religious and cultural beliefs of Iranians. Prophet Mohammad says, "Who so hides the defect of his Muslim brother in the world and does not disgrace him, Allah hides his defect at the day of Resurrection" (Siyoti, 1981). This religious virtue, and probably other similar ethical beliefs, act as a shield against revealing sex scandals in the Iranian context. In addition, talking openly about sex (especially if the target is a high-ranking political personality) is taboo in Iranian culture although it might not be in other cultures.

The Tenacity-target pattern (example 13) also shows the long-term ideology of the Iranian political system.

**Example 13** Some donkey was asked, "How are things with you"?

He said, "My food is scarce and my load is enormous, but I'm submissive and thankful".

They said, "Truly, you are a donkey"!

How familiar!!!!!! (Value: Tenacity; Target: the nation).

In this example, the Iranian nation has implicitly been introduced as cowardly and gutless, willing to accept all kinds of miseries but doesn't dare to object to the problems they constantly suffer. This kind of target-value, context-bound pattern, depicts the socio-political condition of the targeted society. Billig (2005, pp. 201–202) maintained that "in addition to the simple act of giggling or mocking, as a practice humor also involves various socio-political purposes. In other words, it has been argued that social life is dependent on the practices of ridicule." Cowardice has been copiously illustrated through Iranian humor. Such pusillanimity can be due to the despotism the Iranian nation has experienced during its long history and, as Moradi and Abrishamchian (2017) conclude, expecting the effect of 2500 years of despotism to be abolished is nothing but a naive dream.

#### 10.3.3.3 Socio-Political Context Effect

This section reports the ways in which the Iranian socio-political context shapes the attitudes of the humorists to evaluate their targets. It should be noted that a small percentage of the jokes in our database (5.17%) revolved around minor scattered topics on which the coders could not arrive at a unanimous decision. Thus, we considered them as miscellaneous and disregarded them in our analysis. Table 10.5 presents political humor based on our socio-political model.

About 62 percent of Iranian humor was non-aggressive. The findings show that the existing political system (whether bounded or unbounded) affects the public attitudes adopted in political humor. Accordingly, seen from the perspective of our analysis, political humor needs to be evaluated while having an eye on three meaning-affecting factors; the type of targets, the socio-cultural context, and the attitude embedded (openness model). The analysis also shows that the usual patterns are acted upon as illustrated in Table 10.6.

As shown in Example 14 below, Iranian socio-political considerations controlled the HRT–attitude (current president—negative veracity) pattern to be presented non-aggressively.

Table 10.5 Socio-political distribution of Iranian political humor

|  | Non-aggressive (%) | Aggressive (%) |
|---|---|---|
| Self-mocking | 31 (10.91%) | 14 (4.92%) |
| Other-mocking | 145 (51%) | 80 (28%) |

**Table 10.6** Target—tone patterns in bounded contexts

| |
|---|
| High Ranking Target (HRT)—conservative humor (non-aggressive, other mocking) |
| Low Ranking Target (LRT)—conservative and conflictive (aggressive, other mocking) |
| Self-Targets (ST)—aggressive (provoker) and non-aggressive |

**Example 14** Although the dust is annoying the people of Khuzestan, we are glad to hear that the "intended person in Tehran" is crying for us … (conservative: non-aggressive, other-mocking, bounded).

The factors that helped shape the Iranian bounded, socio-political context, besides the 2500 years of despotism, originate from a variety of post-revolutionary ideological and cultural forces. These forces have been the target of a wide range of humor. For instance, as claimed in the following conservative bounded piece of humor (Example 15), there are forces of political pressure that come into action to control social and political affairs. These forces are often anonymous and ununiformed, and due to their wide scope of authority they are allowed to intervene and act creatively.

**Example 15** Before the ISIS attack on the parliament, I had never seen from behind the running of the ununiformed troops; in all the memories recorded in my mind, they always used to run toward me.

Freedom of expression, according to Shokohi (2017), was a basic ideal sought by the Iranian revolution. However, some factors led to various changes in the revolution's ideals. The first factor was the groups who took arms against the young Islamic Republic. Another factor was the presence of some narrow-minded/intolerant/radical movements and prominent personalities within the founders of the revolution who thought freedom of speech harms the unity of the country and troubles the political space. This was stated humorously in the following non-law-abiding joke (Example 16) in which it is claimed silencing voices is the highest priority. As a strategy to silence conflicting voices, such movements drew a sacred halo around some of the officials in the system, entrenched behind religious values.

**Example 16** Intelligence agencies have more important tasks, such as arresting Telegram admins, dissidents, and journalists. There is no time for terrorists!!!

Example 17 below depicts an instance of a self-targeting, non-aggressive piece of humor. However, the main targets of this joke are the police and the radical personalities who have been mocked in restrained fashion for restricting the freedom of speech. The long-lasting fear of the adverse consequences of free expression gradually became part of the common culture, passed from generation to generation.

**Example 17** One day a person rushed into the police office and said: My parrot is missing. The policeman said that this issue is not related to us. The poor guy said: I know, but I came to say that in case you find it, everything it says is its own political opinion and I strictly disagree with it.

## 10.4 Conclusion

The findings of the current study are in line with a good number of previous studies. They similarly have found that humor is inhibited by repression, political threat (Hart, 2007), dogmatic ideology (Bayat, 2007), and historical background (Javadi Yeganeh, 2009). Empirical evidence has also shown that to bypass such inhibitions, political humor in authoritarian administrations becomes peripheral and hidden (Merziger, 2007; Shehata, 1992; Swart, 2009; Tuene, 2007). Consequently, as confirmed in this study, in closed contexts political humor that might be used to "offer an account of how people perceive political actions and decisions and how they evaluate them" (Tsakona, 2017, p. 152) becomes less direct and less aggressive. The findings also show degrees of similarity with Kaplan's (1966) model of contrastive rhetoric. A generic typology of cultural writing patterns suggests that while North American (English) argumentative writing is linear, direct, and to the point, Semitic and Oriental styles tend to be zigzag (parallel propositions, embedded in stories, not in hierarchical progression) and circular (respectful, indirect, non-assertive, but authoritative), respectively (Kaplan, 1966).

Political humor is a "crucial part of society's political discourse" (Peifer, 2012, p. 268), reflecting the public perception of, and reaction to, officials' decisions in response to high-stakes issues (Hart, 2007). The attitudes adopted in political humor disclose the public's feelings toward their politicians. They also illustrate how the public evaluate politicians and their performance. The analysis of the data here showed that the attitudes were presented in sets of exclusive, context-bound, target-value patterns. The study also showed that a bounded socio-political context affects the tone of political humor (aggressive, non-aggressive). In addition, the study indicated that political humor relies heavily on the attitudes embedded explicitly and implicitly.

## References

Abdoli, I. (2015). All banned publications in Rouhani government. *Bartarinha Online*, 1–8. http://www.bartarinha.ir/fa/print/169987. (in Farsi).
Apte, M. L. (1985). *Humor and laughter: An anthropological approach.* Cornell University Press.
Bayat, A. (2007). Islamism and the politics of fun. *Public Culture, 19*(3), 433–459. https://doi.org/10.1215/08992363-2007-004
Billig, M. (2005). *Laughter and ridicule: Towards a social critique of humour.* Sage.
Brottman, M. (2004). *Gershonlegman and the psychopathology of humor.* Analytic Press.
Caufield, R. P. (2008). The influence of "infoenterpropagainment": Exploring the power of political satire as a distinct form of political humor. In J. C. Baumgartner & J. S. Morris (Eds.), *Laughing matters: Humor and American politics in the media age* (pp. 3–20). Routledge.
Chafe, W. (2009). *The importance of not being earnest: The feeling behind laughter and humor.* John Benjamins.
Chen, L. (2004). Evaluation in media texts: A cross-cultural linguistic investigation. *Language in Society, 33*(5), 673–702. https://doi.org/10.1017/S0047404504045026

Dascal, M. (1985). Language use in jokes and dreams: Sociopragmatics vs psychopragmatics. *Language and Communication, 5*(2), 95–106.
Davies, C. (1991). Ethnic humor, hostility and aggression: A reply to Eliott Oring. *Humor, 4*(3/4), 415–422. https://doi.org/10.1515/humr.1991.4.3-4.415
Davies, C. (2008). Undertaking the comparative study of humor. In V. Raskin (Ed.), *The primer of humor research* (pp. 157–182). Mouton de Gruyter.
Davies, C. (2011). *Jokes and targets.* Indiana University Press.
Davies, C. (1990). *Ethnic humor around the world: A comparative analysis.* Indiana University Press.
Davies, C. (2002). *The mirth of nations.* Transaction Publ.
Don, A. (2016). It is hard to mesh all this: Invoking attitude, persona and argument organisation. *Functional Linguistics, 3*(1), 1–26.
Erdbrink, T. (2019). Iran faces worst economic challenge in 40 years, president says. *NYTimes.com.* https://www.nytimes.com/2019/01/30/world/middleeast/iran-economy.html
Fazeli, N. (2006). *Politics of culture in Iran* (1st ed.). Routledge.
Fine, A. G. (1983). Sociological approaches to the study of humor. In P. E. McGee & J. H. Goldstein (Eds.), *Handbook of humor research* (Vol. 1, pp. 159–181). Springer.
Hart, M. (2007). Humor and social protest: An introduction. *International Review of Social History, 52*(S15), 1–20. https://doi.org/10.1017/S0020859007003094
ISNA. (2014). Ahmadinejad's government banned 46 publications. *Hamshahri Online.* http://hamshahrionline.ir/details/240753 (in Farsi).
Jalilifar, A., Savaedi, S. Y., & Don, A. (2021). The battery dies quicker than a black guy: A thematic analysis of political jokes in the American and Iranian contexts. *International Journal of Society, Culture & Language, 9*(3), 1–15.
Javadi Yeganeh, M. (2009). Iranian political culture: Behaviors and attitudes. *Andisheh Club.* www.mrjavadi.com/Default.aspx?PageName=Print&id=7739. (in Farsi).
Kaplan, R. (1966). Cultural thought patterns in inter-culture education. *Language Learning, 16*(1–2), 1–20. https://doi.org/10.1111/j.1467-1770.1966.tb00804.x
Kuipers, G. (2008). The sociology of humour. In V. Raskin (Ed.), *The primer of humor research* (pp. 361–398). Mouton de Gruyter.
Kuipers, G. (2006). *Good humor, bad taste: A sociology of the joke.* Mouton de Gruyter.
Liu, X. (2010). An application of appraisal theory to teaching college English reading in China. *Journal of Language Teaching and Research, 1*, 133–135.
Martin, J. R., & Rose, D. (2003). *Working with discourse: Meaning beyond the clause.* Continuum.
Martin, J. R., & White, P. R. R. (2005). *The language of evaluation: Appraisal in English.* Palgrave Macmillan.
Merziger, P. (2007). Humour in Nazi Germany: Resistance and propaganda? The popular desire for all-embracing laughter. *International Review of Social History, 52*(S15), 275–290. https://doi.org/10.1017/S0020859007003240
Mietusch, D. A. (2013). *Humor across cultures: Research on transcultural humor in intercultural coaching and training settings.* GRIN Verlag.
Moradi, H. Q., & Abrishamchian, M. R. (2017). *Despotism in Iran.* Dorrance Publ.
Moreno, C. (2013). Can ethnic humour appreciation be influenced by political reasons? A comparative study of the Basque Country and Catalonia. *European Journal of Humour Research., 1*(2), 24–42. https://doi.org/10.7592/EJHR2013.1.2.moreno
Naghdipour, B. (2014). Jokes in Iran. *Folklore, 59*, 105–120.
Owen, H. L. (2002). Humorous communication: Finding a place for humor in communication research. *Communication Theory, 12*(4), 423–445.
Pearce, K. E., & Hajizada, A. (2014). No laughing matter - Humor as a means of dissent in the digital era: The case of authoritarian Azerbaijan. *Demokratizatsiya, 22*(1), 67–85. https://demokratizatsiya.pub/archives/22_1_B158221228502786.pdf
Peifer, T. J. (2012). Can we be funny? The social responsibility of political humor. *Journal of Mass Media Ethics, 27*(4), 263–276. https://doi.org/10.1080/08900523.2012.746110

Rezvani, H. (2016). The right to freedom of expression, and the responsibility of states for it. *Foreign Policy Quarterly, 4*, 65–92. (in Farsi).

Sepehrifar, T. (2019). Maximum pressure. *Human Rights Watch*. https://www.hrw.org/report/2019/10/29/maximum-pressure/us-economic-sanctions-harm-iranians-right-health.

Shehata, S. (1992). The politics of laughter: Nasser, Sadat, and Mubarak in Egyptian political jokes. *Folklore, 103*(1), 75–91.

Shokohi, A. (2017). Factors that restricted freedom of expression in the age of revolution. *Iran Online*. http://www.ion.ir/news/260706/

Siyoti, J. (1981). *The little encyclopedia* (2nd ed.). Tebyan. (in Farsi).

Speier, H. (1998). Wit and politics: An essay on laughter and power. *American Journal of Sociology, 103*(5), 1352–1401.

Swart, S. (2009). The terrible laughter of the Afrikaner-towards a social history of humor. *Journal of Social History, 42*, 889–917. https://doi.org/10.1353/jsh/42.4.889

Test, G. (1991). *Satire: Spirit and art*. University of South Florida Press.

Tsakona, V. (2017). "This is not a political party, this is Facebook!" Political jokes and political (mis)trust in crisis-ridden Greece. *The European Journal of Humour Research, 5*(4), 136–157. https://doi.org/10.7592/ejhr2017.5.4.tsakona

Tuene, S. (2007). Humor as a guerilla tactic: The West German student movement's mockery of the establishment. *International Review of Social History, 52*(15), 115–132.

Wan, Y. N. (2008). The exchange of interpersonal meaning in call center conversations. *Odense working papers in language and communication, 29*, 825–839.

Young, D. G. (2014). Theories and effects of political humor. *Oxford Handbooks Online*. https://doi.org/10.1093/oxfordhb/9780199793471.013.29_update_001

Zahedi, A. (2019). The Islamic penal code: Approved 22-3-2013. (11th ed.). *Jangal*. (in Farsi).

Zlobin, N. (1996). Humor as political protest. *Demokratizatsiva, 4*(2), 223–231. https://demokratizatsiya.pub/archives/04-2_Zlobin.PDF


**Alireza Jalilifar** is Professor of Applied Linguistics at Shahid Chamran University of Ahvaz, Iran, where he teaches discourse analysis, applied linguistics, and advanced research at MA and PhD levels. He has published and presented numerous papers on academic discourse. He was the leading researcher at Shahid Chamran University of Ahvaz in 2009, 2010, & 2020. His recent co-authored publication is Appliable Approaches to Analyzing Texts in Academic Discourse, published by Cambridge Scholars Jalilifar has supervised more than 70 MA and 35 PhD theses in Iran. His main interests include non-native language writing, genre analysis, and academic discourse.

**Seyed Yousef Savaedi** Ph.D in Applied Linguistics, is an instructor at Farhangian University of Ahvaz, Iran. He mainly teaches writing and research methods at the BA and MA levels. He has published and presented papers on political discourse and EFL issues. He has been the head of English language teachers at Khuzestan Education Organization since 1998. His main interests include political discourse analysis and TEFL.

# Chapter 11
# Mocking the Powers that Be: The Case of Culture and Political Humor in Malaysia

**Debbita Ai Lin Tan**

**Abstract** Political humor, foremost a linguistic phenomenon, plays a key role in how we perceive politics. It resides in research literature due to its unique obligation to sensitize audiences while entertaining. It deserves more attention because it will become pervasive, if not already so. This chapter covers staged comedic acts with a Malaysian framing, performed by local comedians and accessible via YouTube. The cultural characteristics of a country, together with its legal expectations, normally govern the flavor of its humor and I have therefore included these aspects in my discussions. The essence of culture here is the localized concept of being polite, civilized, and cultured [*berbudi bahasa*], the notion of maintaining/saving face [*menjaga air muka*], and Malaysia's home-grown brand of English—Manglish. The works of Douglas Lim and Jason Leong (released in 2021) were used for analysis. Referring to Brown and Levinson's (*Politeness: Some universals in language usage*. The Press Syndicate of the University of Cambridge, 1987) framework on politeness, the off-record and negative politeness strategies prevail on the whole with respect to Lim's parody, while Leong's jests exhibit the qualities of bald on record and negative politeness. None of the analyzed contents can be construed as ingratiating, but in both cases restraint is observed (as is Manglish use). Directions for future research are suggested.

## 11.1 Introduction

Humor is exceedingly useful. One can invent or distort with it, and one can also serve up very inconvenient truths encased in comedy. Humor remains one of the avenues through which social and political commentaries are amply made, and Malaysia is not an exception. Political humor in this multiethnic country is typically safe comedy, shadowed by the specter of the law that can be summoned—sometimes rather liberally and at times quite understandably—in the name of national security.

D. A. L. Tan (✉)
School of Languages, Literacies and Translation, Universiti Sains Malaysia, Penang, Malaysia
e-mail: debbita_tan@usm.my

Humor of the political variety is generally taken without much humor by Malaysian governments, but this has so far only encouraged some of its local talents. Cartoonist Zunar is one example. In a *Free Malaysia Today* report (Nambiar, 2021), Zulkiflee Anwar Alhaque, better known as Zunar, said that he was called in by the police to be investigated for mischief and abuse of the internet over a caricature depicting the state of Kedah's chief minister, Muhammad Sanusi Md Nor. He was allegedly told that he was being probed for making statements conducive to public mischief with the intent to incite the community, as well as for abuse of network services.

The caricature depicts a larger-than-life Sanusi gripping a butcher's knife stamped with the words "No Thaipusam Holiday" [in Malay *Tiada Cuti Thaipusam*] and chopping a table down the middle, shocking the people of various races on either side of it. The accompanying blurb reads: "Kedahans lived peacefully before he (Sanusi) came..." [*Orang Kedah hidup aman damai sebelum dia ni mai...*]. Sanusi had announced in January 2021 that there would be no state public holiday declared for Thaipusam (a Tamil Hindu festival) that year, given the COVID-19 pandemic-related Movement Control Order. This gave rise to protests slamming Sanusi's move as disrespectful and hurtful to minorities (*New Straits Times,* 2021).

According to a report by the Malaysian news portal *The Vibes* (Annuar, 2021), Zunar had mentioned that as a public figure Sanusi ought to take any criticism in a positive light. He also called Sanusi a "dictator" for being unable to accept criticism.

Zunar has courted trouble before and was repeatedly targeted by a former government for his cartoons, often mocking then prime minister Najib Razak and his luxury-loving wife (*The Straits Times*, 2018). Among his artistic expressions is one of Najib wearing underwear over his pants, holding a bag of money and saying: "Welcome to Malayshia" ("shia" here can be interpreted as alluding to the Mandarin language), against a backdrop of national landmarks with their names altered (from, for instance, *Dataran Merdeka*/"Independence Square" to *Dataran Beijing*/"Beijing Square"), implying the "selling" of Malaysia to China by the premier.

Visual rhetoric targeting the powers that be is not new in Malaysia and it continues to inform, entertain, and persuade the people. To a large degree, this is a pleasing continuity because political cartoons are visually entertaining while delivering biting thoughts or accusations. They engage the human penchant for context, drama and the occasional absurdity, as well as the persistence of Us-versus-Them.

Political cartoons deserve at least a mention in any discourse pertaining to political humor, but more so the staged comedic acts that have become more accessible, relatable, and thus inescapably popular.

The digital realm has risen to prominence as a platform for political discourse and through humorous messages, social media outlets offer more access to political content and permit the masses to participate in political culture, in particular the younger generation (Kasmani, 2022). Kasmani (2022) noted that according to the *Internet Users Survey 2020* report by the Malaysian Communications and Multimedia Commission (2020), Facebook remained the most widely utilized social media site in Malaysia, used by more than 90% of the population. Internet users in Malaysia mainly comprised those in their 20s and 30s, at 46% and 21.2% respectively. Other sites such as YouTube, Instagram, and Twitter also saw an increase in their user base. YouTube in particular experienced the most significant increase from 48.3% in 2018 to 80.6% in 2020. The survey revealed entertainment and humorous contents as the most shared contents in the country. These contents included parodies, satires, jokes, and playful memification.

Within the confines of this chapter, political humor refers to narratives that concern political topics, events, actors/players and institutions, manifested with the intention to elicit mirth or laughter, even at the expense of causing offense. The chapter focuses chiefly on staged comedic acts with a Malaysian framing, performed by local comedians and accessible via YouTube. It is also almost impossible to divorce humor from culture. The cultural characteristics of a country, be it social norms or political practices, often dictate the flavor of its humor. I have therefore included this dimension as well in my discussions—most notably, the concept of *menjaga lidah dan tingkah laku* ("to be careful with one's speech and behavior") that to some extent governs Malaysia's brand of comedy.

In Malaysia, safe comedy is the norm, with attempts at political humor by and large not harsh or crude. If anything, one is more likely to witness unsavory discourse playing out in one of the country's highest offices. Over time, Malaysia's parliamentary discourse has both amused and disgusted the public. Take for instance an incident involving Bung Moktar Radin (Member of Parliament/MP for the state of Sabah's Kinabatangan constituency), who in 2007 on the subject of a leaky ceiling in the parliament building alluded to a woman's menstrual cycle, using the word *bocor* ("leak"). Female MP Fong Po Kuan (Batu Gajah constituency) was targeted: "Where is the leak? Batu Gajah MP also leaks every month" (*Today Online*, 2017). Another MP, Idris Haron, was of the opinion that Fong should not have perceived the remark as a gender issue and accused her of using it to get publicity, saying that it should have been taken as a joke and not as a personal attack (Wong, 2007).

Political humor is essentially a linguistic phenomenon, an intrusion into the affairs of the political order, and mockery in Malaysia can be fairly viewed as an art form that criticizes within the bounds of acceptability. In my estimation, it is also an art form that deserves more attention in contemporary research literature due to its pervasiveness and obligation to sensitize audiences in the course of entertaining.

## 11.2 The Politics of Humor

Anyone who makes you laugh is
always doing more than just that
(Provenza & Dion, 2010, p. 17).

Tsakona and Popa (2011) argued that humor can have a serious intent, adding that political humor conveys criticism against the political status quo and/or recycles prevailing views on politics through different genres, including cartoons and impersonations. From another perspective, they observed how humor can be manipulated in public debates and used by politicians as a means of public positioning and attacking political adversaries. The latter is exemplified in an utterance made by former health minister Khairy Jamaluddin against Anwar Ibrahim during Malaysia's 2008 general election campaign. He had reportedly used the phrase *main belakang* ("to play from the back") which suggested that Anwar was a homosexual and a person of low moral character; Justice Darryl Goon said that the remark, in the choice of analogy and figure of speech within the natural and ordinary meaning, was capable of being defamatory to Anwar (Yatim, 2022) because Anwar was charged with sodomy in 1998 and 2008. Khairy was ordered to pay damages and in what can be best described as an interesting turn of events, Khairy is now a DJ (reportedly a humorous one) and Anwar, the 10th Prime Minister of Malaysia.

All forms of political discourse made public are suasive in nature and political comedy is a frontrunner in this aspect, often serving as calls to view political realities repositioned and see the powerful derided. The degree of repositioning and ridicule varies, of course, from the mild to the extreme and everything else in between. American comedian Stephen Colbert's 2017 invective against Donald Trump is an example of the extreme:

> Sir, you attract more skinheads than free Rogaine. You have more people marching against you than cancer. You talk like a sign language gorilla that got hit in the head. In fact, the only thing your mouth is good for is being Vladimir Putin's c–k holster (Otterson, 2017).

Such unrestrained behavior, if applied within the Malaysian context, would have shocked many Malaysians with language so explicit and misaligned with the social convention of *berbudi bahasa* ("to be polite, civilized, and cultured"). In Colbert's case, he faced backlash for the joke he made about Trump because the last line (the one involving Putin) was deemed homophobic (Otterson, 2017).

The Malaysian brand of comedy, whether aimed at political figures or quality of governance, is generally more in keeping with the following example taken from local comedian Jason Leong's (2021) act entitled "Minister of Propaganda wishes Singapore a Happy National Day":

> Everything is Singapore, Singapore, Singapore. […] Singaporeans always boast about their world-class public transport system. Well, the Malaysian LRT (Light Rail Transit) is also very good, okay? Your MRT (Mass Rapid Transit) is on time, ours arrive ahead of time. So early that two of them had a head-on collision. That's efficiency. Singapore got or not?

Political humor is a collective protest against what is perceived as problematic. In nations that demonstrate little tolerance for blatant dissent, it becomes almost imperative to cloak disapproving discourse in jocularity. The laughter that accompanies each worthy salvo is a retaliation of sorts—against the inept, poor governance, and injustice—and a nod to creative critique made possible only by seriously taking on interpretive commitments.

## 11.2.1 No Laughing Matter

According to Human Rights Watch (2021), Malaysia's Penal Code, Sedition Act, Peaceful Assembly Act, and Communications and Multimedia Act all contain overbroad and vaguely worded provisions that allow the police to investigate or arrest people for a wide range of activities that the government disapproves of. Recent cases have targeted people for organizing public protests, reporting on allegations of police abuse, drawing cartoons, and posting a satirical response to a controversial tweet, in the form of a jealousy-themed Spotify playlist.

With a government that dislikes so many things and shows little promise in terms of treating criticism as something more positive than crime, it is little wonder that political comedy here is not more bold. If the state decides what is (in)appropriate public discourse, then every discourse is at risk of being on the wrong side of the divide at the state's convenience.

Human Rights Watch (2015) reported that during Najib Razak's first term as prime minister (between 2009 and 2013), the Malaysian government rescinded several laws including the draconian Internal Security Act that had been regularly used to restrict civil and political rights, including freedom of expression. In the campaign leading up to the 2013 elections, Najib promised to also repeal the notorious Sedition Act. However, confronted with declining popularity and increasing public discontent, he responded by cracking down on critics and supporting new laws, such as the 2015 Prevention of Terrorism Act (POTA) that legalized preventive detention and restricted certain fundamental liberties enshrined in the Constitution of Malaysia (Ahmad & Dhillon, 2022).

In November 2014, Najib reneged on his promise to repeal the Sedition Act and announced that the law would instead be strengthened and made more effective, and the government in April 2015 pushed through amendments providing for harsher penalties and further restrictions on speech, particularly on social media (Human Rights Watch, 2015).

## 11.2.2 Safe Comedy

> Making jokes, poking fun and free speech through humour and satire will no longer be a laughing matter, after Putrajaya (the administrative and judicial capital of Malaysia) tightened its laws on sedition to clamp down on alternative views and online comments (Zachariah, 2015).

Zachariah (2015) reported that the amendments to the colonial-era Sedition Act led to satirical news outlets toning down narratives and becoming more cautious in poking fun at politicians and government bodies.

In 2020, the chairman of the Malaysian Communications and Multimedia Commission addressed the issue of parody accounts and described their use as a new trend to deliver fake news, mock, or insult (Article 19, 2020). He also stated his concern about the possibility of a particular account misleading its followers;

the account in question, @bermanadotcon, clearly stated in its bio: "Your Source of Parody News. Nothing to do and not affiliated with @bernamadotcom," a reference to a state news agency (Article 19, 2020).

There is a placatory flavor in Malaysian political humor. Reproval and appeasement interweave in a fashion that has become acceptable to, and perhaps even encouraged by, society at large. Such caution is understandable and while there may be parties that call for a lesser degree of it, it remains that social conventions also influence the nature of local discourse, funny ones or not, in the same way that local political practices naturally provide fodder for comedians.

The following sections concern Malaysia's social and political landscapes, including also the dimension of Manglish. Manglish is a localized variety of English that makes regular appearances in Malaysian political humor and is seen as part of the nation's culture. Jason Leong's "Singapore got or not?" in the excerpt presented earlier is an example of Manglish usage. The reason for indulging in these landscapes is to provide a backdrop against which subsequent data can be mapped and better understood.

### 11.2.3 The Local Temperament

Lim (2017) opined that the meaning of speech in society is not solely regulated by what is said but more crucially, how it is said. Lim added that social intelligence calls for a way in which human differences can be navigated without fracturing harmony.

Although etiquette varies across cultures, the common threads are respect and good manners. The notion of politeness is almost pedestalized in Malaysian society; a lack of it, manifested verbally or physically, is generally considered a faux pas. More often than not, manifestations of incivility are attended by expressions of disapproval that might include labels like *biadap* ("rude") or *kurang ajar* ("ill-bred" or literally, "not taught enough").

On this matter, what is unacceptable to Malaysian society is perhaps best illustrated by Jocelyn Chia's recent behavior. On June 16 2023, *New Straits Times* (2023) reported that the controversial U.S. stand-up comedian told Malaysians to "keep going" as more international media outlets were featuring her in their news. Taking to Twitter, Chia stated (*New Straits Times,* 2023): "I'm on the front page of BBC.com now. Interviewed by @CNN, @nytimes @BBCWorld and going to be on @FoxNews this Sat. So actually Malaysia, you can keep going," she said, ending it with a laughing emoji.

The former lawyer had tried joking about Malaysia being a developing country and also made reference to Malaysia Airlines Flight 370 (MH370) which disappeared in March 2014. Flight MH370 left Kuala Lumpur for Beijing but never arrived. To date, the plane and its 227 passengers and 12 crew members have not been located. All 239 are presumed dead. This excerpt is from Chia's performance at New York's Comedy Cellar (Shah, 2023):

> My country is Singapore. After we gained independence from the British, we were a struggling little nation. In order to survive, we formed a union with a larger, more powerful country, Malaysia. When my prime minister went on TV to announce that you guys had dumped us, he cried because he thought we were not going to survive without you. But then, 40 years later, we became a first-world country. And you guys? Malaysia, what are you now? Still a developing country.

That there was hardly a punchline is one thing, but her body language, facial expressions and use of expletives came together quite unbecomingly, making her appear more angry than funny. In any case, Chia then referenced the MH370 tragedy in her discourse about Malaysia seeking to rekindle ties with Singapore (*The Star*, 2023):

> Why haven't you [Malaysia] paid me a visit in 40 years?," she said in a monologue. "I tried, but you know, our airplanes can't fly," she replied in another voice as a graphic of a Malaysia Airlines plane flashed on the screen. This drew several gasps from the audience but Chia pushed on: "What, Malaysia Airlines going missing is not funny, huh? Some jokes don't land."

Singapore was quick to apologize to Malaysians and made it clear that Chia was no longer a Singaporean, while Malaysia's foreign affairs minister condemned Chia for her lack of sensitivity and empathy, stating also that her behavior was "contrary to the values of Asian countries that are known for their manners and morals" (Ng, 2023a, 2023b).

Even so, Chia was not without at least one fan. Local comedian Jason Leong expressed his support for her performance and was (predictably) slammed by netizens for this, including those who admitted to being his past fans (Chua, 2023). As for Chia, she had this to say (Ng, 2023a, 2023b): "Americans can appreciate humour that is harsher, edgier and more in-your-face, as compared to in Asia where the stand-up comedy scene is still in its early days. You won't find a lot of edgy comedy in Asia."

## *11.2.4 Of Virtue and "Saving Face"*

In Malaysia, virtue is referred to as *budi*. It is viewed as associated with wisdom, understanding and discretion, and is not disengaged from manners and morals. The word is derived from Sanskrit's *buddhi* and according to Lim (2003), the concept of *budi* can be observed but cannot be fully explicated. Within the context of communication, it might be best to marry it to the concept of *bahasa* ("language") which includes the aspects of customs, values, and beliefs. An individual who is *berbudi bahasa* is therefore a person of virtue and culture, abiding by social etiquette in manner and speech. Latif and associates (2018) saw the practice of *berbudi bahasa* as an effective formula for multiracial Malaysia, with its religious and cultural diversities, to ensure that unity is not undermined.

Ramli (2013) noted that the practice of *berbudi bahasa* is part of everyday life in Malaysia for both verbal and non-verbal communication. A less direct manner of speaking is also often regarded as the result of sensible upbringing in Asian communities, deemed necessary for avoiding ill feelings, humiliation, or awkwardness. Haji Omar (1992) suggested beating about the bush and the employment of imagery as types of indirect elements in the Malaysian communication style.

*Menjaga air muka* ("to maintain/save face") is another part of local culture. There is a repertoire of "face-saving" practices in Malaysia, used for the benefit of one's own dignity or that of others. Most notably in Asian countries, directness can be perceived as offensive and so the practice of "maintaining/saving face" is rather pervasive in social interactions. In short, high-context communication—in which a great deal of information is implied rather than made explicit—tends to be the preferred mode among Asians. Within the boundaries of humor, however, there is more tolerance among Malaysians and while the measure of this tolerance cannot be objectively described as extraordinarily generous, it is fair to say that directness presented as cheeky "foot-stamping" against the government or any other entity of choice is normally perceived as acceptable.

### 11.2.5 *This One Not Funny Lah*

Manglish is Malaysia's home-grown brand of English. It is an informal English-based creole characterized by the presence of the country's more dominant languages: Malay, Chinese dialects (e.g., the Hokkien dialect), and Tamil. Besides the mixing of words from these sources, Manglish includes as well the use of different syntaxes. For instance, English can be spoken in Malay or Chinese syntax. Another prominent feature of Manglish is the presence of discourse particles like *lah*, *leh*, *lor* and *meh* that are not found in standard English and that are often cryptic to foreigners. Hassan and Hashim (2009, pp. 43–44) explained that the particles serve to convey emotions and attitudes, such as "to soften a directive, place emphasis on a statement or word, and affirm a statement or turn a statement into a question."

Manglish is widely used by locals in less formal and completely informal situations, not excluding comedic acts. It is not merely a tool for functionality, but is also a cultural badge. Malaysians essentially see it as simple and effective, infused with enough local flavors to also project their identities and give them a sense of belonging. The following exemplifies basic Manglish use in Malaysian political humor, taken from Douglas Lim's (2021) parody entitled "Press conference annoying *giler*!" ("An insanely annoying press conference!")—a spoof of a press conference involving Prasarana Malaysia's then chairman who was also a local politician:

> Chairman, *Perang* ("War")-sarana: So I *terus* ("immediately") rush here second thing in the morning. […] First thing breakfast *lah*. […] You see, what happened was there was a missile […] and there was a building. And they kiss each other. […] *Kalau* ("If") Boyzone *ada* ("has") boy, war zone *ada* ("has") war *lah*. […] [Giggles]

Victims of 2021's LRT train collision have filed a civil lawsuit against Rapid Rail and Prasarana Malaysia for alleged negligence. According to the statement of claim,

Prasarana's then chairman Tajuddin Abdul Rahman made bad jokes during a press conference relating to the incident, said the trains "kissed" each other, and was seen laughing on live telecasts (Khairulrijal, 2023). Prasarana Malaysia is a state-owned enterprise.

### 11.2.6 Fodder for Comedy

Malaysia is not remarkably unique in terms of quality of governance and political slip-ups. Every country has its fair share of shortcomings and gaffes, although some may argue that Malaysians have had to endure more in recent years. Economic crises, the COVID-19 pandemic, and overt power struggles—they each influenced the way the country was run in the last decade or so, at times resulting in Malaysia being in the spotlight for the wrong reasons.

Corruption and incompetence continue to bedevil the nation, so much so that the public can sometimes only retaliate with a sarcastic "Malaysia *boleh*!" ("Malaysia can!"; this phrase denotes disappointment and functions to mock the government or fellow Malaysians for their questionable acts). In January 2023, it was reported that Malaysia fell four points in the latest Trust Index by global communications firm Edelman that measures respondents' trust in local institutions to do what is right; the 2023 Edelman Trust Barometer showed that Malaysia was among the countries with the most significant decline of trust in the government (Ayamany, 2023).

Furthermore, Malaysia continued to head in the wrong direction in terms of fighting corruption, dropping to 47 points in the 2022 Corruption Perception Index and, as observed by Transparency International Malaysia's president, was positioned "even below countries such as Namibia" (Carvalho, 2023).

The political goings-on of a country naturally provide fodder for humor. Authority, with its inconsistencies, scandals, foibles and blunders, is an endless source and Malaysia is not an exception to the rule. How can it be when a health minister used "Spanish fly" in reference to the Spanish flu, and a ministry advised women to giggle coyly and speak in a Doraemon-like voice?

Admittedly, the meeting of politics and humor may leave both unchanged, but at the very least one can agree that many such encounters have left Malaysians either giggling (none too coyly) or laughing out loud, as a collective voice against what they believe to be problematic.

## 11.3 Research Approach

This study draws on the works of local comedians Douglas Lim, 46, and Jason Leong, 38. Both videos (Case A and Case B) were released in 2021 and are, at the time of writing, available on YouTube. Lim and Leong primarily used English, with instances of Manglish, and expressions in Malay have been translated into English using the

**Table 11.1** Politeness: Brown and Levinson's (1987) framework

| Strategy | Description |
| --- | --- |
| Bald on record | • Made without ambiguity, redress |
| Off-record | • Provision of hints, association clues<br>• Use of understatements, metaphors, irony, rhetorical questions<br>• Meaning is to some degree negotiable |
| Positive politeness | • Oriented toward acts of praising, offering sympathy and understanding<br>• Use of claiming common ground, in-group identity markers<br>• Potential "face threat" is minimized |
| Negative politeness | • Characterized by compromise, restraint<br>• Use of redressive actions<br>• Little or no direct imposition |

semi-literal translation method to attain better conveyance of meaning. Due to space constraint, non-salient elements/utterances are excluded (without compromising the gist of key messages).

The motivation behind the selection of these videos was fourfold: their position of novelty in research literature, relevance to the notion of political humor, length (approximately 10 min in total), and popularity. At the time of writing, Lim's video had garnered close to 428,700 views and Leong's, close to 120,700.

The analytical approach of the study is presented in Table 11.1, based on Brown and Levinson's (1987) framework on politeness.

## 11.4 Analysis and Discussion

### 11.4.1 Case A: Douglas Lim (2021)

**Caption/Description**: "This is the press conference with the Chairman of *Perang-sarana*. If you know, you know. If you understand, you understand *lah*. Aduhhhh [expression of disappointment tinged with frustration]… While waiting for the vaccine website, watch this video first *lah*. #nowords #douglaslim #stupid/sillyjoke #kisseachother #firstthinginthemorning" [*Ini dia press conference dengan Chairman Perang-sarana. If you know, you know. Faham-faham lah. Aduhhhh… Sementara tunggu website vaccine, layan video ni dulu lah. #nowords #douglaslim #lawakbodoh #kisseachother #firstthinginthemorning*].

> Chairman, *Perang*-sarana [Douglas Lim, henceforth "Chairman"]: Ah, what is it?
>
> Reporter 1: Why you were not there when this thing first happened?
>
> Chairman: You must all understand. I only heard about this war late last night, *ya*? So I immediately rush here second thing in the morning. […] First thing breakfast *lah*. There is even the word "first" in it. […] You understand English? [Giggles]

11 Mocking the Powers that Be: The Case of Culture and Political Humor … 233

Reporter 2: So how many buildings were demolished because of rocket fire?

Chairman: You see, what happened was there was a missile […] and there was a building, *ya*. And they kiss each other. […] Now I don't know why kiss you think is an act of war? It's an act of love, right? When I kiss my wife it's an act of love. Maybe when you kiss your wife it's an act of war *lah*. [Giggles]

Reporter 3: So as chairman, what actions have you taken so far?

Chairman: What question is this. Chair *lah*, sofa *lah*. […] I don't like this. […] What next? Carpet? […] You want to ask, ask properly. [Giggles]

Reporter 4: I heard there was execution of prisoners of war […]

Chairman: See, again. […] What cushion, cushion? […] See, there were […] bullets […] and there were people. And they had a gathering. That's all. [Giggles] Understand?

Reporter 5: We heard some land mines killed soldiers that were patrolling […]

Chairman: This is a war zone. […] Okay, so there was a land mine […] and there were some soldiers. Okay? And I heard it went very well. I heard they had a blast. [Giggles] […] Quiet all. Shut up. […] Now, Ronan Keating, Stephen Gately, Keith Duffy, Michael Graham, Shane Lynch. What are they? Boys. If Boyzone has boy, war zone has war *lah*. Right? [Giggles] Okay, I want to go to the toilet. […] Of course to pee, because as you can clearly see, I don't give a shit.

Standing against a backdrop depicting a war zone, armed with a microphone, a bowl on his head, and a disposable container strapped to his face with rubber bands, Douglas Lim delivered an act praised by netizens, who lauded him for accurately imitating Tajuddin Abdul Rahman's mannerisms (Chua, 2021). An indication of *Barisan Nasional* ("National Front", the political coalition with which Tajuddin was affiliated) can also be observed in the blue hue of the shirt Lim wore.

A parody is fundamentally an art form that intentionally copies the original in a manner that makes the features or qualities of the original more noticeable in a way that is humorous. In this respect, Lim's work does not disappoint. In each of the extracts presented, one sees the build-up (the provision of a setting) and the punchline (a twist to the narration which includes a humorous conclusion), and through these, the blunders of the original are actually made more manifest.

Tajuddin was sacked with immediate effect as Prasarana Malaysia's chairman following the press conference he held in the wake of May 2021's accident involving two LRT trains which left more than 200 passengers injured. The politician had sparked outrage over his ineptness, mocking of a foreign journalist, tasteless humor, for laughing, and for being condescending. A petition calling for his resignation garnered over 100,000 signatures in less than 24 h and the authorities slapped him with a fine for failing to wear a face mask at the press conference (he only sported a face shield).

Going by Brown and Levinson's (1987) framework on politeness, the off-record and negative politeness strategies prevail on the whole in Case A. Each extract contains identifiable allusions and these are particularly relatable to Malaysians who possess knowledge of Tajuddin, his mannerisms and behaviors, and the infamous press conference. In terms of fidelity to the original, the extract involving Reporter 2—in which a missile and a building are said to have "kissed" each other—comes closest to the actual event (Tajuddin had remarked with a laugh that the LRT trains "kissed" each other). The subsequent extracts, in which bullets and people "gathered," and a land mine and soldiers "had a blast," can be interpreted as creative additions to the original.

The negative politeness strategy is apparent in that there is no direct attack and thus no direct "face threat." Implied meanings are the norm in Malaysian political humor, falling in line with the nation's social conventions and its legal expectations. In essence, it is still safe comedy. Even Lim's YouTube caption/description abides by this. However, his work does display a degree of clearer defiance (see last line: "… I don't give a shit.") against a political culture inherent in many countries including Malaysia—a devil-may-care attitude among a number of politicians who continue to misbehave despite rebuke, and those who continue as unmitigated disasters.

## 11.4.2  Case B: Jason Leong (2021)

**Caption/Description**: Happy 56th National Day to all my friends and fans in Singapore! Hope you enjoyed this video, and find some amusement during these dark times. Best wishes from your envious neighbour! Also, please follow my good friend Sam See @mrsamsee on FB, Twitter, IG and Twitch! #sgnationalday #singapore #nationalday2021

> Sam [talk show host]: How are you qualified to be a minister?
> Minister of Propaganda/Missed Information of Malaysia [Jason Leong, henceforth "Minister"]: Well Sam, in Malaysia, to be a minister you barely need any qualifications. In fact, the more qualified you are, the less likely you will get the job.
> 
> Minister: Let me tell you about some of the good things Malaysia has done. Now you already know that our health minister is taking credit for Philippines' Olympic gold medal in weightlifting because we got her vaccinated while she was training here. […] we are also taking credit for Joseph Schooling when he won the gold in the 2016 Olympics. […] because when Joseph Schooling trained in the swimming pools in Singapore, Malaysia provided the water.
> 
> Sam: Look, why is it that we must always have this uncomfortable rivalry?
> Minister: Everything is Singapore, Singapore, Singapore. […] Singaporeans always boast about their world-class public transport system. Well, the Malaysian LRT is also very good, okay? Your MRT is on time, ours arrive ahead of time. So early that two of them had a head-on collision. That's efficiency. Singapore got or not?
> 
> Sam: But recently hasn't Malaysia gotten some bad press because parliament was suspended?
> Minister: That is our effort to ensure Malaysians […] our dear MPs, have work-life balance. We gave them time off so that they can relax, serve their constituencies, and exercise. […] Like the long jump, high jump, party jump.
> 
> Sam: But aren't there concerns that democracy and freedom of speech is under attack in Malaysia?

Minister: Nonsense! [...] Every Malaysian is free to express whatever praises they have about the government and whatever grievances they have about the opposition.

Sam: Also I heard about how some politicians betrayed their voters in a hotel?
Minister: That is our program to propel Malaysia towards becoming a high-income nation. We pay our Members of Parliament very well. Or at least, some of them. It's called the "Federal Remuneration of Government Support Scheme", AKA the "FROGS Scheme". Now I can't confirm but some offers may be in the millions. Cannot confirm *ah*. [...] But this shows that Malaysia can become a high-income nation. Or like my Cantonese uncle says: "When it comes to income, Malaysia is really *sohai* (a rude and vulgar Cantonese term)." [...] No, he meant "soar high."

Minister: A civil servant in Malaysia with just a salary of 4,000 ringgit per month, or five Sing (Singapore) dollars per month, can own a Rolls Royce, a Mustang, a Range Rover and even an Audi, all together! There are no limits to what you can achieve in Malaysia. That's why our slogan is "Malaysia *boleh*." [...] Yes, Malaysia is excellent at corruption! Both in magnitude and frequency. Our corruption is world-class. [...] And that's why many countries use Malaysia as an example to educate themselves on how to combat corruption.

Minister: And Malaysia will continue to work hard to achieve our own dreams. In fact, by my estimate, in less than five years our journey to fully realize Malaysia's potential will be complete. [...] Yes, in five years' time, Malaysia will be finished. And in the spirit of friendship on your national celebration [...] let me just say that whatever Singapore wants to achieve in the future, Malaysia will always have your back. [...] because Malaysia will always be behind Singapore.

By Malaysian standards, Case B may be considered bold because it calls out the country's political goings-on, largely naming them in no uncertain terms. It speaks of corruption, nepotism and cronyism, incompetence and poor governance, and of power (dis)plays, along with disrespect for the electorate. In each of the extracts presented, a national "plague" is brought forth in humor, albeit bitingly, and it is this acerbic quality that permits Jason Leong's work to be placed to some extent under Brown and Levinson's (1987) categorization of bald on record.

Bald on record discourses are chiefly without ambiguity and redress. Leong's jokes are direct utterances in which the communicative intent is clear. As for redress, a redressive action is one that "gives face" and in the case of Leong's jests, linguistically and contextually, the targeted group is clear: problematic Malaysian governments, with no explicit attempt to counteract this "face damage." However, there is also no personally identifiable information (i.e., no political figure is named), except in the second extract regarding a health minister, and this restraint situates Leong's work within the province of negative politeness that is basically avoidance-based. It is characterized by compromise, softening, and "face-saving" mechanisms, with little or no direct accusation.

Case B's extracts are more than just passing judgments. They serve to resist what is incongruent with good governance. Good governance, applied to any nation, means heading in the right direction when it comes to fighting graft and associated bad conduct, having a worthy cabinet, and showing higher regard for the people and their decisions at the ballot box. Leong's themes are relatively exhaustive, covering not only corruption, incompetence, and freedom of speech, but also more specific issues.

One instance is the discussion on Malaysia becoming a high-income nation; instead of Malaysians soaring higher together, the narration reaches into the realm of power plays and money in politics. The Sheraton Move, a backroom political maneuver, is alluded to. Another instance is a cheeky quip that appears to equate 4,000 Malaysian ringgit to five Singapore dollars. The ringgit's performance has indeed been dismal and while it is true that external factors have contributed to the slump, it would be remiss to dismiss the role of local politics.

Party-hopping, for one, was especially concerning in Malaysia. "Leaping politicians" are always symptomatic of power shifts, that can trigger political instability, social unrest, and in turn a slew of economic drawbacks. This facet of "frog politics" was addressed in 2022 when the anti-hopping law took effect, but observers noted that it will not guarantee stability in the short-term as it does not prevent an entire party from shifting its allegiance (Ariffin & Yang, 2022).

The final extract on Malaysia having Singapore's back is likely to (have) hit some nerves. I believe it is because Malaysians do love their country despite its flaws and wounds, and the suggestion of it coming to a sorry end can induce a very rational fear. Sometimes it does take comedy, with its pivots and punchlines, to drive home a point, discomfort its audience, and start a process of change.

## 11.5 Conclusions

Malaysian political humor is essentially safe and sanitized comedy. This is attributable to the country's sociopolitical culture. At its core, humor is very much a free agent, an advocate of democracy and a promising catalyst for change. We like to believe that political humor should be unrestricted and as liberal as liberal can be in any modernizing/modernized country. And yet, we also know that this is not necessarily ideal, more so when we realize that not every comic can utilize liberty tastefully. By the same token, not every comic can comprehend the cost of laughter that leads to grave discord. The stakes are higher in multiracial countries and like it or not, the jokes in such countries can only be as "democratic" as their politics.

So, do we tickle more or punch harder? As demonstrated by Douglas Lim's and Jason Leong's acts, there are often differing degrees of a middle way. None of the jokes analyzed can be classified as too placatory and while they do mock and ridicule, they most certainly do not qualify as sick or harsh comedy—the kind that elicits more shock than mirth, and more backlash than applause. There is a balance in which restraint and more caustic discourse are each accorded a footing, resulting in the brand of comedy that Malaysians have become so used to.

Comedy challenges the status quo. It carves out a space for audiences to become disarmed, reconsider issues, and respond to them. Comedy also does the opposite. It can refuse to encourage new ways of thinking and instead delegitimize progressive voices and reinforce oppression. Whichever path it takes, the nature of publicized humor, political and otherwise, normally reflects the customs of its home country. Palatability is crucial and in countries where politeness influences acceptability, comedians typically elect to stay on the safer side of the divide, especially if crossing the divide also means sailing too close to the wind. Lest we forget, some countries will tolerate a fleet of laws that can be enacted quite swiftly in the name of national security.

Culture permeates all walks of life. In Malaysia, the concepts of *berbudi bahasa* and *menjaga air muka* are part of the national culture. Any conduct that departs from these concepts is seen as going against the grain of good manners and morals. Even when real political circumstances are brought forth humorously and a higher level of tolerance is hence granted, deviations from politeness still appear as guarded moves. Allusions are popular, criticism is measured, and stinging remarks are tempered with anonymity. Within the sphere of this chapter, Leong's work packs more punch and Lim's parody derides in subtler fashion. Both used Manglish (another feature of Malaysian culture) and Lim's work is more saturated in this aspect than Leong's. Neither touched on highly sensitive topics.

Brown and Levinson's (1987) framework offers four strategies: bald on record, off-record, positive politeness and negative politeness. The present study's analyses revealed the employment of the first two strategies as well as the last. In other words, Lim and Leong did not oblige by way of ingratiation. It is also necessary to emphasize that although criticism is observed, it is manifested through restraint, but none of the contents studied may be construed as sympathetic or apologetic. On the whole, the jests are as anticipated—relatable (with sufficient wit, and each with its own strain of boldness) and polite enough for the Malaysian setting.

This chapter complements current literature and its limitations afford directions for future lines of inquiry. First, to arrive at more comprehensive conclusions the corpus can be made more inclusive by taking into account the narratives of other local comedians or by comparing verbal and visual rhetoric. Second, context is rarely immaterial and it would be interesting to see, for instance, if humor by parliamentarians is necessarily more cutting than the political humor served up by stand-up comedians. Cross-country comparisons in this regard are worthwhile as well. Finally, another useful area of research involves estimating the utility of different types of comedy for political change and social justice. The specifics of these two facets should naturally comprise discourse pertaining to cultural influence.

# References

Ahmad, A. R., & Dhillon, S. K. (2022). Must the prevention of terrorism entail the violation of human rights? The case of Malaysia's Prevention of Terrorism Act. *UUM Journal of Legal Studies*, *13*(1), 243–266. https://doi.org/10.32890/uumjls2022.13.2.10

Annuar, A. (2021, May 7). Cops quiz Zunar, seize phone over Kedah MB Thaipusam cartoon. *The Vibes*. https://www.thevibes.com/articles/news/26579/cops-quiz-zunar-seize-phone-over-kedah-mb-thaipusam-cartoon

Ariffin, A., & Yang, C. (2022). No more political frogs? Malaysia's anti-hopping law doesn't stop parties from switching sides. *Channel News Asia*. https://www.channelnewsasia.com/asia/malaysia-anti-hopping-law-political-frogs-3083576

Article 19. (2020). Malaysia: Humour and satire must be protected. *Article 19*. https://www.article19.org/resources/malaysia-humour-and-satire-must-be-protected/

Ayamany, K. (2023, January 24). Study: Malaysia among countries with biggest drop in trust from last year, especially towards the govt. *Malay Mail*. https://www.malaymail.com/news/malaysia/2023/01/24/study-malaysia-among-countries-with-biggest-drop-in-trust-from-last-year-especially-towards-the-govt/51635

Brown, P., & Levinson, S.C. (1987). *Politeness: Some universals in language usage.* The Press Syndicate of the University of Cambridge.

Carvalho, M. (2023, January 31). Malaysia slips in corruption perception index score. *The Star*. https://www.thestar.com.my/news/nation/2023/01/31/malaysia-slips-in-corruption-perception-index-score

Chua, D. (2021, June 8). #Showbiz: Douglas Lim's MCO parodies a hit with netizens. *New Straits Times*. https://www.nst.com.my/lifestyle/groove/2021/06/696898/showbiz-douglas-lims-mco-parodies-hit-netizens

Chua, D. (2023, June 9). #Showbiz: Angry netizens give Dr Jason Leong an earful on his Facebook page. *New Straits Times*. https://www.nst.com.my/lifestyle/groove/2023/06/918327/showbiz-angry-netizens-give-dr-jason-leong-earful-his-facebook-page

Haji Omar, A. (1992). *The linguistic scenery in Malaysia*. Dewan Bahasa dan Pustaka.

Hassan, N., & Hashim, A. (2009). Electronic English in Malaysia: Features and language in use. *English Today, 25*(4), 39–46. https://doi.org/10.1017/S0266078409990435

Human Rights Watch. (2015). Creating a culture of fear: The criminalization of peaceful expression in Malaysia. *Human Rights Watch*.

Human Rights Watch. (2021). Malaysia: Free speech under increasing threat. *Human Rights Watch*. https://www.hrw.org/news/2021/05/19/malaysia-free-speech-under-increasing-threat

Kasmani, F. (2022). Persuasive political humour on social media: A study of Najib Razak's Facebook posts. *SEARCH Journal of Media and Communication Research, 14*(1), 1–17.

Khairulrijal, R. (2023, March 27). 2021 LRT crash victims sue Rapid Rail and Prasarana for alleged negligence. *New Straits Times*. https://www.nst.com.my/news/crime-courts/2023/03/893338/2021-lrt-crash-victims-sue-rapidrail-and-prasarana-alleged

Latif, T. A., Saedin, M. S., Buhari, N., & Ibrahim, I. M. (2018). *Berbudi bahasa* practices: A study on civilizational values among Malaysian society. *Sains Insani, 3*(2), 68–73. https://doi.org/10.33102/sainsinsani.vol3no2.62. (in Malay).

Leong, J. (2021, August 9). Minister of Propaganda wishes Singapore a Happy National Day. *YouTube*. https://www.youtube.com/watch?v=CWTXLEiUuwo

Lim, B. S. (2017). Malay sayings as politeness strategies. *Journal of Modern Languages, 15*(1), 65–79.

Lim, D. (2021, May 26). Press conference annoying *giler*! (An insanely annoying press conference!). *YouTube*. https://www.youtube.com/watch?v=T2GBSjgEPVA

Lim, K. H. (2003, July). *Budi* as the Malay mind. *The Newsletter* (International Institute for Asian Studies). https://www.iias.asia/sites/default/files/2020-11/IIAS_NL31_31.pdf

Malaysian Communications and Multimedia Commission. (2020). *Internet users survey 2020*. Malaysian Communications and Multimedia Commission.

Nambiar, P. (2021, April 28). Zunar hauled up over cartoon on axing of Thaipusam holiday. *Free Malaysia Today*. https://www.freemalaysiatoday.com/category/nation/2021/04/28/zunar-hauled-up-over-cartoon-on-axing-of-thaipusam-holiday/

*New Straits Times*. (2021, January 22). 'Kedah MB's cancellation of Thaipusam holiday disrespectful, irrational'. *New Straits Times*. https://www.nst.com.my/news/nation/2021/01/659706/kedah-mbs-cancellation-thaipusam-holiday-disrespectful-irrational

*New Straits Times*. (2023, June 16). #NSTviral: Jocelyn Chia, basking in media spotlight, tells Malaysia to 'keep going'. *New Straits Times*. https://www.nst.com.my/news/nst-viral/2023/06/921012/nstviral-jocelyn-chia-basking-media-spotlight-tells-malaysia-keep

Ng, H. S. (2023, June 8). Singapore apologises to Malaysians for comedian Jocelyn Chia's MH370 joke. *Channel News Asia*. https://www.channelnewsasia.com/singapore/jocelyn-chia-malaysia-mh370-singapore-comedy-offensive-comments-high-commissioner-3546331

Ng, K. (2023, June 14). Jocelyn Chia: US comedian calls Malaysia's reaction to MH370 joke 'ridiculous'. *BBC News*. https://www.bbc.com/news/world-asia-65900089

Otterson, J. (2017, May 2). Stephen Colbert in hot water over 'homophobic' Donald Trump joke. *Variety*. https://variety.com/2017/tv/news/late-show-stephen-colbert-homophobic-donald-trump-1202406991/

Provenza, P., & Dion, D. (2010). *Satiristas: Comedians, contrarians, raconteurs & vulgarians*. Harper Collins.

Ramli, R. (2013). Culturally appropriate communication in Malaysia: *Budi bahasa* as warranty component in Malaysian discourse. *Journal of Multicultural Discourses, 8*(1), 65–78. https://doi.org/10.1080/17447143.2012.753895

Shah, A. (2023, June 7). Singaporean comedian Jocelyn Chia's MH370 joke doesn't land with Malaysians. *New Straits Times*. https://www.nst.com.my/news/nation/2023/06/917476/singaporean-comedian-jocelyn-chias-mh370-joke-doesnt-land-malaysians

*The Star*. (2023, June 8). Jocelyn Chia deactivates social media accounts following MH370 joke backlash. *The Star*. https://www.thestar.com.my/news/nation/2023/06/08/jocelyn-chia-deactivates-social-media-accounts-following-mh370-joke-backlash

*The Straits Times*. (2018, July 30). Malaysia drops sedition case against political cartoonist Zunar. *The Straits Times*. https://www.straitstimes.com/asia/se-asia/malaysia-drops-sedition-case-against-political-cartoonist-zunar

*Today Online*. (2017, April 7). When Malaysian MPs' remarks in parliament shocked Malaysians. *Today Online*. https://www.todayonline.com/world/asia/when-malaysian-mps-remarks-parliament-shocked-malaysians

Tsakona, V., & Popa, D. E. (2011). Humour in politics and the politics of humour: An introduction. In V. Tsakona & D. E. Popa (Eds.), *Studies in political humour: In between political critique and public entertainment* (pp. 1–30). John Benjamins.

Wong, C. W. (2007, May 13). There they go again. *The Star*. https://www.thestar.com.my/opinion/columnists/on-the-beat/2007/05/13/there-they-go-again/?pgno=3

Yatim, H. (2022, February 7). Khairy loses appeal against Anwar for 'main belakang' remark in 2008. *The Edge Malaysia*. https://theedgemalaysia.com/article/khairy-loses-appeal-against-anwar-main-belakang-remark-2008

Zachariah, E. (2015, April 23). Toning down satire, humour after amendments to Sedition Act. *The Malaysian Insider*. https://www.malaysianbar.org.my/article/news/legal-and-general-news/legal-news/toning-down-satire-humour-after-amendments-to-sedition-act

**Debbita Ai Lin Tan** serves as Senior Lecturer at the School of Languages, Literacies and Translation, Universiti Sains Malaysia. She is keen on interdisciplinary research and her current areas of interest include language and media/political studies, translation difficulties, and the relationship between psychology and linguistic nuances. For more information, https://ppblt.usm.my/index.php/lecturer-profile/163-debbita-tan-dr.

# Part III
# Political Humor in the Print Media

# Chapter 12
# Politically Related *Senryû* Verses in Daily Newspapers as a Manifestation of Humor in Japan

**Ofer Feldman and Ken Kinoshita**

**Abstract** It is often suggested that the Japanese do not have a sense of humor. Seriousness is regarded as one of the most important elements of success in society. Yet, through its long history, Japan has developed a culture that enjoys laughter, reflected in traditional drama and literature. *Senryû*, satirical and humorous verses that deal with common people in everyday situations, is one of the expressions of this tradition. This chapter focuses on *senryû* verses as an exemplar of humor in Japan. It examines *senryû* verses contributed by general readers as they were published in the opinion and commentary pages of two national dailies, *Yomiuri* and *Asahi*, between April 1, 2022, and March 31, 2023. The chapter reveals that 1,623 of the total 3,443 verses that were published then focused on political issues, processes, and decisionmakers. The ensuing discussion details distinguishing features of *senryû* as a vehicle revealing public sentiments towards political institutions and leaders, policy initiative and decisions, and the society as a whole—using on the one hand such rhetorical devices as satire, irony, and ridicule, and on the other hand expressions of optimism, hopes, and empathy.

## 12.1 Introduction

This chapter examines political humor and its relationship with Japanese culture, detailing in particular *senryû*,[1] or satirical verses that referred to political events and episodes as they were written by readers and published in two Japanese national

---

[1] In Japanese, vowels can either be short or long; a diacritical mark, for example, â, ê, î, ô, or û over the vowel indicates that it is a long vowel. Personal names are given in the Japanese order i.e., family name first.

O. Feldman (✉)
Faculty of Policy Studies, Doshisha University, Kyoto, Japan
e-mail: ofeldman@mail.doshisha.ac.jp

K. Kinoshita
Faculty of Social and Environmental Studies, Fukuoka Institute of Technology, Fukuoka, Japan
e-mail: kinoshita@fit.ac.jp

© The Author(s), under exclusive license to Springer Nature Singapore Pte Ltd. 2024
O. Feldman (ed.), *Communicating Political Humor in the Media*,
The Language of Politics, https://doi.org/10.1007/978-981-97-0726-3_12

dailies—*Yomiuri* and *Asahi* (circulation of about 7 and 4.5 million copies a day, respectively, in 2021), during a period of one year, April 1, 2022 through March 31, 2023. Considering *senryû* as an important manifestation of political humor, the chapter aims to describe and categorize the nature and the content of these *senryû* verses, specifying their distinguished features as a means of echoing the way the public makes sense of politics, a tool to voice the public's views and feelings toward political events and politicians.

It is our intention to demonstrate in the ensuing discussion that through sharp and witty expressions, *senryû* verses reveal the two-fold public sentiments towards public affairs. On the one hand, by using such rhetorical devices as satire, irony, sarcasm, and ridicule, readers reveal their discontent regarding the function of the government and the ruling coalition of parties, and the way the prime ministers and his cabinet members run the country; their frustration from the opposition parties and their inability to provide a viable alternative to the government; criticism toward individual politicians and their involvement in unethical activities; dissatisfaction with government bureaucracy, from political processes as well as social events; economic stagnation; and even readers' antipathy toward international leaders and their conduct. On the other hand, *senryû* verses also include optimistic, positive expressions, mirroring readers' wishes that current social problems will be solved, revealing expectations that policymakers will listen to public needs and demands and respond accordingly, and that Japan will be a better place in which to live. Neutral verses, conveying no emotions, are also identified.

In its structure, the chapter is divided into five sections. In the second section we detail cultural aspects affecting humor in general and political humor in Japan in particular, offering some explanations for the relatively less pervasive political humor in this country. The third section details historical and social factors that are at the center of Japanese humor, also detailing the characteristic of *senryû* and its role in Japanese culture. The fourth section focuses on the analysis of the data gathered from the two dailies with representative selection of verses published in the examined period. The conclusion section offers some observations on *senryû* as reflecting Japanese (political) humor and discusses selected methodological issues related to the current study.

## 12.2 On Humor in Japanese Society

The common thread that runs through studies conducted in Japan since the 1980s is the notion that a growing number of political, economic, and social issues have given rise to public criticism and dissatisfaction focusing on the way political leaders run the country, increasing political malaise with the decision-making processes, and apathy regarding the political and economic systems.[2] Among these issues, the public was discontented with the worsening economic recession, increasing unemployment

---

[2] This section and the ensuing one draw upon Feldman (2000, 2004).

and job insecurity, the escalating incidence of administrative corruption and political scandal involving syndicated crime and members of the Japanese National Parliament (Diet), lack of leadership, integrity, and competence of the country's prime ministers, and the government's inability to advance political reform.

Whereas all these issues could have become potential targets of laughter, one found at that time significantly fewer expressions of political humor in Japan than in many Western societies. Even these days, jokes about leading politicians, Diet members, prime ministers, or government bureaucrats are rare. Jests about the emperor are unthinkable. Politically oriented graffiti in public places such as walls around public institutions, or in public toilets, can scarcely be found. Political satire, such as performed by *THE NEWSPAPER* (*THE NEWSPAPER*, n.d.), a social satire comedy group consisting of nine members that specializes in current affairs, and which has appeared on the stage since 1988, is extremely rare.

There are a few reasons why political jokes and satire are not as widespread in Japan as they are in Western societies. Political humor lies deep within a society's psyche, drawing on common experiences, socialization processes, attitudes, and stereotypes from that society and its culture. It also reflects general attitudes that citizens have towards political authority, institutions, and the political system. In this sense the dearth of political humor in Japan can be attributed to the fact that the psychological involvement of individuals in politics is relatively low as politics is not generally perceived to be as important or central as it is in other societies. Another reason is related to the fact that politicians, along with other civil servants and authority figures, are granted an unusually large measure of social esteem, and enjoy attitudes resembling the one directed only towards God in the West. They are generally addressed in respectful manner, and one rarely sees the level of suspicion, criticism, or hostility toward these public figures that one finds displayed in Western countries, regardless of what negative feelings Japanese may feel toward their political leaders (Feldman & Watts, 2000).

Japan's relatively less pervasive political humor might also reflect general attitudes not only towards the political system and politicians but also towards humor and laughter in general. One prevalent view in this regard is related to communication style, as Japanese tend to hide or control their emotions internally, do not express their spontaneous emotions, and repress their laughter and smiling when they are with other people.[3] As a result, they are often seen as being unable to understand or appreciate humor. This communication ethos is attributable to six factors.

First, traditionally, in Japan there is a strong tendency to look down on laughter (Inoue, 2003, p. 5) that has typically been regarded as implying impudence, imprudence, cruelty, and/or complicity that hurts others and causes them discomfort. Because Japanese tend to be cautious about the feelings of others, to avoid giving offense and shy away from "loss of face," that is loss of self-respect and dignity

---

[3] I distinguish here between humor and the "Japanese smile." Japanese often laugh nervously or smile at times that seem inappropriate to non-Japanese. Apparently, they smile to conceal anguish, to spare others sympathetic pain, and to cover embarrassment or discomfort. Their smiles may cover up sorrow, anger, or inconvenience, or they may serve as a polite signal to stop discussing a certain topic or to stop a particular action.

for both speaker and listener due to public humiliation or embarrassment (e.g., Feldman & Kinoshita, 2017, p. 154; 2019, pp. 53–54), individuals are not supposed to laugh at all in front of other people (Fukusaku, 1977, pp. 27–29). Thus, whereas adults are supposed to feel social pressure that keeps them from laughing and makes them self-conscious with such behavior, children are the only ones in Japan who are allowed to laugh at any time (Sotoyama, 1976, pp. 141–156).

Second, laugher was customarily viewed as a threat to the harmony and conformity of the community—two elements that Japanese greatly value and strive for in every social interaction (Feldman, 2021, pp. 210–211). For example, extended families used to live together in one house. The small size of this house and its thin wood or paper walls enabled talking, and especially laughter, to be easily heard from one end of the house to the other. These sounds often interrupted the peaceful, quiet atmosphere of the home. As such, Japanese developed a particular sensitivity to laughter as something having the power to disrupt the calmness and tranquility of one's house and the community overall (Fukusaku, 1977, pp. 31–32).

The third factor is related to the vertical structure of Japanese society. Japanese social relations are hierarchical, based on superior-subordinate relations such as boss-employee, master-follower, or senior-junior (Feldman, 1999a, p. 6). This superior-subordinate structure is the primary basis of the social order, shaping attitudes and behavior, and affecting character, personality, and ability. For the superior to tell a joke to an inferior might be inviting unwanted intimacy; for an inferior to tell a joke to a superior, such as their employer or business associates, would be presumptuous. Accordingly, Japanese consider activities involving humor, such as telling jokes, to be appropriate only among equals. Since much of the social interaction involves people who aren't equals, exchanging jokes is less prevalent in Japan than it is in other, less hierarchical, societies. In other words, only a closer interpersonal relationship between the jester and the listener e.g., family members, friends, and partners, are considered appropriate for such activity.

Historically speaking, until late in the nineteenth century Japanese society was strongly dominated by vertical relations defined by status, class, and authority. The Tokugawa government (the military government during the Edo period from 1603 to 1868) intentionally created a social order called the four divisions of society, or the four-tiered class system [*shinôkôshô*] that would stabilize the country. This made it imperative for people to maintain strict social codes. The four classes were based on ideas of Confucianism that spread to Japan from China and were not arranged by wealth or capital but by what philosophers described as their moral purity. By this system, the non-aristocratic remainder of Japanese society comprised samurai warrior class [*shi*], farmers and peasants [*nô*] artisans [*kô*], and merchants [*shô*]. The rigid social hierarchy of the time required that members of each social caste behave in a manner befitting their status.

As members of the highest group, samurai were expected to exhibit the most exemplary behavior. Samurai warriors valued taciturnity, staidness, and solemnity; laughter was construed as a vice that was offensive to others, which thus had to be suppressed as much as possible, resulting at times in punishment. Because people in those days were always conscious of one another's position or authority, laughter was perceived as an insult that was sometimes sufficient cause to start a fight (Inoue, 2003, p. 15). The samurai also believed it was a virtue not to reveal any thoughts or emotions through facial expressions, including smiling (Sotoyama, 1976, p. 141–142). Even after the samurai era, following the Meiji Restoration of 1868, soldiers were forbidden to laugh, and any who did laugh in front of a superior would be subject to severe punishment.

In addition, the Tokugawa Shogunate feared the potentially subversive effects of popular entertainment forms that looked critically at the ills and oddities of society. Political authorities were afraid that satire, which exposes society's structural flaws and troubling social relationships, might have a demoralizing effect on the public and encourage immoral acts. Therefore, the Shogunate attempted to control public opinion through a series of edicts that regulated popular entertainment. An edict issued in 1816, for example, denounced lighthearted material as unsuitable for viewing and of little socially redeeming value (Sekine, 1967). Also, after the Meiji Restoration, officialdom viewed some types of popular entertainment with suspicion. Consequently, the Meiji government issued many edicts against such entertainment, similar to those formulated by the Tokugawa Shogunate.

The fourth factor is related to Japanese education. Perhaps one of the cultural aspects that determines the scarcity of humor is the focus on "seriousness" in society and especially in education, perceived as the most important element in climbing the social ladder. Since the Meiji era, the Japanese have been driven by such slogans as "work, work" and "be serious, be serious" and every hour's value was considered very important to carry out work. Laughter reflected one's "unseriousness," and "unskillfulness" (Inoue, 2003, p. 12–13). From an early age teachers suppress the tendency of pupils to laugh, advocating a society in which people think that laughter reflects "inauthenticity, playfulness, and laziness" (Inoue, 2003, p. 11). Instead, social pressure is put on students since childhood in the educational sphere where the whole learning process is characterized by overheated competition to study seriously and enter college, particularly to go to a "good" college. Pupils must study hard to pass the examinations to get into junior high school, senior high school and then to enter a "good" college that will pave the way to a "good" workplace. In many cases, college graduates are more likely to be in management positions and can be promoted to the top, while high school graduates are largely relegated to factories and attain much lower positions and income.

In comparison to youngsters in other countries, Japanese children have a hard curriculum and very busy schedules in school. There, they must follow strict rules and regulations regarding dress code and the length and the color of their hair, for example. Following the Japanese hierarchical social structure, students are taught to look up to and talk respectfully to their teachers, school administrators, and superiors in general, including their schoolmates in higher grades. High value is placed in school education on harmony in interpersonal relations, group norms and goals above personal and individual goals, and the ability to cooperate and endure hardship with others, all reflecting the stronger emphasis on seriousness in the Japanese educational system in which there isn't much opportunity for wittiness and jesting.

Moreover, in contrast to their counterparts in Western societies, Japanese teenagers devote more time to formal schooling and to their homework, and many of them commute to cram schools [*juku*] and prep schools specializing in college entrance [*yobikô*], where students learn how to pass entrance examinations. Even during their vacations teenagers study hard by preparing homework and participating in projects related to school. Teachers, parents, and schools all put pressure on students to do well on tests, by suppressing all other aspects of education, especially individual and intellectual growth, all which results in a serious frame of mind. Because they have to attend school and cramming, youngsters have limited free time for leisure, parties, picnics, or activities that help foster individuality and creativity, or to meet friends with whom they can share their inner thoughts and feelings, including humor (Feldman, 1998).

Fifth, another factor related to the relatively less pervasive political humor in Japan is the seriousness of politicians themselves, especially Diet members, and in particular members of the government. Events such as U.S. President Ronald Reagan entertaining members of the public and members of the Congress with a wide range of jokes are unimaginable in Japan (The Reagan Foundation, n.d.). Likewise, Japan never had something similar to the informal gatherings as the White House Correspondents dinner, the traditional annual event organized by the White House Correspondents Association of journalists who cover the White House and the president of the U.S., where humorous and satirical remarks are made by comedians, entertainers, and the president.

Most Japanese politicians would refrain from telling jokes altogether while speaking in public out of concern that their speech would be perceived and interpreted differently from their intention by certain segments of the public or the media. During election campaigns many politicians or political candidates tend to "spice up" their lectures in front of supporters with humorous comments on a variety of social issues, revealing funny anecdotes and personal episodes as they try to go beyond the dry details of politics with the purpose of entertaining the listeners at hand. Indeed, this results in frequent laughter, applause, and or encouraging shouts (Feldman & Bull, 2012). There were, however, numerous occasions where such remarks of politicians or aspiring politicians drew attention from the media, causing political ripples, criticism, condemned, and provoked anger from such segments as women's groups, elderly and sick people and their families, and members of political parties who didn't like either the topic or the content of a certain statement; instead of funny remarks they perceived certain utterances rather as debasement. In this way, casual and humoristic remarks made by politicians during political meetings resulted in embarrassment to the speakers and their political groups. Eventually they had to retract their remarks and apologize; some even had to take responsibility and resign their position either within the government or their political parties, discouraged from telling jokes altogether when making public lectures (Feldman, 2021, 2023).

Last, the news media, in particular the daily newspapers, include very few laughter and humor-related columns. In addition to the regular coverage of political, social, economic, and international news, newspapers also include editorials columns and feature stories written by professional reporters, and other articles explaining current issues written by experts in various fields. All these articles and commentary are serious, with formal reportage and analysis based most often on selected sources of information (Feldman, 2011). In addition to these columns, the dailies, especially the national ones, include political caricatures in articles on politics, comic strips, and *senryû*. Some columns are written by individual readers and not by journalists. These include some satire on social and political events, and amusing observations, yet they are not giving very much weight in the newspaper. Some of these writers use pen names to remain anonymous, an age-old Japanese tradition for writers, with such names often including a humorous pun or twist (Feldman, 1999b).

### *12.2.1 "Regional Distinction" and Shared Style of Humor*

Whereas the above section underlines the socio-historical aspects that oppressed humorous expression in Japan to the extent that it is not as widespread as in Western societies, Japanese do not totally lack a sense of humor. It is only a matter of "understanding humor in Japan" (for a detailed exploration see Davis, 2006). They exchange jokes, albeit not nearly as frequently as Westerners do, and probably not in the same style—a short third person narrative and a punch line. Rather, Japanese jokes are told in a story form, as an episode, recounting a personal experience, with the aim to share a common occurrence and a sense of relating to each other. During election campaigns, for example, and as mentioned, candidates for political office use this method of telling personal experiences, especially humorous episodes, as an effective way of getting a reaction, generating laughter from their audience, and through this to create followers and gain voters' support (Feldman & Bull, 2012).

Historically speaking, even during the second half of the nineteenth century, Japanese literature included various forms of parody and satire such as *modoki* (satirical mockery), *chakashi* (making fun of in a joking manner), *ugachi* (expressions of events and happenings in the world from a backward or oblique point of view, rather than looking at them in straightforward fashion), *mitate* (enigmatically depicting the object of satire in terms of something else), *mojiri* (changing lyrics in parts of a song to make it humorous or allegorical), and *keiku* (an epigram i.e., short, interesting, memorable, and sometimes surprising or satirical statement) (Brink, 2001).

Furthermore, it has been suggested that Japanese humor can be distinguished along "regional" lines between "the humor of the East and the humor of the West" (Inoue, 1987). The East refers to the Tokyo region [*Kantô*] and the West to the Osaka region [*Kansai*]. Even though there are no major differences in lifestyle in various parts of Japan, including Tokyo and Osaka that are less than three hours apart by train, differences between eastern and western Japan persist as *Kantô* has retained the culture of the samurai, while *Kansai* has retained the culture of merchants (Inoue, 2006).

As pointed out above, in the samurai culture (that Tokyo retained), people were highly conscious of one another's social position, and laughter was construed as a form of offense, insult, or dishonor. During the Edo era (1603–1868), samurai dominated the whole country. In Osaka, the second largest city in Japan that has for a long time been a city of economic importance and the gateway for foreign culture and trade, the samurai class was small compared to the number of ordinary citizens. This in comparison to Tokyo that facilitated the more horizontal social structure. In the merchants' culture that continued in Osaka during that time, merchants' livelihood depended on wholesalers as well as regular and prospective customers, so that the ability to get along with fellow townspeople was extremely important. This required skill at negotiation, verbal creativity, and an ability for lightening the mood with comic remarks (Inoue, 1984, p. 204) that could only evolve in horizontal and egalitarian relationships. Humor thus came to play an important role in daily life.

As a center where the various laughter arts have been cultivated for centuries, even these days Osaka boasts more comedians than any other city in Japan. Osaka differs from Tokyo in its comedic style, selection of materials, and the use of different dialects, as their material seems deeper and more sophisticated in comparison to comedians from Tokyo who use standard Japanese and tend to play set roles, seldom revealing their true character (Inoue, 1984, pp. 42–53).

Beyond the distinction between the style in humor in these two areas in Japan, there are forms of humor and satire that speak in the same manner to people all over the country. This includes such comedy genres as *kyogen* (traditional Japanese comic theater), *niwaka* (impromptu joke, witticism, or pun), *chaban* (theatrical farce, skit, or slapstick), *karukuchi* (light story), *saru mawashi* (monkey show), and in particular: *rakugo, manzai, kigeki,* and *senryû*.

*Rakugo* is a popular form of comic monologue, a Japanese sit-down comedy, as opposed to Western countries' stand-up comedy. In this form of comedy, a storyteller [*rakugoka*], usually sitting down on a *zabuton* (a cushion for sitting), creates an imaginary drama and portrays various characters through episodic narration and skillful use of vocal and facial expressions. Typically, the storytellers use no scenery; their only musical accompaniment is a shamisen, flute, or brief drum roll heard as the *rakugoka*, dressed in a plain kimono, enters and sits on a *zabuton* at center stage. There they remain, delivering comic monologues about social events, episodes involving married men and their wives or lovers, and anecdotes related to society in general. Often, they take the roles of two or three people, using only a small towel and a fan as props.

*Manzai* is a dialogue containing comical wording and gestures. It is usually performed by a team of two or three comedians [*manzaishi*] in a stand-up style comedy. They act out humorous incidents or tell a series of loosely connected funny stories. When it involves two performers very often one of them asks questions that the other answers, playing the role of a funny man [*boke*, literally, stupid, unaware, clueless, or senile], reflected in the tendency for absent-mindedness and misinterpretation, and the other plays a straight man [*tsukkomi,* literally, run into, roll into, or butting in, and other actions to enter with unusual movement], correcting the *boke*'s errors. Their dialogues reflect all kinds of current affairs, from family matters to social events, and most of the jokes revolve around mutual misunderstandings, inappropriateness, double-talk, and other verbal gags. *Kigeki* are comic plays performed by troupes of comedians. They reflect common social situations involving neighbors, police, gangsters, and family members.

Senryû,[4] or satirical verse (often translated also as "comic verse," "comical poem," or "satirical poetry"), is a genre of Japanese short poetry popular for its humorous qualities and ability to draw laughs from the readers (Ueda, 1999, p. viii). It consists of 17 syllables (or *morae*, i.e., the syllabic unit in Japanese speech; Kubozono, 1999 for details), in three syllable-based components, five-seven-five, that give rhythmical percussion to Japanese ears. The seventeen syllables form is similar to *haiku*, a style of aesthetic poetry aimed at conveying the beauty of nature during the four seasons in Japan (Shirane, 1998). Both *senryû* and *haiku* originated from the same earlier form, the *renga* (linked verse),[5] and both are regarded as the shortest poetic forms in the world (Fukumoto, 1999, p. 14). Despite being classified as a form of poetry, both are quite different from English verse: they are very short, written in one line, have no foot, no meter, no rhyme, no assonance, and no repeated consonant sounds (Kumei, 2006, p. 29).

Although *senryû* and *haiku* have similar origins and similar structure, the two have several different characteristics, and are treated today as quite different forms of poetry. One of the major differences is their tone, content, and vocabulary. *Haiku*

---

[4] The word *senryû*, literally means "river willow," derived from the name of Karai Senryû (1718–1790), the pen name of Karai Hachiemon, who lived in the downtown district of Edo, the former name of Tokyo, whose humorous poems were first published in 1765. Karai started as a totally unknown *tenja* (referee) in winning entries in *senryû*'s contests, beginning with the first contest in 1757 and covering the next seven years. In 1757 he became a *maekuzuke* (literally, "adding to the front verse") master. *Maekuzuke*'s format consists of two parts: The initial part *maeku* (previous verse), usually containing two lines of seven Japanese syllables each (totalling 14 syllables in sections of 7-7); and *tsukeku* (following verse) consisting of three lines in total of 17 syllables with 5-7-5 syllable patterns. At the verse-writing poetry contest, the master, or referee, would announce the *maeku* part first before the contest entrants wrote the *tsukeku* in such a way that the two verses combined would make a good poetic sequence. The amateur poets who submitted verses to those contests had to pay a small entry fee. In return, they could win prizes such as cotton fabric, a set of bowls, or a tray. The winning verses were printed and distributed to various poets' groups that helped in advertising the contest and collecting entries.

The contests judged by Karai became immensely popular, and the finest *tsukeku* selected by him and reflected his personal taste became widely known to the public in an anthology called *Yanagidaru* of 756 winning verses from the contests (published in 1765). It was followed by 22 more of the same title, also compiled by Karai, and a further 144 volumes compiled by his successors to the tradition. The type of *tsukeku* Karai chose came to be recognized herewith as a new genre of poetry known as *senryû*, with stand-alone seventeen syllables, without its *maeku* part (For a detailed discussion see Fukumoto, 1999; Kobayashi, 2006; Shirane, 1998; Ueda, 1999).

[5] *Renga* was established by the fifteenth century. In a *renga* gathering, popular among the rising merchant class during the 16th and early seventeenth century, each member presented a *hokku* (starting poem), comprising 5-7-5 syllables, hoping his would be selected among many as a starter of *renga*. In this gathering, participants collaborated to produce 100 in sequence: one person makes a first part, the second the latter half, then the third the next first. Reflecting the spirit of the merchant class, *renga* at that time were comical, supportive, and down-to-earth, with plain, everyday vocabulary (Kumei, 2006). *Hokku* was considered important, and eventually it became an independent poetry form, from which both *haiku* and *senryû* developed, the former by the end of the seventeenth century, the latter becoming recognized as an independent poetic form in the latter half of the eighteenth century.

has a more serious tone whose favorite subjects are related to nature and seasons. It typically contains a *kigo* (seasonal words) i.e., seasonal reference that indicates a season of the year, to set the tone of the poems and to provide keys to their deeper meanings. *Haiku* also includes a *kireji* (cutting word) or verbal *caesura*.

On the other hand, *senryû* has no rules except the syllabic form five-seven-five. It does not need to contain a word that represents a season, and it has no *kireji*. *Senryû* is typically satirical, ironic, or humorous in tone. It deals with human foibles and social mores, with human feelings and behavior in everyday situations, including between young lovers, between husband and wife, between parents and child, and between family members of different generations, topics that are generally overlooked by poets in other genres. In doing so, *senryû* mixes humorous, often cynical, or darkly humorous aspects with wit, and even gentle satirical or sarcastic reflection on people, events, and human nature and relationships.

Furthermore, *haiku* is relatively archaic, where classical words and phrases are used, and is regarded as a lyric genre and as a higher and more sophisticated literary genre than *senryû* (Fukumoto, 1999, p. 18). In the latter, modern Japanese language is used, and is seen as a critical genre, stylistically much freer than the elegantly refined *haiku*. One need not be a specialist to compose *senryû*. As we see in the following study, the local and national dailies have columns dedicated to *senryû* and publish almost daily the so-called *jiji senryû* (*senryû* on current affairs), composed by readers, that capture the social, economic, and political events of daily life in a timely manner.

It is estimated that as many as ten million people enjoy reading and composing *haiku* in Japan. The *senryû* writing population is not as large, yet it remains a popular form of expression in Japan. Testifying to its versatility and popularity are the different kinds of *senryû* available in Japan today. These include *eko senryû* (environmental/ecological *senryû*), through a contest organized since the beginning of the century by local governments and companies (including Japan Automobile Federation) to raise awareness of global warming, and appropriate use of recycling and waste disposal; *kodomo eko senryû* (children's ecological *senryû*), inviting elementary school students to send their *senryû* to the above contest; *otaku senryû*, composed by *otaku*, one the subcultures in Japan, consists of group of youth community media and technology enthusiasts, including popular media such as *manga* (Japanese comics), *anime* (Japanese cartoons), online video games, computers, and other related genres; *sararîman senryû*, popular among middle class, white-collar Japanese corporate workers whose income is guaranteed in the form of a monthly regularly paid salary ("salaryman"). *Sararîman senryû* reflects the climate of white-collars workers, their views on their companies and changing working conditions, their families, and other important aspects within Japanese society, economy, and education (e.g., Spinks, 2011). Last, published by the national dailies, are the *Asahi senryû and Yomiuri jiji* (contemporary) *senryû* that are at the center of this chapter with their nature and characteristics discussed in the next section.

## 12.3 *Senryû* Verses in the Dailies

### 12.3.1 Methodology

The ensuing analysis focuses on *senryû* verses published in two Japanese national dailies, *Yomiuri* and *Asahi*, during one year period—April 1, 2022 through March 31, 2023. Along with other national and local newspapers, these dailies publish *senryû* verses from their readers almost every day. *Asahi* usually publishes seven verses in its *koe* (opinion) page under the title of *Asahi senryû*. *Yomiuri* publishes usually six *senryû* verses in the education page under the title of *Yomiuri jiji senryû*. In the first, verses are selected in different days either by a columnist or a former editorial writer, and they include a one-word commentary on each of the verses; in the second, a reporter from the cultural desk selects the verses and refers to all the verses in one general commentary.

Using an online database of both newspapers, the second author working closely with graduate and undergraduate students, collected all the *senryû* published during the above-mentioned period (in total: 3,443 verses). Based on the main focus of the verses they were first categorized and broadly divided into the following five categories: (1) Politics (including verses that referred either directly or indirectly to political affairs, policy issues, policymaking, political processes such as election, issues related to politicians and government officials, political parties and factions, political ideology, political corruptions, and international affairs and leaders); (2) Economy (e.g., cost of living, consumers issues, business, trade, and technology); (3) Society (e.g., lifestyle, inequality, work, education, aging, welfare and health); (4) Sports and entertainment; and (5) Other (items included here were later reexamined and integrated in one of the other four categories to construct a total four clusters of *senryû*. See Table 12.1).

Before presenting a random sample of *senryû* verses for selected categories (and subcategories, as they appear in Table 12.3), a word is in order about the challenging task of translating the verses into English. Some of the *senryû* presented in the newspapers were easy to translate, requiring no need for detailed explanation mainly because they dealt with "universal" or "widespread" issues that speak "equally" to members of different cultural backgrounds. Consider for example such a "worldwide" phenomena as corruption. Many verses in both newspapers focused on the scandal involving the 2020 Tokyo Olympic (held in 2021 after a pandemic-driven postponement). During 2022 and 2023 Japanese prosecutors arrested a former deputy executive director of the organizing committee for suspected breach of antitrust laws. At the same time, prosecutors also arrested executives at six advertising and event-planning companies, including the country's biggest advertising agencies Dentsu and Hakuhodo, who have been indicted on charges of bid-rigging [*dangô*] for contracts connected to the Olympics Games. The companies also have had a complaint filed against them by Japan's Fair-Trade Commission. The arrests come after months of

**Table 12.1** Distribution of *senryû* verses along the examined period by months

| Topic/month | Politics | Economy | Society | Sports and entertainment | Total |
|---|---|---|---|---|---|
| April 2022 | 147 | 28 | 66 | 50 | 291 |
| May 2022 | 114 | 18 | 111 | 25 | 268 |
| June 2022 | 129 | 34 | 106 | 28 | 297 |
| July 2022 | 138 | 25 | 103 | 25 | 291 |
| August 2022 | 146 | 20 | 105 | 32 | 303 |
| September 2022 | 167 | 18 | 87 | 25 | 297 |
| October 2022 | 152 | 19 | 74 | 38 | 283 |
| November 2022 | 144 | 21 | 85 | 47 | 297 |
| December 2022 | 133 | 11 | 72 | 47 | 263 |
| January 2023 | 111 | 21 | 103 | 39 | 274 |
| February 2023 | 121 | 30 | 101 | 19 | 271 |
| March 2023 | 121 | 7 | 113 | 67 | 308 |
| Total | 1,623 | 252 | 1,126 | 442 | 3,443 |

investigations into alleged corruption in the planning and sponsorship of the international sporting event. Here are a few related verses that we believe do not need explanation beyond a simple "literal" translation:

> *Gorin mada owattenai to tokusô-bu* (literally: The special investigation division [of the public prosecutor office stated that] the Olympics are not over yet) (*Yomiuri*, August 2, 2022).
>
> *Dangô mo kyôgi shumoku to naru gorin* (Olympics where bid-rigging is also an athletic event) (*Yomiuri*, November 23, 2022).
>
> *Gorin ni wa mamono to kiseichû ga iru* (There are demons and parasites in the Olympics) (*Yomiuri*, December 4, 2022).
>
> *Soshiki-i ga nyûsatsu made mo soshiki shite* (The organizing committee also organized the bidding) (*Yomiuri*, December 19, 2022).
>
> *Kiji ga noru tabi ni yogorete iku gorin* (The Olympics are getting dirtier with every published [newspaper] article) (*Asahi*, January 31, 2023).

On the other hand, less "universal" verses need extended socio-cultural, historical, and political explanations to be fully grasped by those who aren't familiar with the Japanese political context and contemporary circumstances. Therefore, we explained the background and nuances of these verses to facilitate understanding. Consider the following example:

> *Seijika wa shiranu ga hotoke wo shinkô shi* (Politicians believe in Buddha even though they do not know him) (*Yomiuri*, August 30, 2022).

This *senryû* is derived from the Japanese proverbs *shiranu ga hotoke* (knowing nothing is like being a Buddha), and *shiranu ga hotoke, shiru ga bon'nô* (ignorance is bliss, but knowing is trouble). Both proverbs suggest that not knowing is the supreme happiness; knowing is a source of anxiety as it increases one's trouble. This means that one can remain calm like Buddha if one doesn't know the facts. At base, the proverbs aim to mock those who are unperturbed and unaware of their own ignorance.

By itself the verse ironically criticizes Japanese politicians' repeated response that they "didn't know," whenever they are asked about dubious activities, trying to evade their accountability to misconduct that they are linked to. The *senryû* refers in particular to Diet members from the Liberal Democratic Party (LDP, one of the coalition government parties), who constantly claimed they didn't know that some of the staff in their offices who supported their campaign activities, were actually members of the Unification Church, formally known as the Family Federation for World Peace and Unification,[6] that has become the source of controversy since the fatal shooting on July 8, 2022 of former Prime Minister Abe Shinzô (who also served as the President of the LDP), during an election campaign speech. For several months after the assassination of the former prime minister, members of the party continued to deny they knew about their relationship with the Unification Church's members. Obviously, they did so to avoid criticism from the media, the public, and especially voters from their constituencies, for contacting members of this antisocial group, and perhaps even to secure their seat in the upcoming election. Yet, at the same time the media disclosed photos of leading LDP Diet members, including the Speaker of the House of Representatives, meeting officials of the group in various occasions. The above verse thus ridicules such a situation in which high-echelon politicians were trying to avoid being held accountable for such involvement with the cult by pretending they weren't aware of meeting officials from the Church.[7]

Finally, there are *senryû* using words that sound similar to other words, or have several different meanings, that without detailed explanation their meaning is lost. Consider the following verse:

> *Gorin-go ni miru kuchikiki no seika rirê* (The negotiators' results of the relay that is seen after the Olympics) (*Yomiuri*, September 13, 2022).

This verse is related to the Olympic games' scandal. Like other *senryû* it also consists of a play on words: The word *seika* (here spelled intentionally as the word *results*) is written in different letters from a word more appropriate in this context i.e., *torch* (that in Japanese has the same sound i.e., *seika*). Instead of referring to attention given to the Olympic *torch relay*, the verse refers to public attention regarding the post-Olympic games' *activity of the negotiators* (those who were allegedly involved in corrupt affairs).

With these thoughts about translation in mind, here is a random collection of *senryû* addressing different themes:

---

[6] The Church founded in South Korea in 1954 by the late Sun Myung Moon. It was labeled a cult by critics and has become a social problem for its mass weddings and "spiritual sales," in which people are talked into buying jars and other items for exorbitant prices.

[7] In September 2022, LDP's internal survey disclosed that 379 members, around half of the LDP Diet members, including high ranking members of the party, had dealings with the controversial religious group. Soon after, members of the party were instructed to cut their ties with the Church.

### 12.3.1.1 *Senryû* Verses on Politics

(1) Domestic Politics

**Individual Prime Minister**

> *Kishida japan oungôru de 3 shitten* (Kishida's Japan scored three self-goals) (*Yomiuri*, November 23, 2022).

> *Tadashi sugi sôri no eri wa yoreyore ni* (The prime minister's too straight collar is too shabby) (*Yomiuri*, November 25, 2022).

These two verses ridicule Prime Minister Kishida Fumio and the poor political performance of his Cabinet members. Both address the same issue and were published two days apart following the news on November 20, 2022, that the Minister of Internal Affairs and Communications resigned, in fact was ousted, from the government, after a magazine accusing him of misusing political funds.

The first *senryû* used the soccer metaphor as it was published at the time of the World Cup 2022 taking place. In an analogy to the Japanese national soccer team called *Moriyasu Japan*, using the name of the team manager Moriyasu Hajime, the government of the current prime minister was described as *Kishida's Japan*. The three self-goals, as the team's own actions, refer to the fact that three ministers, the Minister of Economic Revitalization, the Minister of Justice, and the Minister of Internal Affairs and Communications, appointed by the prime minster, blundered and resigned (in fact, a fourth minister resigned later, see below). By using a metaphorical soccer expression, the *senryû* sarcastically questions the leadership of the prime minister regarding the way he selected his ministers and manages his cabinet.

The second *senryû* uses the idiom *eri wo tadasu* (straightening one's collar), referring to adjusting disordered clothing, or by implication to the prime minister changing his attitude and tightening his mind. The metaphor of *collar* (along with *sleeves*) is often used by political pundits in Japan: *Collar* (and *sleeves*) of a shirt, are parts that stand out clearly from the main body, used to symbolize leaders who naturally do (or should, at least) stand at the top of other people, and are looked upon as a good model (Feldman, 2004, p. 116). Here the prime minister who has "straightened his collar too much" suggests that he has dismissed the three ministers in his cabinet. By describing the collar as "too shabby," the *senryû* implies that support for the Cabinet is declining even after the ministers were removed from their office.

**Political Scandal**

Here is a selection of verses that express readers' cynicism and sarcasm probably a result of frustration from the unethical activities of officials involved in the organization of the Olympic games:

> *Yoku mireba gorin man'naka kuroi wa de* (Looking closely, a black ring can be seen in the middle of the Olympics [rings]) (*Yomiuri*, August 21, 2022).

> *Seisan wa owatte nan bo gorin-fû* (Liquidation is over and done with, in Olympics style) (*Yomiuri*, September 6, 2022).

*Kasabuta no dekiru ma ga nai gorin kizu* (Olympics' wound that doesn't have time to form a scab) (*Yomiuri*, November 30, 2022).

*Gorin-go ni zokuzoku juyo no kuro medaru* (Black medals awarded one after another after the Olympics) (*Yomiuri*, February 14, 2023).

*Kisowazu ni shôsha wo kimeru ura gorin* (Backdoor Olympics negotiations determined the winner without competing) (*Yomiuri*, February 15, 2023).

### Coronavirus

*Ni kara go he seiseki-hyô nara monku nashi* (No complaint if the grading scale is changed from two to five) (*Asahi*, January 28, 2023).

The verse refers to the government decision to shift its attitude toward the coronavirus by officially downgrading the status of the pandemic from class 2, similar to severe infectious diseases such as SARS and tuberculosis, to class 5, the same as rubella and seasonal influenza (the change in the Infectious Diseases Control Law was announced in January to be effective from May 8, 2023). As a result of this change, a range of coronavirus measures has been removed, including the restrictions on leaving the house when infected with the virus. In this *senryû*, modifying the numbers from 2 to 5 is seen as a positive change, resembling grades in education where most schools in Japan have a numerical grading system ranging from 1 to 5, with 5 being the highest grade and 1 the lowest. Probably recalling school days, whatever is upgraded to 5 is a welcome and desirable development.

(2) **International Politics**

*"Majogari" to jibun de iu hito uso kusai* (People who speak of "witch hunters," stink of lies) (*Asahi*, September 6, 2022).

This is a verse full of irony referring to U.S. President Donald Trump who had tweeted the words "witch hunt" over 300 times since his inauguration in an attempt to portray his opponents as witch-hunters. Here the *senryû* implies that those who use such a term (i.e., President Trump) are in fact not to be trusted.

#### 12.3.1.2 *Senryû* Verses on Economy

### Cost of Living

*Kakeibo ga moete orimasu shôbôsha* (A burning household's account book [needs] a fire truck) (*Asahi*, October 20, 2022).

*Hangeki no nôryoku motanu waga kakei* (Our household is without the ability to fight back [increasing prices]) (*Yomiuri*, December 28, 2022).

*Yachin ka to mimachigau yôna denki-dai* (Electricity bill that could be mistaken for rent) (*Yomiuri*, January 27, 2023).

These three *senryu* are about the increasing cost of living during 2022. They reflect anger and frustration with increasing expenses and with difficulties managing household accounts. The first verse is about the shortage of money at home (equivalent to another unique expression *kakei wa hi no kuruma* i.e., household finances are on fire). The third verse sarcastically reveals that the sharp increase in electricity prices (of seven Japanese electricity companies) makes the bills as high as the monthly rent of the apartment.

### Economic Leaders

*Kôtai su kareha wappen haru mae ni* (Before shifting position put on a leaflet badge) (*Asahi*, January 28, 2023).

This is a humorous, somehow neutral verse referring to the news on the planned change of leadership in the automotive manufacturer Toyota Motor Corporation. On April 1, 2023, it was announced, the current Toyota president will step down and become chairman of the board just before turning 70. The verse advising the retired president (who might not be able to have the use of a driver now) to put, like any other "commoner," a senior citizen marking on his car (in Japan, after the age of 70, drivers are obliged to use a maple and four-leaf markings on their car).

### 12.3.1.3  *Senryû* Verses on Society

### Education

*Shin daigaku mezasu zo ra ra ra kagaku no ko* (Aiming at a new college, la la la, science child) (*Yomiuri*, January 22, 2023).

This verse followed the news (e.g., *Yomiuri*, January 19, 2023) on the decision to merge, in fiscal 2024, two national universities—Tokyo Institute of Technology and Tokyo Medical and Dental University—into a new university named Tokyo University of Science. The phrase "la la la science child" is famous in Japan as it appears in the lyrics of the theme song of Astro Boy, an android young boy with human emotions, a science fiction *manga* series published from 1952 to 1968, one of the most successful *manga* and *anime* franchises in the world. It is also the title of Yahagi Toshihiko's novel *La La La Science Child*, published in 2004. This book is about a protagonist who is guilty of attempted murder of a police officer during the student movement (1968–1969), flees to China, spends 30 years there in bitterness, and then returns to Japan by smuggling himself out of the country and soon realizes to his dismay that while everything seems to have changed, nothing has really changed in Japan. The *senryû* might skeptically indicate that either like the *manga* there will be not much science in this unification of the two universities (probably only *fictional* science), or, like the book, nothing will really change (in terms of science in these institutions) even after their merger.

## Lifestyle

*Shiretoko ni namida no ryojô chinkonka* (Tearful requiem for a journey to Shiretoko) (*Yomiuri*, April 27, 2022).

*Naze omowan modorenai hodo aretara to* (Why didn't [they] think they wouldn't be able to come back if it gets so rough) (*Asahi*, April 29, 2022).

Both verses express resentment and irritation following the Shiretoko cruise ship's sinking accident. In April 2022, a sightseeing boat sank off the Shiretoko Peninsula in Hokkaido, a national park and world heritage site. The boat operators decided to sail despite the forecast of bad weather, including strong winds and high waves, and against the advice of local fishermen. This decision was fatal as the waves overturned the boat, leaving 20 passengers including children and crew members dead, and six others missing. The second *senryû*, in particular, reveals the reader's anger towards the boat operators for their problematic decision that cost people's lives.

*Muryô-ka wa sora tobu kuruma fukyû-go ni* (Free access [on the highway] will come only after the spread of flying cars) (*Yomiuri*, January 20, 2023)

The Ministry of Land, Infrastructure, Transport and Tourism decided to amend the law and to extend the deadline for collecting expressway tolls, from 2065 to 2115. This was criticized as a de facto reversal of the 2005 proposal to make expressways free of charge. In response to this news, out of frustration and hopelessness, this verse cynically condemns the decision with a view that expressways would be toll-free only after flying cars will start to be in use (that is, only when there will not be any need to use the expressways).

## Agriculture

*Niwatori ga masuku yokose to naiteiru* (Chickens are crying [begging for] for a mask) (*Asahi*, January 11, 2023).

*Tori infuru ni-rui ni kaku wo agete kure* (Upgrade bird flu to the second category) (*Yomiuri*, March 7, 2023)

The verses reflect contrasting views, as both refer to bird flu, the disease caused by infection with bird influenza viruses. During 2022–2023, Japan faced a major, nationwide avian influenza outbreak, affecting 26 out of its 47 prefectures. In 16 out of 26 prefectures there was not enough land to dispose of culled birds properly. The largest number of birds culled on record in a single season until then was 9.8 million in 2020, but that was surpassed with 10 million birds culled as of January 10, 2023. Along with emergency disinfection at poultry farms nationwide, the government called for thorough quarantine measures to be implemented, including draining reservoirs near farms with outbreaks to prevent wild birds gathering there.

The first verse cynically suggests that the birds yell for masks to use as a measure to prevent the spread of the influenza virus, the same way masks were used to slow the spread of the coronavirus. The second verse expresses hope that the bird flu will soon be "upgraded" to the next category, becoming something like a seasonal influenza B virus that affects human beings, that is less harmful and causes less severe disease than influenza A.

**Emperor and the Imperial Family**

> *Karuizawa no tenisu kôto mo toshi wo heru* (Karuizawa's tennis court is also aging) (*Asahi*, October 21, 2022).

This verse followed media coverage of the 88th birthday celebration of the empress emerita and related programs on her life-course events, showing among other things the tennis court in the town of Karuizawa, Nagano Prefecture, where she met the emperor emeritus for the first time in August 1957 (at that time the now retired emperor was the crown prince, and the former empress was a commoner. They married in April 1959). The *senryû* expresses nostalgia, noting that like the tennis court the empress emerita had also aged.

> *Ten'nô wo zenritsusen ga chikashiku shi* (Prostate is approaching the emperor) (*Asahi*, November 11, 2022).

The verse refers to the news that Emperor Naruhito has been found to have an enlarged prostate and would undergo a tissue examination for confirmation. The verse expresses empathy for the emperor who was once (before the end of WWII) regarded as a living God and now affected by health issues as much as any other aging regular "human being."

### 12.3.1.4 *Senryû* Verses on Sports and Entertainment

> Ôtani to nazukete miru ka rokketo ni (Let's name the rocket after Ôtani)
>
> (*Yomiuri*, March 10, 2023).

This *senryû* was written in response to the news that the first launch of the Japanese H3 rocket on March 7, 2023 ended in failure. It ironically suggests naming future such rockets after Ôtani Shohei, a Japanese, professional, superstar baseball player in U.S. Major League Baseball, who is widely regarded as the best baseball player in the game today. Just like Ôtani's ability to pitch and bat at the highest level, the rocket named after him would probably be as successful and perform as perfectly as does Ôtani.

Following the first stage of categorizing and dividing the *senryû* verses according to the above-mentioned four categories, the second stage in the analysis involved detailed examination, especially of the politically related *senryû*, identifying 51 categories specified in Table 12.3.

## 12.4 Results and Discussion

Table 12.1 provides a general outline on the distribution of the sample of the *senryû* verses during the examined period. It reveals the number of verses ranged from the lowest number (263) in December 2022 to the highest (308) in March 2023 (verses were published between 24 to 27 days in each month). The distribution of verses referring to politics was not equal during that time, ranging from 111 in January 2023 to 167 in September 2022. On some days, few politically related verses were published, while during other days there were several politically related verses.

No explanation was offered by the dailies as to why sometimes they tended to publish more and other times fewer politically related verses. It can be assumed that this is a result of the number of *senryû* that were sent to the newspapers; at times readers might send more and at other times send fewer verses. The fact that in different days there are varying numbers of verses dealing in politics illustrates that the number and frequency of verses regarding a certain theme (in this case politics) might reflect the general climate and developing events related to the subject of the verses. Growing attention and news items and stories in the media to a particular issue probably generates more *senryû* related to this issue. In this sense, *senryû* resemble other columns in the news media, such as political cartoons, that reflect the frequency, content, and nature of the news published by the media. Regarding politics, then, related verses and their frequency thus reflect the political mood and events at a given historical moment as well as perhaps the general feeling and attitudes of the public towards politics.

As detailed in Table 12.2, during the examined period the two dailies together published 3,443 verses, covering all areas including politics, world affairs, economics, society, and sports and entertainment. Of the total, the largest group of *senryû* (47%) related to the political process, activity of politicians, and policy matters on the domestic and the international levels. These were followed by 32.7% of the verses which referred to society, issues of lifestyle, science and technology, among other things, and close to 13% and 7% of the verses were concerned with issues related to the economy, and sports and entertainment, respectively. The table shows the high proportion of political verses that appeared in *Asahi* in comparison to *Yomiuri* (close to 64% and 36%, respectively), whereas the latter had more verses than the former in the other three categories.

Table 12.3 indicates the breakdown of only the political-related *senryû* verses. It shows that 51 categories of verses regarding a given theme were identified. Table 12.4 further reveals the way we clustered the 51 categories into 19 clusters that represent verses on related issues. Here are selected *senryû* verses that dominated this list of clusters.

**Table 12.2** Number and percentage of each category of *senryû* in the dailies

|  | Politics | Economy | Society | Sports and entertainment | Total |
|---|---|---|---|---|---|
| *Asahi* | 1,038 | 92 | 429 | 105 | 1,664 |
| % within daily | 62.37 | 5.53 | 25.78 | 6.31 | 100% |
| % within category | 63.96 | 36.51 | 38.09 | 23.76 | 48.33 |
| *Yomiuri* | 585 | 160 | 697 | 337 | 1,779 |
| % within daily | 32.88 | 8.99 | 39.18 | 18.94 | 100 |
| % within category | 36.04 | 63.49 | 61.90 | 76.24 | 51.67 |
| Total | 1,623 | 252 | 1,126 | 442 | 3,443 |
| % within dailies | 47.13 | 7.32 | 32.7 | 12.84 | 100 |
| % within category | 100 | 100 | 100 | 100 | 100 |

## 12.4.1 Policy Issues

### 12.4.1.1 On National Security

*Teki kichi wo uteba dô naru kikasete* (Let me know what happens if you shoot the enemy base) (*Asahi*, April 13, 2022).

*Teki kichi wo nerau kotchi mo teki kichi da* (Aiming at the enemy base, ours is also an enemy base) (*Asahi*, April 22, 2022).

The two verses reflect a sense of insecurity and anxiety regarding national security and the defense of the country, especially in light of the military buildup by North Korea and China. In the same month that these *senryû* were published, North Korea in particular test-fired a new, short-range missile reportedly aimed to "enhance the efficiency in the operation of tactical nukes," marking the first time North Korea had linked a specific system to tactical nuclear weapons use. Sirens blared across northern Japan and residents were told to "evacuate immediately," schools delayed their starting times, and some train services were suspended, as the government announced Pyongyang's repeated missile launches pose a "grave and imminent threat" to Japan's security. With tensions growing in the region, and the increasing missile barrage that North Korea has already fired by April, many Japanese started to worry about their ability to counterattack and what might be the outcome of such a response.

### 12.4.1.2 On Coronavirus

*Zensû no minaoshi sekai ichi kaihi* (Reassessing the total number will [enable us] to shun the world's number one) (*Yomiuri*, August 30, 2022).

*Dekinunara tomete shimaou zensû hâku* (If [the government] can't do it, let's stop it) (*Yomiuri*, August 26, 2022).

**Table 12.3** Breakdown of political *senryû* (51 categories)

| Theme of the *senryu* | Asahi | Yomiuri | Total |
|---|---|---|---|
| 1. Russia (invasion of the Ukraine) | 145 | 122 | 267 |
| 2. Prime Minister Abe Shinzo's death (related national funeral, Unification Church | 137 | 41 | 178 |
| 3. National security, peace, self-defense forces | 107 | 23 | 130 |
| 4. Diet members' personal qualities, grievances | 81 | 30 | 111 |
| 5. Prime Minister | 70 | 20 | 90 |
| 6 China (including President Xi Jinping, the Chinese Communist Party (CCP), "zero covid" policy, and human rights issues) | 35 | 47 | 82 |
| 7. Covid 19 policy | 60 | 14 | 74 |
| 8. Japanese diplomacy | 34 | 27 | 61 |
| 9. Ruling coalition of parties | 46 | 8 | 54 |
| 10 Government bureaucracy | 39 | 13 | 52 |
| 11. Olympic corruption | 30 | 22 | 52 |
| 12. Elections | 28 | 23 | 51 |
| 13. North Korea (including military abilities, buildup of nuclear weapons, and nuclear tests) | 22 | 25 | 47 |
| 14. Ministers (functioning and resignation of ministers) | 31 | 14 | 45 |
| 15. United States of America | 22 | 21 | 43 |
| 16. Ukraine (war with Russia) | 18 | 21 | 39 |
| 17. Nuclear energy policy | 21 | 8 | 29 |
| 18. Local autonomy | 16 | 14 | 30 |
| 19. Consumption tax increase | 19 | 11 | 30 |
| 20. United Kingdom | 7 | 14 | 21 |
| 21. Opposition parties | 10 | 9 | 19 |
| 22. My number (The Individual Number Card, an identity document for citizens of Japan); the usage related to this card | 8 | 5 | 13 |
| 23. South Korea (Japan-Korea relationship; meeting between the leaders of the countries) | 5 | 8 | 13 |
| 24. Declining birthrate | 3 | 9 | 12 |
| 25. Ministry of Health, Labor and Welfare | 6 | 3 | 9 |
| 26. Ministry of Economy, Trade, and Industry | 7 | 0 | 7 |
| 27. UN and other international organizations | 3 | 3 | 6 |
| 28. Philippines | 4 | 1 | 5 |
| 29. Turkey | 2 | 3 | 5 |
| 30. Ministry of Justice | 2 | 3 | 5 |
| 31. Brazil | 1 | 3 | 4 |
| 32. Finland | 1 | 2 | 3 |
| 33. France | 1 | 2 | 3 |

(continued)

**Table 12.3** (continued)

| Theme of the *senryu* | *Asahi* | *Yomiuri* | Total |
|---|---|---|---|
| 34. Germany | 1 | 2 | 3 |
| 35. LGBT | 3 | 0 | 3 |
| 36. Italy | 2 | 1 | 3 |
| 37. Ministry of Land, Infrastructure, Transport and Tourism | 1 | 2 | 3 |
| 38. Constitution | 2 | 1 | 3 |
| 39. Sri Lanka | 1 | 1 | 2 |
| 40. The right of a married couple to use separate surnames | 2 | 0 | 2 |
| 41. *Go to travel campaign* (to encourage travel around Japan from July 2020 onwards) | 0 | 2 | 2 |
| 42. Cool Japan (part of Japan's strategy, aiming to disseminate Japan's attractiveness and allure to the world) | 0 | 2 | 2 |
| 43. Digital agency | 1 | 1 | 2 |
| 44. Iran | 1 | 0 | 1 |
| 45. Honduras | 1 | 0 | 1 |
| 46. Hungary | 0 | 1 | 1 |
| 47. Syria | 0 | 1 | 1 |
| 48. Indonesia | 1 | 0 | 1 |
| 49. Afghanistan | 0 | 1 | 1 |
| 50. Sweden | 0 | 1 | 1 |
| 51. New Zealand | 1 | 0 | 1 |
| Total | 1038 | 585 | 1623 |

These two verses capture the irony of the government's stance reconsidering its grasp of the total number of coronavirus cases. From the onset and spread of the virus the Japanese government had been keeping track of the exact number of people infected with the coronavirus, making Japan the country with the highest number of infected people internationally. In a bid to reduce the administrative burden on hospitals and local health centers, in August 2022 the government decided to revise its policy on tracking the virus cases, and to simplify its reporting system by targeting elderly and high-risk people. Against that backdrop, the first *senryû* reveals that reassessing the total number means that the precise number of infected people will become unknown, enabling Japan to avoid the negative label of being the world's "number one" infected country. The second *senryû* is critical of the government decision, stating that if the government doesn't plan to follow the exact number of infected people, it would be better to stop counting altogether.

**Table 12.4** Breakdown of political-related *senryû* verses (19 clusters)

| Theme of the *senryû* verses | Asahi | Yomiuri | Total |
|---|---|---|---|
| 1. Policy issues (including national security, coronavirus, diplomacy, nuclear energy, consumption tax increase, declining birthrate, the right of a married couple to use separate surnames, LGBT, Constitution, *Go to travel campaign* (to encourage travel around Japan from July 2020 onwards), Cool Japan (part of Japan's overall brand strategy, aiming to disseminate Japan's attractiveness and allure to the world) | 251 | 97 | 348 |
| 2. Russia-Ukraine war (invasion to Ukraine) | 163 | 143 | 306 |
| 3. Prime Minister Abe Shinzo's death (related national funeral, Unification Church) | 137 | 41 | 178 |
| 4. Diet members' personal qualities, grievances | 81 | 30 | 111 |
| 5. Prime minister | 70 | 20 | 90 |
| 6. China | 35 | 47 | 82 |
| 7. Government bureaucracy (including Ministry of Land, Infrastructure, Transport and Tourism; Ministry of Health, Labor and Welfare; Ministry of Economy, Trade and Industry; Ministry of Justice; Digital Agency) | 56 | 22 | 78 |
| 8. Ruling coalition of parties | 46 | 8 | 54 |
| 9. Olympic corruption | 30 | 22 | 52 |
| 10. Election | 28 | 23 | 51 |
| 11. North Korea | 22 | 25 | 47 |
| 12. Government ministers | 31 | 14 | 45 |
| 13. United States of America | 22 | 21 | 43 |
| 14. Variety of countries and international organizations (including Philippines, Turkey, Brazil, Finland, France, Germany, Italy, Sri Lanka, Iran, Honduras, Hungary, Syria, Indonesia, Afghanistan, Sweden, New Zealand, UN, and other international organizations) | 20 | 22 | 42 |
| 15. Local autonomy | 16 | 14 | 30 |
| 16. United Kingdom | 7 | 14 | 21 |
| 17. Opposition parties | 10 | 9 | 19 |
| 18. My Number (The Individual Number Card, an identity document for citizens of Japan) | 8 | 5 | 13 |
| 19. South Korea | 5 | 8 | 13 |
| Total | 1,038 | 585 | 1,623 |

## 12.4.2 Russia-Ukraine War (Invasion of the Ukraine)

"Kougeki" wo "hangeki" to yobu shita no saki (The tip of the tongue that calls "attack" a "counterattack") (*Asahi*, April 23, 2022).

Pûchin no "shôri" ni dorehodo no bohyô (How many tombstones are needed until to Putin's "victory") (*Yomiuri*, February 16, 2023).

The two verses follow media reports on Russia's invasion of the Ukraine. The first *senryû* reveals sarcasm as it refers to Russia's attempt to deceive the world with its leader's own glib tongue in presenting this invasion as a "counterattack" rather than an "attack." The second verse ironically indicates that Russia's victory will be decided by massive killing of thousands of civilians (and injuring many thousands more).

### 12.4.3 Prime Minister Abe Shinzô's Assassination

*Owaru made dasenu kokusô haumatchi* (How-much [money] can't be put out until the state funeral is over) (*Yomiuri,* September 2, 2022)

*Kokumin no kane to na wo kari jimin-sô* (Borrowing people's money and reputation for the Liberal Democratic [Party's] burial) (*Asahi*, September 28, 2022)

Former Prime Minister Abe's state funeral was held on September 27, 2022, costing 1.24 billion yen. In August, the cabinet decision had pegged the cost at 250 million yen, but it was pointed out that it was unclear how much would be spent on guarding dignitaries and staffing for security. The government then estimated on September 6 that it would cost 1.66 billion yen (eventually the cost was less than this amount). Since the national funeral would be paid for entirely with government funds, there was a wave of public criticism, most vocally from opposition parties and political pundits objecting to this national funeral. The verses above can be taken as satirically criticizing the fact that the price of a national funeral is unknown and that even though it is a national funeral, it can also be regarded as the funeral of the Liberal Democratic (Party). The last part of the verse appears as a play on words with the same sound: instead of the *jimin-tô* (the Liberal Democratic Party) it is written *jimin-sô* (Liberal Democratic's burial).

### 12.4.4 The Prime Minister

*Kishida-shi ga dappi to mieru "kentôshi"* (It looks as if Mr. Kishida is shedding his skin on "deliberation envoy") (*Yomiuri*, July 26, 2022).

*Zuibun to shippo no ôi chin-shu desu* (A rare species with quite a lot of tails) (*Asahi*, January 5, 2023).

These are two sympathetic verses in terms of their attitude towards the prime minister. The first is an optimistic view of the leadership style of Prime Minister Kishida who has been nicknamed the "deliberation envoy" (*kentôshi*) because of his frequent use of the phrase "to consider" (e.g., his views regarding policies, as opposed "to decide"). Following the upper house election in July 2022, the government geared up to embark in earnest with economic policies (which Kishida termed "new capitalism"), along with other measures. There were growing expectations among politicians and political pundits that Kishida himself would change his discourse, and by this also his activity, to be more practical. The verse mirrors the hope that the prime minister will amend his rhetoric the same way an animal changes their appearance (Kishida in fact changed his speaking style using such words as "to explain," and further changed it in the first months of 2023 including such words as "to determine").

The second *senryû* describes the same prime minister as being able to pull through difficulties in his administration and maintain political power. From October through December 2022, four ministers resigned or were forced to resign from Kishida's cabinet; in addition to the three mentioned above, the Minister for Reconstruction was also forced to resign following a political fund scandal. All these troubles within the administration raised doubts about the prime minister's leadership ability as well as questions within his own political party about his political future. In addition, during this term of office, criticism regarding possible tax hikes (i.e., corporate, income, and cigarette taxes) to finance the increase in defense spending contributed to the decline in Cabinet support, damaging Kishida's public approval ratings (in November, 43.5% of the public expressed disapproval). Despite all this, the prime minister was able to preserve his political authority. The *senryû* depicts Kishida (resembling a chameleon) and his skill to survive and function through the consecutive troubles he suffers with these resignations and the talk about increasing taxes (cutting off the tails).

## 12.4.5 China

*San-ki-me wa shûshin made no ichiridzuka* (Third term is a milestone toward lifetime [appointment]) (*Yomiuri*, October 21, 2022).

*Te wo tataku dake ni atsumaru san zennin* (Three thousand people gathered just to clap their hands) (*Asahi*, March 7, 2023).

Both verses, published five months apart, express an ironic and cynical view of the Chinese political system and especially regarding the general meeting of the 20th Central Committee of the Communist Party of China (CPC) that was held on October 16, 2022, inaugurating General Secretary Xi Jinping's third term in power. The verses noted that Xi's election for a third term was unusual, suggesting that his reelection indicates staying in this position forever. On March 10, 2023, during the 14th National People's Congress, Xi was elected President of the State and Chairman of the Central Military Commission. In response, the second *senryû* cynically reveals that 3,000 people gathered at this meeting only to applaud Xi's election to the position, as in fact the Congress didn't have any other candidate and that the results were obvious and known in advance.

### 12.4.6 Government Bureaucracy

*Shôeki no yûsen no mae seigi kie* (Justice disappears before prioritizing the interest of the Ministry [of Justice]) (*Asahi*, June 10, 2022)

This *senryû* sarcastically criticizes the Ministry of Justice's response to the death of Wishma Sandamali, a Sri Lankan woman who died in March 2021 while in custody at an immigration detention facility in Nagoya, after her requests for provisional release and adequate medical care were denied. In June 2022, after looking at this incident, the Nagoya District Public Prosecutors Office dropped the case against the senior immigration officials in charge at the time, whom the bereaved family accused of allegedly committing murder, or negligence as her guardian resulting in death. The exact reason for this decision was not disclosed, and as the family of the Sri Lankan woman demanded to know why prosecutors dropped their case, the *senryû* writer offered their view that justice was disappearing, believing that the Ministry of Justice was trying to conceal the truth in favor of the ministry's own interests.

*Zaimushô shiboreru mono wo mata mitsuke* (Japanese Ministry of Finance finds something to wither again) (*Yomiuri*, November 10, 2022)

The verse expresses irony at the request of the Ministry of Finance to increase users' nursing care burden. On November 7, 2022, a committee of the ministry proposed that the user's 10% burden regarding nursing care services would be increased to 20%, or the target of people eligible for 20% and 30% would be expanded. In response to the ministry's attempt to collect a larger share from long-term care insurance users, the *senryû* condemns the government for repeatedly raising the amount collected from various sources, as it now "again found" another "target" for revenue.

## 12.5 Conclusions

Several observations can be made, first regarding this particular study, and second the *senryû* verses as a stylistic device, a technique for readers to convey their emotions and thoughts through the print media (arguably, perhaps without an intention to provoke an emotional response among readers).

First, the verses referring to politics represent a large portion of the published *senryû*: More than 47% of the total verses that appeared during the examined period concerned political events, activity, and decisionmakers. With ever-increasing political issues placed on the national agenda in Japan and the growing number of topics, from policy issues to political events and activities on the local, national, and international levels, this figure might be taken as obvious. Yet, this proportion contrasts with the finding of an earlier study on political *senryû* in another national daily the *Mainichi*: Of the total of 5,846 verses that appeared during the period of one year, January through December 1997, only 145 verses (2.5%) referred to the political process and decision-making, policy issues, and the activity of politicians (Feldman, 1999b). It is also noticeable that in this study there was a difference between the proportion of politically related verses published by the two newspapers: 64% by *Asahi*, 36% by *Yomiuri*. These findings lead to two possible explanations.

First, in the past, as in the period covered in this chapter, readers indeed sent a large number of *senryû* related to politics, but the persons who selected them for publication in the *Mainichi* preferred for some reason to publish only a portion of them, allocating more space to verses regarding society, economy, or sports and entertainment.

Another explanation that can be offered regarding the small proportion of political *senryû* as observed in the previous study is that the number of related *senryû* sent from the public was in fact small. If so, this might be due to two reasons. First, in comparison to recent times, readers back then did not consider politics as a topic to compose *senryû* about. Perhaps they considered public affairs as too serious a domain to address in light, witty expressions, preferring to write about "less serious" and more appealing easy-to-write-about topics, such as society and the economy.

Yet another reason can be proposed: the public did not closely heed politics, as they do these days, and showed less interest in political activity and policy issues. The public's decreasing political interest in politics was in fact reported at that time in many studies of political attitudes in Japan, following voters' feelings of alienation and increasing expressions of distrust toward politicians and bureaucrats (Feldman, 1995). This might have been mirrored in the limited number of *senryû* in the newspaper. Those who sent verses on politics reflected the general mood of cynicism toward the ability of politicians, criticism of policy issues and decision-making processes, and the increasing ethical issues related to politics including politicians' corruption and the increasing amount of money in politics. These were the major categories of the *senryû* published by *Mainichi* some 35 years ago. Psychological distance from politics could account for less politically related *senryû*. This notion suggests that further content analysis of the *senryû* published at different times, perhaps even in different print media channels (including journals), could more finely detail the role, function, and effect of this reader tool (as a form of political participation) in political communication in Japan.

Our second observation is related to the humor expressed in these *senryû*. As we indicated throughout this chapter, the humor expressed (and often hinted) in the *senryû* ranged from irony, cynicism, sarcasm, and ridicule (revealing irritation, anger and frustration) towards political leaders and government officials, and the way they handle social, economic, and health issues, all the way to expression of support, hope, optimism, and empathy addressed to (for example) to the prime minister and the emperor. This two-fold structure of *senryû* verses demonstrates the scope and versatility of (political) humor conveyed by *senryû*. Clearly, however, it is dominated by a type of "black humor," a satirical expression of sentiments toward politics, politicians, and political events and issues.

Conspicuously, not only do these verses include a wide range of viewpoints and emotions, but they also refer to a wide range of issues and topics. For *senryu*, nothing is taboo. To put this notion in the right context, it is noteworthy to mention one aspect on the working of the Japanese media. Reporters and editors always consider the possible impact of their stories on specific groups of readers. To avoid evoking an adverse emotional reaction from readers, editors have to carefully filter information. The result is that daily newspapers tend to be "fringe-exclusive." Anything controversial that might irritate the foundation of Japanese society or culture is very easily discarded or carefully filtered before publication. This includes stories about taboo subjects like the imperial family, minority groups, and religious groups and cults (Feldman, 2011, p. 187). By contrast, all these issues are detailed (some of these discussed above) in the *senryû*, without fear or reservation. In this regard, these verses are probably the most democratic expressions of opinion in the Japanese media.

Last, from a methodological standpoint, many of the verses examined in this study appeared as falling into two categories. The dilemma we faced with a large number of verses was the main message the writers tried to convey: is it about the trigger (the background behind the writing of the verse e.g., the decision of the ministry, categorized as political verse) or the outcome of the decision (e.g., the effect on lifestyle, categorized under society or economic sections)?

In addition, we also noted that *senryû* verses appear to be short lived, perhaps like political cartoons. In other words, as time passes, the context to which the *senryû* referred to is forgotten and the *senryû* loses its witty characteristic. This is the ephemeral nature of these verses. To understand the *senryû* and its context there is a need to search for the news and events that took place around the time they were published. Other *senryû* are more general, referring not to particular and specific events but to routine, even universal, types of political activity and philosophy that can appeal to readers at all times and in different cultures. Both types illustrate the unique characteristics of *senryû* as satirical poetry that deserve further scholarly research.

**Acknowledgements** Financial support for the writing of this chapter came from a Grant-in-Aid for Scientific Research by the Japanese Ministry of Education, Culture, Sports, Science, and Technology (2023–2025), to the first author (Grant number 23K01245).

# References

Brink, D. A. (2001). At wit's end: Satirical verse contra formative ideologies in bakumatsu and Meiji Japan. *Early Modern Japan: An Interdisciplinary Journal, 9*(1), 19–46. https://kb.osu.edu/bitstream/handle/1811/668/v9n1Brink.pdf?sequence=1&isAllowed=y

Davis, J. M. (Ed). (2006). *Understanding humor in Japan*. Wayne State University Press.

Feldman, O. (1995). Political attitudes and the news media in Japan: Effects of exposure and attention to the news media on political involvement and disapprobation. *Howard Journal of Communication, 6*(3), 206–225. https://doi.org/10.1080/10646179509361697

Feldman, O. (1998). Materialism and individualism: Social attitudes of youth in Japan. In M. W. Watts (Ed.), *Cross-cultural perspectives on youth and violence* (pp. 9–25). JAI Press.

Feldman, O. (1999a). Introduction to political psychology in Japan. In O. Feldman (Ed.), *Political psychology in Japan* (pp. 1–23). Nova Science Pub.

Feldman, O. (1999b). "*Senryû*" as political participation: On the nature and content of "*senryû*" in the Japanese media. *Naruto Kyoiku Daigaku Kenkyu Kiyo, 14*, 85–90. (in Japanese).

Feldman, O. (2000). Non-oratorical discourse and political humor in Japan: Editorial cartoons, satire and attitudes toward authority. In C. De Landtsheer & O. Feldman (Eds.), *Beyond public speech and symbols: Explorations in the rhetoric of politicians and the media* (pp. 165–191). Praeger.

Feldman, O. (2004). *Talking politics in Japan today*. Sussex Academic Press.

Feldman, O. (2011). Reporting with wolves: Pack journalism and the dissemination of political information. In T. Inoguchi & P. Jain (Eds.), *Japanese politics today: From karaoke to kabuki democracy* (pp. 183–200). Palgrave Macmillan.

Feldman, O. (2021). Decoding Japanese politicians' rhetoric: Socio-cultural features of public speaking. In O. Feldman (Ed.), *When politicians talk: The cultural dynamics of public speaking* (pp. 203–220). Springer. https://doi.org/10.1007/978-981-16-3579-3_12

Feldman, O. (2023). Challenging etiquette: Insults, sarcasm, and irony in Japanese politicians' discourse. In O. Feldman (Ed.), *Political debasement: Incivility, contempt, and humiliation in parliamentary and public discourse* (pp. 93–116). Springer. https://doi.org/10.1007/978-981-99-0467-9_5

Feldman, O., & Bull, P. (2012). Understanding audience affiliation in response to political speeches in Japan. *Language & Dialogue, 2*(3), 375–397. https://doi.org/10.1075/ld.2.3.04fel

Feldman, O., & Kinoshita, K. (2017). Do important questions demand respectful replies? Analyzing televised political interviews in Japan. *Journal of Asian Pacific Communication, 27*(1), 121–157. https://doi.org/10.1075/japc.27.1.07fel

Feldman, O., & Kinoshita, K. (2019). Political communicators and control in political interviews in Japanese television: A comparative study and the effect of culture. In O. Feldman & S. Zmerli (Eds.), *The psychology of political communicators: How politicians, culture, and the media construct and shape public discourse* (pp. 31–55). Routledge.

Feldman, O., & Watts, M. W. (2000). Authority and political authority in Japan: Cultural and social orientations in non-western society. In S. Rippl, C. Seipel & A. Kindervater (Eds.), *Authoritarianism: Controversies and approaches in authoritarianism research today* (pp. 147–171). Leske & Budrich. (in German).

Fukumoto, I. (1999). *Haiku and senryû: How to think and enjoy laughter and sharpness*. Kodansha. (in Japanese).

Fukusaku, M. (1977). *Japanese laughter*. Tamagawa Daigaku Shippanbu. (in Japanese).

Inoue, H. (1984). *Laughter as a human relation*. Kodansha. (in Japanese).

Inoue, H. (2003). *Osaka culture and laughter*. Kansai Daigaku Shuppanbu. (in Japanese).

Inoue, H. (2006). On the "culture of laughter" in Osaka: Laughter and the culture of life of the Osaka people. *Forum Gendai Shakaigaku, 5*, 57–68. https://www.jstage.jst.go.jp/article/ksr/5/0/5_KJ00008433922/_pdf (in Japanese).

Kobayashi, M. (2006). *Senryû*: Japan's short comic poetry. In J. M. Davis (Ed.), *Understanding humor in Japan* (pp. 153–177). Wayne State University Press.

Kubozono, H. (1999). Mora and syllable. In N. Tsujimura (Ed.), *The handbook of Japanese linguistics* (pp. 31–61). Blackwell.

Kumei, T. (2006). "A record of life and a poem of sentiments": Japanese immigrant "senryu," 1929–1945. *Amerikastudien/American Studies, 51*(1), 29–49. http://www.jstor.org/stable/41158196

Reagan Foundation. (n.d.). The best of President Reagan's humor. https://www.youtube.com/watch?v=Pgs-LaWyUJI

Sekine, M. (1967). *Considerations of storytelling and rakugo*. Yuzankaku. (in Japanese).

Shirane, H. (1998). *Traces of dreams: Landscape, cultural memory, and the poetry of Basho*. Stanford University Press.

Sotoyama, S. (1976). *Everyday words*. Mizumi Shobo. (in Japanese).

Spinks, W. A. (2011). In the midst of transition: Salaryman *senryu* poems and the perception of workplace change. *Contemporary Japan, 23*(2), 187–212. https://doi.org/10.1515/cj.2011.010

THE NEWSPAPER. (n.d.). https://ja.wikipedia.org/wiki/%E3%82%B6%E3%83%BB%E3%83%8B%E3%83%A5%E3%83%BC%E3%82%B9%E3%83%9A%E3%83%BC%E3%83%91%E3%83%BC (in Japanese).

Ueda, M. (1999). *Light verse from the floating world: An anthology of premodern Japanese senryu*. Columbia University Press.


**Ofer Feldman** is Professor of Political Psychology and Behavior at the Faculty of Policy Studies, Doshisha University, and an Affiliated Professor at the Center for Southeast Asian Studies, Kyoto University, Kyoto, Japan. His research centers on the psychological underpinnings of mass and elite political behavior in Japan. He has extensively published journal articles, books, and book chapters on issues related to political communication and persuasion, political leadership, and political culture. His books include *The Rhetoric of Political Leadership* (2020, edited), *When Politicians Talk* (2021, edited), *Adversarial Political Interviewing* (2022, edited), *Political Debasement* (2023, edited), *and Debasing Political Rhetoric* (2023, edited). In 2021 he was elected Honorary Chair of the Research Committee on Political Psychology, International Political Science Association.

**Ken Kinoshita** is an Associate Professor at the Faculty of Social and Environmental Studies, Fukuoka Institute of Technology, Fukuoka, Japan. He has published several books and journal articles on the working of the Japanese Diet, local councils, and political communication, including *Chihô gikai kaikaku no susumekata* (How to proceed with improving the functions of local councils?) (2020, in Japanese), *Seijika wa naze shitsumon ni kotaenaika* (Why Politicians Equivocate?) (2018, in Japanese, co-authored with Ofer Feldman), and *Niinsei-ron* (Bicameral Theory) (2015, in Japanese). His most recent book *Japanese Politicians' Rhetorical and Indirect Speech* (2023) focuses on the relationship between politicians' interview replies and facial displays.

# Chapter 13
# Depicting *"La Grieta"*: The Role of Political Satire and Humor in Argentinean Polarization

**María Isabel Kalbermatten**

**Abstract** This chapter explores *"la grieta"* in Argentine society, the deep and irreconcilable division, primarily between Kirchneristas and Anti-Kirchneristas, that fragments and polarizes the nation. It significantly shapes political, social, cultural, and even personal relationships in the nation. Introduced by Jorge Lanata during the 2013 Martin Fierro Award Ceremony, *la grieta* extends beyond politics, impacting friendships, families, and workplaces. Argentina's main newspapers align themselves with different sides of *la grieta*, made evident in their satirical approaches in political columns and editorial cartoons. *Página 12* takes a progressive stance, *La Nación* leans conservative, and *Clarín* leans center-right. These newspapers reinforce existing beliefs, deepening the ideological and political divide. Selected texts like "Life begins at 30: The beautiful Página" (*Página 12*), "Cristina vs. Alberto: Call the firefighters!" (*La Nación*), and "Let the rift not wane" (*Clarín*) shed light on how satirists portray *la grieta* as a problematic phenomenon. Political satire both reflects and critiques the polarizing aspect of the division in Argentine society. This analysis provides perspectives on the role of satire in addressing societal wrongs within the context of *la grieta* in Argentina. Understanding the impact of this division can provide deeper insights into the social, cultural, and political dynamics of Argentine society.

## 13.1 Introduction

The term *la grieta* in Argentine Spanish has evolved metaphorically to symbolize a profound and irreconcilable division, characterized by opposing political and ideological factions, primarily between Kirchneristas (who support the policies of the

---

M. I. Kalbermatten (✉)
Gustavus Adolphus College, St. Peter, Minnesota, USA
e-mail: mkalberm@gustavus.edu

Kirchner family's political movement,[1] emphasizing social justice and state intervention), and Anti-Kirchneristas (who oppose these policies for reasons including concerns about corruption and concentration of power). This divide, while not stemming from a single specific issue, is fueled by historical political rivalries, economic inequalities, differing social perspectives, and varying attitudes toward governance. Media influences, perceptions of corruption, and the legacy of populist policies also contribute to this rift. *La grieta* encompasses a complex interplay of factors, reflecting a deep-seated polarization within Argentine society. It represents a significant cultural factor that profoundly shapes relationships throughout the country, thereby also exerting an influence on political satire within Argentina's three main newspapers. While the primary focus lies on the current social and collective structures in Argentina, it is crucial to acknowledge that the term *la grieta* possesses deep historical roots. Jorge Ernesto Lanata, an Argentine journalist,[2] first introduced this notion during the 2013 Martin Fierro Award Ceremony,[3] describing it as "an irreconcilable division in Argentina" that "represents the most detrimental issue we are facing." Lanata further emphasizes that "even beyond the current government,[4] that will eventually come and go, Florencia, Máximo, Néstor Iván,[5] or whoever may follow, '*la grieta*' will persist. It has evolved beyond mere politics; it has become a cultural divide in the broadest sense, influencing our worldview. It has managed to separate friends, siblings, couples, and work colleagues." Consequently, all Argentinians find themselves aligned with one side or the other of *la grieta*, often influenced by their family backgrounds.

The country's main newspapers—*Clarín*, *La Nación*, and *Página 12*—clearly position themselves on different sides of *la grieta*, and their opinion pages reflect their perspectives and attempts to influence and manipulate the population toward their respective viewpoints. Each newspaper maintains a distinct political stance, evident in their editorial cartoons (Kalbermatten, 2016) and satirical opinion columns. *Clarín* adopts a center-right editorial line, *La Nación* leans more conservative, while *Página 12* is a more progressive newspaper. Their primary contribution has been to reinforce their readers' existing beliefs, thereby deepening the divide that characterizes the social, cultural, and political discourse of the country.

---

[1] The Kirchner family is a political family in Argentina. Néstor Kirchner was President from 2003 to 2007, known for center-left policies. His wife, Cristina Fernández de Kirchner, followed as President from 2007 to 2015. They're associated with the Justicialista Party and their policies had an impact on Argentina's political and economic landscape.

[2] He is known for his work in investigative journalism, literature, documentaries, television fiction, and magazine theater. He has been involved in founding newspapers (*Página 12* and *Crítica de la Argentina*) and has contributed to various magazines.

[3] The Martín Fierro Awards, organized annually by the Argentine Television and Radio Journalists Association (APTRA), recognize outstanding achievements in Argentine radio and television programs as well as presenters.

[4] Lanata refers to Cristina Fernández de Kirchner, president of the country at that time.

[5] They are the daughter, son, and grandson, respectively, of former president Néstor Kirchner and his wife, Cristina Fernández de Kirchner.

Since early societies, the role of the satirist has been to critique and expose perceived wrongs or societal ills within a given society (Caulfield, 2008, p. 7). To explore how the concept of *la grieta* is addressed and condemned within the political satire columns of various newspapers, a careful selection of texts has been made. These texts, including "Life begins at 30: The beautiful Página" by Rudaeff from *Página 12*, "Cristina vs. Alberto: Call the firefighters!" by Reymundo Roberts from *La Nación*, and "Let the rift not wane" by Borensztein from *Clarín*, shed light on the satirists' portrayal of *la grieta* as a problematic and divisive phenomenon within Argentine society.

## 13.2 La Grieta as a Metaphor of Argentine's National Division

The term *"grieta"* as defined in the 2022 edition of the Dictionary of the Royal Spanish Academy (2022) encompasses three distinct meanings. First, it refers to "an elongated indentation in the earth or any solid body." Second, it describes "a shallow indentation formed on the skin or mucous membranes of various body parts." Last, metaphorically it represents "a difficulty or disagreement that threatens the solidity or unity of something." This metaphorical usage draws upon the concept of a long and deep notch or recess from the physical realm and applies it to the social sphere. Zullo (2021) utilizes Lakoff and Johnson's (1980) metaphor theory and posits that, in Argentine Spanish, *la grieta* functions as both a conceptual and an orientational metaphor. The author argues that the former symbolizes a divided society, while the latter positions individuals or groups on opposing sides (Zullo, 2021, pp. 14–18). Within the context of Argentine society, *la grieta* has come to symbolize a profound and irreconcilable division, encompassing both ideological (conservatives versus progressives) and political (Kirchneristas versus Anti-Kirchneristas) aspects. It has led to a fragmented and polarized state within society.

Lanata is widely credited with popularizing the metaphorical usage of *la grieta* in the Argentine media. A decade has passed since he first introduced this expression in 2013, and he recently commemorated its anniversary with an article titled "May you have a miserable birthday: 10 years of division, and how long will we continue like this?" published in the *Clarín* newspaper (Lanata, 2023). In a somewhat ironic twist, Lanata sarcastically wished the term a miserable birthday while reflecting on the prolonged endurance of this division. In the initial paragraphs, he delved into the origin and context of the term, providing a detailed account. He recounted an incident during the Martin Fierro Awards ceremony where he observed a deep-seated division among the attendees that he believed mirrors the profound societal divide between Kirchneristas and Anti-Kirchneristas in Argentina. Lanata attributed the genesis of this division to the political legacies of former presidents Néstor Kirchner and Cristina Fernández de Kirchner, accusing them of promoting their monopolistic perspective on representing the entire nation.

The conceptual metaphor of *la grieta* portraying a divided society emerged in the speech when Lanata characterized the country as "two halves of Argentina." He regarded *la grieta* as a comprehensive "cultural rift" that significantly shaped individuals' perception of the world. This cultural phenomenon not only fragmented society but also strained relationships among friends, siblings, partners, and colleagues. This fragmentation is what he saw during the Martin Fierro Awards party, and what he tried to describe with the word *grieta*. Despite facing accusations of exacerbating the division, Lanata maintained that his role has been solely to describe the existing situation. However, his 2013 speech marked a significant turning point in the popularization of the expression in Argentina.

While the widespread recognition of the phrase is often attributed to Lanata's utilization in 2013, he acknowledged in his recent column that the expression was not novel at that moment,[6] as he had previously employed it to describe a distinct division within the country. He had used the expression on two separate occasions (García et al., 2019, p. 7). In 2006, he produced the documentary *La Grieta*, that focused on Argentina's Process of National Reorganization[7] from 1976 to 1983. Within this documentary, Lanata utilized the metaphorical meaning of *la grieta* to represent the division in Argentine society between two "streams of opinion, the division between those who longed for the years of dictatorship and those who, on the contrary, defended democracy as a right that should never be lost again" (García et al., 2019, p. 7).

Three years later, in an interview with *La Nación* newspaper, Lanata revisited the metaphorical concept to shed light on a different division within Argentine society. This division emerged after the severe economic crisis of 2001, which had lasting impacts on the social fabric of the country. He used the metaphor to highlight the significant gap between segments of the Argentine people as well as antagonism towards their political leaders, stemming from deep disillusionment and mistrust. He argued that the division was fueled by a lack of competent, accountable, and trustworthy leadership, hindering the formation of a united and inclusive society.

As previously mentioned, *la grieta* is an orientational metaphor that envisions people or groups within an imaginary space divided into two symmetrical and parallel parts, devoid of any contact between them (Zullo, 2021, pp. 14–18). The two instances presented demonstrate the underlying schema of the orientational metaphor, as described by Zullo (2021, pp. 15–18). According to the author, this metaphorical framework consists of a binary division, with individuals in Argentina being situated on one side or the other of this divide due to their past, present, and future. Zullo argued that this polarization is deeply ingrained in Argentina's societal fabric. Lanata, in the 2006 documentary, emphasized that this division is not a

---

[6] In fact, Lanata used the metaphor in a 1989 article titled "*La Grieta*" published in *Página 12* to discuss a referendum held in Uruguay regarding the revocation of the amnesty law for perpetrators of the previous dictatorship (Fabbro, 2021).

[7] The National Reorganization Process, also known as "*El Proceso*," was a military dictatorship in Argentina from 1976 to 1983. It was governed by a military junta comprising representatives from the Army, Navy, and Air Force. The junta appointed different officials as Presidents of the Nation with executive and legislative authority.

recent phenomenon but rather an extension of longstanding divisions in the country's history. These divisions have been characterized by deep-rooted animosity, hatred, and conflict, as evidenced by significant events such as coups, revolutions, and acts of violence. In his 2013 speech, Lanata drew parallels to the 1950s in Argentina,[8] considering it a historical precursor to the present state of *la grieta*.

As Zullo (2021, p. 15) highlighted, the conceptual metaphor of *la grieta* implies the presence of an agent responsible for the division. In attributing blame for this division, Lanata singled out the political class, specifically former presidents Néstor Kirchner and Cristina Fernández de Kirchner. During his 2013 speech, he made direct accusations against the Kirchner administration, alleging their deliberate efforts to sow discord in society and stigmatize dissenters as traitors to the nation. According to him, this was not a mere coincidence, but a calculated strategy employed by the Kirchners. He argued that Kirchnerism was rooted in the philosophical notion of creating an adversary, thereby intentionally fostering the existing rift within society. Once this division took hold, reconciliation seemed increasingly unattainable, as both sides became more polarized, and anti-Kirchnerism reached an intolerable level. In a recent radio interview, Lanata attributed the origin of *la grieta* to Cristina Fernández de Kirchner, asserting that she wielded her position of power to vilify journalism and position it as an enemy to society.

Even a decade later, the persistent existence of *la grieta* in Argentina continues to be a subject of concern. Lanata perceives this situation as irrational, characterized by intense animosity and hostility, resulting in a fractured society and a collective sense of disillusionment. During a television interview in March 2021, he asserted that significant differences within the government contribute to the exacerbation of this divide. Moreover, he observed that the political opposition's discourse further intensifies the rift, making it challenging to find common ground. According to Lanata, addressing the divide becomes nearly impossible when it is promoted both from the top (government) and the bottom (opposition).

The concept of bridging this divide gained prominence in early 2023, becoming a central topic in media discussions. The imperative to unite both sides and overcome this division is seen as crucial for the nation's overall improvement. Lanata, in his column, echoed this sentiment, emphasizing the necessity of national unity to ensure a smooth transition in governance for the upcoming president. In a recent radio interview, he highlighted the crucial role of justice in closing the rift by addressing grievances and ensuring accountability. However, he expressed skepticism regarding the near-term possibility of achieving resolution.

Over the years, Lanata's concept of *la grieta* in Argentina underwent changes, reflecting the evolving dynamics within the country. Initially centered around the divide between supporters and opponents of the Kirchner governments, the rift was largely defined by ideological differences. However, as time has passed, the composition of the two sides has expanded to include new political actors and emerging

---

[8] The 1950s in Argentina were marked by intense political polarization between Peronistas, who supported Peronism, and opposition factions, including conservative groups and the military. This polarization laid the groundwork for future political conflicts and divisions in Argentine society.

social issues, broadening the scope of the divide. Moreover, the perceived causes of the division have evolved beyond mere policy disagreements, incorporating concerns such as corruption, economic challenges, and democratic institutions. This complex interplay of factors underscores the need for a nuanced understanding of *la grieta* and its multifaceted nature in Argentine society.

The dichotomy between Kirchneristas and Anti-kirchneristas, known as "la grieta," is fueled by multiple elements. A substantial wellspring of discord revolves around economic policies. Kirchnerismo is closely associated with the prioritization of social welfare programs, subsidies, and intervention in the economy. Conversely, Anti-kirchneristas critique these policies as unsustainable and deleterious to long-term economic stability. Divergences also arise regarding the extent of governmental involvement across various sectors. Kirchneristas tend to advocate for heightened government participation, particularly in domains like energy, transportation, and telecommunications, whereas Anti-kirchneristas lean towards more market-oriented and deregulated approaches.

Corruption allegations have targeted both Kirchnerista and Anti-kirchnerista factions, although they have been particularly salient within Kirchnerista governments that have grappled with numerous scandals and investigations. Kirchnerismo is linked with endeavors to address human rights abuses during Argentina's military dictatorship (1976–1983), although Anti-kirchneristas at times critique the government's selective and politically motivated approach to justice. The division also encompasses apprehensions about media manipulation and freedom of expression. Certain Anti-kirchneristas accuse Kirchnerismo of exerting control over media outlets and stifling dissenting voices.

The Kirchnerista movement is frequently characterized as populist, with supporters viewing it as an empowerment tool for marginalized groups and the working class, whereas critics perceive it as a strategy to consolidate power and secure a loyal voter base. Discrepancies in foreign policy and international relations contribute to the chasm, as Kirchnerismo has assumed a confrontational stance with specific international organizations and nations, whereas Anti-kirchneristas emphasize diplomacy and cooperation. Finally, the animosity is compounded by the rhetoric and communication style employed by both sides' political leaders, thereby further deepening the schism among the populace.

## 13.3 *La Grieta* as Cultural Polarization

In recent years, an increasing body of research across disciplines such as sociology, political science, and media studies (Fabro, 2021; García et al., 2019; Kessler et al., 2020; Moltó, 2021; Nigro, 2021; Obradovich, 2021; Schuliaquer & Vommaro, 2020; Svampa, 2019; Tagina, 2014; Waisbord, 2020; Zullo, 2021; among others) has emerged to examine the phenomenon of *la grieta* as a form of polarization. These scholars dedicate their research efforts to conducting thorough investigations into the multifaceted manifestations and societal consequences associated with this divisive issue. For instance, Moltó (2021, p. 67) argued that polarization in Argentina is deeply rooted in a society divided into two exclusive groups: Kirchneristas and anti-Kirchneristas. These groups hold divergent perspectives on social, political, and economic realities, with each side attributing blame to the other for the country's challenges. The author further suggested that perceiving the "other" group as morally inferior impedes collective efforts to overcome present challenges and construct a more prosperous society. This dynamic reveals a disheartening tendency to assign fault to the opposing group for an unsatisfactory and unjust situation.

A subset of researchers (García et al., 2019; Nigro, 2021; Zullo, 2021) specifically focused on exploring the role of the media in popularizing and perpetuating the concept of *la grieta* through mass media platforms and social media. They delve into the ways in which the media contribute to the dissemination and reinforcement of this divisive phenomenon, aiming to shed light on the mechanisms through which *la grieta* becomes entrenched in society, influencing public discourse, political dynamics, and social interactions.

According to García and his associates (2019), the concept of *la grieta* emerged as a media construct encompassing the representation of two opposing ideological-political perspectives, leading to polarization within Argentine society. The authors have sought to explain the expansion of the term and its role in creating division, arguing that the expression *la grieta* gained traction in media discourse due to its strong emotional associations and attributions. Lanata's perspective portrays *la grieta* as a construct extending beyond the media, permeating everyday life, and generating a sense of unease. Furthermore, it depicts a fractured society devoid of possibilities for resolution in the foreseeable future, characterized by antagonistic relationships, animosity, and severed ties. *La grieta* can be understood as a concept associated with discomfort stemming from diverse political perspectives and a rejection of conflict (García et al., 2019, p. 9).

Zullo (2021, pp. 8–9) argued that the media, particularly political journalism, bears responsibility not only for the emergence of the term *la grieta* but also for perpetuating a confrontational and polarized view of politics and society. The author suggested that this polarization creates a specific representation of the political arena and its actors, extending to other areas of information, proposing a binary and oversimplified model of reality based on the metaphor of *la grieta*. Zullo highlighted the metaphorical use of *la grieta* as a symbol of political, and ideological polarization, embraced by both extremes within Argentine journalism.

Lastly, Nigro (2021, p. 36) emphasized that polarization involves the adoption of two opposing and nearly antagonistic perspectives on reality, manifested through language, particularly the use of pronouns such as "us" and "them," establishing a sense of belonging within conflicting groups. Nigro's article aimed to demonstrate that Argentine political journalism, especially in opinion columns, reinforces polarization rather than fostering national unity. Additionally, Nigro argued that the digital dissemination of political columns facilitated by social media platforms has the potential to significantly amplify the negative consequences on citizens' critical consciousness. Political polarization, stemming from various issues of instability within democracies, has consequently led to the emergence of more homogenous narratives in public opinion through social media, albeit in diverse manifestations.

In conclusion, these studies highlight how the media have played a significant role in shaping relationship dynamics within Argentine society through its utilization of the concept of *la grieta* in the presentation of events in the country.

## 13.4 *La Grieta* and the Role of Political Satire in Three Argentinian Newspapers

According to Young (2017, p. 873), political satire holds a unique position within the vast landscape of political humor, noting that "political humor" encompasses a wide-ranging notion that includes various comedic forms related to officials, institutions, events, processes, or political issues. The characterization of satire has proven challenging since it is found in conventional genres such as poetry, drama, fiction, and essays, as well as in tragicomedies, allegories, and grotesque literature. Earlier, several authors (Elliot, 1962; Feinberg, 1968) advocated for a prototypical definition of satire that incorporates shared attributes among the various works representing this phenomenon. In line with the recommendations of Elliot (1962) and Feinberg (1968), Test (1991) proposed a list of four shared traits that comprise modern satire in its diverse forms. These traits serve as necessary but not sufficient conditions for the classification of different works as satire and encompass attack, judgment, play, and laughter.

A consensus among scholars (Caufield, 2008; Feinberg, 1968; Gray et al., 2009; Test, 1991) asserts that satire primarily aims to assail the injustices and maladies prevalent in society. Satirical writers direct their attacks at individuals, institutions, and processes within the social systems they inhabit. The scope of satirical targets, such as political institutions, societal obsessions, and public vices, is broader than that of political humor that often centers on political candidates, government officials, and public figures. Conventional political humor commonly seeks to elicit laughter at the expense of others, whereas satire is crafted to induce laughter at oneself and others, facilitating an awareness of a broader array of systemic flaws.

Furthermore, satire necessitates passing judgment on a societal aspect to inspire its rectification (Caufield, 2008). Young (2017, p. 973) posited that the essence of satire lies in its capacity for judgment and critique, distinguishing it from the broader concept of political humor. The author contended that satire, in contrast to certain political jokes that refrain from questioning the existing social and political order, presents a vision of what the order could or should be. Young concluded that while satire may exhibit biting and even aggressive tonality, its underlying premise often retains an optimistic tone, implying that the collective deserves better.

Lastly, aggression and judgment intertwine with playfulness, leading to audience laughter. Caufield (2008) contended that satire employs a unique strategy by blending wit, humor, and "play" to captivate the audience's attention. It is this playfulness that enables a clever interaction between the satirical writer and the audience. By constructing a form of "game" with the audience, satirical writers guide the audience toward the aggressive judgments they present. This playfulness within satire manifests itself in various forms, including wordplay, irony, and more (Caufield, 2008).

Caufield (2008, p. 9) additionally introduced a fifth characteristic of political satire that, in her view, combines all the aforementioned characteristics. The author posited that for individuals to engage with play established by the satirist they must possess a certain level of pre-existing knowledge. Caufield concluded that effective satire demands an informed audience that actively participates in the satirical experience and arrives at their own conclusions. Individuals lacking sufficient knowledge to comprehend the satire are excluded from the comedic intent (Caufield, 2008, p. 99). In essence, satire necessitates reader involvement in the wordplay and independent discernment of the judgments presented.

The following political humor columns exemplify political satire that critically examines the prevalent use of the *la grieta* metaphor by the mass media to explain polarized situations within the country. It is worth noting that each of these columns adopted a distinct perspective that aligned with the political orientation of the newspapers where they were published. *La Nación*, Argentina's oldest and most traditional newspaper, has historically maintained close ties with the agricultural and industrial sectors, thereby reflecting their interests. In terms of ideology, *La Nación* leans towards a fusion of liberalism and conservatism. In recent years, the newspaper has exhibited a clear inclination towards Macrism,[9] referring to the ideology of "Cambiemos," the political party that achieved victory in the 2015 presidential elections. In contrast, *Clarín* emerged as the dominant media conglomerate in Argentina, exerting substantial influence across various domains, including free-to-air and cable television channels, film, and TV production companies, radio stations, telecommunications, digital content platforms, and print publications. Notably, all entities under the umbrella of the *Clarín* group have consistently demonstrated an anti-Kirchner stance over the past fifteen years. On the other hand, *Página 12*, established in 1987, represents a relatively recent addition to the newspaper industry. From its inception, *Página 12* has consciously aligned itself with the more progressive and intellectual segments of society, catering to the interests and perspectives of this particular demographic. While maintaining a critical outlook, the editorial line of *Página 12* aligns with Kirchnerism, the political ideology associated with the administrations led by Néstor Kirchner and Cristina Fernández de Kirchner.

---

[9] Macrism in Argentina refers to the political ideology and policies of Mauricio Macri during his presidency from 2015 to 2019. It focused on market-oriented economic reforms and attracting foreign investment but faced criticism for economic challenges and social inequality.

### 13.4.1 "Life Begins at 30: The Beautiful *Página*," by Marcelo Rudaeff (Rudy)

In an interview with *Revista Viento Sur* of the University of Lanús (2017), Rudaeff criticized Lanata, whom he preferred not to name and described as a pseudo-journalist, for his lack of honesty in using the term *la grieta* to describe the political and ideological division in Argentina. He argued that the term fails to capture the historical reality of a preexisting division that dates to 1492 and even earlier. Rudaeff noted that the arrival of outsiders in 1492, bringing conflict and power dynamics, refutes the notion of a unified state that suddenly cracked. The author contended that the perpetuation of violence is rooted in power imbalances, with certain individuals exploiting the vulnerable. As a humorist, he embraces the role of employing absurdity to shed light on this complex issue within the context of an ongoing cultural struggle, wherein influential actors skillfully manipulate language and ideas to shape prevailing narratives.

The satirical column titled "Life Begins at 30: The Beautiful *Página*" (Rudaeff, 2017), published in *Página 12* on July 2017, is a clear example of political satire that critically scrutinizes the pervasive employment of the *la grieta* metaphor by the mass media to explain any polarized situation within the country. The focal point of the column revolved around the 30th anniversary of the *Página 12* newspaper, as implied by its title. Employing his customary conversational style, Rudaeff started the column by inquiring into the reader's well-being, consistently maintaining this engaging tone throughout the text. This technique serves to actively involve the audience in a thought-provoking discussion concerning various topics pertinent to the intricate social and economic challenges encountered by the nation during the presidency of Mauricio Macri.[10] Argentina confronted a multifaceted social and economic landscape in July 2017, prompting the government to pursue a series of reforms aimed at fostering investment and revitalizing the economy. However, the nation grappled with persistently high inflation rates and elevated levels of unemployment, thereby exacerbating the existing socioeconomic challenges. In response to this pressing concern, social assistance programs were implemented to specifically target vulnerable segments of the population. Consequently, these initiatives generated diverse responses within the populace, giving rise to divergent perspectives regarding the effectiveness of the reforms in terms of enhancing living standards and mitigating societal inequality.

In the column, Rudaeff subtly addressed the presidency of Mauricio Macri by exploring the notion of "changes" in the lives of his readers, making an implicit reference to the former president's coalition, "*Cambiemos*" ("Let's Change"). Rudaeff compiled a list of rights, such as employment, wages, freedom of speech, and social assistance, that citizens supposedly lost as a result of the political transformations enacted during Macri's tenure. Furthermore, the author delved into the communication of these changes to the public by the media, making specific mention of the

---

[10] Mauricio Macri was the President of Argentina from 2015 to 2019. He continues to be involved in Argentine politics as an opposition figure.

*la grieta* phenomenon. Rudaeff emphasized the importance of communication that enlightens readers about the country's reality and recalled the historical significance of the phrase "The people want to know what it's about!" during Argentina's 1810 independence, symbolizing a call for transparency and active participation in shaping the nation's destiny. As Rudaeff stated in his column of July 17, 2017:

> The communication that does not numb the brain, that awakens it, can distress, it can cost us more, but it's worth it!
> Look how much it's worth it, that the first cry for freedom in our national history was, "The people want to know what it's about!"
> And French and Beruti[11] were handing out blue and white ribbons, and perhaps if some current media had existed back then, they would have accused them of "widening *la grieta* between criollos and Spaniards, having a subversive attitude towards the poor viceroy, and not understanding that independence from Spain meant isolating oneself from the world."
> And in reality, *la grieta*, that was never a grieta, entered the Cabildo[12] where it already existed. And the same representatives, the same First Junta,[13] probably didn't take five minutes to divide themselves into "Saavedra[14] supporters and Morenists.[15]" Because it wasn't that everyone was united and then started to divide (that would be a *grieta*, something that breaks and creaks), but, in my opinion, the history of humanity is almost the opposite: we are all separated, and we come together as best we can.
> But well, these are opinions. Ways of communicating.

> [La comunicación que no adormece la neurona, que despierta, puede angustiar, puede resultarnos más cara, pero ¡Lo vale!
> Miren si lo vale, que el primer grito de libertad de nuestra historia nacional fue "¡El pueblo quiere saber de qué se trata!".
> Y French y Berutti repartían cintitas celestes y blancas, y quizás si hubieran existido entonces algunos medios actuales, los hubieran acusado de "ensanchar la grieta entre

---

[11] French and Berutti were important figures in the early stages of Argentina's struggle for independence. Their contributions to the revolutionary cause helped pave the way for the establishment of an independent Argentine state.

[12] El Cabildo in Argentina refers to the historic building in Buenos Aires that served as the seat of colonial government. It played a pivotal role during the May Revolution of 1810, leading to the establishment of the First Junta. Today, it stands as a museum and symbol of Argentina's fight for independence.

[13] La Primera Junta was the first governing body established during Argentina's May Revolution in 1810. It marked a shift in power from Spanish colonial rule and laid the foundation for Argentine's self-governance, eventually leading to the country's declaration of independence in 1816.

[14] Cornelio Saavedra (1759–1829) was an Argentinian military leader and politician. He played a key role in the May Revolution of 1810 and led the patriot forces to victory. Saavedra was the president of the Primera Junta, Argentina's first independent government.

[15] Morenists were supporters of Mariano Moreno, an Argentine lawyer, journalist, and politician. He was a key figure in Argentina's independence movement and a strong advocate for equality and freedom of the press.

criollos y españoles, tener una actitud destituyente con el pobre virrey, y no entender que independizarse de España llevaba a aislarse del mundo"

Y en realidad, la grieta que nunca fue grieta, entró al Cabildo donde ya estaba. Y los mismos representantes, la misma Primera Junta, no deben haber tardado cinco minutos en dividirse entre "saavedristas y morenistas". Porque no fue que todos estaban unidos y se fueron dividiendo ( eso sería una grieta, algo que se rompe y va crujiendo) sino que, a mi entender, la historia de la Humanidad es casi al revés, estamos todos separados, y nos vamos juntando como podemos.

Pero bueno, son opiniones. Maneras de comunicar].

In the above excerpt, Rudaeff employs absurdity when he describes how certain Argentinian media would have covered the May Revolution of 1810 in Buenos Aires. The absurdity lies in the fact that media in 1810 did not exist in the manner portrayed. He humorously suggested that if such media were present, they would have used the notion of *la grieta* to describe the event and accused the revolutionaries of widening the divide between the criollos and Spaniards. Additionally, Rudaeff posited that the media would have labeled the revolutionaries' attitude as subversive, expressed sympathy toward the "poor" viceroy, and argued that independence from Spain would isolate the colony from the world. The sentence Rudaeff employed to depict the media's hypothetical coverage is a parody of the arguments used by the current media (that he criticizes) to defend Macri's policies. Subsequently, Rudaeff offered his own perspective on *la grieta*, as discussed previously. He asserted that there was never a real divide between the two main members of the First Junta. Instead, he contended that the history of humanity suggests the opposite: individuals are inherently separate and come together as best they can. Rudaeff acknowledged that these are his opinions and noted the existence of different modes of communication. By doing so, he distinguished himself from the media outlets that believe in the concept of *la grieta* and who actively promote it. Rudaeff concluded his column by celebrating the anniversary of *Página 12*.

In summary, Rudaeff's text exemplifies a political satire piece, wherein he critiqued the media's utilization and propagation of the notion of *la grieta*. Notably, the media become the target of his critical analysis. Political satire, as employed by Rudaeff, serves as a means to critique the audience as well, prompting them to be conscious of a broader set of systemic shortcomings within society. This is evident when Rudaeff urged readers to engage their intellectual faculties and critically evaluate the information conveyed by the media. By employing absurdity, Rudaeff created humor while simultaneously urging readers to reflect upon the existence of *la grieta*, often leading to discomfort as they recognize their own complicity in perpetuating such divisions.

## 13.4.2 "Cristina versus Alberto: Call the Firefighters!" by Carlos M. Reymundo Roberts

The column's title, "Cristina vs. Alberto: Call the firefighters!," published in *La Nacion* on November 2020 (Reymundo Roberts, 2020), emphasizes the conflict between Argentina's President, Alberto Fernández, and his Vice-President, Cristina Fernández de Kirchner. The use of "vs." (versus) implies a sense of confrontation or rivalry between the two. The subsequent phrase, "Call the firefighters," serves as a metaphorical indication of the existing problem or tension between them, and the necessity of calling for help.

Reymundo Roberts started the text by examining the initial promise made by the current president during his electoral campaign to bridge the well-known *grieta* in Argentine society. However, instead of fulfilling this promise, the columnist accuses Fernández of exacerbating the existing division. Nevertheless, the president is not the sole focus of the columnist's critique. The Argentinians, who cast their votes for him and embraced his vow to reconcile the schism, also face criticism for their credulity.

> Like every candidate, Alberto traversed the campaign trail brimming with promises. Nothing too serious, because he knew that we knew he wasn't someone to be taken literally. After assuming office, he continued with that habit. In fact, there were moments, back in April, when we even considered him a promising president. Now, that is serious: our oversight. You see, the professor promised us, as the main goal of his term, to bridge the divide. I remember tears of emotion streaming down my face as I heard him say that. Eleven months after those moving words, the country is more divided than ever. We've even just inaugurated the most concerning rift of all: the one that has appeared between him and Cristina. A geological fault that, I admit, surprised me and fills me with fear. I'd say it's time to call the firefighters.
>
> [Como todo candidato, Alberto transitó la campaña llenándose la boca de promesas. Nada grave, porque él sabía que nosotros sabíamos que no es una persona para tomar al pie de la letra. Después de asumir siguió con esa costumbre. De hecho, hubo momentos, allá por abril, en que llegamos a considerarlo un presidente prometedor. Eso sí que es grave: nuestro despiste. Pues bien, el profesor nos prometió, como principal objetivo de su mandato, cerrar la grieta. Recuerdo que me cayeron lágrimas de emoción al escucharlo. A once meses de esas palabras conmovedoras, el país está más dividido que nunca. Incluso acabamos de inaugurar la grieta más preocupante de todas: la que ha aparecido entre él y Cristina. Una falla geológica que a mí, lo reconozco, me sorprendió y me mete miedo. Yo iría llamando a los bomberos].

In the final three sentences of the introductory paragraph, Reymundo Roberts presented the central theme of his column, namely the growing divide between the president and his vice-president. He emphasized the severity of this new division within the political landscape, employing expressions such as "worrying" and likening it to a "geological fault." These evocative phrases serve to underscore the significant divide that emerged between those responsible for governing the country, prompting Roberts to figuratively suggest the intervention of firefighters to address the situation.

The second paragraph commenced with an invitation to analyze the various divisions within the Peronist Party,[16] stating: "Let's first review the map of fractures in Argentina under the Fernández administration. I will probably forget some, as it seems like something breaks every day. I hope not to confuse you." Through the utilization of the metaphorical expression "map of fractures," Reymundo Roberts anticipated, albeit through exaggeration, the extensive catalog of conflicts that emerged among key figures, including the president, vice-president, her son, the governor of the province of Buenos Aires, political organizations, the secretary of economy, and the labor unions. The implication was that this list of confrontations appears boundless, creating a landscape in which the map of Argentina is riddled with cracks. In the subsequent paragraphs, the columnist proceeded to present additional enumerations of divisions, encompassing the clashes between the president and his ministers and the governor of Buenos Aires Province, as well as among the members of the opposition coalition "*Juntos por el Cambio*" (Together for Change).

In the concluding paragraphs, Reymundo Roberts returned to the central theme of his column, namely the deep division between the president and his vice-president that he characterized as an "*abyss*" separating them.

> I will now satisfy the readers' curiosity: the abyss that is beginning to separate Alberto from Cristina. Let's see, she has already played her hand with the card—the burofax, as Jorge Liotti would say—and she is preparing her weapons: The Senate, the majority in the Chamber of Deputies, La Cámpora, the main power bases, the territorial organization, Justicia Legítima, the conurbation, the province, the votes, the ideas. As for the professor, he has been showing signs of autonomy: the October 17th event, designed by governors and the CGT as a platform to rescue the President; the photo with Vilma and Massa, the refusal to rush cabinet changes, Guzmán's meeting with AEA... At any moment, he might say that Maduro is a dictator, that Nisman was murdered, and that soybeans are not a weed.
>
> This scenario will delight millions. As a fearful person, I am not at ease. Because Alberto is Alberto. And Cristina is Kirchner.
>
> [Voy a satisfacer ahora el morbo de los lectores: el abismo que empieza a separar a Alberto de Cristina. A ver, ella ya cantó sus cuarenta con la carta –el burofax, diría Jorge Liotti–, y vela sus armas: el Senado, la mayoría en Diputados, La Cámpora, las principales cajas, el armado territorial, Justicia Legítima, el conurbano, la provincia, los votos, las ideas. En cuanto al profesor, viene dando muestras de autonomía: el acto del 17 de octubre, pensado por gobernadores y la CGT como plataforma de rescate del Presidente; la foto con Vilma y con Massa, la negativa a apurar cambios en el gabinete, la reunión de Guzmán con AEA... En cualquier momento dice que Maduro es un dictador, que a Nisman lo mataron y que la soja no es un yuyo.
>
> Este escenario hará las delicias de millones. Yo, asustadizo, no me quedo tranquilo. Porque Alberto es Alberto. Y Cristina es Kirchner].

The term "*abyss*" carries metaphorical weight, underscoring the profound extent of their disconnection. The columnist proceeded to present a series of factual examples illustrating how each of them independently governs the country. Notably, Reymundo Roberts used irony when discussing the current president's display of

---

[16] The Partido Peronista was a political party in Argentina centered around Juan Domingo Perón. It championed the working class and implemented social welfare measures. Peronism remained influential in Argentine politics even after Perón's death.

autonomy through his solitary participation in various events. Moreover, the columnist employed satire by predicting that the president, mockingly referred to as "the professor," might even adopt three notions that would contradict previous questionable statements made by Cristina Fernández de Kirchner. These questionable ideas include Kirchner's assertion that Nicolás Maduro, the incumbent president of Venezuela, is not a dictator, that the late prosecutor Alberto Nisman[17] was not murdered, and that the soybean is a weed. By employing these rhetorical devices, Reymundo Roberts accentuated the divergence between the president and vice president. He encouraged the president, tongue in cheek, to be somewhat bolder, while simultaneously undermining the credibility of the vice president through the use of satire and ironic juxtaposition.

In conclusion, Reymundo Roberts' text serves as a critical commentary on the numerous fractures within Argentina's political landscape. The primary focus of his critique is directed towards the politicians themselves. Through his adept use of metaphors, exaggeration, irony, and sarcasm, the columnist employs humor as a rhetorical device. However, it is important to note that beneath the surface of these humorous elements lies a profound concern for the unity of Argentina. Reymundo Roberts employs these rhetorical strategies to capture the readers' attention and draw awareness to the potential risks posed by these divisions. Through his text, the columnist seeks to highlight the gravity of the situation and the need for cohesive action to safeguard the unity of the nation.

### 13.4.3 *"Let the Rift not Wane" by Alejandro Borensztein*

The article titled "Let the rift not wane" was published in *Clarín* on December 23, 2022 (Borensztein, 2022), and delves into two significant events that took place in Argentina towards the end of that year. The first event revolved around the triumphant victory of the Argentine national soccer team in the World Cup held in Qatar. The second event of significance pertained to President Alberto Fernandez's declaration to defy a Supreme Court ruling mandating the return of funding to the opposition-controlled government of Buenos Aires. This decision ignited an institutional crisis and served as the culmination of a week fraught with political setbacks.

Borensztein's column adopted an initial satirical tone, employing irony to present the president's rejection of the Supreme Court ruling as a peculiar yet striking way to conclude the year by endangering the Republic. The primary focus of the columnist's criticism was directed towards the president whom he reproached for displaying inappropriate conduct related to this matter.

> The government disobeying a Supreme Court ruling and once again jeopardizing the Republic is a beautiful way to end the year.

---

[17] Alberto Nisman, an Argentine prosecutor, gained prominence for his investigation into the 1994 bombing of the AMIA building. His accusations, controversial death, and unwavering pursuit of justice have left a lasting impact on Argentina's history.

[El Gobierno desobedeciendo un fallo de la Corte Suprema y poniendo otra vez en riesgo la República es una hermosa manera de terminar el año].

In subsequent paragraphs, Borensztein addressed the atmosphere of joy and unity that permeated the country following the victory of the national male team in the World Cup. The prevailing positive atmosphere in the country prompted Borensztein to contemplate the possible ending of *la grieta* after two decades of longstanding division. Employing irony, the columnist asserted disingenuously that it is essential for Argentines to maintain and preserve this division by recognizing its significance and safeguarding its existence.

> Beyond the joy that the players gave us, the massiveness of the popular celebration revealed a concerning fact: the divide may be going out of style. While *la grieta* is a phenomenon that divided us, destroyed us, and ultimately eroded the little remaining trust in the country, it must be acknowledged that it kept us entertained for 20 years. Therefore, it is crucial to become aware, value it, and defend it.
>
> [Más allá de la alegría que nos dieron los jugadores, la masividad de la fiesta popular dejó un dato muy preocupante: la grieta estaría pasando de moda. Si bien la grieta es un fenómeno que nos dividió, nos destruyó y terminó de demoler la poca confianza que quedaba en el país, hay que reconocer que nos mantuvo entretenidos durante 20 años. Por eso es muy importante tomar conciencia, valorarla y defenderla].

In the next paragraphs, Borensztein attributed the continued existence of *la grieta* to the president's rejection of the Supreme Court ruling. While the columnist condemned the president for reigniting the divide, he also criticized the opposition, particularly Macri's supporters, for displaying a comparable level of intolerance as Kirchner's followers. Notably, Borensztein acknowledged the distinct approach of Larreta, the mayor of Buenos Aires and a potential presidential candidate, who refrained from employing the polarizing concept of *la grieta*. However, the columnist did not exempt Larreta from scrutiny and directed criticism towards his decisions regarding specific construction projects in the capital city of Argentina.

In conclusion, Borensztein's column offered a critical analysis of the persistent divide between the population and political leaders in Argentina. He attributed the perpetuation of *la grieta* to the actions of the political leaders, who he suggested are responsible for jeopardizing the stability of the Republic. Through his use of irony, Borensztein prompted readers to reflect upon this divide by drawing a sharp contrast between, on the one hand, the unity and collective joy experienced in the country following the national soccer team's victory in the World Cup, and on the other hand, the national tumult involving the president's rejection of the Supreme Court decision.

## 13.5 Conclusions

The concept of *la grieta* has been a pivotal cultural factor in Argentinian society. While it is widely acknowledged by a considerable portion of the Argentine populace as a deeply entrenched division that has shaped the nation's history and continues to define Argentine society, there are dissenting voices that contest the existence of *la grieta*. These individuals argue that it is an oversimplification, failing to fully capture the diverse range of opinions and perspectives within the country. Nonetheless, the prevailing perception of *la grieta* as an inherent element of the Argentine experience remains, with successive administrations unable to bridge the enduring divide.

An important aspect in perpetuating and intensifying this division is the role played by the media, particularly through their continued utilization of the expression *la grieta*. The three major newspapers in Argentina, namely *Clarín*, *La Nación*, and *Página/12*, align themselves distinctly with different sides of *la grieta*, evident in their respective satirical opinion columns. These columns not only serve as a platform for expressing the newspapers' perspectives but also as a means to sway and direct public opinion, effectively advocating their own agendas. The primary contribution of these newspapers lies in reinforcing the existing beliefs of their readership, thereby deepening the chasm that characterizes the social, cultural, and political discourse of the country.

While "la grieta" may play a role in shaping certain discussions and debates, it is the multifaceted viewpoints put forth by individual columnists that truly fuel the fire of political satire. The columnists bring their own unique perspective to the table, often influenced by the stance and ideology of the newspaper they write for. This diversity of viewpoints is what enriches the discourse surrounding political matters and enables a more comprehensive exploration of different angles. As these distinct viewpoints are disseminated through various publications, they work in tandem to influence how the audience perceives and understands "la grieta." This dynamic interplay of perspectives serves as a catalyst for shaping public opinion and challenging preconceived notions.

Through the vehicle of satire, these perspectives can be exaggerated, juxtaposed, and dissected, providing a lens through which readers can critically examine the complexities of "la grieta." By doing so, political satire helps redirect and reshape the audience's perceptions, encouraging them to reconsider their initial notions and embrace a more nuanced understanding. In essence, while "la grieta" may set the stage, it is the synergy of individual viewpoints and the skillful use of satire that truly mold the discourse, making it a powerful tool for steering public awareness and promoting a deeper engagement with political dynamics.

## References

Borensztein, A. (2022). Let the Rift not Wane. *Clarín*. https://www.clarin.com/opinion/grieta-decaiga_0_t9dnDN6Qsu.html (in Spanish)

Caufield, R. P. (2008). The influence of "infoenterpropagainment": Exploring the power of political satire as a distinct form of political humor. In J. C. Baumgartner & J. S. Morris (Eds.), *Laughing matters: Humor and American politics in the media age* (pp. 3–20). Routledge.

Elliot, R. C. (1962). The definition of satire: A note on method. *Yearbook on comparative and general literature*, 11. Indiana University Press.

Fabbro, G. (2021). The journalistic rift: A preliminary investigation. *Fopea*. https://www.fopea.org/wp-content/uploads/2022/02/FOPEA-La-grieta-periodistica-Una-investigacion-preliminar.pdf (in Spanish)

Feinberg, L. (1968). Satire: The inadequacies of recent definitions. *Genre, 1*, 31–37.

García, L. A., Córdoba, D. M., & Escalante, A. M. (2019). Feeling the divide: Its construction and installation in the television medium. In XXI° Congreso de la Red de Carreras de Comunicación Social y Periodismo. Escuela de Ciencias de la Comunicación, Facultad de Humanidades, Universidad Nacional de General Sarmiento. https://www.aacademica.org/21redcom/21 (in Spanish)

Gray, J., Jones, J., & Thompson, E. (2009). The state of satire, the satire of state. In J. Gray, J. Jones, & E. Thompson (Eds.), *Satire TV: Politics and comedy in the post-network era* (pp. 3–36). New York University Press.

Kalbermatten, M. I. (2016). Political humor and manipulation in two Argentine newspapers. In L. Aranda & T. Leão Vieira (Eds.), *The senses of humor: Possibilities for analyzing the comic* (pp. 63–84). Verona. (in Spanish).

Kessler, G., Focas, B., Ortíz de Zárate, J. M., & Feuerstein, E. (2020). The divergent in a scenario of polarization: An exploratory study on the 'non-polarized' in controversies about crime news in Argentine television. *Revista SAAP, 14*(2), 311–340. https://doi.org/10.46468/rsaap.14.2.A3 (in Spanish)

Lakoff, G., & Johnson, M. (1980). *Metaphors we live by.* Cátedra. (in Spanish).

Lanata, J. (2023). "May you have a miserable birthday": 10 years of division, and how long will we continue like this? https://www.clarin.com/opinion/-cumplas-infeliz-10-anos-grieta-vamos-seguir_0_7BgBBbF8JD.html (in Spanish)

Moltó, M. (2021). La grieta in Congress. Exploratory analysis and methodological proposal to investigate political polarization in legislative debates in Argentina. *Revista Enfoques, 19*(35), pp. 66–89. http://www.revistaenfoques.cl/index.php/revista-uno/article/view/551/pdf_100 (in Spanish)

Nigro, P. (2021). The responsibility of journalism in the political polarization of social media audiences. *Más Poder Local, 44*, 34–53. https://www.maspoderlocal.com/index.php/mpl/article/view/periodismo-polarizacion-politica-mpl44 (in Spanish)

Obradovich, G. (2021). The beginnings of social and political polarization in Argentina. Rethinking the agricultural conflict. *POSTData, 26*(2), 339–370. https://www.revistapostdata.com.ar/wp-content/uploads/2021/10/postdata-26-2-t-obradovich.pdf (in Spanish)

Reymundo Roberts, C. M. (2020). Cristina vs. Alberto: Call the firefighters! https://www.lanacion.com.ar/opinion/cristina-vs-alberto-llamen-bomberos-nid2502033/ (in Spanish)

Royal Spanish Academy. (2022). *Dictionary of the Spanish language.* https://www.rae.es/ (in Spanish)

Rudaeff, M. (2017). Life begins at 30: The beautiful Página. *Página*. https://www.pagina12.com.ar/40247-la-bonita-pagina (in Spanish)

Schuliaquer, I., & Vommaro, G. (2020). Political polarization, media, and social networks. Coordinates of a developing agenda. *Revista SAAP, 14*(2), pp. 235–247. https://doi.org/10.46468/10.46468/rsaap.14.2.I (in Spanish)

Svampa, M. (2019). Post-progressivisms, polarization, and democracy in Argentina and Brazil. *Nueva sociedad, 282*, 131–134. https://nuso.org/articulo/posprogresismos-polarizacion-y-democracia-en-argentina-y-brasil/ (in Spanish)

Tagina, M. L. (2014). Politics and polarization in Argentina: A study of the behavior of elites, political parties, and public opinion. *Revista Derecho Electoral, 17*, 185–212. https://www.researchgate.net/publication/280569286_Politica_y_polarizacion_en_Argentina_un_estudio_del_comportamiento_de_las_elites_los_partidos_politicos_y_la_opinion_publica (in Spanish)

Test, G. (1991). *Satire: Spirit and art.* University of South Florida Press.

University of Lanús. (2017). Humor in interesting times: Marcelo Rudaeff, Rudy. *Revista Viento Sur, 15*. http://vientosur.unla.edu.ar/index.php/el-humor-en-tiempos-interesantes/ (in Spanish)

Waisbord, S. (2020). Is it valid to attribute political polarization to digital communication? On bubbles, platforms, and affective polarization. *Revista SAAP, 14*(2), 249–279. https://doi.org/10.46468/rsaap.14.2.A1 (in Spanish)

Young, D. G. (2017). Theories and effects of political humor: Discounting cues, gateways, and the impact of incongruities. In K. Keski & K. Hall Jamieson (Eds.), *The Oxford handbook of political communication* (pp. 871–884). Oxford University Press.

Zullo, J. (2021). Polarization as a metaphor: The use of the rift in two Argentine newspapers. *Revista Latinoamericana de Estudios del Discurso, 21*(1), 4–22. https://doi.org/10.35956/v.21.n1.2021.p.4-22 (in Spanish)

**María Isabel Kalbermatten** is Associate Professor of Spanish at Gustavus Adolphus College, USA. Her research interests are centered in two areas: Discourse Analysis, involving the use of verbal irony, sarcasm, parodyhumor, and gender in real conversations; and, Applied Linguistics, developing strategies to help students improve their writing and reading skills in Spanish. She has numerous scholarly publications and has participated in many national and international conferences regarding the use of verbal irony in conversation, the use of humor in political manipulation, and other related topics.

# Part IV
# Conclusion

# Chapter 14
# The Complexity of Media Political Humor: Research Considerations

**Sam Lehman-Wilzig**

**Abstract** The present anthology of studies in political humor offers a rich buffet of research methodologies. However, they only scratch the surface of the complexities involved in examining the topic. This concluding chapter expands on several methodological questions regarding the sub-field of political humor research, especially: (1) In any given society, to what extent is political humor addressed to both/all sides of the political spectrum—the question of *"balance"*; (2) What are the factors underlying the *influence* of political humor? (3) Assuming political humor is effective, is its influence greater on governmental policy, personnel, and/or ideology, *or* on the general public (or segments thereof)? (4) To what extent does the specific *medium* through which the political humor is expressed have influence—and for each medium, on whom? These and other ancillary variables are discussed here as a sort of "road map" for future scholars studying this fascinating (and smile-generating), but under-researched, topic.

## 14.1 Introduction: The Question of "Balance"

In the accompanying book to this double volume on political humor, the spotlight was placed on the humor generated by political leaders and other functionaries within the regime. The present volume looks at the other side of the coin: how the "Fourth Estate"—the media—use forms of political humor to shed light on the doings of those leading the system. As such, one could expect that the media's approach would be somewhat more objective and balanced.

Clearly, as most chapters in this volume make clear, such expectations are not realized. Each medium and the specific purveyors within that overall medium, are no less partisan than the politicians that they skewer. In and of itself, this is not necessarily a "flaw," if and when each newspaper, TV/radio station, news site, blogger, etc., is counter-balanced by others who hew to the opposite ideological, policy, or partisan line.

---

S. Lehman-Wilzig (✉)
Department of Communications, Peres Academic College, Rehovot, Israel
e-mail: ProfSLW@gmail.com

Some chapters here suggest that occasionally this is the case. For instance, in Chap. 5 we see how three different satirical magazines take quite different approaches to the Turkish system: one is anti-government, another is basically pro-government, and a third specializes in a specific policy area (feminism) from a socially critical perspective. As the author notes throughout, these three satirical venues deal not merely with "political" issues, but also with the cultural foundations underlying such politics. In other words, such satire aspires to much more than mere political change; it seeks profound cultural transformation as well—whether in a liberal or neo-conservative direction.

Another example of overall ideological balance: Argentina (Chap. 13), in which three newspapers employ satire to advance their ideological position: conservative, progressive, and center-right. However, here the problem is reader insularity. If the public were to read all three on a steady basis, such comprehensive humor could be enlightening; however, almost all readers stick to only newspaper, thus merely reinforcing their already predetermined political position. The result, as the author notes: "Their primary contribution has been to reinforce their readers' existing beliefs, thereby deepening the divide that characterizes the social, cultural, and political discourse of the country." Nevertheless, these "ideologically" balanced media situations are the exception to the general rule, as can be seen in most of the other chapters in this book.

### 14.1.1 Why Satirical Balance is not Always Present

Having said that an ideal situation occurs when political satire is balanced by humorists and satirists of different policy or ideological positions, managing to reach supporters and opponents alike, clearly such "balance" is not always possible, whether the situation being several media employing such humor or only one medium. There are a few reasons for this.

First, media supporting the government will not be eager to use humor to skewer the leadership. Thus, as opposed to more "centrist" media that will shoot barbs at all politicians left, right, and center, pro-government media (especially if funded or regulated by the state) will tend to impale only the opposition.

Second, perhaps in a specific country there aren't any worthy satirists working in every political camp. It bears mentioning that notwithstanding the impressive number of countries represented in the present two complementary books, the editor Prof. Feldman approached far more scholars in other countries. True, some had prior obligations etc., but it is also probable that in some of those non-responsive countries political humor is simply not a significant force in public, political life.

Third, satirizing political leaders can be personally dangerous (as in the attack on Salman Rushdie; the murder of the Charlie Hebdo magazine staff; etc.), limiting the number of potential satirists who worry for their life—a situation even more palpable in a quasi-democratic country (i.e., semi-autocratic: Brazil under Bolsonaro—Chap. 4) and certainly in a fully autocratic political system (Brazil half a century ago:

ditto). For as U.S. best-selling author Neil Gaiman (2015) sadly noted: "How important are free speech and satire? Important enough that people will murder others to silence the kind of speech they don't like."[1]

Nevertheless, there is no dearth of brave political satirists in the world, as this book clearly shows. As the British novelist and film critic Penelope Gilliatt (2015) opined: "A satirist, often in danger himself, has the bravery of knowing that to withhold wit's conjecture is to endanger the species."[2] Or at least to endanger the continued rule of the political leaders.

All leaders understand this, especially in authoritarian regimes. As shown in Chap. 10, the Iranian regime had no compunctions about silencing its media critics: "…during two governments Ahmadinejad's government suspended or closed 46 publications, whereas… the more moderate government of Rouhani also suspended seven newspapers."

Fourth and finally, a national culture might frown on overly aggressive satire (e.g., Japan as noted in Chaps. 2 and 12); without a tradition of barbed humor, political satire might not flourish because the public is not ready for it. Nevertheless, when done correctly, satire can avoid public antagonism by being subtle:

*Satire should,*
*Like a polish'd razor keen,*
*Wound with a touch,*
*That's scarcely felt or seen.*
(Lady Mary Wortley Montagu, 1733) [3]

Thus, even if the ideal "satirical balance" is not reached in a nation, one-sided political humor still serves a very useful purpose, especially when pointing out the foibles, flaws, and fakery of those running the country. This is because as Lord Acton (1887) famously noted: "Power tends to corrupt and absolute power corrupts absolutely."[4] The longer it stays in power, and especially when there hardly exists any check on leaders' action, discourse, or policy, the government tends to lose its political and even moral bearings. Political satire and other types of acerbic humor, among other things, reminds the public that they are being led not by "Gods" but by flesh-and-blood human beings prone to error (and worse).

In short, political "balance" is not a requirement for the proper functioning of a political system, and we should not criticize a situation in which all political humor is channeled in one direction—and certainly the humorist should not be attacked for what s/he does. For as the famous Doonesbury cartoonist Garry Trudeau (1988) has (humorously) argued: "Satire is supposed to be unbalanced. It's supposed to be

---

[1] Gaiman (2015), https://twitter.com/neilhimself/status/552861305334276096.

[2] Gilliatt (2015), https://www.azquotes.com/author/50240-Penelope_Gilliatt.

[3] Montagu (1733), https://jacklynch.net/Texts/montagu2.html.

[4] Acton (1887), https://oll.libertyfund.org/quote/lord-acton-writes-to-bishop-creighton-that-the-same-moral-standards-should-be-applied-to-all-men-political-and-religious-leaders-included-especially-since-power-tends-to-corrupt-and-absolute-power-corrupts-absolutely-1887.

unfair. Criticizing a political satirist for being unfair is like criticizing a 260-pound nose guard [large U.S. football player] for being physical."[5]

## 14.2 How Effective is Political Humor? Methodological Complications

The media arsenal at the satirists' disposal is vast: *text* (social media comments [Chaps. 9 and 10], newspapers, pamphlets, essays, books, poetry verses [Chap. 12]), *graphics* (cartoons [Chaps. 3, 4, 5 and 6]; manga and comics [Chap. 2]; animation [Chap. 7]); *multi-media* (videos [Chap. 7], TV satire [Chap. 8], sketches [Chap. 8]), movies, theater); and *audio* (songs, podcasts). Similarly, there are many forms of humoristic, political expression: caricature, irony, slapstick, burlesque, lampoon, mockery, and parody among others. All have the same basic purpose, as encapsulated pithily by the group that presents the Garry Trudeau (1988) each year: "…make people laugh, and then make them think."[6]

This is a fine line to walk: to be not overly aggressive or brutal that could put off many citizens, but also not to be so subtle that the humor doesn't lead to (political) thinking (see Chap. 10 on Iran, as an example of this approach under a pseudo-democratic regime). Which leads to a major research question that was not much addressed in this anthology (in Chap. 3 on Indonesia, Sect. 3.1.1 does refer to a few past studies on this question): how *effective* is political humor in leading to some change among the populace or the government? The unknown author's comment (2023) regarding the U.S. presidential election outcome is certainly pithy : "Kennedy didn't beat Nixon. Satire beat Nixon!"[7] But writ large as a statement of political humor, in general how accurate is it?

### 14.2.1 Variables Influencing the Influence of Political Humor

There are quite a few variables and questions to account for when studying the effectiveness of political humor. Indeed, a preliminary question for anyone studying the influence of political humor is to ask: what effect(s) are we looking for? This need not necessarily be the usual one of electoral or policy change; there are more general, but certainly no less important, outcomes stemming from political humor. As Chap. 8 (Poland) notes, political humor can also involve "*cultivating citizenship* by demystifying the processes behind the exercise of power on the one hand, and in *diminishing trust* in politicians and *depoliticizing the citizens*" (my added emphasis).

---

[5] Trudeau (1988), chrome-extension://efaidnbmnnnibpcajpcglclefindmkaj/https://niemanreports.org/wp-content/uploads/2014/04/Fall-1988_150.pdf (page 8).

[6] Nobel Prizes (2023), https://improbable.com/ig/2023-ceremony.

[7] Unknown author, https://quoteinvestigator.com/2023/09/01/satire-beat/.

So that researchers must make clear from the start what effect they are looking for, as this can affect their choice of corpus selection and methodology. For our purposes here, let's assume that the effect being studied is change of political behavior—whether electoral, behavioral, or attitudinal.

First and foremost, what counts as political humor? How does the researcher decide what is considered funny in any given society? For such a determination, the researcher has to be intimately familiar with the culture and mentality of the society and political regime. This does not necessarily mean a "native born" person; scholars from other societies can (and do!) successfully learn enough about foreign cultures to do such top-flight research.[8] In any case, such a determination cannot be based exclusively on the researcher's "gut feeling." As noted in Chap. 13 (Argentina) regarding various background reasons, multiple meanings, and expansion of key terms over time: "This complex interplay of factors underscores the need for a nuanced understanding of *la grieta* and its multifaceted nature in Argentine society." (Note: *la grieta* itself is not "humorous," but it is the core on which much humor is anchored over there.)

How, then, to attack the challenge inherent in much political humor? One good example of how to do so, in light of semantic complexity and change, can be found in Chap. 9 (Montenegro): "The present study opted for the methodology of analyzing audience reactions, specifically the reactions of Facebook users. Thus, comments were considered humorous if they received a laughing emoji or a 'ha-ha' (or similar) reply ('hahaja,' 'ahahah,' 'xaxa,' 'LOL,' and laughing GIFs of various kinds)." With a little creative imagination, other forms of relatively "objective" criteria can be used to decide what is suitable for the corpus under study e.g., focus groups; popularity of the cartoonist; reputation of the standup comedian; ratings of the TV satire program; and so on.

Second, how many people actually see/hear such humor? A million people watching a satirical YouTube satire sounds like an impressive number—but might not have much electoral impact in a country of over fifty million (e.g., Germany, France, England). As can be seen by almost all the studies in this book, political humor lends itself far more to *qualitative* Discourse Analysis, as it is heavily based on the semiotics of a "text" (the different ways it can be interpreted; see my comments further below). Nevertheless, this doesn't negate the need for understanding the *extent* of political humor in any given society. The number of people exposed, and the frequency that such items appear in the public space, can certainly make a difference. For instance, to take but two studies in this book, an entire country exposed to—and talking about—a corpus of satire over half a century (*Forges* in Spain: Chap. 6) will obviously have a greater impact than the finding that a mere 8% of humorous Facebook comments in Montenegro are sexist (Chap. 9). Thus, quantitative analysis—frequency of expression and extent of audience exposure to political humor—should be added (where possible) to complement the qualitative research that will always remain the core of

---

[8] Indeed, the editor of this series, Prof. Feldman, was born, raised, and educated in Israel, but has spent the last four decades living in Japan, becoming a respected expert on its culture and forms of political discourse, as his numerous studies on Japan clearly show.

such studies. A good example of quantitative analysis complementing a core, qualitative methodology can be found in Chap. 10 (Iran); Chap. 12 (Japan) manages to study the *entire* humorous corpus of a specific type of text (*senryu*).

Third, who are the people exposed to such biting humor? Are they all from the opposition? (In which case, it will have little electoral impact.) Or are many of them government supporters? Or, perhaps most likely, most are from the broad, impressionable middle-of-the-electoral-map, in which case such satire etc., could be electorally significant. And if "only" a narrow segment of society, are they opinion leaders (in which case the spirit of that satirical humor will continue to expand outwards in ever-growing waves) or common folk without much personal influence further on? Most perplexing of all (in a research context), as noted in Chap. 6 (Spain): "…not all recipients will reach the same interpretation, as they will follow different inferential processes depending on their own cognitive schemes and the spatial–temporal context in which they access the cartoon [or any medium, for that matter]." Thus, even a seemingly "homogeneous" audience will not necessarily "understand" the humor in the same way or with the same level of effectiveness because of their different ways of seeing the *explication*, the *implicated premise*, and/or the *implicated conclusion*.

Fourth, as we know from psychology studies, people almost never change their mind when exposed to a one-time piece of evidence that goes against their long-standing mindset; our mental tools to protect against cognitive dissonance are too strong for that. As noted in Chap. 8 (Poland): "…potential effects of political humor are gradual rather than instant." Therefore, the next question becomes: does such political humor have staying power? In other words, is the satirist engaged in a *campaign* of humorous criticism (e.g., daily caricatures or op-ed columns), or is such political humor sporadic and infrequent? How long does a non-partisan member of the public have to be exposed to continual political humor for it to be effective?

Fifth, are there specific types and modes of political humor that are more effective in changing public opinion and attitudes than other types? If so, does this depend on the individual's socio-economic variables? And/or perhaps it is (also) related to the nation's general culture (aggressive: Poland [Chap. 8]; or circumspect: Japan [Chaps. 2 and 12]), or its specific, traditional modes of humor (textual, aural, visual)?

Sixth, are there specific types of media that are more successful in using political humor to influence the public? Such a question, of course, is time dependent. The answer to this question studying the 1980s might well find that back then the most influential medium in this regard was television (and in the 1940s, newspaper cartoons). However, by the second decade of the twenty-first century, clearly internet web sites and perhaps more specifically social media reach a much broader audience given their virality i.e., ability of every citizen to "spread the joke." Chapter 3 on Indonesia (Sect. 3.1.1) notes this, citing no less than seven references; Chap. 10 on Iran is completely devoted to social media in a country where traditional media are totally under the thumb (and the eye) of the authorities.

There is also an ancillary element to this media chronology: each generational cohort grows up with its own specific medium. Therefore, in asking "which medium has the greater influence?" we might well have to add: "on Generation X (or Y, or Z etc.)." Even today, Baby Boomers in the U.S. (those born immediately after WWII) tend to read print newspapers at much higher levels than millennials whose adolescence was formed by the internet and thus tend to avoid "legacy media" (even Facebook has become passé for many youngsters today!).

Seventh, researchers also should turn their attention from the bottom to the top—from the public to the politicians (the focus of the previous companion book). Here the question becomes: to what extent, if any, does political humor really affect the political behavior or policies of those being satirized and held up to ridicule? In other words, are there cases where we can tangibly see a change in government action due to such humorous attacks? Clearly, this is not simple or easy to do; there will always be several variable factors besides political humor that can cause modification of political behavior or policy. However, this shouldn't free the researcher from trying to assess in some systematic fashion whether indeed specific political humor in the media does more than merely provide the public with a vicarious way of letting off steam—or make political leaders angry without any change emerging out of their irritation.

Eighth and finally, on whom exactly does political humor focus? As just hinted at, most research in this field is addressed to politicians running the country. However, this is not always the case. For example, in Chap. 8 regarding political satire in Poland, the authors note: "The performers routinely engage in stylizations that tend to be very crass in the case of accent and garb, especially as regards Polish historical 'others': Germans, Russians, Americans, Czechs, Arabs, Jews." Similarly, in Australia (Chap. 7), extreme right-wing humor is mostly directed at native (aborigine) Australians and blacks in general. In short, political humor does not always have a positive goal of changing leadership policy or personnel; it can also negatively reinforce social stereotypes or lead to civic "disenchantment" (Chap. 8), causing citizens to withdraw from politics. Thus, any systematic attempt to understand the effects of political humor, has to first determine the satirized addressee to be analyzed and how that affects public perceptions and activity, as well as (or) the political leaders' policies.

Altogether, this is an extremely complex field of study involving not only many straightforward methodological issues, but also a great deal of subjective evaluations that should be "objectified" as much as possible. For those who wish to further study the overall question of possible methodological avenues to pursue in researching the influence of political humor, especially from a quantitative and cross-comparative perspective, see my complementary, companion piece—the Conclusion chapter in the first book of this series on political humor (Lehman-Wilzig, 2024), especially Sect. 13.4.2.

## 14.2.2 Further Complexity: Two Types of Addressees; Cross-Cutting Variables

As if the number of methodological considerations listed above was not "headache" enough, another aspect should be taken into account: all the above research questions can be split into two quite different categories of participants: political humor by *non-politicians* (humorists, satirists, comedians etc.)—the focus of the present book; and humor expressed and presented by the *politicians themselves* in the heat of electoral (or even normal political) battle—the focus of the earlier, companion book. These two forms can be mutually reinforcing, if used by critical commentators and opposition politicians—or supportive humorists and coalition politicos. Alternatively, the two groups' humor can cancel each out by being mutually negating e.g., funny commentators railing against the government, but simultaneously bitingly humorous coalition members verbally spearing the political opposition.

Clearly, none of these questions can be answered in complete fashion, mainly because in the messy and complex world of politics there are always other dynamics and variables at work beyond cutting humor—true for influence on the general public (receiving inputs from non-humorous sources) and on the politicians (various internal factors e.g., coalition considerations, constituent pressures).

Moreover, some of the question categories above are influenced by other ones. Two such examples: first, the answer to "which medium's political humor has greater influence?" is directly affected by the nature of the political regime, given that social media provide greater anonymity (using VPNs etc.) against autocratic regime censorship as opposed to print, radio, and television. Second, the type of audience will usually be connected to a certain type of medium: opinion leaders reading elite newspapers; "influencers" on social media; the average citizen watching televised comedy sketches; and so on.

## 14.3 Concluding Thought: Political Humor and Veracity—The "Fake News" Conundrum

The famous military historian Barbara Tuchman (1978) noted a core element of her profession—equally relevant to journalism in general, and political humor specifically (especially media-created): "Satire is a wrapping of exaggeration around a core of reality."[9] In words that are more attuned to contemporary politics, how do we relate to political humor that by definition uses exaggeration and other forms of distorting reality to express their idea of "political truth"?

We are all aware that when politicians talk (or otherwise employ political discourse in its various guises), we should take what they say with several grains of salt, if edible

---

[9] Tuchman (1978) https://www.goodreads.com/quotes/9847912-satire-is-a-wrapping-of-exaggeration-around-a-core-of.

at all. On the other hand, when it comes to the media—especially institutional (i.e., not social media)—we do have an expectation of hewing to some semblance of reality.

Nevertheless, in the very heart of political humor lies a conundrum. On the one hand, we have Doctorow's (2007) perspicacious statement: "Satire's nature is to be one-sided, contemptuous of ambiguity, and so unfairly selective as to find in the purity of ridicule an inarguable moral truth."[10] This is paradoxical: how can something that avoids the messiness of life and its multifarious elements also be considered a "moral *truth*"? Here we once again arrive at human psychology. Most people are far more prone to listen to a *simplistic* "take" on the news (or any aspect of reality) than to a complex, multi-sided picture. This is where political humor excels, by distilling the flaw of the politician (or policy etc.) into its basic core and attacking it without considering "mitigating circumstances" or other complexities.

What does this mean for the researcher of political humor? Two contradictory things. On the one hand, political humor is not to be viewed (perhaps should *never* be considered) as a *reliable* source of information regarding the political system and/or politicians or policies within the regime. Put simply, political humor in all its variations is not a journalistic news report. On the other hand, it definitely has to be considered an important element in a country's political system with potential influence over the country's leadership (the degree of which depends on all the variables listed here earlier) and perhaps even more so among its general audience (readers, listeners, viewers etc.). To that end, I will offer here a quote that (in my opinion) is only partly true: "A man is angry at a libel because it is false, but at a satire because it is true" (Chesterton, 1911).[11] Such satire might be true "in spirit" but is hardly true "in fact"—precisely because by its very nature it must exaggerate or distort in order to be funny and effective.

This sets the researcher of political humor apart from most academic counterparts (other than those who study disinformation, propaganda, and the like). Political humor in the media should *not* be viewed as a necessary *reflection* of a country's political health, but rather as a very useful *distortion* of its socio-political situation. This renders it no less influential than journalistic reporting.; indeed, one can say that it turns traditional journalism on its head. The news delivers essential political information; political humor offers necessary political criticism. The former seeks truthfulness regarding what is; the latter, provides distortion (exaggeration, imbalance, etc.) to create what should be—something no less important to guarantee the continued health of any political system.

---

[10] Doctorow's (2007), http://www.notable-quotes.com/d/doctorow_e_1.html.

[11] Chesterton, (1911), https://libquotes.com/g-k-chesterton/quote/lbc1x6z.

# References

Acton, Lord. (1887). Lord Acton writes to Bishop.... https://oll.libertyfund.org/quote/lord-acton-writes-to-bishop-creighton-that-the-same-moral-standards-should-be-applied-to-all-men-political-and-religious-leaders-included-especially-since-power-tends-to-corrupt-and-absolute-power-corrupts-absolutely-1887

Chesterton, G. K. (1911). *Five types: A book of essays*. Kessinger Publishing, LLC. https://libquotes.com/g-k-chesterton/quote/lbc1x6z

Doctorow, E. L. (2007). *Creationists: Selected essays, 1993–2006*. Random House. http://www.notable-quotes.com/d/doctorow_e_l.html

Gaiman, N. (2015). How important are free speech and satire? *Twitter*. https://twitter.com/neilhimself/status/552861305334276096

Gilliatt, P. (2015). *To wit: Skin and bones of comedy*. Scribner. https://www.azquotes.com/author/50240-Penelope_Gilliatt

Ignoble Prize. (2023). The 33rd first annual Ig Nobel Prizes. https://improbable.com/ig/2023-ceremony/

Lehman-Wilzig, S. (2024). Political humor: Theoretical questions, methodological suggestions. In O. Feldman (Ed.), *Political humor worldwide: The cultural context of political comedy, satire, and parody* (pp. 239–248). Springer.

Montagu, Lady M. W. (1733). *Verses addressed to the imitator of the first satire of the second Book of Horace* (Edited and annotated by Jack Lynch). https://jacklynch.net/Texts/montagu2.html

Quote Origin. (2023). Quote origin: Kennedy didn't beat Nixon. Satire beat Nixon. *Quote Investigator*. https://quoteinvestigator.com/2023/09/01/satire-beat/

Trudeau, G. (1988). Garry Trudeau faces news executives and talks about his comic strip and their prerogative to delete. *Nieman Reports, XLII*(3), 4–8, 54. https://niemanreports.org/wp-content/uploads/2014/04/Fall-1988_150.pdf

Tuchman, B. (1978). *A distant mirror: The calamitous 14th century*. Alfred A. Knopf. https://www.goodreads.com/quotes/9847912-satire-is-a-wrapping-of-exaggeration-around-a-core-of

# Index

**A**
Abe, Shinzô, 36, 255, 266
Absurd, 8, 29, 102, 126, 166, 168, 172
Aggressive
 anecdota, 24
Aggressive function (of humor), 5
*Anime* (Japanese cartoons), 252
Anti-Kirchneristas, 273–275, 278, 279
Appraisal model, 16, 203, 204, 209, 212
Argentina
 culture, 299
Argentinean
 polarization, 273
 society, 273
*Asahi* (Japanese newspaper), 244, 252–254
Audience, 13, 22, 46, 50, 54, 55, 66, 75, 83, 89, 96, 108, 112, 114, 123, 136, 140, 146, 148–151, 157, 166, 167, 174, 175, 178, 180, 188, 196, 223, 225, 229, 236, 249, 280–282, 284, 289, 299, 300, 302, 303
Australia, 15, 146–149, 151, 154, 156, 186, 212, 301
Australian
 culture, 145–148, 150, 156, 157
Authoritarianism, 84, 95

**B**
Balkan modern patriarchy, 197
*Bayan Yanı* (Turkish satirical magazine), 93, 102, 104, 108, 113
Bemiller, Michelle, 184, 186, 189, 190, 198
"Black humor", 7, 15, 93, 102, 114, 269
Bolsonaro, Jair
 government, 15, 73–75, 77–84, 86–89

Brazilian
 culture, 75
 politics, 88

**C**
Cabaret, 165–167, 170, 172, 174, 178, 179
*Campana de Gràcia* (Catalan weekly magazine of satire), 121
Caricatures, 1, 22, 41, 45, 46, 51–54, 58, 60, 65, 68, 75, 77, 103, 114, 120, 150, 152, 153, 157, 170, 183, 188, 224, 249, 298, 300
Carnivalesque, 28, 29, 31, 40, 41, 97, 170
Cartoon
 symbolism, 45, 56, 59
Cartoonist, 7, 14, 21, 22, 24, 29, 46, 47, 50–58, 60, 62, 64–67, 73–75, 79, 82, 88, 94–96, 99, 109, 119, 121, 123, 124, 134, 135, 140, 152–154, 224, 297, 299
*Chaban* (theatrical farce, skit, or slapstick), 250
*Chakashi* (making fun of in a joking manner), 249
China, 224, 246, 258, 262, 267. *See also* Communist Party of China
Civic Platform, Party, 167
Comedians, 172, 178, 179, 223, 225, 226, 228, 229, 231, 237, 248, 250, 251, 298, 299, 302
Comic effect, 15, 131, 165–169, 175, 178–180
Communist Party of China (CPC), 267
Comprehensive theories (of humor), 5
Conflict theories, 207

Conservatism, 281
Constitutional revisionism, 24
Coronavirus. *See also* Covid-19
Coutinho, Laerte, 73, 74
Covid-19. *See also* Coronavirus pandemic
Critical Discourse Analysis, 14, 15, 45, 48, 145, 146, 149, 150, 184, 187, 189
*Cu-Cut!* (Catalan illustrated satirical magazine), 121
Culture
    patriarchal, 15, 36, 94, 97, 102, 108, 183–185, 188, 194, 196–198
    samurai, 249
    sociopolitical, 236
Cynicism, 169

**D**
*Dajare* ("wordplay"), 8, 9
Defensive function (of humor), 7
Delegitimization, 184, 187
Devaluation, 186, 190, 191, 194, 197, 198
Diet members (Japanese politicians), 245, 248, 255
Distortion, 76, 82, 303
Documental Image Analysis, 73

**E**
*Eko senryû* (environmental/ecological senryû), 252
Election campaigns, 96, 153, 248, 249
*El Jueves* (Spanish weekly satirical magazine), 121, 139
*El País* (Spanish-language daily newspaper), 122, 124, 130, 140
*El Papus* (a Spanish weekly anarchist satirical magazine), 121
Erdoğan, Recep Tayyip, 99
Ethnic stereotype, 7, 166, 168, 171
Exaggeration, 38, 41, 50, 52–54, 65, 67, 68, 82, 83, 89, 104, 123, 179, 286, 287, 302, 303

**F**
Face
    loss of, 245
    saving, 16, 223, 229, 230, 235
Facebook, 13, 15, 154, 183, 184, 187, 188, 190–198, 211, 224, 299, 301
Fake news, 75, 179, 227, 302
Far right
    communication, 145, 146, 148, 153, 157
    humor, 145, 148, 149, 154, 157, 158
Female politicians, 15, 16, 183–189, 191–198
Fictionalization of Politics, 157
*Folha de São Paulo* (Brazilian newspaper), 74, 75, 77, 88
Fraguas, Antonio (i.e., Forges), 15, 119, 121, 139
Freedom
    of expression, 46, 67, 94, 95, 104, 122, 206, 214, 219, 227, 252, 278
    of speech, 59, 67, 176, 178, 204, 206, 207, 219, 234, 235, 282
Freud, Sigmund, 8
*Fûshi* (satirical manga), 22

**G**
*Gekiga* ("dramatic pictures"), 30
Gender
    equality, 86, 93, 94, 97, 183, 185
    stereotypes, 10, 35, 38, 41, 102, 152, 180, 184–186
Gezi Protests, 94, 97, 99, 104
Górski, Robert, 166, 172, 174
Graffiti, 1, 245
Grotesque, 36, 41, 280

**H**
Haiku, 251, 252
Hanson, Pauline, 151
*Hermano Lobo* (a Spanish humor magazine), 139
Humor
    disparaging, 8, 184, 185, 187
    provocative, 208

**I**
Impersonation, 169, 174, 226
Incongruity Theory (of humor), 4
Indonesia, 7, 14, 45–52, 54, 56, 57, 59–61, 65, 68, 71, 298, 300
Indonesian humor, 45
Intellectual function (of humor), 8
Interdiscursivity, 150, 156
Internet memes, 146, 153, 155, 169
Intertextuality, 29, 150, 156
Iran, 16, 102, 104, 205, 206, 208, 214, 216, 298, 300
Irony, 16, 30, 41, 50, 65, 80, 121, 122, 139, 146, 150, 166, 176, 178, 191, 243,

Index

244, 257, 264, 268, 269, 281, 286–288, 291, 298
Islamic humor magazines, 98, 108, 109
Istanbul Convention, 97, 103, 104, 108, 109

**J**

Japan, 7, 12, 14, 21, 22, 24, 26–30, 35, 36, 40, 41, 243–246, 248–253, 256–259, 262, 264, 268, 269, 272, 297, 299, 300
Japanese
  culture, 14, 21, 25, 27, 30, 41, 243, 245, 249, 250, 270
  politicians. *See also* Diet members
  society, 14, 16, 21, 22, 25, 31, 35, 36, 40, 243, 245–247, 250, 253, 261, 269, 270, 273–275, 299
Jests, 16, 223, 235, 237, 245
Joke, 1, 3, 5, 8, 10–13, 77, 83, 89, 93, 121, 148, 149, 151, 152, 155, 157, 169, 178, 179, 186, 187, 206–208, 211, 212, 214, 219, 225–227, 229, 231, 235, 236, 245, 246, 248–250, 280, 300
*Joshiraku* ("female *rakugo*"), 31
Journalists, 2, 13, 14, 94, 95, 119, 122, 170, 219, 233, 248, 249, 274, 282
Justice and Development Party (JDP), 95

**K**

*Kami-shibai* ("picture card street theater") storytelling, 24
*Karukuchi* ("light story"), 250
*Keiku* (an epigram), 249
*Kigeki* (comic plays performed by troupes of comedians), 250
Kirchner, Cristina, 277, 281, 285–287
Kirchnerism, 277, 281
Kirchner, Néstor, 274, 275, 277, 281
Kishida, Fumio, 256
Kitazawa, Rakuten, 24, 40
*Kodomo eko senryû* (children's ecological senryû), 252
*Kyogen* (traditional Japanese comic theater), 250

**L**

*La Esquella de la Torratxa* (Catalan illustrated satirical magazine), 121
*La grieta*, 16, 273–279, 281–285, 288, 289, 299

Lanata, Jorge, 273, 274
*La Traca* (Spanish satirical weekly magazine), 120
Laugh, 3, 8, 13, 40, 77, 225, 234, 245–247, 251, 298
Laughter, 2–5, 9, 30, 35, 40, 41, 74, 76–78, 83, 89, 130, 148, 169, 172, 188, 203, 204, 225, 226, 236, 243, 245, 246, 248–250, 280
Law and Justice, Party, 166, 167
Leong, Jason, 223, 226, 228, 229, 231, 234, 235
Lim, Douglas, 223, 230–233, 236

**M**

Macri, Mauricio, 281, 282
Macrism, 281
*Mainichi* (Japanese newspaper), 268, 269
Malaysia, 223–231, 233–237, 239
Malaysian comedians, 16
*Manga* (Japanese comics), 2, 14, 21, 25, 28, 252
Manga media, 40
Manglish, 223, 228, 230, 231, 237
Mannerism, 52, 68, 168–170, 174, 175, 179, 233
*Manzai* (a dialogue containing comical wording and gestures), 250
Meiji Restoration (of 1868), 247
Mental hygiene, 179
Metaphor
  conceptual and orientational, 275–277
  visual, 45, 55, 56, 60, 120, 133
*Misvak* (Turkish satirical magazine), 98, 108, 110, 113
*Mitate* (enigmatically depicting the object of satire in terms of something else), 249
Mockery, 89, 133, 148, 204, 225, 249, 298
*Modoki* (satirical mockery), 249
*Mojiri* (changing lyrics in parts of a song to make it humorous or allegorical), 249
Monşer, 110
Montenegro, 15, 183–185, 188, 191, 194, 195, 197, 201, 299
Morreal, John, 5
Muhammed cartoon, 22

**N**

Narrative device, 165, 166, 175, 177
National character, 11, 14

National identity, 76, 147, 168
Neoliberalism, 75, 78, 79, 88, 133
*Niwaka* (impromptu joke, witticism, or pun), 250

**O**
Ôno, Kôsuke, 33
Openness Model, 206, 218
*Oyaji gyagu* ("old man gag" or "old man joke"), 9

**P**
Palatability, 236
*Papitu* (Catalan illustrated satirical magazine), 121
Parody, 1, 2, 12, 14–16, 27, 31, 32, 35, 40, 41, 50, 80, 89, 133, 152, 165, 166, 169, 170, 180, 223, 227, 228, 230, 233, 237, 249, 284, 291, 298
Poland, 7, 15, 165–168, 170–177, 298, 300, 301
Polishness, 175
Politeness, 16, 223, 228, 232–237
Political
  campaign, 22, 59, 82, 87, 148, 153, 154, 226, 227, 249, 300
  candidates, 14, 46, 86, 130, 177, 213, 248, 249, 280
  cartoons, 1, 6, 7, 13–16, 21, 22, 24, 40, 41, 45–60, 62–68, 73–77, 81, 88, 89, 93, 94, 98, 104, 109, 110, 112, 113, 119, 120, 122–124, 131, 137–140, 148, 150, 152, 153, 157, 224, 227, 270, 274, 298, 300
  culture, 1, 2, 14, 15, 21, 24, 27, 35, 40, 51, 63, 73, 75, 84, 94, 97, 102, 108–110, 113, 114, 119, 121, 140, 145–150, 152–154, 156–158, 166, 170, 183–186, 189, 197, 198, 203, 212, 214, 216, 219, 223, 224, 228, 234, 237, 244, 249, 270, 297, 299
  cynicism, 169, 256, 269
  discourse, 1, 2, 7, 24, 28, 30, 32, 40, 41, 46, 48, 50, 51, 55, 56, 67, 94–99, 104, 109, 110, 114, 117, 120, 122, 126, 135, 144, 146, 149, 150, 156, 158, 167, 184, 186, 187, 201, 203, 204, 224–230, 235–237, 267, 274, 277, 279, 289, 296, 297, 299, 302
  humor, 1–16, 21, 22, 24, 27, 30–32, 35, 38, 40, 41, 46, 50, 51, 54, 73–77, 80, 83, 85, 88, 89, 93–98, 102, 104, 108, 109, 112, 114, 119–122, 126, 127, 129, 130, 139, 140, 145, 146, 148–151, 154, 155, 157, 158, 166, 167, 169, 170, 172, 174, 177–180, 184, 186–188, 191, 196, 198, 203–208, 210–220, 223–225, 228, 230–233, 235–237, 243–246, 249, 269, 280, 281, 284, 291, 295–303
  leaders, 1, 7, 16, 50, 57, 65–67, 95, 166, 167, 170, 171, 173, 180, 214, 243–245, 253, 256, 258, 269, 276, 278, 288, 295–297, 301, 302
  legitimacy, 2, 205
  opposition, 15, 94, 97, 108–110, 112, 135, 174, 235, 244, 277, 282, 286–288, 296, 300, 302
  satire, 1, 2, 6, 7, 14–16, 21, 22, 27, 40, 41, 46, 50–52, 55, 57, 59, 65, 67, 94, 96, 123, 146, 150, 152–154, 157, 165, 166, 168–170, 174, 179, 225, 227, 244, 245, 247, 249, 273, 274, 280–282, 284, 287, 289, 296–300, 302, 303
  scandal, 52, 55, 113, 167, 217, 231, 245, 253, 255, 256, 278
Popular Party, 129–131, 135
Populism, 94, 109, 112
*Por favor* (a humor magazine published in Barcelona), 121
Prejudice, 1, 10, 58, 120, 176
Puppet show, 168, 170

**R**
Rajoy, Mariano, 132
*Rakugo* (a popular form of comic monologue, a Japanese sit-down comedy), 31–33, 250
Relevance Theory, 119, 120, 122, 124, 140
Relief/Release Theory (of humor), 4, 5
Republic of Türkiye (Turkey), 15, 93
Ridicule, 5, 16, 30, 65, 76, 82, 83, 87, 89, 97, 123, 148, 153, 174, 175, 178, 180, 213, 218, 226, 236, 243, 244, 255, 256, 269, 301, 303
Right-wing comedy, 301

**S**
Safe comedy, 223, 225, 227, 234
*Sararîman senryû* (middle class, white-collar Japanese corporate workers' satirical verses), 252

Sarcasm, 50, 51, 65, 121, 139, 244, 256, 266, 269, 287, 291
*Saru mawashi* (monkey show), 250
Satire, 6, 7, 13, 15, 21, 27, 28, 50–52, 58, 65, 93, 152, 166–169, 173, 243, 245, 273, 275, 280, 281, 284, 287, 296, 297, 299, 301, 303
Satirical
   humor, 6, 7, 13–17, 21, 24, 29, 40, 41, 45, 50, 51, 68, 73–76, 87, 88, 93, 94, 96, 98, 108, 109, 119–121, 139, 151, 166–169, 173, 178–180, 226, 243, 244, 249, 250, 280, 281, 296–300
   representation, 7, 21, 52, 56, 59, 60, 65, 67, 74, 75, 149, 166, 169, 177
Schneider, Rachel, 184, 186, 189, 190, 198
Self-stereotype, 168
*Senryû* (or satirical verse), 243, 251
Sexism, 108, 157, 184, 186, 195, 196, 198
Sexist humor, 15, 183–188, 190, 195, 196, 198
Sexual function (of humor), 6
Sexual objectification, 16, 183, 186, 191, 198
SNS, *see* social networking services
Social
   commentary, 7, 14, 16, 22, 45, 46, 50, 56, 59, 60, 65, 66, 169, 183, 184, 187, 249
   critique, 14, 27, 45, 49, 50, 52, 55–59, 65, 66, 80, 94, 129, 175, 178, 226, 275, 278, 280, 284
   network, 12, 16, 75, 184, 203, 215
Social function (of humor), 6, 41
Socialist Party, 131
Socialization processes, 245
Social Networking Services (SNS), 14–16
Spain, 7, 15, 119–122, 125, 129, 132, 135, 139–141, 144, 283, 284, 299, 300
Staged comedic acts, 223–225
Stereotypes, 1–3, 11, 15, 36, 41, 165, 172, 173, 178, 179, 185, 186, 301

Superiority Theory (of humor), 3, 184

**T**
Taishô Democracy, 24
Television, 13, 15, 33, 96, 137, 138, 165, 172, 191, 206, 274, 277, 281, 300, 302
Tezuka, Osamu, 24, 28, 40, 41
Thematic Analysis, 15, 145, 146, 149, 150, 155, 166
Tokugawa Shogunate, 247
Trump, Donald, 13, 148, 175, 226, 257
Turkey. *See also* Republic of Türkiye

**U**
*Ugachi* (expressions of events from a backward or oblique point of view), 249
U.S., 12, 13, 15, 148, 153, 154, 228, 248, 260, 297, 298, 301
*Uykusuz* (Turkish satirical magazine), 93, 94, 97–99, 102, 104, 113, 114

**W**
Widodo, Joko, 14, 45–47, 59

**Y**
Yamafuji, Shôji, 22, 41
*Yomiuri* (Japanese newspaper), 244, 253, 255–259, 261, 269
*Yonkoma* ("four cell strips") *manga*, 24
YouTube, 13, 15, 16, 172, 174, 223, 225, 231, 234, 299
Yudhoyono, Susilo Bambang, 14, 45, 46, 51

**Z**
Ziv, Avner, 5

Printed in the USA
CPSIA information can be obtained
at www.ICGtesting.com
CBHW071713310724
12489CB00002B/18

9 789819 707256